Praise for *Mrs. Woolf a̶*

"The historian offers us an invaluable glimpse into the hidden history of domestic service in an absorbing narrative, beautifully written with the sensibility of a poet."
                                                          —*Times* (UK)

"A fascinating and elegantly written book."
                                    —*Daily Mail* (Critic's Choice)

"A scintillating meeting of biography, social history, and literary criticism."
                                                      —*Observer* (UK)

"An authoritative, detailed account of the dynamic relationship between Virginia Woolf and the domestic help that was so crucial to her existence as a woman and a writer. Alison Light is clear-eyed and wise about her chosen topic."   —*Washington Times*

"Light is a first-rate scholar, using literary criticism, biography and social history to give readers both an intimate view of one extraordinary household and a larger view of the role of service and class in British society."   —*Howard County Times*

"This is a bold, impressive and important rewriting of a slice of British social history."
                                                      —*Guardian* (UK)

"Do we really need another book on Bloomsbury? The answer is, resoundingly, yes. Especially *Mrs. Woolf and the Servants*. Light doesn't take away from Bloomsbury's legacy. She adds the dignity and intelligence of the people who made all those conversations, all those books possible."   —*Los Angeles Times*

"Superbly researched, often passionately eloquent, and enthralling throughout . . . Light's signal achievement in her compelling book lies in divvying up her pages equally between the lives of the servants and that of their mistress. *Mrs. Woolf and the Servants* is no dryly academic sociological study. It is an inquiry into the fundamental nature of human intimacy."   —**Michael Dirda**, *Washington Post Book World*

Mrs. Woolf and the Servants

An Intimate History of
Domestic Life in Bloomsbury

Alison Light

BLOOMSBURY PRESS
NEW YORK BERLIN LONDON

Published by Bloomsbury Press, New York

All papers used by Bloomsbury Press are natural, recyclable products made from wood grown in well-managed forests. The manufacturing processes conform to the environmental regulations of the country of origin.

LIBRARY OF CONGRESS CATALOGING-IN-PUBLICATION DATA

Light, Alison, 1955–
Mrs Woolf and the servants : an intimate history of
domestic life in Bloomsbury / by Alison Light.
p. cm.
Includes bibliographical references and index.
ISBN-13: 978-1-59691-560-2 (alk. paper hardcover)
ISBN-10: 1-59691-560-9 (alk. paper hardcover)
1. Woolf, Virginia, 1882–1941—Employees. 2. Authors, English—20th century—
Biography. 3. Women domestics—Great Britain—Biography.
4. Bloomsbury (London, England)—Social life and customs.
5. Bloomsbury (London, England)—Biography. 6. Bloomsbury group. I. Title.

PR6045.O72Z787 2008
823.912—dc22
[B]
2008008086

Originally published in Great Britain in 2007 by Penguin Books Ltd.
First published in the United States by Bloomsbury Press in 2008
This paperback edition published in 2009

Paperback ISBN: 978-1-59691-694-4

1 3 5 7 9 10 8 6 4 2

Typeset by Palimpsest Book Production Limited, Stirlingshire, Scotland
Printed in the United States of America by Quebecor World Fairfield

for Fran Bennett

And sit we upon the highest throne of the World,
yet sit we upon our own tail.

Michel de Montaigne, 'Of Experience'

Contents

List of Illustrations and Picture Credits

Picture Credits

Preface

If I were reading this diary, if it were a book that came my way, I think
I should seize with greed on the portrait of Nelly, and make a story
– perhaps make the whole story revolve around that – it would amuse
me. Her character – our efforts to get rid of her – our reconciliations.

(December 1929)

When I first read Virginia Woolf's diaries, I was shocked but also
fascinated by how viciously she wrote about her cook, Nellie
Boxall.* Nellie had come as a live-in servant in 1916 and was to
stay until 1934. Those eighteen years were to prove a battle royal
between Nellie and Virginia, a battle in which the running of
the house became a constant struggle for control and for mutual
understanding. Nellie was a 'mongrel', Virginia wrote, after one
of their many rows, with her 'timid spiteful servant mind',
exhibiting 'human nature undressed'. Yet in the next breath, she
was also 'poor dear Nelly' of whom her mistress was very fond.
In turn – according to Virginia – Nellie exasperated her by
wielding whatever weapons she had: she constantly threatened to
leave, then equally capriciously withdrew her notice; she resorted
to emotional blackmail, begging to be kept on when Virginia
tried to sack her; she accused her mistress of heartlessness before

---

* Woolf and her subsequent biographers and critics refer to 'Nelly' Boxall, but, as
I discovered, she is 'Nellie' on her birth and death certificates, she always signed
herself as 'Nellie', and that is how her relatives spelt her name. Virginia Woolf,
the writer, was 'Mrs Woolf' to her contemporaries or even 'Mrs Leonard Woolf';
that usage is now archaic so I generally refer to her as 'Woolf', except where it
might confuse her with Leonard, and use 'Virginia' elsewhere, often to put her
on a par with Nellie.

gossiping about her to the other servants; worst of all, Nellie seemed to relish the endless tearful 'scenes', which degenerated into breast-beating and mutual recriminations and left them locked in an exhausted stalemate. It was 'sordid', wrote Virginia, 'degrading' and a 'confounded bore'. But for all the dramas, Nellie never left the Woolfs and Virginia could hardly bear to part with her. After all those years of living together they were like a husband and wife who ought to divorce but can't; they were deeply, hopelessly, attached.

Taking my cue from Woolf – who never did write her 'portrait of Nelly' – I wanted to tell their story. I wanted to understand what they rowed about and what was at stake in this situation which tormented them so much. What interested me was the ferocity of the feelings involved. Virginia wrote obsessively about Nellie in her diaries and letters; she felt sick after their arguments, furious, guilty, bewildered and disgusted by it all; sometimes she anxiously sought to appease Nellie, sometimes she burst out violently and defensively. 'The poor have no sense of humour,' she decided, on one occasion. Here, it seemed to me, was a unique record, however one-sided, of the painful and defensive relationship between mistress and maid, which had rarely been written about but which echoed down through the ages and into our own day. This was a story about mutual – and unequal – dependence but it was also about social differences, about class feelings and attitudes which were generated and sustained by women at home and indoors rather than by men in their workplaces.

And what of Nellie? Would it be possible to learn anything about her and her side of the story? What was it like to work for Virginia and Leonard Woolf, both writers, both considered rather advanced in their views, compared to many of their day? And what did Nellie actually do for them? I wanted to know how much Nellie and Virginia's story was special to them and how much it was an inevitable product of the servant relationship. This was a story of Britain in the 1920s and 30s. Were Nellie and Virginia's set-tos representative of larger social changes, part of the zeitgeist as older expectations of service from the Victorian age began to crumble? I needed to expand my reach and investigate the other servants in Virginia Woolf's world if I was to understand what servant-keeping meant to her and to ladies like her. As an upper-middle-class girl Virginia Stephen had grown up in the late nineteenth century in a house with a staff of seven or so, all living in. Any facts about her nurse and nursemaid had all but disappeared, but one figure had remained steadfast in Virginia's life and imagination: Sophia Farrell, always known as Sophie, who worked for Virginia's parents as their cook-housekeeper, followed Virginia and her siblings when they made their own homes in the 1900s and remained in the family's employ for most of her life. Here was the 'prehistory' of Virginia's relation to Nellie.

Until I began to read about domestic service in Britain, I hadn't really grasped just how central it was to the history of women in this country. In fact, it's hard to resist the conclusion that the history of service *is* the history of British women. Millions of women had either been servants at some point in their lives or kept servants. I was particularly interested in the period from the late nineteenth century onwards, but what historians call the 'feminization' of service was actually in evidence from the mid-seventeenth century and by 1806 women outnumbered men in service by eight to one; by 1850 approximately 80 per cent of servants in middle-class households were women. At the beginning of the twentieth century domestic service was still the largest single female occupation. It remained so until at least 1945. Added to this were the vast numbers of other women, casual workers, such as washerwomen or chars, who eluded the census. Even though the majority of servants were temporary and saw domestic work as just a phase or a staging post, usually on the way to marriage, nonetheless the service relationship was at the heart of most women's lives in nearly all periods of British history.

Domestic service is extremely difficult to generalize about as conditions of work varied enormously (in my Prologue I try to pull some of these threads together). I decided to concentrate on live-in service and find out what I could about those who worked for the Woolfs: their lives would roughly span a century. Sophie

Farrell grew up in the 1860s, and was a country girl who came to work in London. She was representative of thousands of other migrants, though her story is her own. Gradually too, Lottie Hope, the parlourmaid to Nellie's cook, began to emerge from the shadows. A chance reference in Virginia Woolf's letters spoke of her as a foundling and I wanted to find out more about her past: orphans and charity girls made up another huge group of servants and I hoped her story would cast light on the Victorian inheritance which became such a burden to Virginia Woolf's generation. By way of scene-setting, *Mrs Woolf and the Servants* consequently begins with the household into which Sophie Farrell arrived, which was under the command of Virginia's mother, Julia Stephen. Lottie's story provides another 'prehistory': the relation between mistress and maid which philanthropy had enabled and which was to disappear as the twentieth century progressed. Lottie went on working in the Woolf milieu until the Second World War. One of my aims was to find out, if I could, what happened to her and Nellie in the 1950s and 60s.

Among the veritable mountain of material about Virginia and Leonard Woolf in the archives, there's almost nothing on the servants. I had a couple of photographs of them and a handful of their letters to go on. On the other hand, there are innumerable passages about the servants in the diaries and letters of Virginia Woolf, her husband and their circle; so many, in fact, that editors have been embarrassed by their superfluity – at one point in the 1910s Virginia and her sister, Vanessa Bell, write every day about their servants' doings. I was helped by a scattering of dates of birth and death which editors had provided (though they sometimes turned out to be inaccurate) and by the discussion in Quentin Bell's biography of Woolf, from which I also learnt that Nellie and Lottie had been recorded by BBC radio. Frequently in my research I was hampered by the convention of omitting servants' surnames. For a while I assumed that the Mabel and Flossie (Selwood) who worked for Vanessa Bell in the 1910s were the same Mabel and Flossie (Haskins) who 'did' for Virginia and her sister in the 30s. Such muddles are bound to occur where documentation is scarce. Even so, there is a long history of not noticing or valuing servants, seeing them as functionaries or mere types. It rankled with many servants at the time and continues to annoy some of their descendants, as I was to discover. Percy Bartholomew, for instance, was Leonard Woolf's gardener for twenty-odd years, but Leonard discusses his character in his auto-biography without once giving his surname. Percy's son, Jim, remained furious about this. Other commentators, who could be scrupulous in checking the details of a number of Bloomsbury's casual acquaintances, were often far less assiduous in tracking down the servants who were part of the Woolfs' daily lives for years. My aim in this book was to give the servants back their dignity and the respect they deserve.

I wanted to restore the servants to the story but not only for their own sakes. Virginia's relationship with Nellie was as enduring, intimate and intense as any in her life, but it was at an oblique angle to it. Far from seizing on the story 'with greed', as she imagined her reader might do, most literary critics have kept it at arm's length or shunted it off into social history. Virginia's dependence on her servants plays havoc with any easy celebration of either her or her sister, the painter Vanessa Bell, as bohemian, free women, creating a new kind of life. The servants don't usually feature in accounts of 'Bloomsbury's women'. Idealizing visions of them as heroines often go hand in hand with a romantic view of art which imagines it to be the product of lonely genius. But without all the domestic care and hard work which servants provided there would have been no art, no writing, no 'Bloomsbury'. Virginia Woolf's own feminist sympathies led her to champion the need for much more writing by and about women whose lives had long been obscured. In her best-known essay, *A Room of One's Own*, she asks, 'Is the life of the charwoman who has brought up eight children of less value to the world than the barrister who has made a hundred thousand pounds?' Yet her polemical, political writing about women sits uneasily alongside the obnoxious views of Nellie or Lottie which she expresses in her letters and diaries. As Hermione Lee notes in her biography of Woolf, the 'problem' of servants 'gets into almost all the novels'. But how? One further aim of this book was to put those literary representations, in the fiction and essays, alongside the flesh-and-blood servants and see what happened. My purpose is not to debunk or devalue Virginia Woolf or her writing but to argue that the figure of the servant and of the working woman haunts Woolf's experiments in literary modernism and sets a limit to what she can achieve.

★

Virginia Woolf's prejudices about her servants and the 'lower orders' in general were typical of the day. Between the wars the English were not incidentally class-conscious; it was how their society was structured, and one was as likely to meet snobbish attitudes in the station-master or the postman, the country solicitor or the businessman, as the smart London florist or the cockney. The offensive passages in Virginia's writing about the poor or the suburban, about 'the Jew' or 'negroes', can be matched by others equally vile in the work of many of her contemporaries. But she was highly unusual in examining many of her reactions and feelings, probing her sore spots, especially in her diaries. If Woolf was right in thinking that from 'the spectacle of oneself, most of us shy away', she was one of those who stayed put and stared hard. This combination of narrowness (in social experience, for example) and extreme self-awareness is one reason why her diaries are so compelling. When I first acquired my copies of the five volumes of Virginia Woolf's diaries, I did what probably many readers do. I turned immediately to the end, searching for portents of the suicide to come. Instead I found a life, unfinished, and Leonard about to do the rhododendrons. One incident, though, stayed in my mind. In early March of 1941, a couple of weeks before her suicide, Virginia went to the ladies lavatory at the Grill restaurant in Brighton. She had just been with Leonard to see her doctor because she was in a perilous mental state, deeply depressed, as she often was, by finishing a book, already half-starving herself, at this, the worst point in the war with Germany. Back home she wrote about the trip and how she had sat listening to the other women in 'The Ladies', peeing as quietly as she could (or 'p-ing', as she put it euphemistically). She recorded the talk in the cloakrooms laced with a vitriolic mixture of fury and disgust at the 'tarts' she'd overheard there. But that was far from the end of it. Her manuscripts reveal that she then drafted a sketch, 'The Ladies Lavatory', and in a sudden leap of the imagination she included a mysterious central figure, the lavatory attendant, who watched and heard everything. What, Virginia asked, would her memoirs be like? Then she turned the sketch into a short scene, with a more poetic, ambivalent title, 'The Watering Place'. She cleaned up the draft and the lavatory attendant, part-muse, part-artist, disappeared.

The imaginary lavatory attendant became the tutelary spirit of this book. That Virginia Woolf, daughter of South Kensington respectability, should try to identify with the woman at the bottom of the pile, still strikes me as extraordinary. It's typical too that she should delete her. The shadowy outlines of the poor and of servants can be seen in many of the earlier versions of Woolf's work. Why did she so often blue-pencil them out? Was it simply censorship? And what is simple about censorship? Certainly when Leonard Woolf came to publish selections from Virginia's journals in *A Writer's Diary*, a decade or so after her death, he bowdlerized the visit to Brighton with its 'spasms of irritation'. By so doing he made it harder for the reader to see how often Virginia's work was driven by the urgent need to handle and reshape what she found unaesthetic, even repulsive, especially when it concerned the life of the body. What was censored, avoided or voided rears its ugly head many times in this book: the place of hate in creativity; the force of hateful feelings in the making and destroying of our selves. Like other modernists experimenting in the art of fiction, Virginia Woolf often wrote from the darkest places in herself and from her least acceptable feelings; she frequently felt disconnected from others and feared the solipsism which resulted. She hoped to transform what separated her from others into forms of connection through art.

Virginia Woolf was a writer to whom the life of the mind, of consciousness, of feeling and memory, was paramount. In 'Sketch of the Past', her memoirs written towards the end of her life, Woolf called all those forces which act on an individual and make her or him a person in time and place 'invisible presences'. She was thinking of her mother in particular, whose absence filled her life for so long. Among all those internalized others – parents, siblings, friends, lovers – were also the servants, those women who were meant to be invisible but whose presence disturbed her so much. Woolf's childhood experiences, her mental instability (however it is categorized), her fraught relation to her body, made her especially sensitive to the issue of dependence. The idea of becoming independent – economically, but also emotionally and psychologically – powerfully motivated many of her generation of women as they emerged from Victorianism, and it certainly fuelled Woolf's feminism. I try to write about the ways in which the figure of the servant reminded Virginia Woolf that this enabling fantasy of independence, the idea of the fully self-directed, autonomous individual, remains just that, a fantasy.

What Virginia Woolf called 'the question of Nelly' was inseparable from a history of domination and servility in British cultural life. She was writing at a point when British society began to face the prospect of democratization and a better chance in life – in housing, health care and education – for the majority of British people. Her own world was under threat. At times she yearned to 'have no screens' between herself and others; at times she was furious at their invasion of her space. The competing claims, the different voices of different social groups, could sound to her ears like a mere cacophony, dissonant and harsh; in her later work she searched for forms through which to orchestrate a kind of polyphony, if not a harmony. Writers are especially prone to hear voices in their heads but that experience is not peculiar to them. In a famous formulation the psychoanalyst D. W. Winnicott once wrote that there was no such thing as a baby – only a baby and its mother. Equally we might say that there is no such thing as an individual, only the social relations by which we know our selves and our limits. Inside our selves, inside that room which can feel so much our own, is a society, a whole field of folk.

★

I have my own personal reasons for wanting to write this book. My grandmother, my mother's mother, Lilian Heffren, was a live-in servant for a time and her memories, which I grew up with, were always at the back of my mind. Like Nellie Boxall, she was born in the last decade of the nineteenth century. She too went into service as a young girl barely in her teens straight from the orphanage (the local workhouse), where she'd been placed after her parents' deaths. Her memories were grim and she often talked of being 'treated like dirt' by other women. In her first job she was a 'skivvy' or kitchenmaid, the lowest of the low: up at five to black the kitchen-range and lay the fires, scrubbing pans in the scullery all day, sweeping, cleaning, doing all the filthy jobs, until she dropped into her bed last thing at night. She had had a breakdown at sixteen, I was told, and her hair went white (when I found my first grey hair in my twenties, I imagined it was part of that legacy). She found life easier as a 'tweeny', or between-stairs maid, answerable to cook and housekeeper, but she had nothing good to say of service, or not that I recall. Though her story was as remote to me as Cinderella, it was one to which I was umbilically tied. I wanted to write this book to get to the bottom of some of those feelings which I associated with the 'class consciousness' I had grown up with. Not the feelings of solidarity and belonging, which were also there, but the messy, painful, intimate, damaging feelings of inferiority, envy, deference and belligerence.

When I first had the idea for this book a dozen or so years ago, I found it hard to think of domestic service except as exploitation, a species of psychological and emotional slavery – 'dependency', with its pejorative overtones, would be a more appropriate term. Writing the book has brought home to me how various and different servants' experiences were, and I have tried to see service

in terms of what it had to offer them, and what they made of it.
My own life underwent a seachange during those years. As I was
about to embark on the research my first husband, Raphael Samuel,
was diagnosed with cancer. A vigorous, strong-willed person, he
was quite Bolshevik about his illness, defying many of the conventional strictures, and acknowledging his limits only when he had
really tested them, so that his last months were lived as fully as he
could. Even so, despite his phenomenal energy, he had to suffer the
gradual, relentless erosion of his powers, as muscles wasted and gave
out, and I had to witness this. The circumference of life kept
shrinking at the insistence of the body, no matter how expansive
the mind and spirit remained. The process, as no doubt many readers
will know, was like that of premature ageing and brought with it,
as ageing itself does, the terror of loss, and the fear of being treated
like a child, patronized and turned into an object by others. It was
my first experience of looking after someone else's every need since
I was not a mother. Unlike mothering, in this case at least, the
helpless person became weaker, despite one's best attentions. I can
only gesture here at what this meant. I am still trying to make
sense of it, but I know that it affected this book when I finally
returned to work on it after Raphael's death. It made me think
and feel differently about the place of mourning in Virginia Woolf's
life and it seemed important to write about how that affected her
in becoming a writer. It also made the question of our dependence
on others look and feel different: this suddenly had an inevitability
about it, which I had seen face to face. Dependence was no longer
a question of whether, so much as when. And I also came to think
that the capacity to entrust one's life to the care of others, including
strangers, and for this to happen safely and in comfort, without
abuse, is crucial to any decent community and to any society worth
the name.

As the book became increasingly peopled, the solitary business
of literary criticism gave way to the more sociable pursuit of
biographical material – unpublished letters, interviews and the
visits to houses and places where the servants had worked. I met
local historians and I advertised for information in the press and

on the radio; there were several strokes of luck and several dead-ends. As the literary figures – famous or not – gradually became real people who lived in historical time, they became more, not less mysterious, more complicated as individuals, and I felt greater responsibility towards them. There are no saints or martyrs, no outright villains or heroines in what follows. I wanted to tell the stories in ways which would be satisfying and pleasurable but I also have tried to resist inventing motives or filling in gaps where I did not have the evidence, particularly of the servants' lives. Virginia Woolf's life provides the backbone to the book but the italicized paragraphs at the beginning of each section freed me to fictionalize a little, moving backwards and forwards over time as it suited me. Inevitably I've limited what I say about her writing and her life to what touches my subject most nearly. Virginia Woolf was full of gaiety as well as seriousness, hugely curious about other people, a writer with a vivid sense of humour, often at its most hilarious in the diaries, where her views are also at their most offensive (but isn't that part of our pleasure in reading them?). For a fuller picture of her the reader must go to the biographies.

What I found out about some of those who worked for the Woolfs is summarized in short biographical sketches in the Appendix at the close of the book. Writing about the servants' lives I've tried to upstage those of their employers but the relationship is not symmetrical and cannot be: I don't have the servants' versions of the story. Elsewhere I have included some passages from the autobiographies and memories of former servants but I have treated them gingerly. Many were produced or collected long after the events described and they need a fuller attention than I can give them here. As the book began to expand and take on the complexity of the lives under scrutiny, I felt more and more sure that a book about the servants' own feelings would have to be part of a much wider analysis and understanding of their lives and of the histories of the poor than I could attempt here. Food for thought, and for another volume, I hope.

Prologue

Down ill-lit corridors the servant scurries, disappearing into darkened chambers, hurrying back to the kitchens or the courtyards, a blur on the edge of vision. Servants form the greatest part of that already silent majority – the labouring poor – who have for so long lived in the twilight zone of historical record. Their voices are rarely heard and their features seldom distinguished. In the servant's case, though, anonymity often went with the job.

In mid- to late-nineteenth-century Britain, when live-in service was at a peak, servants' labour was meant to be as unobtrusive as possible. Relegated to the basements and the attics, using separate entrances and staircases (their activities muffled and hidden behind the famous 'green baize door'), segregated in separate wings and outbuildings, servants lived a parallel existence, shadowing the family members and anticipating their needs. In the grander households the lower servants were often unknown 'above stairs'. They might be hailed by their work-titles such as 'Cook' or 'Boots', or, if their own names were considered too fancy, given more suitable ones: 'Abigail', 'Betty', 'Mary Jane' were all in vogue at one time. Uniform also minimized individuality. Deportment and body language – the bowed head, the neatly folded hands – all aimed at self-effacement, preventing the servant from 'putting themselves forward'. The best servant was a kind of absent presence.

But that is only half the story. Though they might be obscured as individuals, servants were nevertheless always a visible sign of their employers' status. The aristocratic town houses or country estates sported an ostentatious retinue of hundreds. In particular the hefty footman was a piece of human furniture, paid by height and build; his quantity of unused muscle a measure of his master's opulence. His livery signalled that he was someone else's 'creature', but it also drew attention to him. At the other end of the social scale, even a wretched maid-of-all-work was evidence of her employers' respectability, of their aspirations to gentility, if not of their actual wealth. As the history of painting and portraiture confirms, a servant in the background puts the master in the centre of the frame. Any actual physical proximity – waiting at table, helping one to dress – was mitigated by social distance.

Over the centuries servants learnt to be amphibious. None more so than the live-in servant, moving between the classes, making a home within a home, a halfway house between kin and strangers. The pattern of going into service, taking a situation in another's household with board and lodging included (or 'diet and lodging' as it was known in the eighteenth century), is as old as service itself. Servants frequently encountered a different world from the one into which they had been born: they observed new codes of dress, manners and behaviour; they saw how the other half lived. If they had their wits about them, they managed to live a double life, adopting their employers' standards, but remaining outsiders, enjoying only a portion of the domestic comfort they made possible. The live-in servant had divided loyalties. Many worked in order to send their earnings home to relations whom they were seldom able to visit. Servants were expected to pin their colours to their employers' masts but they usually kept a foot in both camps.

Servants are everywhere and nowhere in history. Their very numbers have made any history of service nigh on impossible: in medieval times up to 60 per cent of the population were likely to work as servants and from its inception the great city of London was a city of servants. By the eighteenth century servants consti-tuted the largest single workforce in the capital – around 14 per cent of its entire population. A hundred years later, according to another estimate, one person in eleven was in service throughout Britain. But though they were legion, so much about servants was singular. Legally seen as the dependants of their employers, they were in principle free to leave. Their hours of work, their time off and their wages were often unregulated and the quality of their board and lodging, like the 'perks' or 'perquisites' which went with the job, varied enormously. The housekeeper in an affluent family, with responsibility for several staff, might have little in common with the lodging-house skivvy. Yet even a kitchenmaid could improve her life by moving to another, more generous mistress. In the big houses servants were often a self-sustaining community set apart from their fellows. Their personal dependence on their employers, who provided the roof over their heads and the food they ate, identified them with the status quo. Servants had no guild or trade union and rarely spoke up for their own interests as a group. Working in comparative comfort behind closed doors, deferring to their employers, and perhaps apeing them, the figure of the servant seems the opposite of the articulate, organized or collectively minded 'worker'. The work of the average housemaid might be every bit as backbreaking, and her hours every bit as long, if not longer, than that of the fieldworker or the miner, but she has little of their dignity; she hardly seems as victimized or exploited as the factory-hand returning home to a crowded slum-dwelling. The search for a better situation, the putting by of earnings with a view to marriage, are not rousing themes for banners or songs. The kitchenmaid's story has not yet found its place in accounts of how the English working class was made.

Service, in other words, has always been an emotional as well as an economic territory. The valet, the housekeeper and the slopper who emptied the chamber-pots all knew this as they stepped over the threshold of someone else's house. Service could be brutalizing and estranging; it could also be affectionate and devoted, but, however unequal the parties, it was always something more, or less, than a purely financial arrangement. Servants handled the worldly goods of their employers; they knew every nook and cranny of the house. They were the first up, getting the family out of bed in the morning; they kept them warm, they guarded and chaperoned; they fed, washed and clothed the people they worked for. They scoured the grease and hairs from the bath; they tried on new shoes to save their masters' feet. Marriages were played out before them; rows and lovemakings overheard; the upbringing of children, disputes between the generations – household crises were their staple fare. They were witnesses and eavesdroppers, allies and sometimes friends, whose emotional and sexual lives were entangled with those who gave them orders. Ruled by the cash-nexus, service was a relationship of trust which involved a mutual dependence. The servant, however vulnerable, wielded a precarious power.

For what is entrusted to the servant, be it only the crockery, is something of one's self, and being taken care of by a person who is seen as subordinate, an outsider or an inferior, is never without its anxieties and fears. Servants may leave only vestigial traces in the official histories of the past but they have always loomed large in the imagination of their employers. Inside every servant, or so it seems, is a sorcerer's apprentice whose rough magic is enough to send the rhythms of domestic order and of social life spiralling out of control: the slave who knows more than his master, the trickster turning the tables or getting the upper hand, the 'uppish' servant reappears in different guises through the ages. The figure of the servant casts a long shadow, disturbing the hearts and minds of all who like to think themselves in charge. But the servant was never only a species of agent provocateur, fomenting rebellion. Their intimacies with their betters knew few bounds. Servants were the body's keepers, protecting its entrances and exits; they were privy to its secrets and its chambers; they knew that their masters and mistresses sweated, leaked and bled; they knew who could pregnate and who could not get pregnant; they handled the lying-in and the laying-out. Servants have always known that the emperor has no clothes. No wonder they were dubbed both the scum of the earth and its salt, as they handled the food and the chamber-pots, returning dust to dust.

From medieval times to the middle of the twentieth century live-in service was the scaffold supporting life in the British Isles. For century after century most women expected either to be servants or to keep servants. Yet change did come. As momentous as women cutting their hair for the first time, as children leaving home before they got married, the disappearance of the live-in servant from the majority of British homes is a powerfully suggestive fact. When Virginia Woolf, who noticed it happening, declared that since her youth in the 1900s 'all human relations' had changed, she readily included those between 'masters and servants'. For her generation, what it meant to be British, at home and abroad, what it felt like to be a person, had always depended on having or being a servant. Had human character, as she hoped, at last changed?

ONE

The Family Treasure

Does housekeeping interest you at all? I think it really ought to be just as good as writing, and I never see — as I argued the other day with Nessa — where the separation between the two comes in. At least if you must put books on one side and life on t'other, each is a poor and bloodless thing. But my theory is that they mix indistinguishably.

Virginia Stephen to Violet Dickinson, December 1906

For Virginia Woolf the past was a house. It was a high old house of several storeys off a narrow, quiet cul-de-sac in a respectable and prosperous part of London: 22 Hyde Park Gate in South Kensington was her home until she was twenty-two and she returned to it constantly in her imagination and in her writing. It was a house full of 'small, oddly shaped rooms', which accommodated her parents' three families – the older Duckworth children from Julia Stephen's first marriage, the younger four Stephen siblings all born there, and Laura Makepeace Stephen, the child of Leslie Stephen's first marriage to one of Thackeray's daughters, 'the idiot', who ended her life in an asylum. Crowded, shared, but also segregated, the house was a space divided between parents and children, men and women, masters and servants. A place of retreat, it was also a workplace. Seven people waited on another eleven; they slept and ate there, in the attics and the basement, living a parallel life. This was the house with its unthinking, pellmell family life, like a great ship packed to the gunnels or a ship of fools, which sailed on blithely for thirteen years of Virginia Stephen's life only to be shipwrecked by her mother's death, 'the greatest disaster that could happen'.

As a child Virginia Stephen was amused and irritated by the servants, the first Pauline, for instance, slow and ruminative, with her odd English-German, fancying herself too good for a maid ('too hard work for that cow' Virginia had scribbled wickedly in her journal when she was fifteen), the clumsy second Pauline with the creaking boots, or the Irish slopper, shrinking when one passed. Jenny, Ellen, Florrie, Maud – they were so straitlaced it was fun shocking them with swearwords and naughtiness or trying to light fires better than they, but really one was too busy with one's own affairs (she was reading Carlyle on the French Revolution, borrowed from her father's library). They were such silly creatures, moved to tears and stillness, 'like tamed beasts', when they listened to music outside the drawing-room door. Yes, she wrote knowingly, their silence was what one craved above all.

Like other upper-middle-class girls, Virginia Stephen lived a cosseted existence, cared for by the servants. She'd been kept clean, fed and watered by them ever since the nursery. She woke to find the curtains drawn and jugs of water placed beside her wash-basin; her clothes – mended, laundered, brushed – were laid out for her; there was help on hand for buttoning boots or putting up her hair with the wretched pins. Of course no one in her circle shopped for food, let alone cooked an egg, or picked up their own clothes from the floor. For young ladies like Miss Stephen servants were largely unremarkable, simply the backdrop to the greater and more interesting drama of growing up. In the diary with which she was experimenting they naturally had the bit-parts, allowing her the lead role. Mocking their antics or foibles was a matter of playacting or showing off, a bravura performance, since for all her condescension Miss Stephen was more dependent than the skivvy: she couldn't give notice to leave. And 'Ginia' or Jinny, as her father called her, was especially vulnerable since she was prone – as she noted gaily in her journal – to 'lose her wits'. Writing about the servants was light relief, it turned life at Hyde Park Gate into a silly domestic comedy like those French plays at the Criterion or the Playhouse which her father took her to. Servants belonged to a commonsensical world of order and structure, while what happened in the family – madness, death, mourning – took place in a more brutal universe. At times in the Stephen household the drama of growing up seemed worse than tragic: life seemed senseless and shapeless; it had no plot.

Most of the servants at Hyde Park Gate came and went. The Stephens were merely a chapter in their own busy lives. Sophie Farrell, the family cook, was the exception. She joined the household in the 1880s and went on working for the family for fifty years. Her life spanned Virginia's, and she kept alive the connection with the values and habits associated with Virginia's long-dead parents, and especially her mother. Virginia kept in touch with Sophie through the years. She became 'old Sophy', an archaic figure in Virginia's imagination, a relic or survival from the past. For Sophie Farrell the celebrated Mrs Leonard Woolf was 'Miss Genia', a nervous, cheerful and sweet little girl.

In the late 1930s when Virginia began her memoirs, she was, like many of us, tempted into nostalgia. Reliving the long warm summers of childhood when the whole family decamped from London to Cornwall, she conjured up feelings of the 'purest ecstasy', of lying in the nursery listening to the waves break on the shore. But immediately she halted this drift. Childhood was also the place of suffering and despair, of waves that smashed rather than lulled. Few now were left who had shared or remembered those early years. She thought of Sophie Farrell, who had always gone with them to St Ives, and how as children up in the nursery they had lowered down a basket on a string to the kitchen; if Sophie was in a good mood she would fill it with treats, if in a temper she might cut the thread. Now, half a century later, Virginia wondered how the servants had stood their lives. The differences were so horribly apparent – the black beetles and the darkness in Sophie's basement, the threadbare carpet in the maids' attics which had embarrassed even her mother. Only in childhood was it possible to turn a blind eye. Perhaps not even then. Even then the obstinate presence of other people broke in on one's longings and fantasies; the basket came back empty rather than full.

SOPHIE FARRELL AND JULIA STEPHEN

Among the very few mementoes of the servants which can be found in the Virginia Woolf archives at Sussex University are four letters from Sophia Farrell, written to Virginia in the 1930s. After Sophie had retired, Virginia sent her an annual gift of £10, though Sophie had not been in the service of the Stephens for many years but had been working for the Duckworths, the other branch of Virginia's family. 'You are much too good to me,' Sophie writes over and again in her Christmas thank-you letters. 'I don't deserve such kindness. I am sure I don't.' 'I feel so unworthy of it all,' she reiterates. 'What a dear good generious [*sic*] lady you are to be so good & kind to me.' Sophie writes as she talks and spells 'by ear', her careful hand taking pains to be read. Her script belongs to an age when the majority of poor children were lucky to get their 'letters'. Virginia's flowing hand, by contrast, has all the casual illegibility of the socially confident. Always Sophie signs herself 'your obedient servant' or 'yours obediently, Sophia'. A conventional enough tag, 'I remain your obedient servant' might have been found at the bottom of letters from solicitors or officials well into the twentieth century. In Sophia Farrell's case it was not merely a form of words.

In the letters Sophie is both humble and snobbish, frequently mentioning her connection to the family and reminding Virginia how long she has known her: in December 1935, for instance, she calculates 'it will be 50 years on the 8th of next April that I first saw you', which means that she began her service to Julia and Leslie Stephen in the spring of 1886 when Virginia was four years old. The following Christmas of 1936 she mentions again, 'it's 50 years last Friday that I first cooked your Christmas dinner'. What news, she asks, of 'Miss Nessa and her charming children' or 'Master Adrian', how clever 'Master Julian' must be, how grateful she is that 'Mr and Mrs Gerald' (Duckworth) gave her luncheon or that she spent Christmas with Lady Margaret. How could someone who was shunted between members of the Stephen family when it suited them, unceremoniously dropped when they no longer needed her, who earnt a pittance compared to their substantial incomes, and who ultimately was left in old age with handouts and a rented room, be so content with the scraps from their table? Yet not a hint, not a scintilla of resentment; rather the reverse – 'Still I feel young & allway happy. I wish it all could come over again.'

Sophie's letters have a directness and a pathos but even so they make dodgy evidence. Letters are always written with one eye on the recipient, 'to spray an atmosphere round one', as Virginia once put it, and the image of the devoted and loyal old retainer was what Sophie wanted to create. In the old adage a servant is only as good as his master and Sophie's deliberate self-abasement is, paradoxically, the source of her self-esteem. The letters display Sophie's character by offering a testimonial to the family. And each declaration of her long service also celebrates her pride in her own longevity, the fact of survival, an achievement in itself for the labouring poor. 'I allways feel so proud that I was your servant for so many years,' she wrote to the famous author in

December 1939. 'It gives me so much to think of now I am old. For in a little over a year I shall be 80.' After fifty years of being a servant, if Sophie Farrell could no longer believe in the ideals of service and in her own usefulness, what sense would she make of her life?

Hardly any letters from the Woolfs' servants were kept. Live-in servants naturally had few occasions to write them and the rest of Sophie's correspondence has disappeared. Virginia – or Leonard – probably held on to these few because they had passing references to the old days at Hyde Park Gate and St Ives. Virginia's relationship to Sophie was inherited from her mother and was part of her own prehistory, the early years of childhood before her mother's death. In Virginia's fiction and essays the figure of the Victorian servant, shadowy versions of Sophie, conjured a complex mixture of feelings, of longing, of rage and of guilt. In one of her manifestations the Victorian servant was the good servant who gave unstintingly, a nurturing, maternal presence. She was also an embodiment of dependence, which for a later generation looked less like love or loyalty than power and subservience, and for Virginia herself was an acute reminder of her own defencelessness.

★

Nothing is dearer to the conservative imagination, be it that of the master or the servant, than the figure of 'the family treasure', the old retainer become friend, or indeed 'almost a member of the family' (a great deal depends upon that 'almost'). Yet this nostalgic vision obscures how temporary and mobile a form of employment service actually was. Very few of Sophie's generation, born in the middle of the nineteenth century, stayed in their 'places' for more than a year or two; most changed situations far more frequently, and the majority left to get married. In the 1860s there were over a million servants and around 400,000 single-servant households in Britain. Nearly 40 per cent of all women servants were aged under twenty. Like scores of others before and since her time, Sophie Farrell was not born a servant but had service thrust upon her; like so many others, she was a migrant, travelling hundreds of miles to the city to live and work in a stranger's house. She was propelled into serving others by a society which had no other use for poor girls from the country, though she, like the other servants in this book, was fortunate in her employers, and worked hard to make something of what had been made of her.

Though its cities grew at an astonishing rate and the urban population's demand for servants grew with it, Britain in the mid-nineteenth century was still a predominantly agricultural society and work on the land was the largest employer of the nation. Domestic service came second, but it was the chief employer of women. Since the enclosure of land in the eighteenth century, however, with the disappearance of smallholdings and the smaller farms, female servants who had formerly worked in husbandry, as dairymaids, on the land or as house servants, were finding fewer and fewer jobs. Employment at the 'big house' on country estates was always hard to come by and in the last quarter of the nineteenth century the agricultural depression drove more and more country men and women into the towns. Sophie was one of those country girls who made up the staple of urban domestic servants, driven into service by sheer economics as much as by any desire to serve.

Sophia Farrell was born on 13 May 1861 in Ranby, a tiny village on the edge of the Lincolnshire Wolds, whose smooth, rolling chalk uplands, marked by steep hills and dotted with woodlands, were quite unlike the flat stretches of marsh or fen country elsewhere in the county. In Ranby the Farrells lived in one of the cottages at Cross Road, next to the estate of the local landowner, Sir Francis Otter, for whom Charles Farrell, Sophie's father, was a gardener. Her mother, Ann, was a laundress on the estate. Otter was small fry as far as the county went but Ranby with its handful of tenants was effectively his fiefdom. The Farrells had two other little girls, Frances and Mary, Sophie's older sisters, and the census for 1861 also gives another domestic servant as lodging with the Farrell family, Emma Richardson, who was eighteen. Most likely she too worked for the estate. Within two or three years the family had moved to West Barkwith, a few miles away, equally tiny and remote. In the 1860s there were about 150 inhabitants in the village, mostly labourers working for a few farms; there was the church, All Saints, and the rectory. Sophie's father got a job working for the rector, the Reverend Edward Archer (MA, Trinity College Dublin), as a groom, looking after the horses and the garden. Sophie's childhood was spent in the purlieus of the rectory.

In a later sketch of a family cook, based on her talks with Sophie, Virginia Woolf recast her as 'Biddy Brien', once an 'O' Brien' and a Catholic. If the Farrells were originally O'Farrell, the evidence is hard to find. It's just possible that they emigrated from Ireland in the 1820s when the Irish first came over to Lincolnshire in large numbers for the harvest. Sophie's grandfather Michael Farrell can be found in Binbrook, another village on the Wolds, where labourers hired themselves out for seasonal tasks; unlike West Barkwith, it was an 'open' village (with an absentee landlord) and had a history of migration and discontent. Sophie's aunt, Hannah, was born in Binbrook but her father, Charles, grew up in the market town of Louth, and both were baptized Protestants. With its elegant Georgian streets, Louth was a prosperous place with plenty of carriage-folk and coaching inns, and at the time of the census of 1851, when he reached his majority, Charles was living there with Hannah and his brother-in-law Edward, working as a groom. In 1859 he married Ann Brown, a local girl, the daughter of a labourer. She made her mark in the register since she could not write her own name. Charles gave his father's profession as 'stonemason'.

Working for a man of the cloth and living in a tied cottage would have provided a measure of security and a step up in the world. Charles must have been a literate and God-fearing Anglican for he became the parish clerk and sexton at West Barkwith, which usually meant reading the lesson and responses in church, keeping parish records and burying the village dead. The family lived in a cottage close to the rectory for nearly fifteen years. There were eight more children after Sophie – Ellen, Olive, Agnes, Elizabeth, Henry, Rose, George and Charles – all baptized into the Church of England. The last little boy, born when his mother was forty-four, did not survive. Sophie was sixteen years his senior. Like her older sisters, she would have learnt to mind the little ones early on. Yet compared with the hand-to-mouth existence of most rural labourers, the Farrells were in clover. Charles's job meant decent housing, regular work and probably better food than the bread, bacon and potatoes that made up the staple diet of most of the farmworkers. Sophie's prospects were limited but her family were not among the very poor, the day-labourers hiring themselves out and sometimes barely scratching a living, walking miles from their parish because their landlords wanted to save money on the rates by not housing them on their land. Sophie would have been sturdy and independent from an early age, expected to work in the house and join in the fieldwork at harvest time. Though life on the Wolds was hard, there were worse places to have been born in rural Britain. In Dorset she might have starved to death.

The Wolds were different from other parts of the county. On the Wolds agriculture was undergoing a revolution and the tenant farmers were perfecting the most advanced practices, the 'high farming' which mixed arable with livestock or rotated crops to refertilize the land, reclaiming it from acres of uncultivated rabbit warren. Though miles from London, the Wold farmers were nevertheless known to be among the most prosperous and forward-thinking in the country (their agricultural show at Horncastle displaying the latest farm implements and equipment drew visitors from all over Europe). In Lincolnshire the landed estates were much larger than the national average (the Earl of Yarborough, for instance, had over 56,000 acres towards the north of the county), and the tenant farmers, who rented land, were often wealthy and powerful men. Landowners and the larger tenant farmers – the squirearchy – ran pretty much a closed shop. The wealthiest men in the county were also the Members of Parliament and the local magistrates;

they invested in the railways and diverted them at will when they looked like spoiling their land; they made the roads take detours round their property, put up towers and arches in their own names and decorated the churches with plaques in their own memory, fashioned by their workmen. Parish life varied and depended very much upon the landlord. Some landlords liked their tenants to be presentable at all times; they housed them in estate cottages whose architecture neatly matched their own Halls, they liked them to wear corduroy and insisted on their tenants attending church. With a good landlord a tenant might have a cottage, a pig, a little strip of garden; the landlord's womenfolk might help with welfare schemes and invite the farmworkers to plum-bread and tea when a son and heir was born. The press was always fond of printing glowing accounts of feast days when tenants expressed – or were expected to express – their gratitude. But equally it had to report the need for soup kitchens in some districts and dire poverty: these same landlords could evict their tenants at short notice or have them arrested if caught poaching; landlords sat on the bench and sent their former tenants to prison.

Not everyone was prepared to doff the cap. In the 1830s Lincolnshire had its share of 'Captain Swing' riots and forty years later labourers burnt the hayricks again in protest at high prices and falling wages. The farmers soon showed their colours by forming a special division of volunteers to ride against the men. Those in the larger, open villages, without a resident landlord watching their every move, were more likely to turn to Methodism and to self-help – the agricultural trade union began in Lincolnshire – but nonetheless the slow process of learning self-respect took many decades. It would take a century for many 'labourers' to call themselves 'farmworkers'. On the big estates many felt they were comparatively well off since they were not starving and had a roof over their heads, especially the families of 'confined' men, the shepherds and bailiffs and workers with steady jobs and tied cottages. Yet the image of a happy tenantry feeding off cakes and ale provided by their betters has to be reconciled with the mass emigrations from Lincolnshire to Australia and New Zealand. If there were other opportunities, sometimes whole villages voted with their feet.

Sophie was brought up in the heartlands of deference. In county society the Anglican clergy was generally aligned with the most conservative elements of village and parish life and, since West Barkwith had no resident landlord, the rector was the gentry's spokesman and the leading figure in the village. Sundays always gave the parson a chance to bring home the lessons of knowing one's station in life and it was rarely in the interests of a clergyman to rock the boat. Many were themselves the younger sons of the landowners (at Ranby Sir Francis put his second son, John, into the living) – the 'squarsons'. In church the gentry usually had the front pews and the labourers were shunted to the back; they knew their place even in death, when they were frequently buried out of the way on the north side of the churchyard under temporary markers. The parson strongly influenced the village school – if it existed, he managed any public charity work and as a Guardian he administered the hated Poor Law, overseeing the entry of indigent or aged parishioners into the workhouses. Often the local clergy were also Justices of the Peace. There were kindly, charitable and decent parsons who cared for their flock, of course – the diary of the Reverend Francis Kilvert, for instance, reveals how well loved he was by his parishioners in Radnorshire in the 1870s – and many villagers found comfort and consolation in the Church and its teaching. Sophie's childhood, like that of most Victorian children, would have revolved around the church calendar and church attendance, but her father's position put the Christian faith much more firmly in the centre of family life. Charles Farrell might be 'servant to the Rector', enjoying a fuller stomach and a little more respectability than his neighbours, but it was a humble enough position, entirely dependent upon patronage.

As for schooling, Sophie simply missed the boat. In the 1860s few Lincolnshire children were in school after the age of ten. In the towns the larger charitable foundations took pride in training 'the children of the lower orders of society' with a view to 'the useful attainments and moral and religious habits which Servants now under instruction in our National Schools will have acquired'. Where they existed in the villages, schools relied on private initiatives, a 'dame school' taught by a local widow or a poor school run ad hoc by the clergyman or his daughters (Charlotte Brontë has her heroine Jane Eyre set up such a place). Before education became compulsory, through a series of piecemeal changes from the 1870 Act onwards, village children had to take pot luck. They mostly went to school in the winter when there was little work in the fields. Three years before the Elementary Education Act, when Sophie was six, her near neighbour, Edward Heneage, Esq., MP, the local bigwig of Hainton Hall, whose estate of 10,000 acres or so brought in £15,000 in annual rents, was of the opinion that poor children 'should go to school until 9 years of age', after which it should be 'optional'. If Parliament insisted on raising the school-leaving age, 'it will and must be the ruin of all our best labourers', he maintained, 'and will drive them either to the workhouse or out of the country altogether'. Heneage, a widower, kept up a sumptuous establishment, living with his daughter and battalions of servants.

Such a view was necessarily shared by many parents, especially the poorest, who would not be able to make ends meet without the few pence earnt by wives and children. In Lincolnshire women and children went out in gangs to work the fields, much to the disapproval of the clergy, who saw any woman working as liable to be 'light' in morals and also vulnerable, though the girls who worked on the land liked the life, which gave them their evenings and Sundays free. Local children, some as young as six or seven, would be out setting or picking potatoes or 'singling' turnips, 'tenting' or scaring birds, weeding, picking stones and gleaning. Working with the gangs they might earn 6d or 8d a day (around 3p in today's money), though after walking four or five miles there, and working an eight-hour day, they often had to be carried home. Not surprisingly, illiteracy was high in Lincolnshire. Sophie's mother could not write – she'd made a mark on the marriage certificate – though she may have been able to read. Writing was always seen as less 'useful' in the labouring classes though reading was a handy skill for a servant to acquire. Once the new law came in, which encouraged the establishment of elementary schools, Edward Heneage contributed to the founding of a joint-parochial school for East and West Barkwith, which opened in 1873. Too late for Sophie. By then she was twelve and it was time to go into service as her older sisters had done.

'Going into service': what did it mean? All over Victorian Britain girls as young as twelve or thirteen were setting off with their boxes or trunks, trying to be brave as they said goodbye to family, or leaving with the hope of a better existence than their mother's. As a servant they might eat better, dress better, sleep more comfortably than at home; they might put a bit by or send a few shillings home. A girl who had been in service was more marriageable since she had more housewifely skills. She was earning her keep and those few pennies might make all the difference to her family's survival; she had her pride and, for most, service was preferable as a more respectable option than fieldwork. As a social training and one which offered both a wage and a roof over their heads, sending a child into service was frequently chosen by parents as the best thing for their children. Not all girls hated the idea, especially given the alternatives. For many like Sophie Farrell service was their only chance of seeing the world and escaping the poverty at home.

Sometime in the late 1870s the family left West Barkwith. A new rector had arrived and he, perhaps, felt no loyalty towards Charles and Ann. Perhaps the Farrells were simply too many and Charles, now in his fifties, was getting too old to dig graves. The wheel turned. It was the end of their period of stability, it seems, and the family disappears from view for a decade. In 1891 the Farrells can be found back in Louth, with Charles in his sixties, a general labourer. Only Rose and George are left at home, the one a domestic servant and the other, at fifteen, an errand-boy, bringing in a little cash.

In one sense Edward Heneage was right. Lincolnshire's children were leaving and education played its part. A new desire for independence and not to go into agricultural work was blamed for the exodus but it received a major impetus from the agricultural depression in the last quarter of the century. Although the railways had turned some Lincolnshire towns into thriving industrial centres, they also enabled migration and by the 1880s Lincolnshire had become a county of migrants: in many parishes fewer than half who were born there stayed put. There were five trains a day from Louth to London, newspapers and post had improved, and now girls wanting domestic work could advertise and go further afield. Why stand about like cattle in the May Day hirings of the market square having your points judged when there were more civilized ways of getting a job?

How Sophie came to travel to London – a journey of nearly 150 miles – is unknown. She would certainly have needed previous experience before she could move to a large household as a cook. This was a skilled position, at the top of the hierarchy on 'the kitchen side' as opposed to that on 'the house side'. Country girls putting on airs and graces and returning home to flaunt their finery were a popular target for moralists, but town ladies preferred girls like Sophie Farrell whom they felt were more tractable, especially if, like Sophie, they had worked for the gentry in small parishes dominated by the local landowners. Just as well, though, that she was not O'Farrell since prejudice was rife in London against Irish maids. It was expensive to bring a young girl out of the country and might take hours of supervision to polish her manners, though a cook's ways needn't be too dainty since she was largely invisible. She would repay the investment by staying longer if her family were far distant and a girl like Sophie would then be relied on to train up her own kitchenmaids. In the 1880s a cook might expect to earn up to £20 a year in a reasonably affluent London situation, a kitchenmaid half as much – though wages varied enormously depending on the household, the district and the goodwill of the employers. Sophie had had a godly training; she knew her station in the world and believed in duty and hard work. Effectively orphaned and a long way from home, fully dependent on her employers, she had the makings of an ideal servant. Did she ever return to Lincolnshire? Perhaps once a year at least for her holiday. She would surely have gone back for her parents' funerals in the first year of the new century when Charles and Ann both died. Their headstone is one of those now stacked on the west side of Louth cemetery, cleared to make room for other graves.

★

In the 1860s, while her future cook was growing up in Lincoln-shire, Virginia Woolf's mother, Julia Jackson, was already running her first married home in Bryanston Square, north of Oxford Street in central London. At twenty-one she had married a handsome lawyer, Herbert Duckworth, thirteen years her senior. It was a love match. Herbert and Julia were both from that British upper-middle class in which the professions, the county families, administrators and colonial rulers, and a smattering of aristocracy were intermingled and intermarried. His family now owned a house and land in Somersetshire from money originally invested in cotton mills; she had been born among the governing classes in India, where he too had connections, and her mother was one of the seven Pattle sisters, famous in their day for their beauty or their cleverness. Julia grew up in a literary, political and artistic milieu, frequenting her Aunt Sara Prinsep's salon at Little Holland House in Kensington, where one might encounter Browning or Gladstone, Tennyson, Watts and Burne-Jones (both of whom painted Julia), and where she first met Anny and Minny Thackeray, the novelist's daughters, who were to become firm friends. Herbert was, by all accounts, a sweet-tempered and lovable man, and, according to Leslie Stephen, a 'thorough country gentleman', educated at Eton and Trinity College Cambridge, though not, perhaps, the liveliest of intellects. If friends were slightly surprised that the intelligent, beautiful, cultured Julia had fallen for the rather conventional Herbert, no one doubted that the marriage was a very happy one. The Duckworth infants were to be born, if not into the lap of luxury, then into ease and prosperity. Only good fairies were expected to preside over their cradles.

When the Duckworths married in 1867, a new cult of domesticity, with the family at its centre, was well underway. In London terraced houses had become increasingly family-occupied and family-oriented, as opposed to the multiple tenancies and mixed occupation of earlier centuries. Before the Victorian housing boom, Georgian terrace houses had often been divided vertically into separate floors with three or four (or more) families jostling on top of each other. Apartments were sometimes subdivided and sublet with the poorest lodgers taking the basement or cellar. Tenants shared the hall and landings, and it was quite usual for families to cook, wash, sleep and entertain in one or two thinly partitioned rooms. Single lodgers might dine with a resident family, or pay for meals to be cooked by the landlady and brought to their rooms, or have a pie sent up from the local tavern or cookshop. The more affluent, who could afford to rent entire houses, adopted the aristocratic model of giving over different rooms to different activities and times of the day, eating in one, sleeping in another, entertaining in another still. During the nineteenth century this practice extended further into the middle classes, and Victorian houses were built to incorporate this expectation. Kitchens were hived off at the back or sent underground into basements, where now only the servants ate. By the mid-century dinner was eaten at the end of the working day, at six or seven rather than three or four ('luncheon' became a new feature). In Julia's childhood in the early part of the century men often formed a separate group from the ladies at the table; the new fashion was to seat them alternately. Rather than place all the victuals on the table, with the gentlemen frequently helping the ladies, it became stylish amongst the genteel to eat 'à la Russe', bringing in one course after another, and changing the plates and cutlery for each course.

Every room needed its accoutrements and every activity its accessories. There were new standards of personal comfort as Britain's flourishing industries and its Empire produced a greater variety of goods. The old draughty, sparsely furnished rooms or halls of the eighteenth-century gentry now smacked of poverty (their turn would come round again in due course when the moderns recoiled from Victorian knick-knacks and upholstery). Some of the changes to furnishings and fittings were already in place in the grander town houses at the end of the late eighteenth century: fitted carpets rather than rugs, wallpaper covering the wainscoting. Dark mahogany from the Empire was now generally preferred over rustic English oak, and 'mahoganized' skirting boards and doors added depth to a room. The Victorians rearranged the sofas, no longer standing furniture off the carpets and against the walls, so that the hearth, symbol of home and product of industry, with its gleaming fenders and scuttles and irons, came to the fore. Coal was ubiquitous, and hob grates made for a better distribution of heat over the house, though lighting often depended on candles in sconces or upon oil lamps rather than gas, which was expensive and considered unreliable until the Houses of Parliament adopted it in 1852. And just as someone had to bring in the dishes and wait at table, clear, wash and dry the new crockery, scour the pans with sand and furbish up the silver, someone had to sweep the piled carpets, draw back the heavy plush curtains, keep fingermarks off the walnut tables, smooth the antimacassars and plump up the armchair cushions, polish the brass, blacklead the grates and ranges, light the fires – no mean feat in the days of tinder-boxes and feeble sulphur matches – carry jugs and cans of water up and down, rake out the dead ashes and empty the ashcans. By dint of their labour, the servants worked hard to create for their employers the tranquillity and ease which were the essence of home, sweet home. A servant for each task, if one could afford it, and Herbert and Julia could: cook and kitchenmaids, housemaid, parlour-maid, a lady's maid, a nurse and a nursemaid, a gardener. And in the Duckworth circle, a plethora too of casual help from 'the wash' to the knife-grinder, and all the troop of back-door callers who kept the house and its inhabitants up to the mark.

Fewer people – especially in London – now ran their own businesses or workshops at home, and more and more people travelled to town or to the burgeoning City on the new railways.

The idea of home, sequestered from work, a retreat and a refreshment, took on a new emotional and economic power. Herbert didn't need to work for a living but he nonetheless 'practised, not very seriously, at the Bar', while Julia looked after household matters and her growing brood. Though the reality of their lives was never so neat and tidy, men and women were meant to adapt to these 'separate spheres' of life: he to the world of commerce and labour, and she to the 'Queen's Garden' of home, as John Ruskin famously called it, 'the place of Peace, the shelter, not only from all injury, but from all terror, doubt and division', where she might reign supreme. Naturally both Herbert and Julia had grown up with servants and Julia had learnt early the habit of authority, since her mother was invalidish. By all accounts Julia was an ideal wife, beautiful and serene, but also an efficient organizer, rustling in her silks from the top to the bottom of the house, supervising the servants. The 'Angel in the House', that self-sacrificing feminine presence, who always put the needs of others first, was only one half of the equation. She might be gracious and unworldly but she must also exercise firm, if not ruthless, authority. Hers was the little Empire of home, an *imperium in imperio*.

The welter of manuals on 'home management' and advice books on 'domestic expenditure' published throughout the period are evidence of how much effort and forethought, how much constant bustle, was needed to create this ideal haven of domestic calm. As Isabella Beeton put it in the first sentence of her *Book of Household Management* in 1861, the domestic Bible of many homes, 'As with the Commander of an army, or the leader of any enterprise, so it is with the mistress of a house.' With careful timetables and strict superintendence of subordinates, the house was to run like clockwork. Devising menus, ordering food, checking the state of the linen and gently breathing down the necks of her servants to make sure they were doing their jobs properly were all part of her supervisory role. Ideally too – so the advice went – the mistress must be up before her servants and know their work better than they did. The new fashions of crinoline and slippers might hamper a lady's movement but she could always keep her maid on the

go. It did not matter that even the minimal apparatus of respectability – a parlourmaid and cook – was beyond the reach of most
Victorian households. The manuals were largely aspirational, aimed
at a middle class upwardly mobile, if only in their imaginations.
There were contradictions everywhere. In theory the Victorian
lady was not meant to handle money, yet she had to balance the
books; husbands were not supposed to interfere in the housekeeping but ultimately they kept the purse strings. Time and again
the pundits warned against leaving things to the servants; debt
was a serious liability with so many new things to buy and young
women got precious little training in arithmetic (there must have
been many young mistresses like Dickens's hopeless Dora, David
Copperfield's first wife, who lets her pet dog trot over the accounts
and the 'girl' serve them undercooked joints). And how could a
mistress be more knowledgeable than her servants when menial
work of any kind was increasingly seen as degrading or 'vulgar'
and respectable women no longer scrubbed floors or washed their
dirty linen in public?

   In the 1830s and 40s the Evangelical revival in Britain had
reinforced the idea of master and mistress as moral guides and
influences. The lady of the house was to be the emotional and
spiritual heart of family life, a patron and model for her servants,
who would look up to their 'betters' only if they were superior
in sensibility as well as status: only those who knew how to govern
themselves were fit to govern others, and the 'interior government'
of oneself was reflected in the order achieved in one's home.
Conversely, a slovenly home reflected on the morals of the mistress
as much as the maids. At best, mistresses were to be like mothers
to their charges, softening the economic relation and such power
as they actually wielded. However inexperienced themselves,
mistresses were considered responsible for their servants' 'moral
welfare'. A mistress might be shocked, let down, infuriated by her
servants, but she did not feel guilty about entering their rooms,
inspecting their belongings or intervening in their lives. Sexual
misconduct could not be tolerated. With young working-class
girls in the house there must be no hint of scandal. A 'moral

shock' was certainly administered to the household of Thomas Carlyle, the eminent critic and historian, when his wife, Jane, belatedly discovered that a hapless maid had given birth in the china closet and kept it secret. The master had been entertaining a guest in the dining room at the time with 'just a thin small door between!' Mrs Carlyle made a wry joke of it in her correspondence but 'the creature' was instantly sent packing. Thirty-four maids came and went in the thirty-two years the Carlyles lived at Cheyne Row in Chelsea (not counting chars or other temporaries). Thomas Carlyle was an exacting master at the best of times and Jane Carlyle, in keeping with the times, believed it right that she should expend all her energies and considerable talents protecting him from domestic unpleasantness. Even the most liberal-minded mistress could be autocratic: when Elizabeth Barrett Browning's devoted maid, Lily Wilson, married and had a child, Lily was obliged to send him back to England, so as to concentrate properly on the Brownings' own ringleted boy.

Deference and a modest demeanour – never being over-familiar or 'forgetting oneself' – was assumed to be part of the servant's contract. 'A servant is not to be seated, or wear a hat in the house, in his master's or mistress's presence; nor offer any opinion, unless asked for it; nor even to say "goodnight" or "good morning", except in reply to that salutation,' wrote Mrs Beeton, in one of the many inventories of rules for servants. The strictest homes kept time off to a minimum – an afternoon a week at best, and every other Sunday. Alternate Sundays were spent in church though 'servants' church' was usually later in the day so that the family's Sunday dinner might go undisturbed. Morning or evening prayers conducted by the master were a common household ritual. Most tried to institute a 'No followers' rule. Uniform did away with personal vanity as well as putting paid to the anxiety that maids dressed in their mistresses' cast-offs were indistinguishable from them (it also prevented servants from doing a trade in their employers' old clothes which had been a perk in the past). Servants were usually expected to purchase their uniforms themselves. The practice of giving servants more suitable names was another way of making individuals anonymous. Mrs Carlyle, for instance, abbreviated 'Florence' – 'too long and too romantic a name for household use!' she exclaimed – to the more plebeian 'Flo'.

For many working women, service was often an uneasy truce with the values they were meant to share but which made little sense to them: being thrifty, for instance, on their meagre wages, or staying loyal to one household. Complaints were frequently made about the 'roving disposition' of women servants, who moved places as they felt like it. One estimate in 1876 reckoned that 10 per cent of London female domestics were looking out for a new post, and there were clearly servants who relished the chance to direct their own fortunes. Hannah Cullwick, who took on some of the roughest kitchen jobs as maid and scullion, and whose diaries are among the very rare written testimonies of a servant's life in the period, clearly valued her independence and pitied her mistress, mewed up at home: 'that's the best o' being drest rough, & looking "nobody"', she wrote, 'you can go anywhere & not be wonder'd at'; adding, 'I would not be set up for a lady if I could help it, not for a fortune – I'd rather be low & work for my own bread.' Others hoped to save as they grew older in service: house-keepers, nannies and cooks in wealthier establishments were more likely to accept the rules since they had more to gain. Such 'upper' servants generally had the incentive of status and of disciplining and instructing their subalterns.

By the 1880s the novelties of the 40s and 50s had assumed the mantle of tradition. Servants had always, so it seemed, been in uniform, always followed specialized tasks, and had always been paid accordingly in fine gradations. The principles of a well-run home depended upon separation, segregation and subordination – a place for everything (and everyone) and everything in its place. In practice it was far harder to maintain ranks.

★

When Sophie Farrell began work at 22 Hyde Park Gate in 1886 she was twenty-five and would have been working for nearly a

22 Hyde Park Gate

dozen years. Julia was forty and had been managing a home for half her lifetime. She was now Mrs Leslie Stephen. In 1870, when she was twenty-four and pregnant with their third child, Gerald, Julia's idyllic life with Herbert Duckworth had been shattered by his sudden death 'She was as unhappy as it is possible for anyone to be,' Virginia recalled her as saying, and Stella Duckworth remembered that their mother, an undemonstrative woman, used to lie on Herbert's grave. After several years of widowhood, fussed over by friends and family ('oh the torture of never being left alone!' she would say of those years), of devoting herself to 'doing good', nursing and poor-visiting, she moved to Hyde Park Gate in South Kensington. It was there that she gradually accepted the attentions of her bereaved neighbour, Leslie Stephen, who had married Julia's beloved friend Minny Thackeray. Minny had died at the age of thirty-eight in 1875. A Cambridge don and ordained as an Anglican cleric, Leslie had lost his faith and embarked on a literary life as editor, writer and critic. He had become a fiercely anti-Christian polemicist, attacking the delusive consolations of religion, sentiments to which Julia was strongly attracted. She too had relinquished her religious convictions through the long years of mourning. They were married in 1878 though Julia, who felt her own life had been blighted, feared that she could not make this depressed, often morose, widower happy. When Sophie arrived, Julia's three children from her first marriage were in their teens. Leslie and Minny's daughter, Laura Makepeace Stephen, who was sixteen and suffering from a mental abnormality or handicap of some kind, was largely kept confined in the house, eating her meals with her nurse in the nursery. Leslie and Julia had four children, a younger generation who made a confederacy of their own: Vanessa, aged seven, Thoby a year younger, Virginia who was four and Adrian, the baby, nearly three years old.

With its tall white stucco-fronted houses, Hyde Park Gate was (and is) a quiet cul-de-sac, off the Kensington Road, a 'little backwater of a street' Leslie Stephen wrote approvingly, whose 'intrinsic calm' was 'almost like the country'. It had been built in 1843 as part of the huge expansion of the West End of London, providing salubrious town houses for the upper echelons of British society. Kensington, home of Kensington Palace, close to Hyde Park and Buckingham Palace, housed the grandest of London's residents – it became a royal borough in 1901. Together with Bayswater, it was also the home of imperial connection, of the affluent Anglo-Indian families, bankers and investors, who rubbed shoulders with the aristocracy and the ambassadorial class, as well as the artistic milieu in which Julia had grown up. For the upper-middle classes Kensington was a village, 'a little colony' of interconnected family and friends all within walking distance. Herbert's sister, Sarah Emily (known as 'Minna'), lived at 18 Hyde Park Gate, and Anny and Minny Thackeray had grown up in nearby Young Street. Leslie Stephen had been born close by. When he married Minny they moved to Onslow Gardens in South

Kensington. In Leslie's boyhood of the 1830s there had been country fields and market gardens in South Kensington but the Victorians were modernizers, not least in bulldozing eighteenth-century tenements and putting up new housing at a phenomenal rate. Parts of the district were still a building site. The Metropolitan Railway, London's first underground railway, running from Paddington to Farringdon and then extended down to South Kensington, brought the populace to the new 'South Kensington Museum' (later the Victoria and Albert), the Science Museum and the Natural History Museum – all free of charge – which loomed over the neighbourhood in all their dark-red Gothic grandeur. High Street Kensington was home to large department stores, including Barkers, Julia Stephen's favourite venue, Cramer's music shop, Mudie's Select Library and an ABC (Aerated Bread Company) for tea and cake, which often makes its way into Virginia's early journals.

Number 22 Hyde Park Gate had been adapted over the years to accommodate its ever-growing number of inhabitants, adding on two extra floors at the top and a dining-room extension on the lower-ground level at the back. Inside the people were arranged, vertically in their groups, as in a doll's house, coming together at designated times of the day, their movements often regulated by the lighting of fires. High up under the roof, where the stair carpet ran out, the servants had their shabby attic bedrooms; below them was Leslie Stephen's book-lined study – no servant would be there in the daytime to disturb the master while he laboured on the monumental volumes of the *Dictionary of National Biography*; the little Stephen children had their day and night nurseries on the third floor with their nurse; on the second floor were bedrooms and sitting rooms for the almost grown-up Duckworth siblings, while the first floor was given over to Leslie and Julia, their double bedroom, and a room where Julia's mother stayed. Julia had had the woodwork in the house painted black 'under the influence of Titian', as was the mid-Victorian manner, and there were busts 'shrined in crimson velvet' and dark portraits in oils. The ground-floor double-length drawing room was partitioned by folding black doors, lined with red: the front half had its piano and writing table, and was where the ladies of the house sat, served tea at the appointed hour and received visitors; the back half was a retreat for other family activities. There was a small conservatory. Across the hall, with its twisting staircase, was the dining room, smelling of food, wine and cigars, with its heavily carved sideboard and long baize-covered table, where Julia taught the children, sitting upright in the carved oak chairs with their red-plush panels. When the Stephens married, Leslie had moved into Julia's house, bringing his own substantial accumulation of furniture, books, papers and goods. There were built-in china cupboards, mammoth wardrobes and tallboys or chests of drawers squeezed into corners and on landings to house the cumbersome frocks and snowy piles of sheets, pillowcases, tablecloths and napkins without which Victorian domestic life was impossible. There was no electric light. Passages and corridors were crowded and the rooms, which had little natural light, were overshadowed by a Virginia creeper outside, draped over the windows. In other words, the house was typically Victorian in its aesthetics and decoration; it was cloistered and protected, insulated from the cares of the world.

Sophie's domain was the basement. The Stephens' house had its 'backstairs' world. A plush curtain hung over the top of a staircase in the dining room, muffling the servants' activities and keeping the cooking smells, no longer considered suitable for genteel noses, at bay. Down the flight of stairs, in almost 'incredible gloom', Sophie and the maids had a poky sitting room next to the kitchen, with a shiny black sofa and a vast cracked, extremely bad portrait of Julia's parents for company. The view out of the window through the iron railings was of the dusty patch of back garden. The insanitary basement for the six or seven maids was damp as well as dark and cold; the servants' attics were stifling in summer. Years later Virginia remembered one of the maids bursting out to Julia, 'it's like hell' and being instantly banished to the pantry. Her breaking out was the exception, however, since these conditions were fairly standard. There were three water-closets for the seventeen or eighteen people in the house. The servants had their own and it was usual for the gentlemen and ladies to have separate lavatories. Chamber-pots would be used at night, scoured in the 'slop-room' where the row of brass cans stood; the family took their baths in a tin tub in the one bathroom, with a bath that needed filling with cans full of boiled water, each weighing about thirty pounds, carried up several flights of stairs. Servants generally relied on 'a lick and a promise' in cold water from the jug and basin in their rooms.

Sophie would have needed her dozen or so years of experience, though where she worked in the intervening years before the Stephens' house is unknown. Probably she had started as a kitchenmaid and graduated to cooking. As she had no professional training Sophie was known as a 'plain' cook, which meant, nonetheless, being able to turn out three meals a day if needed, bake bread, scones and cake for tea, and cope with the family's entertaining. The cheerful author of *The Management of Servants*, a practical guide written in the 1880s, reckoned plain cooking 'makes but very little work in comparison with professed cooking', describing the meals thus: 'The dinner generally consists of fish, a joint and vegetables, a pudding or tart; and the luncheon is either a joint, vegetables and plain pudding, or cold meat, salad and potatoes.' In a small household the luncheon joint 'answers for the children's dinner, and for the servants' dinner' but at Hyde Park Gate there were five males, five females and six or seven servants – seventeen mouths to feed, with the frequent addition of guests for luncheon, tea or dinner. Julia had an 'at home' on Sunday afternoons. Cooking was done in the basement by the flare of a small gas light, in 'almost complete darkness', and with no running hot water. Though the days of open fires, roasts on spits and pots hanging from 'jacks' or hooks were gone, the new kitchen-ranges or 'kitcheners' needed constant stoking with fuel and could be very temperamental. It was hot and heavy work, needing strong arm muscles. Fuel was kept in the wood cupboard outside the kitchen in the square of yard at the front of the house inside the railings ('the area'); deliveries were made to the kitchen door in the basement. Mealtimes structured the day for all the family and punctuality was crucial. Since ovens had no temperature gauges, Sophie would have tested the heat with her arm or hand. (Another popular manual, *The English House-keeper* (1842), advised keeping the kitchen clock under lock and key lest the cook alter it with a broom handle to suit her purposes.) Sophie had the maids as deputies to fetch and carry food to the table, including a scullery girl who would scrub floors and tables and see to the endless piles of washing-up. In most houses china 'butler sinks' had replaced the old lead ones but they had to be lined with a tea-towel to prevent breakages and, being a foot deep, they made the shoulders and back ache from the continual stooping over them. There was little time off during the day, though the afternoon was generally quieter. The working day ended for the maids when the last dish had been dried and put away on the dresser and either Mrs Stephen or Sophie sent them up to bed.

In the upper-middle-class home lives went on in parallel but there was not much individual privacy except, perhaps, for the master. Julia began the day by descending to the kitchen to discuss the meals. Sophie would order food, go provisioning or send out, take deliveries into the kitchen (in the absence of refrigeration milk was delivered two or even three times a day in warm weather), as well as organize and cook the day's meals. In the mornings the maids performed their cleaning and polishing as discreetly as possible in print frocks and brown aprons, changing into their black wool dresses, with clean, white aprons and caps for the afternoon and evening, unless they worked only in the kitchen. For all its constant cleaning, the Victorian house was one of the dirtiest places to be, particularly in smoke-ridden London, where the furnishings gathered dust, daily smuts and grime. Curtains, rugs and upholstery would be beaten by hand; carpets swept with a brush – sometimes after damp tea leaves had been laid down to help collect up dust. Coming from Puritan stock, Leslie Stephen disliked what was considered unnecessary luxury. On his travels in the USA he had experienced central heating and he had found American plumbing – 'all the water through spouts goes everywhere', as his first wife put it – mildly corrupting. His sister-in-law, Anny, had put in hot water and it had nearly bankrupted her and her husband. It was simpler and cheaper to use servants to carry water-cans and to install a cold tap in the kitchen. In the mornings the slopper went to and fro, emptying chamber-pots into the water-closet and swilling out the dirty water from the basins. No lady would flit along a corridor to use a lavatory at night.

From 1882, the year of Virginia's birth, until 1895, the year of her mother's death, the family took a house in Cornwall for the summer, Talland House in St Ives. The extended break spanned the whole season, often from June to mid-October. Hyde Park Gate was shut up, the dust sheets were thrown over the furniture, ornaments were washed, and the opportunity was taken to give each room a thorough going-over; ceilings might be re-whitened. Like other middle-class Victorian families renting a holiday home, the Stephens took much of their own household with them – books, clothes, pets and servants – though they also hired local people to help out – Jinny Berryman, who did domestic work and supplied chickens, and Mrs Daniels, who took in the family's washing and carried it up the drive to the house in a huge wicker basket. The servants in London would have their holidays staggered throughout the summer months (they were usually expected to work at Christmas) but Sophie always accompanied the family to St Ives. Virginia remembered her lording it over 'her' kitchen, bossing the other girls and the local help, standing at the back door to receive the joints of meat, flying off the handle as cooks were wont to do in the heat of the kitchen, and relying on Julia to defuse domestic crises. Sophie had come a long way. To be a cook was a coveted job and the Stephens' household was a good place to work. She had her perks and her prestige – 'Cook' was often given the courtesy title of 'Mrs' since she had many of the responsibilities of housekeeper. Sophie may have learnt to read and write with Julia's help.

Julia Stephen was seldom off-duty and every year in Cornwall, sometimes with Stella, she visited the poor, the sick and the bereaved in St Ives; one had lost a son mangled by the railways, another drowned in a shipwreck. She offered comfort and practical help, like the gift of a shawl to a woman who was then able to mourn respectably and her charges need not fear that she would press religious consolation upon them. She got up a subscription for a resident nurse for the town. With her calm presence and unaffected manner, time and again she was the person people wanted by them. It made her, however, much less available to her children, though she fussed over her last child, the baby Adrian, and always nursed them when they were ill. Perhaps her gift for nursing came from watching her father, who was a doctor, and from tending to her ailing mother. To her children her long association with sickness and death left a shadow on her life and personality. She could be droll, however. Her one published work, *Notes from the Sick Room*, expatiates on the invalids' worst nightmare – crumbs in the bed. Many people found her charismatic and she was remembered for her vivid presence and distinctive laughter, as well as for her rather grave beauty. It was the 'mixture of absolute compliance with the rules of society and her oddly incongruous sense of humour' which made her very attractive. According to Leslie Stephen, in his *Mausoleum Book*, many of Julia's servants were devoted to her. Sophie seems to have revered her, and when she wrote to Virginia in later life, she always referred to Julia as 'your beloved mother'. It was usual for domestics to move on because they wanted better treatment rather than more money – 'she never gave me a kind word' was a frequent reproach – but Julia inspired loyalty. Suzette, her Swiss maid, had been with her since Julia's first marriage; she stayed on after an operation for cancer until she was eventually sent home to friends in Zurich where she died; the children's nurse was also an old hand. In the lively mock-newspaper produced by the Stephen siblings, *Hyde Park Gate News*, the 'juveniles' duly marked the departure of the housemaid Ellen Eldridge because she too was ill, noting her 'long and faithful services' (with rather more excitement they also announced the arrival of the 'darling dog',

Shag, short for 'Shaggy', as 'he is long-haired and numerous haired', who became the family pet when Virginia was ten, and was very popular in the kitchen).

When the paternalist household worked, parents, children and servants followed the established rituals and naturally found nothing strange in the ceremonies of their tribe. This was the pattern, the accepted rhythm of their lives. At its core was a belief in service as a moral and social good. Service was not simply a throwback to a pre-industrial past; for the mid-Victorians it was an ideal, suffused with the Christian belief in self-forgetfulness and dedication to others, which underpinned public as well as private life. Generations of men found their self-esteem in the idea of serving their country at home or abroad, being a 'public servant' in the new Civil 'Service', in the colonial 'service', as a 'servant' of a bank, or a government 'servant', or in the 'services'. Leslie and Julia Stephen were both agnostics but they believed the meaning of life could be found only in the dedication to something beyond oneself, in work and in family, however transitory that meaning might be. Domestic servants, too, found dignity and pride, and sometimes an affirmation of their religion, in doing their jobs well.

By the end of the nineteenth century the usual anxieties about servant mobility and the commercial cheapening of a relationship of trust were exacerbated by the first signs of an apparent shortage. In the mill and textile towns girls had long avoided domestic service when they could, and even the migration of country girls could not keep pace with the demand from the middle classes in the ever-expanding towns. Girls with a modicum of education began to expect more from life, seeing the glimmer of opportunities opening up in shops and offices as well as factories. In the last years of the century the servant population grew steadily older as younger women started to look elsewhere. Some ladies began to commiserate with their girls in finding service 'menial' and in wanting to 'live out', but Julia Stephen saw such individualism as breaking the maternal bond. She was moved to write rejoinders though she never published them. Her model of service was of friendship, though tempered by the appropriate decorum. In an unpublished essay on 'The Servant Question' she argued that 'our friendly cook' was a tried and trusted ally, who knew exactly what each member of the family liked to eat and who sent up titbits 'with the zeal of a friend to help us back to health'. There were opportunities for kindness, she thought, on both sides. The servant, in her view, was no more dependent than anyone else, less so, in fact, since a working woman had made her own way in the world, relying on her own gumption: 'The woman who earns her bread in domestic service cannot be said, except in a very restricted sense, to be dependent.' Service was, in any case, a shared condition for mistress and maid alike, a matter of 'fellow-feeling': the servant was dependent 'as we all are, on those with whom she lives'. Being dependent was not submission or degradation but a lack of that self-centredness, 'that troublesome speck of self', as George Eliot had put it in *Middlemarch*, which so many Victorians saw as an affliction. Service, Julia urged, was 'the condition of our being', the foundation of the self and of society. 'As surely as we know anything,' she declared with some passion, 'we are convinced that dependence on each other is the most unvarying as it is the happiest law of life.' For Julia there could be no attachment, no society worth the name, without a recognition of mutual dependence.

Julia Stephen and Sophie Farrell were bound into the same pattern of life, which made them both, differently, dependent. They were protected as well as restricted by a life which put men and their needs first. Julia refused to sign a petition in favour of women's suffrage and held to the old-fashioned view of the mistress in the maternal role, looking after her 'girls'. Sophie, who could have knocked her slender mistress down with a feather, looked up to her. The life of service and obedience, of self-denial and caring for others, was the womanly life but between women its demands were unequally distributed and differently valued. The mistress might take on lighter tasks (needlework was favoured) and, in smaller households with only a general servant, this might extend to cooking and even cleaning. But the chain of command was nonetheless paramount.

The house on five floors worked hard to maintain the polar distances between its two tribes of women, but such boundaries were always clearer in the imagination than in daily life, where they were always being broached. Ideally, like Mary and Martha, handmaids to their Lord, mistress and maid played complementary and equal parts. In theory they shared the tasks of ministering to others, dividing the spiritual and the physical between them. Maids and cooks took care of the body, feeding and cleaning, while the mistress supervised and nurtured the emotional life of the household. In practice such divisions were blurred, most obviously by nurses and nannies, and when household members were physically at their most vulnerable. In sickness, in childbirth, when they were elderly or, like Laura Stephen, needed special attention, it would be the servants who were constantly on hand. Though a cook was more remote than a nurse, her role – especially if she remained in the household for years – was also central as a provider. Knowing how to feed the family gave her an intimate and deep knowledge. Sophie knew, for example, that 'like the Master', Miss Geenia [*sic*] only ate properly when she was helped and didn't 'like to be bothered' with carving or serving. In Hyde Park Gate, as in respectable society at large, physical appetites and pleasures were considered lower than the life of the mind. Yet those who seemed merely to be serving the body were also inevitably meeting emotional and psychological needs.

After her death, Julia's daughters hung one of the famous photographs taken by their aunt, Mrs Julia Margaret Cameron, on the walls of their new home. Mrs Cameron's portraits of Julia's face emphasized the otherworldliness which suited the mid-Victorian ideal of chaste feminine beauty (the Pre-Raphaelite painter Edward Burne-Jones had used the pregnant Julia as his model for the Virgin Mary). With the light accentuating her cheekbones and her heavy lidded eyes, Julia appears ethereal and mournful, as indeed she was when Mrs Cameron photographed her in her widowhood. This was the image of self-sacrificial femininity, the Madonna figure, which haunted her daughters, and which Leslie Stephen enshrined in his memoir of Julia, worshipping her

saintlike qualities and paying tribute to her angelic nature in his
Mausoleum Book.

Julia's daughters also kept their photograph albums which
chronicled the family history in its more informal moments,
especially on holiday in Cornwall, when the Stephens and Duckworths unbuttoned a little, playing cricket, hunting moths or
trying out their Kodaks. The servants were ideal subjects, a captive
audience who did not need to be posed too carefully. One
summer's day in 1892 Gerald Duckworth attempted photographing
Sophie Farrell in the kitchen, though according to the rather arch
report in the children's *Hyde Park Gate News*, he 'was not favoured
with a kind reception' and Sophie 'was only made to submit when
the head of the house (who is Mrs Stephen) entered and at once
commanded Sophia to be still'. The photographs of Sophie which
survive are conventional enough, echoing traditions of 'low life'
painting. Shelling peas in 'her' kitchen, she is recognizably 'The
Cook' of earlier genre painting; another which shows her bran-
dishing her saucepan and spoon is a version of those loyalty
portraits in oils which displayed favoured servitors to admiring
visitors, or those group photographs of household staff in their
serried ranks, holding a badge of office – corkscrew for the butler,
broom for the housemaid – ultimately a testimony to their masters'
benevolence. Yet Sophie's portraits are also affectionate pictures,
'snaps', which themselves claim intimacy, taken close up with her
smiling gently into the camera. Of course only a working woman
would be photographed this way, displaying her hefty forearms
and her ample bosom. Such a picture of robust female flesh was
irredeemably lower class. By contrast Mrs Stephen in her spiritualized portraits is disembodied, refined almost out of existence,
barely a creature of flesh and blood at all.

MISS GENIA AND SOPHIE FARRELL

On a summer holiday in the early 1900s Virginia Stephen
watched the Romany caravans at Wilton fair and wrote in her

Mrs Herbert Duckworth, 1867

Sophia Farrell, 1890

journal about houses. Her sentiments might have shocked her mother:

A house that is rooted to no one spot but can travel as quickly as you change your mind, & is complete in itself is surely the most desirable of houses. Our modern house with its cumbersome walls & its foundations planted deep in the ground is nothing better than a prison; & more & more prison like does it become the longer we live there & wear fetters of association & sentiment, painful to wear – still more painful to break.

The holiday was a respite from Hyde Park Gate where her father was slowly dying of cancer. She was twenty-one. Virginia's mother had been dead eight years and her half-sister, Stella Duckworth, who had looked after Virginia in her wake, was also dead. Virginia's home in London was weighted down with mourning and distress. Not surprising, then, that she should feel, 'I never see a gypsy cart without longing to be inside it.' This idealized view of the Romanies' life as the antithesis to bourgeois domesticity was a romantic fantasy which appealed to many writers, the escape to a life which magically evaded social relations and responsibilities. It was especially compelling to a young lady who felt utterly trapped at home. But in Virginia Stephen's respectable world women were not travellers or vagabonds; the freedom of the road, like the freedom of the mind, was usually male. Women could not easily be nomads, not least because the burden of keeping house so often fell on them. They were associated with domesticity, with the ties of affection and social connection, those bonds she now saw as chains. How could a woman's life be uprooted and yet 'complete in itself'?

The Romany caravan is an early version of a 'room of one's own', Virginia Woolf's well-known image of the psychological as well as literal space which she felt a woman needed in order to write. It was one of many spatial metaphors and images which she employed to conjure the life of feeling and thought, and the history of her emotions. Looking back in her fifties, she wrote in 'Sketch of the Past' that her mother was 'at the very centre of that great Cathedral space which was childhood', a space open and airy and yet a sanctum. When she came to describe the years after Julia and Stella's deaths, she flinched as if she were about to be shut in. 'I do not want to go into my room at Hyde Park Gate,' she wrote. Always there was the threat of being 'suffocated by recollection', as if her own interior might shrink or collapse under pressure, become inundated, like the walls of her childhood house which she imagined as 'tangled and matted', 'soaked' with emotion, like a child's hair after crying.

When she recalled 46 Gordon Square in Bloomsbury, where she and her siblings set up home after Leslie Stephen's death, Virginia emphasized 'the extraordinary increase of space'. There was more room to think, and read and write. Yet the life of the mind was hardly a safe haven. From an early age she knew – and was told – that her mind was vulnerable, that she was subject to 'nerves', and needed to mind her own capacities. Words were a tonic but they could overstimulate or intoxicate: in talk she might 'fizz' with excitement and find her thoughts, like her pulse, racing. Reflection could also be dangerous and lead to despair, like the paralysis she felt as a child when she could not step across a puddle in her path and 'the whole world became unreal'. 'Much thinking,' she wrote after her father's death, 'would send me down bottom-less pits.' In a family with more than its fair share of casualties, Virginia Stephen was often the most dependent. After her mother died she suffered depression and a nervous collapse, about which little is known, and a second breakdown followed her father's death in 1904; Virginia attempted suicide then, probably for the first time. In the 1900s her life continued to be menaced by ill-health, by the fevers, headaches, sleeplessness, loss of appetite and other symptoms which relatives and friends feared might herald mental disturbance. Compared to her sister, Vanessa, who was soon bedded down in marriage and motherhood, Virginia's was an unanchored existence. She remained unattached until she was thirty, but her worst years of mental instability were still to come.

Being a writer felt like finding a place to live: 'one gradually sees shapes and thinks oneself in the middle of a world'. Though it was a volatile environment, the life of the mind was to prove extraordinarily habitable. 'I go from one lighted room to another,' she wrote happily in middle-age, feeling that her mind was a house of many mansions where she could wander at will. All her life Virginia Woolf wanted to fashion new shapes in her writing, but neither her work nor her self could ever be secure possessions. They were temporary tenancies, improvised and often precarious. And no matter how powerful the fantasy of self-sufficiency, of a life untrammelled, these interiors would always be shared.

*

After Julia Stephen's death in 1895, the summers at St Ives came to an end; there were no more editions of the boisterous *Hyde Park Gate News*. Julia died of rheumatic fever, aged forty-nine. Two years later, while the household was still reeling with grief, Stella Duckworth, who had become the mainstay of family life, also died. She and Jack Hills had been married three months, although Stella had stayed within reach, as Leslie Stephen required, by setting up home at 24 Hyde Park Gate. She was twenty-eight and died of peritonitis in the early stages of pregnancy. These were the years when Leslie Stephen's children, and his daughters in particular, bore the brunt of their father's misery, his all-consuming demands for sympathy and affection, his plunges into abject grief, his wild rages. As young women Vanessa and Virginia were especially powerless. George Duckworth, now a young man in his early thirties, invaded their bedrooms and directed their social lives, taking them to society dinners and dances in their ballgowns and jewels, where they sat silent in corners 'like mutes longing for a funeral'. 'We ain't popular,' Virginia joked grimly. There had been nothing strange or remarkable about living in a crowded house with a large family and several servants but now the absences of mother and half-sister crammed it full of chaotic emotion. After the deaths of Julia and Stella there was less and less room for the girls to live their own lives.

After Stella died Vanessa, who was barely eighteen, reluctantly took on the mantle of mistress and had to deal with their moody and often histrionic father. Sophie Farrell organized the menus and carried on producing all the meals, a diet that was heavy on meat and cream and naturally expensive. Meanwhile, Vanessa, who had little idea of the cost of groceries, had to manage the household finances, noting down every item in a large accounts book under headings arranged by her father – 'Doctor', 'Education', 'Furnishings' – and so on. She totted up the quarterly and annual expenditure for him to audit and dreaded the weekly ordeal of his vetting 'the books'. He was convinced that they were always on the point of bankruptcy and would storm and rage, while Vanessa stood in mulish silence, weathering his outbursts, waiting for his cheque. After the summer break, Leslie Stephen would be incensed at the pile-up of bills which had come in since they left, so Vanessa and Sophie collaborated, inventing bills for the week of departure and keeping the money secretly in reserve for the autumn. Vanessa had to pay the servants' wages. In 1901, for instance, as the census reveals, there were five live-in staff: Sophie was helped by Ellen Halsey, a 25-year-old parlourmaid from Ireland, Mona Griffin, a housemaid who was twenty-eight, and another housemaid, Maud Chart, who was only twenty and was to stay with the Stephen family for at least fifteen years. Vanessa and Virginia also had the services of a Louise Widmer, a Swiss lady's maid, who was twenty-one. In these sad and oppressed years Vanessa took a number of photographs of the servants sitting at ease in their caps and aprons, off-duty in the garden. A reassuring image of order and female support, perhaps. Sophie Farrell was the Stephen children's staunchest ally.

In later years Virginia Woolf recast the break-up of her family life as a relocation not just in terms of houses and districts but psychologically and personally too. In her telling of it leaving Hyde Park Gate was a story of emancipation, of escape from the grip of the patriarchal family and a flight into modern individuality. But her memoirs took years to write and remained unfinished and unpublished in her lifetime. The story she told was the product of constant revision. From the age of fifteen or so, she grappled with ways of writing about breaks rather than continuities, those times out of time when there is no sense of plot, those states of mind and feeling which are almost unwritable, but whose effects are limitless and formative – the sudden shock of death; the inexhaustibility of grief; the senselessness of suffering, the horror and numbness and impatience at watching a beloved person die slowly; the constant attrition of mourning; the experience, so-called, of breakdown. Her major fiction would often be preoccupied by the shape of an absence, the contours of a loss.

Virginia Stephen decided from a very young age to become a writer and, as her biographer Hermione Lee has suggested, *Hyde Park Gate News* has that characteristic 'vivid, ebullient, attentive flow of comment' on daily life which seems to prefigure Virginia's life-long habit of diary-keeping. Early in 1897 Virginia was allowed to begin her lessons again and diary-keeping was also a measure of her recovery after her mother's death. Diarizing meant putting life at arm's length, inventing one's self as a consistent, convincing entity. Chatty, eager and affectionate, full of unremarkable accounts of family life, of excursions to theatres or galleries, negotiating red buses in order to shop 'steadily' at Liberty's or the booksellers, consuming coffee and hot buttered scones at an ABC, the doings of the family dog – all liberally scattered with silly jokes, family nicknames and an over-fondness for exclamation marks! – her journals are the typically breathless and high-spirited production of an adolescent, if a highly literate one. Yet there is also 'Miss Jan', her alter ego, hopelessly shy at social gatherings, 'tantrumical' and 'contradictious', who allows her to observe her own character, mocking and distancing the world; there is the stark contrast of the entries during the amorphous times of Stella Duckworth's marriage, illness and death, when writing the diary became ever more of an uphill struggle, and she could barely manage even a few lapidary words; there is the obsessive chronicling of Stella's disappearance, going back over the days – her last sightings, the

last time she heard Stella's voice calling out to her – compulsively
filling pages which had originally been left blank. Paradoxically,
the diary is a record of eventlessness, a time when 'one day is so
like another' and 'nothing happened'. But as the terrible year of
1897 came to a close, Virginia noted that it contained 'a volume
of fairly acute life (the first really lived year of my life)'.

For the next few years she kept a journal intermittently, usually
on the country holidays which the four Stephen siblings began
to take as an independent unit in the 1900s. She was practising
as an essayist, writing set pieces on sunsets or local sights, the
change of scene promoting a more intense self-consciousness
about her moods. She reflected too on her passion for reading.
After Stella's marriage, when the night nursery became Virginia's
sitting room at the top of the house, where she later used Stella's
desk as her writing table, she sat ensconced in her 'beloved
armchair', insulated and protected, 'browsing and munching
steadily through all kinds of books'. Books had been 'the greatest
comfort and help' during Stella's illness, but reading was also a
hunger, a voracious appetite which consumed everything from
the 'silver fork' novels of lady authors to Froude and Carlyle. She
'devoured' books rather faster than her father, who lent her works
from his library, liked; she would save up 'big' books to read
('Homer, Dante, Burkes Speeches') for country holidays, describing
in her journal of 1903 the rapture of reading, using her mind as
a source of sensuous, almost orgasmic satisfaction: 'I feel sometimes
for hours together as though the physical stuff of my brain were
expanding, larger & larger, throbbing quicker & quicker with new
blood & there is no more delicious sensation than this.'* This
self-absorbed, solitary activity of reading and thinking was when
she felt closest to others: 'I think I see for a moment how our
minds are all threaded together – how any live mind today is of
the same stuff as Plato's & Euripides'.' It produced an almost

---

* Unless otherwise signalled any oddities of spelling and punctuation in the
quotations from Virginia Woolf's diaries and letters are hers: she generally used
ampersands for 'and', left out apostrophes, as in 'cant' or 'wont' for instance,
and her spelling was often erratic.

mystical belief in the life of the mind and in a disembodied communality: 'It is this common mind that binds the whole world together; & all the world is mind.'

During Leslie Stephen's illness in the autumn of 1903, Virginia was accused of 'making a God of the intellect', though she felt it was a reasonable response to a house which was too much 'a nest of emotion'. Plunged back again into the wearying round of doctors' visits, diagnoses and operations, the Stephen girls also had to play hostess to lachrymose aunts and well-wishers (and all this at the time when George Duckworth became more demanding and irresponsible in his need for affection, wanting fondlings and embraces and 'bedtime pettings' in the night nursery). Virginia's attachment to her father was intense and the prospect of his death appalled her; she spent hours at his side, acting also as his amanuensis, taking down from his dictation the last entry of his *Mausoleum Book*, which he dedicated to Virginia. At her half-brothers' suggestion the young people went 'tramping Bloomsbury' and 'staring up at dingy houses', considering the future. It seemed 'so far away, and so cold and gloomy'. Hyde Park Gate couldn't be bettered – 'Really we shall never get a house we like so well as this,' Virginia wrote, 'but it is better to go.' The flight into freedom did not look enticing at the time – not for Virginia, at least.

'It is all pure loss,' Virginia wrote to Violet Dickinson, as her father approached death in February 1904. Violet was Stella's friend and had replaced her as the maternal presence in Virginia's life. 'We have all been so happy together and there was never anybody so loveable,' Virginia told her, finding it impossible to talk to her brothers and sister about her attachment to her father. His death, like Stella's, was now folded in silence. Virginia spent most of the spring and summer after Leslie Stephen died in breakdown. It was Violet Dickinson who looked after Virginia in her home, where she was kept under the care of three nurses. She was in a perilous condition, alternately violently agitated or depressed, heavily drugged and sedated, hearing voices telling her 'to do all kinds of wild things'. She attempted to kill herself by jumping out of the window. Many of her symptoms may well have been the results of the medication; certainly her original grief seems to have been allowed little expression. Among these reserved English people it was seen almost as a kind of illness.

In Virginia's absence Vanessa packed up Hyde Park Gate and found a new home for the Stephen siblings. That autumn, shuttling between friends and relatives in the country in order to convalesce, Virginia wrote miserable, sometimes angry letters, wanting desperately to be settled back in London. She wrote to Violet that she longed for 'a large room to myself, with books and nothing else, where I can shut myself up, and see no one, and read myself into peace'. Vanessa was still anxious that she wasn't eating enough. 'My own monkey,' she wrote to Virginia in November 1904, 'how I wish you had Sophy's food as I do. Do eat up & take care of your sensitive little organism. Its very delicately made.' Being able to write was again a sign of recovery – 'the oddest feeling', Virginia told Violet, 'as though a dead part of me were coming to life'. She read through her parents' letters and wrote a contribution to Frederick Maitland's life of her father, a labour of love and a work of mourning. Then her longings for home found their way into another, less elevated memorial. Back in London the old family dog, Shag, was run over by a hansom carriage and killed instantaneously. 'Do write his life,' Vanessa urged, 'Sophie tears up wonderfully.' Virginia's sentimental obituary was meant to 'make poor Sophies heart glad'. Sophie, who had accompanied the Stephens across London, was not much taken with Gurth, the younger dog who had ousted Shag. So Virginia told a pathetic story of the old Skye terrier, stone-deaf and half-blind, 'the last of the family to live in the old house', returning from his enforced retirement and making his way back across London to his old home, curling up by the fireside in Sophie's kitchen, before his painless death. If Sophie was identified with this 'faithful friend', Virginia too was like the pining canine, feeling lost and abandoned. The desire to go back and to give up, rather than to move on, was hard to resist. A fantasy of being reunited with the past and returned to the maternal home, nostalgia was also a kind of death-wish and had to be struggled against.

Dogs, of course, were an indispensable part of the Stephens' family life; Leslie Stephen, according to Maitland, his biographer, had been 'unthinkable' without a dog, and Virginia's letters and journals bristle with accounts of being out with Gurth, 'that extraordinarily ubiquitous dog', taking a dog chaperone with her on her many walks into town. In her childhood, animal nicknames – 'pet names' – were one way that these reticent upper-middle-class children could express physical love and warmth. In later life she often signed her letters as a dog, and these soubriquets were part of her flirtatious language with her husband and others. She and Leonard were to have many canine companions: a dog represented, she wrote, 'the private side of life, the play side', harking back to childhood and physical pleasure. But dogs also embodied the Victorian past with their ready capacity to obey authority and respond to discipline. Wherever they appear in her writings – often as a stand-in for that other dogsbody, the servant – dogs arouse the mixed feelings associated with being a dependent and being closer to one's 'animal nature'.

As a young woman missing the comforts of home, writing an article for her servant was one way of expressing painful emotions and displacing them elsewhere. In a literary habit or reflex which was to repeat, servants were the repository for backward-looking desires or for excessive or unacceptable emotions, those which 'overflowed' and which only the emotionally unregulated (like her father or her brother George) would openly display. In 'Sketch of the Past', remembering the day of her mother's death, Virginia believed she had been dry-eyed and afflicted by the giggles; a nurse, on the other hand, had been weeping copiously. 'How seldom I have ever cried,' she later recalled.

All her life Virginia Woolf was a resurrectionist, raising her family from the dead in her novels, and saving people from extinction both as a biographer and an obituarist. Even when they were alive, she liked to pen 'living portraits' as a defence against the void, the unrecorded life, the blank page in history. Most uncanny of all was her posthumous picture of her beloved older brother, Thoby, who died in November 1906, of typhoid contracted on

a holiday in Greece. Virginia kept him alive for almost a month
in her letters to Violet Dickinson, filling in the details of his daily
life and charting his recovery. 'Thoby is going on well; he has
chicken broth of a kind, and will be up by Christmas,' she wrote
when he had been dead over three weeks. It was a protective
gesture, guarding Violet, who was also seriously ill from the disease
caught on the same trip, but Virginia was protecting herself as
well, warding off any further loss, as if the fiction were a primitive magic. Writing also bought her time in which to absorb the
shock and was invested with enormous power. 'I do think all
good and evil comes from words,' she wrote to Violet in the
December after Thoby's death; compared to writing 'flesh is a
cumbersome illustration'. 'I run to a book as a child to its mother,'
she added.

Perhaps all authors in their grown-up daydreaming continue
to feel as omnipotent as children, imagining their fictions can
save lives, including their own. Drawn to rehearse over and again
the traumas of their past, they often seem to play their own version

Sophie, maids and Shag

of that child's game which deliberately repeats the loss of an object in order to have it back again, and master the feeling of its absence. Or, to put it differently, to tolerate dependence while asserting independence. All writing, putting one sentence in front of another, is a delaying tactic, at once memorializing and animating, a holding operation. Writing sustained Virginia Stephen; it was immensely gratifying, a physical as well as mental delight. 'I love writing for the sake of writing,' she noted, enjoying covering the page with ink, the rhythms of writing, which could soothe as well as excite. If writing was a temporary suspension of self-consciousness, it was also a very conscious self-pleasuring. Though she often despaired of what she had produced, and even felt at times 'like one rolled at the bottom of a green flood, smoothed, obliterated', she was amazed to find, going under, that her pockets were still full of words.

★

On 14 January 1905, after eight months of illness following her father's death, Virginia was 'pronounced normal' by her doctor. She was now at Gordon Square in Bloomsbury and beginning to earn money from her writing. She had taken on a weekly class teaching history at Morley College, an institute for working men and women and the *Times Literary Supplement* was sending her books to review. Writing and reading began to structure her daily life. At the end of the year she proudly totted up what she'd read and what she'd published, now a true professional. She ceased diarizing, there was far too much else to write. For now she was settled. Earning money meant she could offset some of what had been spent on her nursing fees. Like her sister she could start to take charge of her life. 'I hate dependence in anyone,' Vanessa had written to her cousin Madge Vaughan during Virginia's breakdown, reversing her mother's dictum. Yet they both depended a great deal on their servants.

When the Stephens moved to Gordon Square, Sophie went with them and so did Maud Chart, the housemaid from Hyde

Park Gate. Sophie had been with the family for eighteen years. Her own parents had died in 1900, within a few months of each other; the rest of her family were far flung. She was in her early forties and dependent upon 'the children' who were now in charge but who knew little about running a house. It was certainly unusual for unmarried Edwardian young people to set up home together, but if Bloomsbury was considered slightly *outré* by Duckworth and Stephen relatives, their domestic life was made respectable by the presence of a cook and parlourmaid. The Stephen siblings were not Bohemians glorying in slumming or in eating scratch meals, though many a Bohemian kept a maid or a manservant as soon as they could afford it. They were of liberal, freethinking stock (their father, like their ancestors, had been fiercely anti-slavery), the brothers destined to become public or professional men like their forefathers, but they were not politically radical. In any case very few socialists were vexed by having servants, even if a Fabian couple or two went as far as sitting down and eating with them. At first Sophie went on ordering and cooking three meals a day, and all the rituals of Victorian eating were observed. The Stephens spent their first Christmas alone together at the close of 1905, digesting Sophie's enormous Christmas tea, eaten on top of a Christmas turkey, though Virginia wrote gaily to Violet about the holiday: 'I never once changed for dinner which is my height of bliss.' When Lady Margaret, George Duckworth's new wife, came to lunch, Sophie rose to the occasion and rustled up a pheasant with all the trimmings.

The new house, like the old house, was on six floors with the typical servant accommodation. Sophie was installed in the basement and Maud's bedroom was in the attic, high up under the eaves. The four siblings, however, had more room to themselves, and as individuals rather than according to their sex. In the Victorian home the ladies occupied the drawing room or parlour; the study or the library was resolutely male. On the ground floor at Gordon Square was Thoby Stephen's spacious study, next to the dining and living room, but it doubled as an informal sitting room and library for them all. The first-floor L-shaped drawing room with its floor-to-ceiling windows, sofas and fires was the apartment into which guests were welcomed and where friends gathered; the second and third floors offered smaller bedsitting rooms for all four Stephens, with Virginia's at the top, occupying a place similar to her father's at Hyde Park Gate – 'the brain of the house' – and looking out on the crowns of the huge plane trees in the square's gardens. Compared to the hushed, narrow cul-de-sac of Hyde Park Gate, where one saw 'Mrs Redgrave washing her neck in her bedroom across the way', the outlook was full of light, the streets bustling and noisy. Indoors, Victorian plush and gloom were avoided. Vanessa distempered the walls white, put a red carpet in the drawing room, bought mirrors and green and white chintz in the modern 'Sargent-Furse' manner, and scattered Indian shawls. Electric light opened up the rooms and made life brighter and easier, though Maud still had to lay the coal fires which fitfully heated the draughty house. Maud cleaned and washed for them, fetching cans of water and collecting the chamber-pots, as well as opening the front door. An invisible network of others went to and fro down in 'the area', collecting the washing, delivering meat, groceries and milk, just as they had in South Kensington. Sophie and Maud were the gatekeepers, protecting their charges from the world.

The Stephens belonged to the rentier class, deriving some of their income from investments and capital, and from landlordship. As young people with only modest private incomes and – as yet – no employment, they soon needed to rein in. The full-blown Victorian meals began to seem absurdly expensive as well as time-consuming when one wanted to write or paint; the tyranny of 'the boiled shirt' and dressing for dinner was soon dispensed with, along with the napkins, minimizing effort as well as laundry bills. Vanessa and Virginia had dismissed their lady's maid, and Virginia liked to regale Nelly Cecil (Lady Robert) with tales of her scruffiness, that her skirt was back to front and hooks undone, because she had to rely on Adrian to maid her. When Thoby, who was reading for the Bar, began inviting his old Cambridge friends for Thursday evenings at home, the men were shabby and some, like Clive Bell, wore soft collars; the ladies sat not in 'white satin or seed pearls' but 'not dressed at all', dispensing whisky, coffee and buns rather than the more respectable tea.

Though it was decades before either Virginia or Vanessa earnt a decent income, they felt they were independent and were perceived as such – Clive Bell remembered them as 'completely independent young women, with a house of their own'. Independence meant being free of family ties and of the expectations of late-Victorian upper-middle-class womanhood. They were not living with parents or under the protection of chaperones, as the daughters of Thackeray had been in the 1860s when they too had been left on their own. They no longer had to mollify society matrons and were no longer 'out' as marriageable young women, having to observe all the niceties of etiquette or the rigmarole of 'calling' – the minute rules of 'good manners' whereby the English went on orchestrating their behaviour for decades. Far more hampered than their male peers by 'iron-boned conventionality', as Virginia called it, they could begin to leave their corsets off. After an initial housewarming their South Kensington cousins were not invited to the Stephens', and Virginia was nervously delighted when she and Vanessa were finally dropped by Margaret Duckworth. 'Now we are free women!' she wrote to Violet in June 1906. 'Any form of slavery is Degrading – and the damage done to the mind is worse than that done to the body!!' To be taken seriously as rational, self-directed beings – that was what independence meant. It helped that many of Thoby's friends were homosexual, though it took Virginia at least a few years to realize that this was why the conversation seemed free of the usual flirtatious nonsense and also why, to begin with, they steered clear of discussions of feelings. As late as 1923, however, Virginia still found it noteworthy that they used Christian names at a party.

Their models of independence were masculine and the desired freedoms those of their male relatives and friends, combining camaraderie and intellectual endeavour. Although Vanessa went to art school and Virginia learnt Greek and Latin privately, they had had little formal education. Virginia had long badgered Thoby for books and conversation, worrying about her 'feminine mind'. Far from being 'Bohemian dissipations', as Virginia teased Violet, Thoby's Thursday evenings took the form of rather solemn arguments about 'the nature of the good', or whether there is any such thing as 'atmosphere' in literature. The ladies mostly listened shyly, but the rational philosophy of the Cambridge young men was absorbed into the Misses Stephen's revolt against Victorian femininity. The new familiarities between the sexes were tame by today's standards but considerable by those of the Edwardians. Virginia's second novel, *Night and Day*, looks back to the pre-war years and captures that sense of release from convention when her awkward, silent heroine meets a young man in his rooms

He made the tea and Katharine drew off her gloves, and crossed her legs with a gesture that was rather masculine in its ease. Nor did they talk much until they were smoking cigarettes over the fire, having placed their teacups upon the floor between them.   (p. 111)

Gloveless hands, crossed legs (legs mentioned at all!), no small talk, no servant, smoking and the sloppy placing of the teacups – all these combined with 'masculine ease' were new freedoms. For Virginia the masculine room to read and write and think was an expanded vision of the self, not cramped and confined by female life. This was the room which she was to imagine as awaiting occupation by the post-war generation after the death of her undergraduate protagonist in her novel *Jacob's Room*.

Though she was following in her father's footsteps, literature was a suitable profession for a lady. In one of her first reviews of 1905, Virginia took issue with a book entitled *The Feminine Note in Fiction* and looked forward to a new kind of woman novelist: with a knowledge of the Classics she would have 'a sterner view of literature which will make an artist of her, so that having blurted out her message somewhat formlessly, she will in due fashion fashion it into permanent artistic shape'. All her life Virginia dreaded being found 'loose', or 'gushing' or garrulous – a kind of verbal incontinence which was both ladylike and 'slovenly', like sloppy housekeeping. She wanted to learn, she said, how to write descriptions without adjectives. 'Writing is an irreticent thing to be kept in the dark like hysterics,' she wrote to Nelly Cecil, a fellow-scribbler, in July 1905, with a memory of her nursing-home days perhaps. Self-control was to be crucial in art as in life.

The ménage of four did not last long. When Thoby died from typhoid at the end of 1906, Vanessa accepted Clive Bell's renewed proposal of marriage two days later. They were married the following spring. Virginia and Adrian were obliged to find another home since the newlyweds were to stay on at Gordon Square. Virginia took Sophie househunting with her and relied on her advice. She repeated Sophie's views on houses and the respectability of individual streets in the neighbourhood in her letters in order to reassure anxious friends and relatives. They found a house in Fitzroy Square – 'Sophie approves of it in every particular,' she wrote to Violet in February 1907 – but the streets surrounding it were 'dingy' if not much different from Gordon Square. There was a house in Upper Montagu Street, but Sophie was dubious: 'She says "it is not a patch on Fitzroy Square and very dirty, but we could manage there".' Virginia did not want to take a house 'which would be unpleasantly disreputable'. Sophie urged Fitzroy Square 'with all the force at her command, and it is considerable: she promises health and happiness, low books and no repairs'. Eventually, in April, Sophie and Maud moved with Adrian and Virginia into number 29 Fitzroy Square, within strolling distance of the Bells.

With Sophie to lean on, Virginia became the mistress of a house for the first time in her life and wrote excitedly to Violet, 'I think housekeeping is what I do best, and I mean to run our house on very remarkable lines.' It was 'life', rather than 'books' but she wanted both to be creative; both needed thought. Being a woman writer working at home would always make it hard to draw lines and Virginia imagined she might blur the distinctions even more. Vanessa, who disliked the whole business of housekeeping, found 'the domestic strain' in Virginia 'very odd' and wondered how to account for it. 'Perhaps it's the sign of real genius,' she wrote to her in July during a tedious stay with her rather proper in-laws. 'If you were only very clever you wouldn't care for such things.' It became a tease between them: Vanessa would live and work more and more cheerfully in dirt and untidiness (though always with a housekeeper), often alongside fellow-artists, while Virginia needed her creature-comforts, peace and solitude in order to write. At Fitzroy Square Virginia put up red brocade curtains and had a spree buying bright green carpets and old furniture. She wanted to 'keep free from armchairs', those stuffy denizens of the drawing room or gentleman's club, though the study was a thoroughly Victorian space with her father's library (now come to her after Thoby's death) – 'great pyramids of books, with trailing mists between them, partly dust, and partly cigarette smoke'. The armchairs reappeared, associated as they were with small islands of reading and retreat. Her sister was to re-cover them and they remained in Bloomsbury.

Virginia's experiments in housekeeping were not very reckless but she became a hostess and lost some of her shyness as she and Adrian tried their own version of Thoby's Thursday evenings. Perhaps more importantly, she was freer to be alone and to enjoy exploring her own mind. This was the only period in her life when she could be truly solitary for stretches of time without a household or a husband. She took frequent short breaks, sometimes near the Bells, moving in and out of London, finding holiday lodgings, and tasting the absolute novelty of a life free of any social engagements. In August 1908 she rented a room in Manorbier in Wales and told Vanessa: 'I never knew I had such a desire to read; and in London it is always fretted and stinted and always will be. I wish one could sweep ones days clean; say not at home, and refuse ever to go out.' 'Having one's read out' meant refusing to 'see' people, and being, by the standards of her upbringing, very unwomanly. She took melancholy walks in all weathers, talking out loud to herself like an eccentric and keeping up a lively conversation in her head. Solitude was lonely and risky, but it could be tempered by demanding a flood of letters from her friends. Perhaps her most wretched experiences of incarceration in the nursing-homes were standing her in good stead. She was learning to look after herself and took close interest in her provisioning when she had to make her own breakfast in her digs, noting that 'milk goes sour very quickly and turns to a smooth kind of custard', whereas butter and bacon 'will keep, with luck, a week'. At the end of the summer Virginia and Adrian talked of letting Fitzroy Square and taking rooms, 'to avoid the burden of a household'.

The pain of Thoby's death remained acute that autumn and winter; it was to resonate throughout the whole of her life (twenty-five years later she thought of her novel *The Waves* as an elegy to him). In its own way, her sister's marriage had also felt like a robbery. Cruelly, but inevitably, both created space. Being alone bore fruit; it allowed her to 'shape infinite strange shapes' for a possible novel in her mind (begun while her sister was pregnant). She wrote a memoir of their childhood, couched as the life of Vanessa, and in some ways a love letter to her. It was also her 'Mausoleum Book', as much obituary as biography, its subject 'the havoc' which death makes 'with innocent desires', the 'mutilations' of their common past. The tone of 'Reminiscences' is uncertain, sometimes pompous and avuncular (its implied reader is her new nephew), sometimes romantic and sentimental, especially when describing her mother. Virginia was vehement, however, when she wrote of that model of feminine behaviour which she and Vanessa had inherited from their mother and half-sister, and which had been travestied after their deaths. Love for others now looked like self-immolation; dependence, which for Julia was fellow-feeling, was seen in a new optic as 'self-surrender', submission to the will of men. These seven years, from 1897 to 1904, were, Virginia wrote, 'the Greek slave years'. She could accept that his daughters were 'to a great extent' unjust to their deaf, wretched father and that 'we made him the type of all that we hated in our lives, he was the tyrant of inconceivable selfishness'. Yet his cruelty still loomed too large to be forgiven. 'Reminiscences' remained unfinished; she was both 'too near and too far'.

Increasingly the therapeutic power of writing lay in self-suppression, an aesthetic of impersonality, in learning to contain oneself. Virginia rewrote 'Melymbrosia', as her first version of her novel was called, many times in the next five years, gradually finding more and more distance from the story of Rachel Vinrace, who sets out on a voyage to South America and whose engagement ends in her death. Though 'Melymbrosia' in its earliest drafts has more social criticism and more raw power, her revisions moved her towards irony and away from the more expressive scenes which bordered on sentiment or melodrama. As it turned into *The Voyage Out*, it became less confessional; her heroine more silent, a blank whose interior life remained her own by being ultimately unfathomable. Rachel's death, an abrupt termination of an unknown future, is left meaningless. Friends who looked at the drafts accused her of being too cerebral or heartless but she knew that women writers, 'authoresses and poetesses', were frequently patronized, infantilized as emotional creatures, read solely in terms of their autobiographies or dismissed as 'artless' – the fate of Mrs Browning and Christina Rossetti respectively. Travelling abroad she soon dissociated herself from those writers whom she met, the faded remnants of the late-Victorian literary life, such as Janet Ross or Alice Meynell ('who somehow, made one dislike the notion of women who write,' Virginia observed in her journal, travelling in Florence in 1909). Her own passion 'for love and humanity', she told Violet, had 'to kindle through depths of green water'.

'What's the use,' asks the heroine in 'Melymbrosia', 'of men talking to women? We're so different. We hate and fear each other.' Although talk had become quite bawdy at Gordon Square, thanks in part to 'the buggers', whose own amours suggested a more casual model of desire, it need not challenge the conventional view that the male sex drive was predatory, overwhelming and uncontrollable. At the beginning of 1910 Virginia volunteered to help with the Adult Suffrage Campaign. Feminists of the period also proposed a number of new ways of living – celibacy, solitude, relations with women, with homosexual men, free love – as ways of keeping the tyranny of heterosexual sex, so often seen as conquest, at bay. Above all, there was work: the relief of dealing in the impersonal, going against the grain of centuries of belief that a woman's being was essentially affective. The free woman would be independent psychologically and emotionally as well as sexually and economically, in order to discover 'herself'.

The independent life of the mind nonetheless needed someone to care for the body. While Virginia was supporting the suffrage, one single woman in three was still a domestic servant and would not get the vote with her mistress in 1918. The Stephens belonged to that upper bracket of British society who kept two or more servants, and they shared the general view of 'the servant question'. Servants were an expense and an intrusion, they might weigh a little on the conscience, but it was not a matter of their 'exploitation'. Few saw domestic work as 'labour'; masters and mistresses thought of giving their live-in maids their 'keep' rather than their pay. The most advanced, if they discussed the problem at all, imagined a utopian future free of domestic chores altogether, or, perhaps, shared communally. The less enlightened were outraged by the Liberal government's National Insurance Bill in 1911, inviting contributions from mistress and maid which then entitled servants to free medical treatment and sickness benefit like other manual workers. Thousands of mistresses and some maids said they would never join the scheme since it belittled the trust on which service was based. The *Daily Mail* led the protest against the measure and Lady Hawarden was one of many who warned against the dangers of invading 'women's own domain' forcing 'obnoxious legislation upon it'.

Neither Virginia nor Vanessa knew how to cook. Both were irked by keeping servants but resigned to it. They thought of taking a country house for the summer months but Sophie seemed 'insuperable' – having no home, she would need to come with them; she was increasingly like an ageing parent, a tie. Vanessa imagined the delights of being 'free to go & come as we liked' and lead a more simple life. 'The more I think of it,' she wrote to Virginia, 'the more it seems to me absurd that we should have, as we soon shall, 5 servants to look after a young & able-bodied couple & a baby.' She had a particular horror of the conventional household of her in-laws, wanting her children to be brought up without 'that awful atmosphere of Sunday and best clothes'. When Virginia and Adrian went to Bayreuth for the Wagner festival in the summer of 1909, Sophie went to the Clive Bells, as she did during the Stephens' other travels, to Spain and Portugal. Virginia asked after her in her letters, and sent her compliments, adding unmistresslike, 'Give her my love.' Sophie meanwhile sent items on just as she had when Virginia had rushed off impulsively to Cornwall or Wales, though she sometimes had trouble replying to Virginia's requests: 'The poor old thing evidently couldnt read your writing & she said it was very like the Master's [Leslie Stephen].' When Sophie was on holiday herself, Vanessa always asked after Virginia's eating habits, 'Is Sophy away now & if so what are you doing for food?'

Vanessa found Sophie a mixed blessing. She admired her dynamism. 'The servants all radiate under her,' she told her sister, and Julian, Vanessa's little boy, devoured her food. 'In fact,' she decided, 'I feel her to me only too perfect.' Nonetheless she preferred 'the rakish qualities' of Myrtilla, her usual cook.

Sophy is keeping us all in very good order. I feel she is in her mettle to be economical & teaches me as much as she can get into my unhousewifely head in a fortnight. I feel an intense atmosphere of respectability around me. It is like having a good balance at the Bank to have her in the house & I see myself go up in the opinion of the others.

But Sophie also made her feel like a child: 'I think that "Madam" is more my present character,' she wrote, 'than "Miss Nessa".' Sophie was now past fifty and very stout. Still wearing the long skirts and formal blouses of the old days, her grey hair piled into a bun, she took careful stock of the world from behind a pair of steel-rimmed spectacles, deciding what would or wouldn't do for

Mrs Stephen's daughters. Sophie took Virginia and Vanessa back to their childhood roles and yet, as she grew older, she increasingly needed looking after. Identified with 'her' children, she too was infantilized.

In the spring and summer of 1910, while Vanessa was pregnant with her second son, Virginia suffered again from severe headaches and sleeplessness; her mental state was fragile. Virginia's doctor, Dr Savage, advised another rest cure and Vanessa finally persuaded her sister into a private nursing-home at Twickenham, where the strict regime of bedrest and 'all the eating and drinking and being shut up in the dark' made her utterly wretched. She threatened suicide and wrote bleakly comic letters, longing to come home and poking fun at the pious spinsters who were in charge of her health – 'they are always wondering what God is up to'. 'I really dont think I can stand much more of this,' she wrote to Vanessa that July, 'you know how you would feel if you had stayed in bed alone here for 4 weeks'. Deliberate 'overfeeding' was part of the rest cure, a kind of sedation. Putting on flesh was always repulsive to her: she felt bovine, yet it may have helped save her life. Alone, she frequently forgot to eat and often associated fleshiness with mental torpor. The inner life could transport her into the kind of rapture which ignored bodily needs; going without food, for a while, could heighten alertness and the senses. At other times, however, her loss of appetite bordered on self-starvation and accompanied a dangerous and depressed state when the body became altogether hateful to her, a gross limitation, even a trap. During Virginia's convalescence, Sophie was on standby to make sure she ate properly, since as Vanessa told Virginia, 'you mustnt simply retreat into your hole and gnaw a bone'. Learning to feed herself and to enjoy feeding would always be bound up with Virginia's relation to the servants who fulfilled so many of the maternal functions. In rejecting food she was perhaps rejecting dependence, however destructive to her own body that might become.

After a walking tour in Cornwall and a holiday spent *en famille* with the Bells and friends at Studland in Dorset, Virginia returned to Fitzroy Square restored. At the end of 1910 she began to look

for a country place out of London where she might write. She
spent Christmas alone in an inn in the small town of Lewes in
Sussex – 'Breakfast was as bleak as a workhouse today,' she wrote
to Vanessa on Christmas Day. She found a house to rent, a semi-
detached redbrick villa in the Sussex village of Firle, which she
named nostalgically after Talland House at St Ives. It was too
suburban for a country place but with room for six – including
Sophie and Maud – it just allowed for weekend visitors. The
countryside gave her a feeling of expansion, she told Clive Bell,
'as though one clapped on a solid half-globe to one's London
life, and had hitherto always walked upon a strip of pavement'.
Sophie and Maud made the house comfortable but also spoilt her
peace, talking as they machined curtains. 'They are very good
humoured,' she wrote to Vanessa, 'though Sophie seems to jam in
the doors rather.' Virginia made jokes about their propriety, and
living at such close quarters she found it 'detestable, hearing servants moving about', a note which was to recur. Servants 'made
everything pompous and heavy-footed' – 'Why we have them, I
can't think,' Virginia lamented. Vanessa could be equally candid,
when she chose. 'My brains are becoming as soft as – yours? – by
constant contact with the lower classes,' Vanessa wrote to her
sister as her holiday in Studland came to an end. 'I shall be glad
to have one floor beneath & one above between me & them
again.'

In London the lease for Fitzroy Square was about to run out.
Again Virginia and Adrian thought of letting rooms and dismissing
their servants, wondering whether to 'expose' a letter explaining
it all to Sophie and Maud and so break the shock that they would
be dismissed. In the end Virginia found it impossible to sack Sophie,
who 'made matters very difficult by her dignified restraint', though
it is hard to imagine how else she might have behaved to make
things easier. In the event the Stephens took a whole house in
another Bloomsbury square, Brunswick, close by, and Virginia
ruefully conceded, 'if you have a house you must have servants.'
Even with servants, it was the cheapest way of living and Virginia
was full of plans. 'I am now undertaking an entirely new branch

Sophie and Maud at Brunswick Square

of life,' she wrote in November 1911 to Violet, who would no doubt be startled by the news that Virginia was now sharing with three young men. Adrian Stephen had the first and Virginia the second floor; the ground floor went as a *pied à terre* to Maynard Keynes, and the top to Leonard Woolf, an old friend of Thoby's who had returned to London after nearly seven years in the Imperial Civil Service in Ceylon. Sophie and Maud were installed as usual in basement and attic, but the collective household was to be otherwise as independent as possible. Maynard and Leonard were to be charged 35s a week, which included electric light, coals, hot baths and service. Much freer now with first names, Virginia sent 'Leonard' a scheme for their communal living: food would be placed on trays in the hall for 'inmates' to collect, carry to their rooms and return. Meals had to be requested in advance by initialling a tablet which hung in the hall, reminiscent of undergraduate arrangements in 'hall': 'tea, egg and bacon, toast or roll for breakfast: meat, vegetables and sweet for lunch: tea, buns, for tea: fish, meat, sweet for dinner', though it was not possible – 'as a general rule' – to cater for guests as well as inmates (in practice the house had a troop of visitors). A box was available for requests or complaints. 'The proprietors' reserved the right to cease service during the holidays though a caretaker would then supply breakfast and do the rooms. Virginia was being considerate to the servants, who certainly had their work cut out. They were, she thought, mostly 'amused' by the new arrangements which also conveniently reduced her need to give orders. The scheme was shortlived, however. In August 1912, nine months after Leonard moved in, Virginia became Mrs Woolf.

★

By the 1910s Sophie had become an old retainer of sorts, a 'treasure', who could prove inconvenient, however valuable, like 'Chailey', the old family servant in *The Voyage Out*, Woolf's first novel. In a brief scene, much rewritten, Rachel, the heroine, is angered that Chailey, a 'competent woman of fifty', is afraid to ask directly for a new cabin aboard ship, but must invent a subterfuge for an interview with her, a fuss about the state of the sheets. In her early drafts Woolf gave the thoughts of both servant and mistress; both are mourning Rachel's dead mother. Chailey imagines Mrs Vinrace's voice, the voice of authority, affectionately chaffing and firmly commanding her servant, an echo, surely, of Julia Stephen, 'Chailey, you old wretch, what d'you come bothering me for?' Feeling neglected and unappreciated, since Rachel is more interested in her music than in the household linen, Chailey silently reproaches her, 'Your mother would have known every sheet in the house.' Chailey misses the fact that there is no one to 'rule' her. In the published version this dialogue is cut and more sympathy is created for the servant. Rachel simply sees Chailey's incapacity as 'lies', dismissing 'the old woman and her sheets' from her mind. The narrator draws our attention to Chailey's 'particular case' in a vignette where she is shown unpacking her motley crew of ornaments in her cabin – 'china pugs, tea-sets in miniature, cups stamped floridly with the arms of the city of Bristol, hair-pin boxes crusted with shamrock, antelopes' heads in coloured plaster, together with a multitude of tiny photographs, representing downright workmen in their Sunday best, and women holding white babies'. Where the early version insisted that 'the tokens of her life ... are not rubbish', the second leaves the reader to imagine the associations, the family attachments and scattered histories (Ireland, Empire) of the migrant poor. Chailey hangs up a portrait of her dead mistress and weeps. Chailey's 'flat expression' is really a surplus of emotion: 'when the lamps were lit yesterday, she had cried; she would cry this evening; she would cry tomorrow. It was not home.' Yet this sympathy also sentimentalizes the servant, her words 'obliterated' by her crying, and her suffering due to her loyalty is safely stowed in a lost past. Chailey, without her first name, is a conventional figure of pathos, deeply reassuring to Virginia's readers, if not to Virginia herself.

Sophie's life became more precarious after Virginia's marriage. At first she was delegated to Adrian Stephen, the baby of the family, and remained at Brunswick Square. When Virginia fell ill,

Vanessa passed on Sophie's advice to Leonard about how much better Virginia ate when she was helped, and sent Sophie temporarily to him. When Adrian in turn married in 1914, Sophie was finally shuffled off after twenty-eight years of continuous service. She was taken on by old 'Aunt' Minna (Sarah Emily, Herbert Duckworth's sister), and trundled back to Hyde Park Gate. Sophie missed the Stephens badly. When she visited Virginia in April 1916, Virginia found Sophie had grown 'quite thin, and very small'. She wrote to Vanessa that Sophie was 'very dismal and affectionate ... she is almost doddering about St Ives, and old furniture and old days, and said she had nothing now to look forward to'. Sophie wrote her melancholy letters – though none has survived – and Virginia decided to ask her back a few months later, though worrying that she might prove too expensive and 'very tyrannical'. But even Sophie had her limits and gave Virginia 'a fearful snubbing'. 'She said she had been very unhappy when Mr Adrian sent her away, and Miss Duckworth had taken her when no-one else wanted her, and she thought it her duty to stay.' Virginia felt she too had done her duty. Visiting her at Aunt Minna's two years later, she was given a 'cool reception' by Sophie, who was busy knitting bedsocks. Virginia, who always enjoyed being rude about her Duckworth relatives, took a small revenge in a gossipy letter to Duncan Grant, a recompense too, perhaps, for the times when she had felt utterly vulnerable to her half-brothers' predations. Sophie, she wrote, had 'turned entirely Duckworth and might indeed be their illegitimate sister. I've always thought them likely to cohabit with stout kitchen maids.'

Nonetheless both Vanessa and Virginia felt worried and responsible when Aunt Minna died in 1918, leaving Sophie, now in her late fifties, without a home or work. The Adrian Stephens felt no qualms in trying to summon her back; they were temporarily without servants. Vanessa thought them very rash as Sophie's Victorian standards of housekeeping would surely ruin them. In the end the Duckworths came to the rescue again and Sophie went next to Lady Victoria Herbert, Gerald Duckworth's sister-in-law. Yet the Stephens went on treating her like a moveable feast and Vanessa 'got old Sophie back' in 1920 and cheerfully left her children and entire household in Sophie's care while she went to Italy with Duncan Grant. Sophie hadn't really settled at Lady Victoria's and finally went to work for George Duckworth and his wife, Lady Margaret. They kept up 'the old game' of domestic service. Virginia's vow to send Sophie £10 a year after Sophie's retirement in 1931 was a measure of her attachment; when she made her will she left Nellie Boxall, her current cook of fourteen years' standing, a mere £10 *in toto*.

In the mid-1920s Maud Chart, who had been parlourmaid to Sophie's cook for many years, had also provided for Sophie's future. Maud had married after the war in 1919 and moved into her husband's house, 43 Tintern Street, in a row of terraces in Brixton, a respectable lower-middle-class London suburb. Maud was in her forties and her husband, John Edwards, was twenty years older. There were other lodgers and no doubt they needed the cash, but Sophie had looked after Maud when she first joined the Stephens as a young woman, and Maud was taking care of Sophie in old age. Sophie retired permanently to Brixton after her seventieth birthday, though she continued to stay with the Duckworths occasionally. When Virginia went to visit her in her room in Brixton in December 1932, she enjoyed the occasion thoroughly. She found 'Maud a stout matron. Sophy presiding like a born lady. "This is more of a party to me" she said. Indeed it was – more than the cocktail one.'

Perhaps with a view to a retirement present Virginia 'dashed off a cook's talk', 'The Cook', a fictionalized portrait which has sometimes been taken as a biography of Sophie. Virginia probably drew on several conversations and stories half-heard over the years, and what sound like Sophie's turns of phrase are reproduced: 'if you don't like it you must loomp it', 'what you save on food you spend on doctor's bills'. Many of the cook's memories come straight out of Sophie's childhood: the growing up in Lincolnshire and hearing about the rick burners and children being whipped to work in the fields; the lack of schooling; a memory of taking milk 'to the Rector' only to receive a dry biscuit herself. But this

is 'Biddy Brien', whose father, a farm labourer, lost the 'O' when
he 'crossed the Channel in the early days'; Biddy in the story is
a Catholic and the oldest of a family of ten, and, what's more,
illegitimate. Sophie, the entirely legitimate offspring of Anglican
parents, was the third girl. Perhaps Sophie, whose family may just
possibly once have been Catholic, though it seems unlikely, had
reverted to the faith of the old country. With what sounds like
the elaborate awkwardness of fact, Biddy tells her listener that
although she had a sweetheart she would never marry because of
her illegitimacy: her father had married his deceased wife's sister
so she had no 'marriage lines'. Did Sophie really tell Virginia this
tall story, fabricate a more highly coloured account in order to
explain her spinsterhood and give herself dignity? Did she think,
as so many do, her own past too dull and unimportant? If she
gave the impression that she was a labourer's daughter, illegitimate
and illiterate, she had surely come a very long way in the world.
But it's much more likely, given how straitlaced Sophie was, that
Virginia made the details up. As with Chailey, Biddy is a senti-
mentalized type, rather than an individual; the sketch is trite
though well-meaning. Even her name seems more appropriate
than 'Sophie', vaguely comic, more biddable (and something of
an 'old biddy').

Like Chailey, Biddy Brien lives surrounded by her mementos,
a relic among relics. Perhaps some guilt at Sophie's reduced
circumstances surfaces in Woolf's observation that her room is full
of 'things that have been thrown away'; like them, she is a lost or
unwanted object. In the series of rooms which for Woolf embody
human interiors Biddy's is part-museum, part-lumber room. But
unlike Chailey, Biddy Brien's detritus belongs to other people,
her employers', and the listener's childhood is deposited in Biddy's
room as though the servant's inner life is an annex of her own.
'Her room is hung with photographs. Her mind is like a family
album'. Gone are the working men in their Sunday best and the
women with babies; 'the family' are those for whom she worked.
Though the servant 'remembers everything' even her memories
are loyally subaltern. Only the slightest hint of disquiet lingers in

the phrase, which implies the listener's different social position, 'It is surprising how much she noticed,' this servant who was so often silent and invisible.

Whenever Virginia felt drawn to idealize the Victorian past – her mother's family, for instance, those beautiful ladies with their glamorous French ancestry, who seemed 'to float in a wonderful air' – she stepped back from the romance. It was 'all a lie, I daresay, concocted because one forgets their kitchens and catching trains and so forth'. When she wrote about Victorian servants it was harder to give up the pleasure of nostalgia. Biddy's inner life is one long happy memory; no sign of those dismal days when Sophie was abandoned by the 'family'. It is impressive that Virginia tried to write Sophie's life, though it tells us as much about Virginia's need to believe – as children do – that Biddy has no other life. 'The Cook' remained unfinished, though it may have informed her thumbnail biography of Lily Wilson, Elizabeth Barrett Browning's maid, appended in a deliberately over-long footnote at the end of Woolf's *Flush*. Like Biddy's, Lily's life is wrapped up in the afterglow of memory, but much more knowingly so.

Rather more uncomfortable feelings appear in Woolf's novel of the 1930s, *The Years*, where Crosby, the old family housekeeper, and the family dog, Rover, are again a more conventionalized portrait of Sophie and Shag, forcibly retired by the younger generation of Pargiters, who sell up the family home. In a scene which harks back to the Stephen siblings leaving Hyde Park Gate Crosby is again a figure of pathos, identified with the 'solid objects', the furniture she spends her life polishing, an anachronism in the modern world. As Eleanor Pargiter prepares to let the house, she is shocked to realize the darkness of the basement to which Crosby had been confined. But the servant, 'following Eleanor about the house like a dog', reassures her: 'It was my home.' Collecting laundry from the youngest member of the family, 'Master Martin', Crosby appears to her employer as 'a frightened little animal', seen 'trotting' into the street. Like her old dog, she is doomed. It is 1913 (the year before Adrian Stephen married) and 'Martin', through whose eyes we watch the sad spectacle of Crosby, feels ashamed and annoyed at his hypocritical way of patronizing her, his hearty, false manner in talking to servants. He blames 'the abominable system' of family life, the old house on six floors, for all these lies. Guilt, pity and rage are intermingled. Although the scenes are set pre-war, the sophisticated analysis of the employers' feelings belongs to hindsight of the interwar period. The scenes may have as much to do with Virginia's dismissal of her cook in the 1930s, Nellie Boxall, as with memories of Sophie. Guilt could itself be a nostalgic emotion, a longing for the good old bad days when master and servant both knew where they were.

Virginia and Sophie kept up a mutually reassuring correspondence. Throughout the 1930s Virginia wrote Sophie 'splendid' letters with 'so much news of everybody that I love to hear of', though none has survived. Sophie became, as the elderly do, a living archive. Her treasure was her wealth of knowledge – 'I feel I want to tell you so much,' she wrote to Virginia. But Sophie's memory was fading and Virginia was also protecting Sophie and, as family historian, keeping Sophie's memory alive. Tintern Street was a long way from South Kensington in every sense, but Sophie kept up the ties. She went frequently to Dalingridge Place, the Duckworths' country home in Sussex; she occasionally spent the holidays there or had her Christmas dinner with 'Mr and Mrs Gerald'. After George Duckworth died in 1934, Lady Margaret gave Sophie some photographs from the family holidays in Cornwall in the 1880s, nearly fifty years before. Typically, Sophie sent them to Virginia. She wrote that she remembered her photograph being taken: 'One day your beloved mother found me in the kitchen shelling peas & said thats what I like to see you doing wait until I fetch Miss Stella to take a snap of you. Then come Mr Gerald [who] said I like to see you stirring with a big spoon. So hear they are.' She asked for the photographs back, then later changed her mind and wanted 'dear Miss Genia' to keep them, generously handing over what was most precious to her – the snaps, she wrote, are 'all Treasures of mine'. Like others trained in self-sacrifice she felt more comfortable giving away what she had. 'I can always see myself in the glass,' she wrote. It was more important to be reflected in Virginia's life.

If Virginia understood Sophie's need for dependence, Sophie's letters also addressed 'Miss Genia', preserving that Edenic time before her mother's death, before the flood. 'I dont feel a bit old,' she wrote, '& you all seem to me just the same children just as dear to me as when you had the funerals for the birds & mice at St Ives. Such happy days.' When she wrote to Virginia that 'there is nobody just like you all are to me', she was telling the simple truth. Virginia drew on Sophie's memories when she came to write her own memoirs for she too was becoming an old biddy, turning the pages of her own photograph album, and mulling over the past. When Stella Duckworth's husband, Jack Hills, died in January 1939, Virginia consulted Sophie to confirm details of his brief time with Stella; writing her 'Sketch of the Past', she wondered who now remembered Stella Duckworth and her short life. Stella's brothers, Gerald and George, were dead, and most of her friends were also gone or scattered. 'Perhaps thus I think of her less disconnectedly and more truly than anyone now living, save Vanessa and Adrian; and perhaps old Sophie Farrell.' In a life full of ruptures, Sophie kept the continuity of memory. Not to have a continuous connection with the past was as bleak for Virginia as being helplessly tied to it.

Sophie was one of the abiding mother-figures in Virginia's life and represented that maternal care which Virginia always sought. Writing to the composer Ethel Smyth, a rambunctious septuagenarian lesbian who was her most intimate friend in the 1930s, Virginia commented, 'What you give me is protection, so far as I am capable of it,' agreeing that this need was 'the child crying for the nurses hand in the dark'. Yet one was at the mercy of carers. Nurses, the original tutelary and maternal presences, feature rarely in Woolf's writing, but their role is ambiguous. Ushering in births, guarding the mad and sitting at deathbeds, they also cut the cords of life. Shadowy figures of reverie, who hold children or the sick safely in their thoughts, they can also menace, like the old women playing cards in Rachel Vinrace's nightmare vision in *The Voyage Out*. In *The Waves*, 'Mrs Constable', with her artistic name, feeds and bathes the children, but also lays down the law. Mothering had its powers and was the source of nourishment. Like the basket which the Stephen children lowered on its string to Sophie down in her St Ives kitchen, and which was such a vivid memory of Virginia's, such nourishment might also be withdrawn, as it had been so violently with Julia's death. To be alone and disconnected, in a helpless state, the state into which all human beings are prematurely born, is the most terrifying of experiences.

In the late 1930s, in 'Sketch of the Past', the last version of her memoirs, Virginia went back to the house of her childhood, able to give house-room to the servants for the first time and to acknowledge that other floor, the 'dark insanitary place' where seven maids once lived. She wrote about her mother assuming 'the frozen dignity of the Victorian matron' when one of them complained, and she wrote more frankly too about her abject bodily feelings: her despair at being bullied by Thoby; and her shame at Gerald Duckworth's sexual exploration of her 'private parts' and about that part of herself which split off, which could always observe events, however terrible. Virginia wrote that she became a writer thanks to her 'shock receiving capacity', which began with the 'mutilations' of her girlhood, a word which carried over from the 'Reminiscences' of thirty years before. She wrote, she said, to 'create wholes', 'to put the severed parts back together again', as if her self, like the house in which she had grown up, had been disaggregated or dismembered all those years. Now, in her late fifties, this was an attempt at an autoanalysis which would try to include the history of her body, that lost object of pleasure. But her memoirs were left unfinished at her death.

There is a scene in Woolf's diary which suggests another side to this story and just how fraught that relation to the body was for the daughters of the middle classes, with their ambitions to be independent of its needs. In September 1918 the Woolfs were visited by the Fabian socialists Sidney and Beatrice Webb, and on a walk across the downs Virginia found herself 'entangled' in a gate and in 'talk' about marriage. Mrs Webb's approval of matrimony was a matter of emotional economy. One needed, she said, one significant relationship in life; it saved spending one's emotions on friends. Marriage was 'a waste pipe for emotion'. Half mischievously Virginia asked, 'But wouldnt an old family servant do as well?' 'Well, yes,' Beatrice replied, and strode on ahead. Woolf's question was deliberately provocative, challenging Mrs Webb's costive account, but it also said much about Virginia's view of service. The old servant might be a reservoir of feeling, but she was also like a drain or a sewer, at best a conduit through whom emotions, like the body's waste, could ideally be flushed clean away. The body, like the basement, could be a dark, insanitary place.

Elevating the mind at the expense of the body was hardly unique to Virginia Woolf. The denigration of the flesh deeply informs the traditions of philosophy and religion in the West. Generations of men and women believed (and still believe) that to be an individual – rational, self-willed, autonomous – meant seeing dependence as dependency, a weak, even terrifying state undermining the ultimate goal of self-government. Virginia's word for the underground emotions she associated with servants was 'subterranean', the baser instincts, so called, of the life of the body and its appetites. In her second novel, *Night and Day*, which looks back to the Edwardian home, the 'subterranean' odour of gossip and bodily titillation is associated with visits to the servants' basement, prompting the heroine's distaste. For Woolf, as for many others growing up in nineteenth-century urban culture, the topography of the house lent itself as an inevitable metaphor for bourgeois identity, with the lower orders curtained off, relegated to the bottom of the house or to its extremities, like a symbolic ordering of the body (in English slang, 'back passage' and 'below stairs' have scatological or sexual connotations, just as 'scrubber' is a colloquial term for prostitute, fusing sex and dirt). The figure of the servant was frequently associated with guilt and shame at a longing for a bodily life devalued as merely animal or low. Even satisfying the most primary of appetites could be shameful: food and drink, after all, turn into waste; it all goes in one end and out the other.

Throughout Virginia Woolf's writing the Victorian working woman might be idealized as a comforting, maternal figure who kept the buried treasure, the lost relation to body, the maternal bond itself: the undifferentiated state when one's pleasure in one's body was without boundary, when the body, 'self' and Other, were seamless and these distinctions did not exist. But that evocation brought terrors too, and violent physical reactions, which were also to find their way into Woolf's writing about 'the poor'.

★

Sophie lived long enough to write Virginia's epitaph, to supply the character reference which only she could give. Like many others, on 3 April 1941 she heard the news on the wireless that Mrs Leonard Woolf, who had been missing since 28 March, was now presumed drowned in the River Ouse near her home at Rodmell in Sussex. Sophie wrote immediately to Leonard, from Dalingridge Place, where she was staying with George Duckworth's widow, Margaret:

> My dear Mr Woolf,
>   Will you please forgive me for writing to you. Just to say I am so very grieved for you for I know how anxious you must be about dear Miss Genia. I do hope so much that she is safe somware & that you will soon have news of her. I have known & loved her ever since she was four years old. She was allways so sweet and good to me. I could never forget her. I should be so thankfull to hear if there is news. I hope so much Sir you will keep well in your great sorrow.
>   May I remain yours faithfully
>   Sophia Farrell

She also wrote immediately to Vanessa, claiming kinship, and saying that she could not bear to feel that 'dear kind Miss Genia' had 'strayed away from you all', like a lost sheep perhaps. To Vanessa she sent her love. In a second letter, after Virginia's death was confirmed, she remembered Virginia's own 'dear letters' which were always 'so bright and cheerfull'. She signed herself affectionately in the old way as 'Sofie', though she remained 'yours obediently'.

Sophie was already very ill when Virginia disappeared. She was still staying with Margaret Duckworth when Virginia's death was confirmed. Margaret Duckworth added a postscript to her own letter of condolence: 'Sophie is very, very grieved.' Soon after, she went back to Brixton and two weeks later into nearby Dulwich Hospital, where she died of cancer, just before her eightieth birthday. Her fellow-servant, Maud, who had given her a home, was there attending to her husband, who was also ill. The pension which Virginia had sent Sophie remained unspent. The letters from Virginia, not the money, had been the treasure. All those thank-yous Sophie had written in reply, saying how much

43 Tintern Street

difference it made to her and how 'usefull it was in these lean times', turned out to be her own piece of fiction. She wanted instead to leave the money to a niece. From years of long training Sophie had denied herself but by saving she also had a measure of control: she had resources. She was not only a photograph in Miss Genia's album existing purely for a family which was not her own. She wanted to make a difference to the future.

TWO

Housemaids' Souls

It is much to be regretted that no lives of maids, from which a more fully documented account could be constructed, are to be found in the Dictionary of National Biography.

Virginia Woolf, footnote to *Three Guineas*, 1939

Despite appearances the ladies of South Kensington were a tough lot. They might be physically fragile but those same delicate creatures sallied forth into the roughest of London streets, armed only with their moral superiority and faith in their capacity to improve the lives of the poor. Virginia Stephen grew up surrounded by 'slummers'. Her mother wore herself to the bone, bussing across London to go poor-visiting, and female relations and friends were all subscribers to good causes, setting up 'ragged schools' for street urchins, being involved in the running of the workhouses, prisons or asylums, offering time and money, dispensing personal charity. In the drawing room at Hyde Park Gate Virginia sat on a stool by the fire surveying the legs of the renowned Miss Hill, who talked earnestly with Stella Duckworth about rehousing the poor. Stella had her own 'philanthropic cottages' in Marylebone, where she hobnobbed with plumbers and carpenters, collected rent and made small talk with the tenants. She was a 'Southwarker' too, volunteering at St Saviour's Union Workhouse in Walworth ('how delightful!', Virginia joked nervously, when the Southwarkers promised to look in at the reception after Stella's wedding). The quiet and submissive Stella went down among the destitute and the desperate, and rolled up her sleeves, administering her 'Pearl Powder', as treatment for the skin infections on the 'foul and itch wards'. While Leslie Stephen groaned among the aspiring young men, female cousins swapped stories of their 'poor-peopling' (the phrase was Miss Florence Nightingale's), of 'their' slums in Whitechapel or Hoxton ('Hogsden' as Virginia enjoyed calling it). Julia's eldest, George, was working for their friend Charles Booth on his vast survey of the London poor. He liked to join the raucous cockneys at the Music Hall in Bow and have the thrill of an evening spent in the slums. Vanessa and Virginia were co-opted too; they took strawberries to old ladies in the local workhouse '& left them chewing happily'.

Even the least adventurous might find some such good works to do.

*Philanthropy need not interfere with home duties; it was womanly to
offer succour and it brought no unseemly remuneration. Any lady who
had trained up her servants, who had run her corner of the little empire
of home, might try that habit of authority and test her moral strength in
the wider world. Indeed, turning dirty little girls into tidy maids was one
of the great aims of Victorian rescue work. Nor was it negligible. Service
was the great route to respectability, an insurance paid by the rich against
the poor's rebellion. In training up future servants, the ladies of the house
were saving the nation from the threat of 'the mob'. In her clean white
apron and cap, the servant kept all kinds of disorder at bay.*

*One need not go east to find darkest London. The 'unknown continent'
of the poor was a mere stone's throw away. There were slums around the
corner from the respectable purlieus of Kensington, where the poor had
their lairs, cringing and growling like* animaux farouches. *Dangers lay
on all sides. To the west, South Kensington degenerated into Earl's Court;
to the north, on the other side of Hyde Park, were dilapidated tenements
and the notorious Notting Dale, a veritable 'Avernus' or hell, where
savage creatures lived in the 'piggeries'. When Stella and the girls went
in search of a reference for a cook and wandered too far from Victoria,
the district became 'impossible' and they had to turn back. All the salubrious haunts of the affluent — the West End theatres, the shops and
town houses — lay cheek by jowl with poverty. And the poor were even
closer than the next street but one. The servants, who ate your food and
wore the right clothes, came from this other tribe. They were in one's
house, handling one's linen, combing one's hair. Behind the security of
the nursery and the comforting figure of the old retainer, there always
lurked the shadow of the rat-eyed, feral poor.*

*So horrible and alien, the poor were nonetheless too familiar a spectacle,
like the cockney trippers Virginia encountered at Hampton Court, 'making
the whole place hideous with their noise and Cockney faces'. Miss Stephen
knew that the poor had been done to death in literature. Gutter novels,
slum novels, rescue novels, underworld novels, social reports, sensational
journalism had all covered the ground. Better to keep the poor out; they
so easily lurched into pathos or melodrama. They belonged to the land
of the penny-dreadful, to the gashed throat and the harsh whisper or,
worse still, the heart of gold. That story of the working girl, 'Slopers Sall',*

which had inched its way into Virginia's novel, had better be scrubbed – a loose woman always dies alone in an upstairs room with the bugs crawling over her face. The insides of others should be left intact. Leave a blank, just the outline of the body, where a victim once had been. If only they wouldn't return as nightmare, as one's lower nature, the beast who stared back from the mirror, the gibbering figure at the end of a wet alleyway, glimpsed in fugue or fever, moments of impure longing.

In the 1900s Julia's daughters rapidly sloughed off their charitable duties (where would they have been if their mother hadn't died?). But philanthropy had made sense of being a mistress. It was a way of managing the differences, the emotional housekeeping, which kept the tensions between rich and poor women under control. When she came to run her own household, Virginia Woolf had neither the confidence of the maternal role nor the faith in fellowship with the poor: all that was claptrap and cant. What justification remained for giving one's orders? Without the moral scaffolding, what would keep poor girls in their place? Stripped bare of the flummery, the fine words and good intentions, all that remained was the nakedness of caste feeling, the dog beneath the skin.

Mrs Woolf could never write about her servants. Yes, survivals like 'old Sophy', could be eulogized or patronized, embodying those older connections from which one had safely and guiltily distanced oneself. Alternately, the housemaid might be a harbinger, the conventional symbol, sweeping away the mess of the past. Yet those actual young women in one's kitchen, younger than their mistress, with their own unruly interiors, there in the flesh and doing the dirty work, they were far more troubling. One would never really have a room of one's own whilst they were in and out. And what if one's housemaids were not so different after all in their dreams and desires? What if they had souls like one's own?

EDITH SICHEL AND LOTTIE HOPE

Of all the Bloomsbury servants, Lottie Hope is the least acknowledged. A fleeting presence, she is easily missed, a first name only, who flits through Virginia's letters and diaries, sounding for all the world like a comedy housemaid: here she is burning a sonnet instead of rubbish, sweeping the lawn with a brush as if she were grooming a small animal; Lottie in her bright stockings ('the yellow legged'), barging into a room, her cropped dark hair 'like a disarranged dahlia', chattering 'like an intoxicated jay'. Time and again, Lottie interrupts but her own character never develops. If Virginia Woolf's diaries were a novel or a play, Lottie's would be the bit-part, sometimes brought in as light relief, sometimes to carry forward the action, as she announces visitors or sets the scene. Even among the servants, Lottie generally played second fiddle to Nellie Boxall's lead, as parlourmaid to Nellie's cook. Yet Lottie worked much longer for Bloomsbury, for thirty-odd years at least.

Through the comic glimpses there are hints of a real life to be read between the lines: Lottie in love with a local farmworker; Lottie riding pillion on a motorbike with the grocer's boy; or looming out of the twilight, wearing a scarlet jacket in a country lane; a glamorous figure with her lipsticked lips and elegant legs, thin as a string bean, 'dancing energetically over her saucepans'. More seriously, when she isn't seen laughing, with her head thrown back, she is remembered for her fury: Lottie's temper 'always unseats her', wrote Virginia, who suffered from her outbursts. In the 20s Lottie quarrelled with Karin Stephen, Virginia's sister-in-law. Years later she lost her job with the Bells in a violent scene: 'loud shrieks during dinner and terror lest a carving knife should be brought into play'. Yet there she is again in Blitzed London, helping the Adrian Stephens move house, 'the faithful Lottie' whom Karin had once turned out. Lottie got away with murder and she was always taken back. A 'wild but in some ways admirable character' was Virginia's summing up. When Lottie was in hospital she wrote Virginia 'long letters, from friend to friend, not at all in the style of old Sophie' – but none of them has survived.

Lottie had her own story to tell, a story with a dramatic opening, which made her special, a creature of intrigue and romance. Everyone knew she was a foundling who had been 'left in a cradle on the doorstep of the Hospital', when only a few days old. Of course, all live-in servants were temporary orphans, especially if they were a long way from home; in the first quarter of the twentieth century employers were *in loco parentis*, and even male servants, like women, children and lunatics, were not considered worthy of the vote. But Lottie was the real thing. Without family, she was literally dependent on the kindness of strangers. Unless she married or found work, she might end up with the tramps and the dossers, in the workhouse, in the 'spikes' or on the streets. All her life Lottie Hope was seen as volatile, a person of extremes whose fears and nightmares were unfounded, the strange or wayward products of 'the servant mind'. Lottie fabricated, they all said, she loved to embroider 'crazy' stories but no one wrote them down. 'By rights,' Virginia noted in her diary, 'Lottie should have a whole chapter to herself.'

What was Lottie Hope's history? The only clue is a casual reference in one of Virginia's letters to 'my parlourmaid, Lottie Hope, a Miss Sichel's foundling'. The name means nothing now, but if Lottie was a nobody, Miss Edith Sichel in her day was quite a personage, a name to conjure with in South Kensington. She was a lady of letters as well as a slummer, worthy of an obituary in *The Times* and two memorial volumes. Like the intertwined lives of Julia Stephen and Sophie Farrell, Edith Sichel and Lottie Hope's different fates were woven together, the warp and weft of mistress and maid. For Miss Sichel, as for Mrs Stephen, the live-in servant, like the charity child, institutionalized the law of life upon which all community was based: the expectation that human beings could look beyond their own kith and kin for respect, for help and care. Yet such idealism drew a veil over the lineaments of rank and power and it began to look threadbare as the fabric of Victorian society unravelled.

★

In the great dustheap of late-Victorian Britain, Lottie Hope was at the bottom of the pile: a pauper without parents, dark-complexioned to boot, with a shock of black, frizzy hair so that people thought she might be a gypsy or have foreign blood. She was destined to

" PLEASE 'M, DO YOU TAKE IN POOR LITTLE GIRLS?"
A GIRL BEFORE AND AFTER RECLAMATION

spend her life skivvying and in the years to come would light enough fires to raze London to the ground, empty enough slops to fill a drawing room with sewage, scrub several acres of floors, and sweep her way up and down mountains. She answered doors and ran errands, brought in food, cleared and scoured the dishes; she washed other people's finery and their dirty underwear, she opened their curtains, smoothed their sheets, stripped their beds; she cleaned their scum off the bath. Unlike Cinderella, she never met her Prince Charming (or if she did she never married him) and she went on working for the sisters (who were beautiful rather than ugly) until her fiftieth birthday had passed. But Lottie was one of the lucky ones. A fairy godmother saved her from poverty and the streets.

Lottie's parentage is unknown. She was one of a vast throng of the infant poor, whose pathetic histories and small ghosts haunt the meticulous records of Britain's workhouses and institutions. In the Whitechapel Union Workhouse, where Edith Sichel was to find her future adoptees, the carefully ruled ledgers with their flowing copperplate script register page after page of 'deserted children': infants wandering the streets or deposited on doorsteps, like one 'Naomi Lambeth', a Jewish child, found by the police; according to the workhouse, 'the usual notices of a "child found"' were circulated' (bills were pasted to lampposts, much as we do today for lost cats and dogs). There were children whose parents left them in shelters or on the workhouse wards and never reclaimed them – Stephen Corbett, for instance, aged one, whose mother, Ellen, had stayed the night with him at Barnardo's and never returned (he died a year later in the workhouse); Maud, Robert, John and Charles Hutton came in with their sick father but he ended up leaving them in the workhouse. Did he ever learn – or care – that his youngest, who lived inside for ten years, died on the wards at thirteen? William Curtis (or Cortez), aged seven, was 'supposed to be the illegitimate offspring of a West End prostitute who placed him with a Mrs Churchill and paid for his maintenance till he was four', but the mother hadn't been heard of since. Older children too were listed, barely children at all, like Mary Ann Brennan, aged fourteen, suffering from gonorrhoea and charged with begging, or the distraught Nellie Radcliffe, aged thirteen, who brought her four little brothers and sisters into 'the house' herself. And among the registers of adult deaths on the wards – from exhaustion or sickness, drink or dementia, starvation, suicide – can be found the screeds of nameless newborns who never even saw the light of day. Compared to these Lottie Hope's fictitious surname was indeed a good omen.

A census on New Year's Day in 1889 revealed that of the 192,000 in Britain's workhouses no fewer than 54,000 were aged under sixteen. Of these, 33,000 were classed as 'orphans and abandoned'. The nineteenth-century term 'deserted child' had gradually replaced the less emotive description, 'foundling', which suggested happy recovery rather than abandonment. Victorians preferred the moral response it provoked, laying the blame on the parents. Who could doubt that many were unquestionably better off 'in the house' for all its harsh conditions and iron discipline? Many, though, were not deserted at all but separated forcibly from parents, despite the best efforts of neighbours and friends to protect or hide them. The end of the nineteenth century saw the founding of many societies and much legislation based on the compassionate view that children could suffer – witness the National Society for the Prevention of Cruelty to Children set up in 1884. Zealous rescue work, however, was liable to be over-protective, assuming that childhood should be a time of sheltered dependence. Just as some poor-visitors argued that working-class life with its extended families and shared beds inevitably promoted immorality, so the working child, even if only running errands or minding younger siblings, was readily seen as a victim, and liable to surveillance. As middle-class observers marched into the tenements, holding up the beacon of a childhood luminous with innocence and unsullied by knowledge of the adult world, they took the moral high ground. They usually had the law on their side.

If Lottie's past was obscure, her future was crystal clear. Though romantic figures in literature and art, foundlings and orphans were not usually on a path to glory. Those waifs and strays, like the 'street Arabs' in Thomas Barnardo's photographs, who tugged at the heart strings of the rich, usually ended up working in their kitchens. In the 1900s nearly all children from institutions went into domestic work if they were girls, on to farms or into the services if they were boys. In 1889 new regulations allowed the placing of children outside the 'union' or workhouse area. In the new foster-homes, where they were 'boarded out', many met with the kindness and affection they craved. Others, though, found it hard to settle, like Billy O'Connor, boarded out at five, shuttling to and fro, and finally dismissed as a fifteen-year-old servant for being 'cheeky' and for tormenting the chickens; or Jane Hall, the subject of official inquiries: at 'Mrs Smith's' the children were well fed and housed but 'kicked and knocked about'. The missus 'only used to hit me,' Jane reported, 'when I deserved it the same as her own children'. At fifteen a girl might earn £10 a year as a 'between maid' living in (a 'tweeny' worked in both the kitchen and the house). A 'garden boy' might rise, as did Daniel Gibb, to the heights of 'houseboy'. First boarded out in

1904, aged seven, at sixteen he eventually earnt £12 a year for cleaning the shoes of 'The Lady Maud Wilbraham' in Chelsea. Disabled children and babies, 'cripples' and 'idiots', later called 'imbeciles' or 'the mentally defective', were hard, sometimes impossible, to find places for. Laundry work was favoured for the 'feeble-minded'. Scores of children were simply disposed of, approved for emigration and shipped, as young as nine or ten, to Canada or Australia. There they worked on farms or became, of course, domestic servants. One estimate puts the number sent unaccompanied from Dr Barnardo's homes between 1868 and 1925 at over 80,000. Only a third of them were orphans proper. Even in kindly homes the child servant performed some of the worst jobs, often as servant to the other servants, or worked the longest hours, like the gardener's lad at the Heligan estate in Cornwall who stayed up all night to keep the braziers alight in the hothouses so that the gentry could be sure to have pineapple to eat. Child labour, which was legislated against in the factories or in commercial enterprises, could be sanctioned in the wholesome atmosphere of home.

Edith Sichel came into contact with deserted children through her work for the Whitechapel branch of a now obscure agency, the Metropolitan Association for the Befriending of Young Servants. The MABYS was one of hundreds of philanthropic initiatives which flourished in the second half of the nineteenth century. Established in 1875 by Mrs Nassau Senior, a close friend of Octavia Hill, its aims were modest and straightforward. Its volunteer visitors would 'befriend' young girls in service, seeking out and talking to maids and their mistresses, inquiring why they had lost their places or left. These were girls who felt, the MABYS reported, 'Nothing to Nobody!'; 'the poor girls are so friendless,' wrote one volunteer, 'and so ready to attach themselves to anyone who will love them.' The work was ameliorative; no cash was ever given to the girls but they were sent to hospital when ill, or provided with safe lodgings, protected from harassment and – the ultimate aim – saved from 'going wrong', prostitution. The girls dubbed the organization 'Mind And Behave Yourself', but as time went on the numbers who turned to these 'moral policemen' increased dramatically. By the mid-1880s the MABYS was a booming concern with some 800 visitors placing over 5,000 girls in domestic service annually. Of its twenty-five branches, Whitechapel could scarcely keep pace with the work, especially as it was the most challenging of the districts for ladies to 'visit'. Here, as elsewhere, the branch was closely connected to the workhouse, where a great pool of potential servants was waiting to be siphoned off. (Miss Louisa Twining's Workhouse Visiting Society had already put thousands of women visitors into the workhouses in the 1860s and 70s with a view to training girls for domestic service.) Edith Sichel worked closely with Henrietta Barnett, or rather, Mrs Samuel Barnett, the wife of the curate at St Jude's in the Commercial Road in Whitechapel. The Reverend (and later Canon) Barnett was on the Board of Guardians at the workhouse, and a prime mover in the charity and settlement world.

South Kensington in the slums was a small world. Leslie Stephen's sister, Caroline Emelia Stephen ('Milly'), was a work-house visitor and had her own 'artisan dwellings' in Church Street, Chelsea (the first occupants were required to hang lace curtains at the windows and tend a pot of geraniums outside the front door). Among her many charitable works, she was involved in the MABYS. Julia Duckworth had met Leslie at the house of Jane Nassau Senior, the founder of the MABYS and the first woman Poor Law Inspector, appointed in Kensington; Julia deeply admired Octavia Hill, who in turn wrote an encomium on Stella Duck-worth's work after her death. Duckworths and Stephens were subscribers to the MABYS and so too were the Thackeray-Ritchie clan who were their kin of sorts: a MABYS report for 1878 advertises a pamphlet, 'Upstairs and Downstairs' by Mrs Ritchmond Ritchie, the former Anny Thackeray, sister of Minny, Leslie Stephen's first wife. At the MABYS Whitechapel branch Emily Marion Ritchie, known as 'Pinkie', who was Anny Thackeray's sister-in-law, offered her services and became fast friends with Edith Sichel. Edith volunteered in 1884 after her father died and

Pinkie Ritchie came to work in the office for a few hours a week. She was thirty-three and Edith twenty-two. Both were accomplished daughters at home, cultured and well read. Edith belonged to a wealthy German Jewish family which had long converted to Christianity; a warm and witty personality, an ardent, though not po-faced believer, who was known for her gaiety and good spirits. Pinkie was a brilliant amateur pianist (whose heart had apparently been broken by Hallam Tennyson, one of Tennyson's sons), she spoke French, German and Italian – as did Edith, who had also studied Latin and Greek. Their lives revolved around their innumerable friends and relations, their cultural activities, foreign travel and charity work. Theirs was one of those intensely romantic Victorian friendships between women, without any hint of impropriety, whose intimacies enchanced their home duties and added lustre to their social positions. 'We seemed destined to belong to each other for life,' Pinkie wrote.

As a MABYS volunteer Edith was expected to listen to the servants' stories and to write notes on the 'cases' she encountered. There were often terrible tales. Many mistresses wanted a servant on the cheap and the Board of Guardians of the workhouse usually paid the outlay for a uniform. The paltry wage of £5 a year might easily be withheld or whittled away once breakages were paid for. Often no one was any the wiser if the girl got no time off or was kept on minimal rations. There were cases of girls kept in rooms as small as broom-cupboards, half-starved to death; of others severely beaten or disfigured. It didn't need the added cruelties, however, for the work to be punishing in the extreme. Some girls said frankly that they would turn to prostitution rather than destroy themselves in conditions where sixteen-hour days, seven days a week, was usual enough employment for a 'general'. It was a mug's game. No wonder the Victorians called their maid-of-all-work a 'slavey'. One estimate of 1889, however, reckoned there were 8,000 slaveys on the books of the MABYS, but across London 'total numbers were incalculable'.

Most people in Victorian and Edwardian Britain wanted a general servant – a maid-of-all-work – who would do the chores and use her common sense. A malleable country girl might be ideal but she was hard to come by. In theory the workhouse girl should be a good substitute. She had grown up in a strictly managed, deferential world and ought – some thought – to be grateful for her existence. The workhouse was a house of industry not of rest, its routine of hard labour meant to deter from entry all but the most needy. As soon as they were old enough workhouse girls pulled their weight in drudgery; they joined the adult women in sweeping and washing floors, doing laundry work or making beds all day. Yet, as the MABYS revealed in their reports, such girls often turned out to be disasters. They were anxious about going into service and unable to settle down. Mistresses complained that the girls were nervy, weepy, clingy, afraid of the dark. They were liable to what appeared to be unwarranted panics. Some were unaccountably mischievous or unruly; subject to 'restless fits' and fidgets, unmanageable. Such girls could be sulky and rebellious, and incompetent; they seemed to have no respect for property. At best they appeared unreliable and idiotic, breaking crockery, tripping over mats – mistresses threw up their hands at this constant comedy of errors. At worst they were foul-tempered (and foul-mouthed), dishonest and irreligious. These were the originals for those stock-characters of hapless drudge or feckless skivvy, who regularly appeared in *Punch* or on the stage, or as a staple in the literature of the day.

The MABYS volunteers, who were familiar with the union workhouses, tried their best to see round the problem. These were girls, who, sometimes from birth, had been shut up in dark, miserable wards without their mothers. They'd been institutionalized so long, used to a life run like clockwork and regimented by bells and shouts, that they couldn't cope on the outside. How could they know the value of possessions when they had never had any? How could they know how to cook a leg of lamb, bleach linen tablecloths, iron collars and cuffs, let alone 'goffer' frills and pleats? They'd eaten the same monotonous diet all their lives, gone to bed without sheets under rough grey blankets, dressed in the same worn dress and ill-fitting boots. In the workhouse they'd used tin plates or rough earthenware and never handled china – no one told them how easily it cracked; some barely knew the use of knives and forks; many had never laid a fire, sat at a dinner table or lived in a family. How could they know its routines and rituals? There were even reports of those who went upstairs backwards in a state of fear (and were heartily laughed at). In the workhouse they'd lived on the ground floor since they were infants. The MABYS offered training at their own Central Home and Laundry, tried to find places where they would not be the only servant, undertook the aftercare of the girls and reported back to the workhouse Guardians on the girls' progress. Often their charges needed rest, food and medication, like 'Nellie Tipples', from the Whitechapel workhouse, who was one of many suffering from ringworm and was, apparently, a difficult case: 'She has been rather naughty lately, rude and disobedient.'

Edith had volunteered for work in the worst districts of London and it must have taken considerable nerve for a young lady of twenty-two to go on long tramps into Whitechapel, searching in lodging-houses, knocking on doors, trying to find missing girls. It was strenuous and sometimes frightening, but she felt entitled by both her social position and her work to enter homes at will. Her letters to Emily Ritchie reveal how shocked and angered she often was by what she encountered, the single rooms where men, women and children were all crowded together, the children without food or proper clothes. She frequently attacked the callous West End 'landlords and parvenus', and she was a close and compassionate observer, noting carefully what women earnt (4d a pair for finishing trousers, 1d for filling twelve dozen boxes of matches), as if she were conducting a social survey. As with others who made the journey into 'darkest London', her traumatic experiences prompted stories and articles making sense of what she saw there. Sichel's writing is conventional, though heartfelt, veering between melodrama, pathos and creaky humour, especially when she depicts 'the characters' she meets in the East End. One of her MABYS reports becomes almost fiction as she describes 'the mad world of Bethnal Green, Shoreditch, or Shadwell' and the farcical search for one

'Eliza Smith', whose 'pitch-black parents' would be at home in Africa (the racial analogy for the 'dark continent' of the East End was a familiar one); the Smiths live in a fog of unknowing (an image borrowed from Dickens), their dirt and confusion like moral squalor, their poverty linked to images of disease and contagion. Eliza is being hit across the shoulders by the son of the house, and Sichel's cheerful comedy allows her to convey 'the sordid and painful facts' in a palatable form. 'A Jubilee Day's Experience', which Sichel published in *Murray's Magazine* in 1887, has an apocalyptic tone, longing for the new dawn of reform. A child guides the narrator into the 'inferno', and as Edith goes 'lower and lower' into the circles of 'a poverty-stricken Hades' she meets people deformed, degraded and soulless. Even the bustling street market with its piano-organ appears dismal to her, 'a travesty of mirth'. Ultimately the hustling, brawling street traders and unkempt girls (always the women have wild, tangled hair) give way to a picture of the calm domestic life inside Miss Hill's 'Model Dwellings'. Here the inhabitants are contented and respectable royalists of the 'mustn't grumble' variety. Edith was to abandon her experiments with fiction but her writing gave her a public voice.

Like other charity-workers who made their way into the tenements, the courts and alleys, Edith Sichel was buoyed up by her religious faith. She was an idealist rather than a theorist and whenever she wrote about the possible solutions to poverty which her contemporaries might propose, she fell back on the gospel of Christian love, on the idea of fellowship and personal equality. In a bold article in *Murray's Magazine* (April 1888) she took issue with George Gissing, pitting him against another 'philanthropic novelist', Walter Besant. She proclaimed the one too bitter and pessimistic, the other too cheerfully optimistic, for her tastes, arguing that although the poor were degraded, they were not hopeless or lost in 'the nether world', they could improve. Her vision was of a moral regeneration that began with individuals. Like Octavia Hill and Julia Stephen, Edith Sichel was dubious about any political intervention or 'doles' and, like them, she took a dim view of women's suffrage. She believed that the poor needed

the moral influence of their betters, as much, if not more than
economic assistance. Self-control, thrift, an orderly, peaceful home
– she looked for domestic remedies to national problems. She
was not blind, however, to the limitations of what she called, in
a letter to Pinkie Ritchie, 'the inconsistencies and hopelessness of
carrying out one's skimpy little systems', but she counted herself
among the run of well-meaning people, neither saint nor martyr,
nor 'noble fanatic'.

Slumming was a 'high enterprise', an adventure, but it was also,
as she saw it, borrowing a phrase of Samuel Barnett's, 'a spiritual
romance' which offered Edith self-discovery by taking her out of
herself and beyond the narrow confines of her well-upholstered
world. 'Slummers', as the slang suggests, were, of course, frequently
disparaged as thrill-seekers or tourists (and some certainly were).
Many ladies, like Edith and Emily, remained daughters at home
but others devoted their entire lives to the poor. They became
'settlers', establishing 'missions' as they did overseas, living among
the poor, sharing their lives, bringing medical aid, running make-
shift clinics for mothers and babies, founding girls' and boys' clubs,
becoming formidable managers, in public or semi-public roles,
and negotiating with other agencies, though usually within a
recognizably feminine sphere; others made the transition into
local government or the new Labour Party. Some, like Marx's
daughter Eleanor, were deeply radicalized. In the harsh winter
of 1887, she visited a desperately poor family with eight children
– 'little skeletons' – living in a cellar in Lisson Grove, the district
where Stella Duckworth was to have her 'philanthropic cottages'.
Eleanor thought it 'extraordinary that these people will lie down
and die of hunger rather than join together and *take* what they
need, and what there is abundance of'. The middle classes, she
thought, lived in 'mortal dread' of this. Philanthropy could never
be enough for Eleanor Marx, who argued that such poverty was
the inevitable byproduct of the ruthless search for profit and
imperial appetite. She joined the factory and dockworkers in the
call for strikes. The tension between those who saw the poor
primarily as a moral project and those who insisted on economic

or political causes of poverty (the dilemma which faces Shaw's Major Barbara in his play of 1905) animated social policy for decades, and, indeed, continues to do so.

Edith Sichel was a small but dynamic figure in that vast landscape. Her commitment to 'poor-peopling' continued after she was forced by ill-health to withdraw from 'the poison of the East End streets'. She had long wanted to finance and manage 'a small home for baby girls to grow up in'. When both she and Pinkie lost their mothers in 1888, they decided to take a country cottage together in Chiddingfold, a tiny village close to the small town of Godalming in the Surrey hills. Edith had visited the area many times with Pinkie – the Ritchies had a family place at nearby Hindhead – and wanted a retreat, though they were to keep their London residences. She found a second cottage in the village, where she placed a widow, Mrs Mary Hill, from the City, who had a number of daughters herself to care for, and then she looked about her for girls and babies to adopt. Most of Edith's little girls would come from the Whitechapel workhouse where the Rev. Samuel Barnett, as its most eminent Guardian, would be able to act as Edith's referee, 'one amongst them having been left as a parcel when a few days old': Lottie Hope.

★

It was not until 1926 that the first Adoption Act was passed in England and Wales, formalizing the role of adopting parents and making adoption legally binding. At the turn of the century adoption was still a relatively casual matter, carried out informally by individuals, agencies or charities. It had long been acceptable, and sometimes imperative, for wealthier relatives to bring up or apprentice the children of poorer members of the family (Jane Austen puts her Fanny Price in this position at Mansfield Park, in the novel of that name). Parents would frequently 'lend' their children if it was to the child's (or their own) advantage. In the nineteenth century those ladies who adopted the children of the poor saw themselves as saving them from poverty, prostitution and even death, much as many of today's affluent Westerners seek to rescue the abandoned children of harsh or war-torn regimes. In the 1860s, Julia Margaret Cameron (Julia Stephen's aunt), approached by a desperate Irish beggar, found the woman a job and took on the care of her daughter, Mary Ryan. Mary worked as Mrs Cameron's maid and posed for her mistress's photographs, eventually making an extraordinary marriage into the upper classes. Other ladies, though, treated their girls and babies like accessories, dropping them when they were no long deemed an asset. Around the same time, Anny and Minny Thackeray, both in their twenties, adopted a little girl called Ellen, simply taking her home with them when they saw 'her tipsy mother' hitting her in the street; she soon disappeared from their lives, presumably passed on to an institution of some kind. The line between adoption and abduction was thin. Few laws existed in the late nineteenth century in relation to homeless children, and many philanthropists, like the most famous rescuer of all, Thomas Barnardo, could be a law unto themselves. In 1889, the year after Edith's move, Barnardo had been brought to trial over the exporting of eleven-year-old Harry Gossage to Canada without his mother's permission. This paragon had sold her son to two organ-grinders in a pub and, when they later abandoned him, she signed for his admission to Barnardo's but not for his emigration. Barnardo was cleared but the result was the 1891 Custody of Children Act, which gave more powers to institutions and to the courts who could now refuse to return children if they thought the parents would ill-use them. The law, which was mocked as the 'Barnardo Relief Bill', would also have eased Edith Sichel's path.

Miss Sichel was not a committee woman and disliked red tape but, even so, the speed at which her private 'adoptions' took place was startling. As the minutes of the Board reveal, in July 1890 she adopted Eleanor Holland, aged eleven months, an 'illegitimate child whose mother is deceased' (her references were given to the Rev. Samuel Barnett and Miss Pauline Townsend, head of the Whitechapel MABYS); a year later, Eliza Smith was adopted, a girl of seven whose mother was still alive but 'is supposed to be getting her living on the streets as an unfortunate' and had apparently deserted her. Each process took less than six weeks. When the Home was well established, the wheels moved even more swiftly and children were simply selected when a letter from Miss Sichel was read out to the Whitechapel Board of Guardians: in one instance, in December 1896, 'Mary Friday', who was only eleven months old, was immediately despatched to Edith for 'present bringing up in her "Home" for little children, Elm Cottages, Chiddingfold'. When the census at Chiddingfold was taken in 1891, the Home included the matron, Mrs Hill, with two daughters, Rosina and Florence, aged sixteen and fourteen, helping out, a couple of older girls, a three-year-old and two tiny babies, of three and one month, names 'not known', whose place of birth was given as Whitechapel. One was probably Lottie. In 1895 Miss Sichel and Miss Ritchie moved to the nearby village of Hambledon, building a new house, Hambledon Hurst, on the cricket green. The 'Baby Cot', as they affectionately dubbed the Home, was then settled in another cottage in the village, on Beech Hill, with Mrs Hill again in charge. All the orphans – including a Betty, Kate, Gertrude, Polly and Patty – were given the surname 'Hope' and their place of birth was registered as 'London Not Known'. According to Pinkie's memoir, 'there were no parents to claim them as they grew up', though this was not strictly the case. Removed to the country and with new names, these girls from the London slums would be very hard to find.

Though it was a private initiative, Edith Sichel's Home was of a piece with changes in workhouse policy. Lady visitors had long played an influential role in monitoring child welfare in the workhouses and improving conditions there; they had been vocal in their support for boarding out and active in the supervision of the fostering of children. Until the late nineteenth century children had usually remained in the workhouse and were then sent to local Poor Law or 'district schools' (known as 'barrack schools', for obvious reasons), effectively set apart from their peers. In the 1890s most workhouses, including Whitechapel and Shoreditch, were now building cottage homes in the country for their pauper children, a more humane alternative to the barrack schools in the centre of London. Barnardo's Girls' Village Home, built on an estate in Essex, had been a model, replacing the old dormitory wards with sixty separate cottages, complete with a village green and a church. In the cottage homes children lived in small groups with a house mother; they had their own kitchens where they might learn domestic skills; there were walks and nature study, and perhaps some horticulture – all good for the soul. Most importantly, a Home was not a vast, impersonal institution and offered the individual attention infants needed. It also clearly fulfilled a need in the benefactors themselves. Like Emily Ritchie, Edith Sichel remained unmarried. Friends noted unapologetically that surrounded by 'her' babies, 'her mother-instinct was fully and beneficently exercised'. This was maternalism with a purpose, however, a natural extension of Edith's work with the MABYS. Sometimes her girls married locally, and when one – 'a regular simple Susan' – brought her child for a visit, Edith was delighted to see her 'joy of a moral grandchild'. 'Almost all the girls,' Pinkie Ritchie noted, 'rewarded Edith's care by becoming excellent young servants.'

Almost all the girls. Again drawing on her MABYS experience, Edith Sichel experimented with a small 'laundry home' in the village. She meant only to have about six older girls – 'Whitechapel generals' – especially those in poor health. She would keep them for a maximum of a year, train them up and find them country situations. She would lay on medical help, lots of fresh air and regular occupation. Laundry work was dear to the heart of many Victorians, who saw it as useful and morally beneficial, as if the very act of producing white linen was a sign of the moral cleansing of women and girls redeemed from vice and dirt. In the 1880s it had become part of the school curriculum and was often seen as remedial work for the 'roughest' type of girl. In the workhouses and training-homes, girls as young as nine or ten might be found in their heavy clogs and thick aprons pumping water and carrying pails, stooping over galvanized baths with their scrubbing boards and soap; lifting the sopping clothes, rinsing, wringing and mangling; wielding the hot and heavy flat irons. Edith bought a shed and converted it, invested in 'a copper' for boiling water and laid in quantities of blue starch, while the gentry sent in their soiled tablecloths and sheets.

The experiment failed and only a few girls found places. They didn't take to the work and got the laundry dirty as soon as they had washed it. In 'The Confessions of an Amateur Philanthropist' (1900), Edith blamed the utterly different set of values between rich and poor, and her mistake of 'taking my normal for their normal'. She was no relativist, however. In part she blamed the anaemia which she believed infected them morally as well as physically, so she took them for nature walks and read them poetry. The girls were listless and walked with their heads down, they missed the shops and the bustle, and were not much interested in birds or Longfellow. 'I had to conclude,' she wrote, 'that I was dealing with people of deficient imagination; people who did not wish to be different, and saw no reason why they should be so; who were wholly lacking in curiosity for anything outside their restricted experiences, and understood no words but their own primitive terms.' And she concluded: 'The Whitechapel mind contains few impressions' and must be worked on by dint of repetition. Studying each of the Beatitudes intensively for a month (imagine!), Edith tried weaning them from Whitechapel behaviour, especially sexual flirtatiousness, which she called 'horseplay'. She offered as comic evidence the girl who thought that being 'pure in heart' meant 'being kind to our young men and not looking at murders in the street'. It seems that Edith Sichel never asked about their lives at home, though she admitted that these girls came to her at fifteen, 'after a good deal of experience about which you have no notion'; nor did she acknowledge that if she were transplanted from her own familiar surroundings, plunged into a steamy workshop and made to drudge all day, then expected to learn piecemeal an alien philosophy, she too would be sullen, lonely, depressed. Edith's advice to other 'amateur philanthropists' was to take only 'little children, as soon after birth as possible' and remove them to the country. Heredity might intervene but at least there would be pleasure in the babies for a while. Ultimately Edith's role was that of the missionary, not the anthropologist. It would take a modern psychoanalyst to suggest that those who had grown up seeing murders in the street might well be listless because they suffered from too many impressions rather than too few.

★

Miss Sichel's babies grew up in the village of Hambledon. Though the records of the Home are missing, the girls can be found in the admissions register of the village school. Lottie Hope is there, enrolled in September 1900, aged ten. She had come from Chiddingfold school already able to read and write. She joined along with Gertrude Hope, but also a Margery Osborne and Christina Halfpenny from the Home – all Lottie's age, Kate Bridget aged twelve and May Goudge, thirteen – so some girls did keep their own surnames. Their parent or guardian was given as 'Miss Sichel'. From the Home on Beech Hill, the crocodile of little girls would have walked hand in hand up the sunken track to school, 'with high banks on either side, and a roof of beech leaves' from 'the most beautiful trees' in the village. Were they aware that Beech Hill was known too for 'one of the loveliest choruses of nightingales in any southern county'? Perhaps on one of her nature walks Miss Sichel would have pointed this out as her charges drank in the obligatory fresh air and longed to scuff up the white dust of the lane with their shoes as the village children did.

Until the second half of the nineteenth century Hambledon, on the border of Surrey and Sussex, was a hamlet with about 500 inhabitants, though some 150 of them had suddenly appeared when a new workhouse for the area was built in the late eighteenth century. Most people worked on the land as labourers or farmers; landowners and gentry were few and far between. With the coming of the railways that began to change. Hambledon was only a mile from Witley station with the main terminus of London's

Waterloo station a mere hour away. The Surrey hills were soon discovered by London's upper-middle classes, especially artists and writers, seeking a rural retreat. Miss Sichel and Miss Ritchie's choice of Hambledon for their second Home was not an accident. They were part of a new wave of incomers to the Surrey villages. In 1876 George Eliot built The Heights, a large redbrick mansion at Witley; the George du Mauriers rented nearby. The Poet Laureate himself had occupied a sumptuous mansion at Aldworth, high up on the downs since 1869, and many of those in Tennyson's orbit rented or built homes in the district. The Ritchies had a place at nearby Hindhead; the painter George Frederick Watts, at Compton. Surrey was one of the Home Counties, whose thatched and timber-framed cottages, village greens and duckponds suggested to the town-dweller a timeless rural peace and a quintessential Englishness (no matter that few of these 'characteristic' village features were found in other English counties). The area around Hambledon proved immensely appealing to Tennyson's friend, the extremely popular artist Myles Birket Foster, who built a new house at Witley which his friend William Morris decorated. Birket Foster and his disciple, Helen Allingham, who also moved to the area, painted delicate, muted watercolours of rustic scenes replete with tumbledown cottages, rosy robins and neat farm girls in clean pinafores. These sentimental views, offering 'a charming, conservative vision of rural delight', were sometimes meant as a protest against the harshness of landlords – Allingham entitled one of her watercolours *The Condemned Cottage* – but all too often any implicit criticism was lost in the picturesque prettiness of the scene. A watercolour of the quaint old almshouses in Hambledon at the bottom of Beech Hill, painted by Birket Foster in the mid-60s, led to the road being renamed Hundred Guinea Lane (after his princely commission). These same cottages later collapsed; they were filthy and unsanitary, and were eventually pulled down. Surrey was one of the most backward of the farming counties in Britain. Its soil – so good for building – was generally poor. The picturesque cottages were often little more than hovels. Hambledon's labourers received less than 10s a week or took odd jobs, while women might expect around 8d a day; infant mortality ran high, typhoid threatened and about half the county's population was illiterate. How could they afford even the few pence needed to send their children to school?

Ironically, until the 1880s the workhouse or charity child was one of the few Victorian infants who was bound officially to receive some schooling. After the Poor Law Act of 1834 a minimum of three hours a day in reading, writing and arithmetic was stipulated, though the first was almost entirely of a religious nature. Village children, on the other hand, must take their chances. In the 1860s the Stephen family cook, Sophie Farrell, had been unlucky in not gaining her letters, but her experience in Lincolnshire was far from unusual given the haphazard state of rural schools, where teaching was often little better than childminding. For much of the century infant education was in a confused state, caught between earlier charitable efforts, older establishments managed voluntarily by national societies or the Church, private 'dame schools' and the increasing interventions of government, offering grants dependent upon attendance and examination performance (Dickens's Gradgrindism or the much hated 'payment by results' system). Hambledon 'National' School had been built in 1852 but not until the Elementary Education Act of 1870 was it more or less compulsory for local children to attend. It was run by the Church of England and a specially elected board of charitable individuals, but also dependent upon Her Majesty's Inspectorate for funds – a situation which made for endless wrangling over the upkeep of the school. HMI monitored progress through the school's 'log book' which the head teacher was now obliged to keep; schools were regularly inspected and had to be approved for government grants to be maintained. Pressure was also increasingly on the teachers and their assistants to be accredited and the new teacher-training colleges began to ensure a steady stream of qualified staff. Inspectors could be sticklers for the timetable and for the standardizing of knowledge but they could also be men of vision, idealists infuriated by the laissez-faire attitude of teachers or the conservatism of the gentry, especially in rural districts where the clergy and the carriage-folk were none too keen on having their labourers get above themselves.

When Lottie Hope joined it there had been nearly fifty years of squabbling over Hambledon School and it was only just beginning to improve. In its first decades attendance was low and conditions were truly dreadful. The one schoolroom, into which all the children were crowded, was dirty and smelly, with pools of water on the floor on wet days and damp on the walls. After miles of walking through the country lanes, the children sat shivering in their coats and boots over a meagre fire. Mostly they worked with slates on their laps, sitting on the floor. Scripture lessons featured largely, and one inspector, a Rev. Peake, noted disapprovingly in the log book for 1889 that the infants 'slurred over' the words of the Lord's Prayer. The teacher never knew whether to expect a hundred pupils or none. Bad weather, bad roads, illnesses such as ringworm, chicken pox, whooping cough or scarlet fever, which sometimes had their origin among the workhouse children and spread easily in the school, frequently kept pupils away. Not surprisingly children would far rather be out of doors helping their parents earn a few pence: in summer and autumn they picked hops, whortleberries, acorns and chestnuts and helped with the harvest. They were also kept off school by the gentry on occasion, during a pheasant shoot, for example, when boys might be employed. Until a village institute was built in 1903 the school was frequently commandeered for village or parochial events, such as dances or concerts, which must have been fun for the community but did little to support the endeavours of the teachers.

Not surprisingly too, the turnover of staff was high. Hambledon School was unrewarding and exhausting and the log books report more than one teacher, like 'Miss Kate Mills' of the infants' department 'ordered to the seaside', too weak and ill to cope with school work. In 1891 Her Majesty's Inspector found that 'the infants are backward and they are taught in a lifeless and unintelligent manner', though conceding that the teachers were 'much handicapped by the crowded state of the room'. In 1894, for instance, the managers were given formal warning that their grant would be withheld unless the infants got a 'proper separation from the older scholars', instead of sitting chanting their tables or alphabet behind a curtain. Hambledon's rector might smile benignly when he examined the children and listened to their parroting of psalms, but the school consistently failed its inspections because of its dilapidated buildings, lack of books and desks, inadequate toilets, or 'offices', as they were euphemistically called. (Until 1946 the school relied on a well in the garden and on earth-closets for the children.) Finally a piano was brought in from the rectory to assist with the singing; in May 1897 the children learnt the Jubilee song 'Victoria the Beloved' and also 'Hurrah for England'. Only in the 1900s did the inspectors judge the school 'satisfactorily efficient'. With the arrival of desks and chairs, the children had to learn to sit up straight, arms folded and no fidgeting. Unruly children who were 'shirking' or 'stubborn' received a 'stripe' on the hand or several stripes on the posterior from the cane, duly recorded in the new punishment book.

By the 1880s school attendance had become obligatory everywhere, though fees were not finally abolished in elementary schools until 1891. In 1899 the school-leaving age was raised to twelve, and again, though permissively, to fourteen in 1900. So Lottie Hope belonged to the first generation of working-class girls entitled to a free state education at elementary level. As the new century began, ten-year-old Lottie would have found her place among the ninety-three or so children on the rolls. There were at last pencils, rubbers, pens and ink, textbooks, charts, a blackboard and easel, new arithmetic books and reading sheets, and even exercise books, though Miss E. J. Leigh-Carter CM (Certificated Mistress) and her two assistants were campaigning for cupboards to put them in. While the infants stood in their pinafores, behind the wooden partition, reciting 'The boy stood on the burning deck' (Mrs Hemans's 'Casabianca') or Longfellow's 'The Wreck of the Hesperus', Lottie practised a new song, 'Rule Britannia', and learnt the year's 'object lessons': tea, sugar, coffee, cocoa, rubber. Empire manifested itself again in the shape of the exotic animals shown on their reading cards – 'camel, lion, tiger, elephant' – and in the more bellicose form of drill, which had the boys marching, wheeling and forming in the playground. According to the school log books Lottie would have bent her head to endless dictation and 'repetitions': Shakespeare's *The Merchant of Venice* was read round the class and great chunks were got off by heart. The children composed their own essays too. More academic subjects, such as geography and geometry, were introduced but arithmetic – multiplication, short and long division – dominated. The girls drew 'natural forms' of flora and fauna out of doors, but they also did a great deal of sewing and knitting, sometimes for a sale of work to the gentry, which brought in funds for the school. While the infants wove mats or worked needlecases, the older girls produced 'fancy work' or more advanced 'specimens' such as shirts. Various practical activities in class, including flower-making, paper-folding and bead-threading, had domesticity in mind, and for the older girls a cookery class existed which Lottie would have attended. In the 1900s the national curriculum put a growing emphasis upon girls acquiring 'the three Cs' – cooking, cleaning and care of clothing – to which some added a fourth: child-care.

What Miss Sichel's girls learnt in the Home was reiterated at school: they should be tidy and diligent if they were to become good domestic workers, whether in their own family or someone else's. Lottie's life, like that of other girls who grew up in institutions, was gregarious and communal; she shared everything and she owned nothing, except perhaps her brush and comb. Though it followed strict routines, it was certainly less regimented and less stigmatized than that of a workhouse child and the school was more relaxed than a London Board School. There were plenty of treats and days off for sports and school trips to the seaside (Southsea on the Hampshire coast was the usual choice). The village had its highdays and holidays. Cricket matches, visiting circuses or gypsy fairs, the village fête or May Day celebrations, harvest homes, tea parties for the most important weddings, all meant a day or an afternoon's freedom, as did village funerals, since the school was just down the lane from St Peter's church and silence must be observed. Miss Sichel's girls would have joined in the festivities for Edward VII's coronation in June of 1902, when the village green was decked with bunting and there were races and tugs-of-war, with even the ladies attempting to balance an egg and spoon, and meat teas provided 'at reasonable prices' before the dancing until dark. Miss Sichel and Miss Ritchie were local luminaries and dropped in at the school from time to time. Sometimes they listened to the singing, and one year Edith offered a prize for the best essay on any historical character (though the log book does not give the results). As an orphan not needed at home or on the farm, Lottie was a steady attender, though, of Miss Sichel's girls, only she and Christina Halfpenny completed their schooling to Standard V. Her fate was a foregone conclusion nonetheless. Only rarely did a child become a pupil-teacher; most boys went on to farms or started at a trade; girls who stayed on like Lottie went straight into service. Lottie Hope left the school on 12 August 1904, aged fourteen. Where she went next, however, is unknown.

There were plenty of places to be had. By the turn of the century motor-buses, bicycles and charabancs had made the Surrey hills even more accessible and the middle classes started to build in earnest. Public schools and prep schools sprang up, businessmen began to travel up to town, leaving their wives and children, and all these prosperous establishments needed servants. Edith and Emily also had their London connections, among whom was a new guest at Hambledon Hurst, the painter and art critic Roger Fry, himself a refugee from Bayswater, South Kensington's stuffy neighbour. He was renting in the area and thinking of building a house, partly because his wife, Helen, who was also a talented painter, was suffering from mental illness and the doctors recommended a country life for her health. He had met Edith Sichel in London and in the autumn of 1908 visited Hambledon Hurst. 'You will like Miss Sichel & her friend Miss Ritchie,' he wrote to Helen after an evening of Pinkie at the piano. 'She plays very beautifully so last night we had a lot of Bach and Couperin.' Fry enthused about the beauty of the

area with its 'undulating woodland', and early the following year
he purchased a sloping plot of land above the nearby city of
Guildford. His house, Durbins, was finished by the end of 1909
and Fry moved in with his two children and his sister, Joan. Helen,
however, was still unwell but was meant to join them soon. Two
local girls, Lizzie and 'Budge' Boxall, came as servants and, when
they left, Nellie, their younger sister, took the job as cook. She
was joined by Miss Sichel's foundling, Lottie Hope, who lived in
as housemaid at Durbins. Thus began Lottie and Nellie's friendship and their long life together working for Bloomsbury.

★

Six-year-old 'Janet Hope' was probably the last of Edith's adopted
babies to go to Hambledon village school, in August 1914. For in
that month, just after the war with Germany was declared, Edith
Sichel died. She left a trust for the maintenance of the Home
until the youngest inmate was sixteen, but by the end of the
following year all her girls had left. Sichel was only fifty-two but
her work earnt her an obituary in *The Times*, not primarily as a
philanthropist but as 'a writer of vivid personality' and the wit
and humour 'generally thought characteristic of the male rather
than the female intelligence'. After abandoning the fiction based on
her East End years, she had found her *métier* writing cultural history
and biography – a life of Catherine de Medici, studies of the French
Revolution and the Renaissance, a biography of Montaigne – as
well as numerous weekly articles for the *Times Literary Supplement*.
In 1918, when Virginia Woolf read the memorial selection of Edith's
writings which Pinkie Ritchie had gathered together at the end
of the war, she was fascinated:

Edith Sichel, whose soul is now open to me through her letters, makes
me determine to write descriptions neither of pictures nor of music.
She makes me consider that the gulf which we crossed between
Kensington & Bloomsbury was the gulf between respectable mum[m]ified
humbug & life crude & impertinent perhaps, but living. The breath of

South Kensington lives in her pages – almost entirely, I believe, because they would not mention either copulation or w.c's.

She wrote to Vanessa that she felt she 'could write pages about her'. She was plagued by feeling that she needed to 'know South Kensington' and to understand its 'humanity'. 'I see outside of that world so clearly, & take a kind of ribald pleasure in putting those figures into action – sending them slumming, to Pops [concerts], to the National Gallery, always full of high thoughts, morality, kindliness, & never seeing beyond High St. Kensington.' It was crucial for the mythologizing of 'Bloomsbury', as she now called it, that Kensington seemed its remote antithesis, but perhaps Edith's world was still too near, rather than too far, to get properly into focus.

Virginia worked hard to put a distance between herself and other literary ladies. Like Sichel, Virginia Stephen had been educated at home, had taken private lessons and attended lectures, and began her literary career reviewing for the *TLS*. She knew Edith Sichel as a writer from the early days of her own apprenticeship, when, in 1905, Virginia's piece on Sichel's *Catherine de Medici* was turned down. Writing to Nelly Cecil, she sneered a little at Edith, whose family had long been Christian, as 'that talented Jewess' who had rather trampled on Mary Coleridge's poems in a posthumous edition Sichel had produced in 1910. Edith's praise for one of Virginia's reviews drew the begrudging acknowledgement that 'the tawny bitch in South Kensington' (surely another anti-Semitic slur) was one of her own kind, 'black to the 3rd finger joint in ink'. Virginia's early writing shared some of that fin-de-siècle savouring of the exquisite moment which suffused much of Sichel's gilded prose, the penchant for painterly descriptions of light and shadow, and the self-consciously literary and allusive (she wisely abandoned 'Melymbrosia' as the working title of her first novel). She would always worry about her own facility for the finely wrought and dreaded being deemed 'a lady-like prattler'. Economy of expression and feeling was paramount to a modern aesthetic. If Edith Sichel's sorties into wit and humour, like her parodies of Browning's monologues, now seemed horribly laboured, her religion was dismissed as saccharine and intrusive. Staunch secularist that she was, Virginia Stephen vetoed anything fictional that smacked of didacticism, including novels with too plainly progressive a politics. She lampooned her contemporaries, such as the novelist May Sinclair, a Fabian whom Virginia mocked as a woman 'of obtrusive, and medicinal morality'.

Edith Sichel had a moral mission to represent the poor, in person and in print. She followed the great Victorian novelists who felt 'compelled', as Mrs Gaskell wrote in *Mary Barton*, to give 'some utterance to the agony which from time to time, convulses this dumb people'. For Sichel the right moral accents and intonation were especially needed as large sections of the poor were far from silent and were voicing very noisy, increasingly political demands. Edith had felt no qualms in her fiction when it came to putting words in her slum girls' mouths; she was a natural mimic and relished reproducing the exotic speech of the 'natives', as she called them, for the benefit of her polite readers. Her story about a general servant, 'Jenny', prefigures George Moore's novel *Esther Waters*, and, like his heroine, Jenny is a sexual victim and a figure of pathos, always in the midst of romance, at the mercy of her desires for love and a better life, but unable to articulate them. Like her later incarnation, 'Gladys Leonora Pratt', the heroine of a story of 1913, Jenny is a mere bundle of vague impressions; any moral sense she has is unconscious. Most other charity-workers, like Sichel, thought the disorderly homes of the poor reflected their disorganized inner lives. The poor frittered their resources because they were too moved by the whims of the present; they never learnt from the past and so could not plan for the future. Teaching history to adults at Morley College in the 1900s, Virginia Stephen had felt something similar. She found the 'nice enthusiastic working women' were 'refreshing after the educated', but they seemed to have no depth: 'so thin is the present to them; must not the past remain a spectre always?' Though Virginia came to distrust the ventriloquizing which other authors assumed as their right, her beggars and chars, like Miss Sichel's

East End girls, were to be centres of feeling but not of consciousness. In this, as in so much else, Bloomsbury and South Kensington
were always much closer to each other than they ever were to
Whitechapel.

Virginia Woolf knew that she knew very little about the poor.
Early in her apprenticeship she determined to avoid 'hackneyed'
descriptions. 'A great imaginative feat it would be to understand
the point of view of a Sussex labourer,' she wrote in her journal
in 1907. 'There is too much of the "pathetic fallacy" in all our
novels; tears in a dog's eyes, joy in an old horse.' When her housemaid, Maud Chart, told her that her brother had had four fingers
cut off by a machine for making sweets, Virginia was sympathetic
and appalled. 'The misery of the lower classes impresses me very
much,' she wrote, but she knew her visions of industrial life were
purely literary. An essay of 1910 on Mrs Gaskell comments on
the problem of always seeing 'the poor in stress of some kind',
which did away with 'the need of subtle understanding'. She
preferred George Gissing's tormented descent into his debased
'Nether World', because he stressed the brutal fact of money, and
'there is no sentimentalism about the fundamental equality of
men in his works'. In her 1912 article on his novels she sounds
like a Miss Schlegel in E. M. Forster's contemporary novel, *Howard's
End*, as she observes that in the slums there was not 'room for
the soul': 'Without money you cannot have space or leisure; worse
than that, the chances are very much against your having either
love or intelligence.' Gissing's dismal philosophy never reassured
the reader; he took risks where others, like the philanthropic
novelists, were constrained by their faith in goodness. Gissing was
a better writer because he could be uncharitable: it was very
much a modern's point of view. But it was equally presumptuous
about the poor.

Virginia's loathing for do-gooders coloured her encounters with
those women who were becoming active in the suffrage or the
Labour movement, whom she often grouped with the philanthropists. During her time spent working for Adult Suffrage, she
wrote to Janet Case, who had once taught her Greek, that she

was suspicious of 'the inhuman side' of politics and found such public women 'bloodless', perhaps echoing her fears about herself as too cerebral and egotistical (the dried-up spinster was a popular stereotype). She could be satirical too about the 'Imperial tread' of women trade unionists and organizers, adding that 'nothing – except perhaps novel writing – can compare with the excitement of controlling the masses'. But she reserved her utmost disgust for the older generation of religious reformers, such as Canon and Mrs Samuel Barnett, Edith Sichel's old friends. Reading Henrietta Barnett's two-volume life of her husband in 1919, Virginia reacted violently against 'the peculiar repulsiveness of those who dabble their fingers self-approvingly in the stuff of others' souls'. As with the radicals, the root of their smugness lay 'in the adulation of the uneducated, & the easy mastery of the will over the poor', adding 'more and more I come to loathe any dominion of one over another; any leadership, any imposition of the will.' Every shred of Woolf's being revolted against the idea of interference; she had herself been constantly subject to the regimes of others – relatives, doctors and nurses, well-meaning religious ladies supervising her convalescences. Not having a philanthropic relationship to the poor was to make being a mistress difficult. And could one be a writer and not dabble in the stuff of other people's souls? An author without authority?

When Mrs Woolf accused Miss Sichel of not knowing 'life', it sounds to twenty-first-century ears like a case of pot calling kettle black. She might be frank in private, but Virginia was not keen to mention either wcs or copulation in her fiction. Certainly the Miss Sichel who had gone into the East End and taken up pauper girls was high-minded and high-handed, but she was involved and active, offering her time, effort and cash. Her Baby Cot flourished for nigh on twenty-five years; she worked as a schools manager and she campaigned for prison reform as a visitor to Holloway, the women's gaol in London. Yes, she saw the 'lowest class' there as little better than 'savages', 'the protoplasm of humanity', and she feared the 'screaming individualism', fostered by a lack of religion, which she felt was fuelling a 'materialistic socialism' and foolish demands for independence. But she proposed literacy teaching for these women, careful case studies of the prisoners and their home lives, and spent her last days reading and talking to them. Miss Sichel surely knew as much, or as little, as Mrs Woolf of life 'crude and impertinent'.

In her memorial volume, Pinkie Ritchie gave a testimonial from one of Edith's girls, who wrote of her 'godmother', 'Heaven knows how heaps of people whom she was a right hand to will miss her more than they can tell.' Each child reared in Edith's Home, so her friends believed, was 'a bit of salvage from the devouring sea of London'. For every Lottie, Gerty, Polly or Janet Hope there were nonetheless thousands who were left to go under. Private initiatives could only be a drop in the ocean. There were also innumerable charity children in less benevolent situations, whose confidence was sapped by being in an institution, whose life in service was pure drudgery and whose intelligence was drained and wasted.

Edith Sichel aged twenty-five

They had nothing good to say of their training 'homes' or of the 'slave-drivers' who ran them. In the end, perhaps, Lottie's temper was a betterr testimony to Miss Sichel's generosity than her gratitude.

MRS WOOLF, MRS BELL AND 'THE CLICK'

When she looked back on the Victorian home, Virginia Woolf saw a gloomy and crowded interior, part-museum, part-mausoleum. Like the Victorian self, it was cluttered and stifling, a hot house with its blinds and heavy curtains drawn. The new rooms which her generation was to imagine would be light, uninhibited places where one might also live differently inside oneself. Yet the past was not so easily got rid of. When the Stephen children left their parents' home, plenty of old things had travelled with them – photographs and paintings, their father's books and even the mantelpiece from Hyde Park Gate. Though 'unwelcomed', their mother's small folding tea table – 'the very hearth and centre of Victorian family life' – around which the daughters of the house had dutifully sat, remained part of their lives. Things were refurbished and relocated, but they were not all abandoned, these totems of a lost tribe. The huge Dutch cabinet that had once dominated the dining room in Kensington eventually presided over Vanessa's studio at Charleston farmhouse and the looking-glass from her parents' bedroom, into which Virginia remembered gazing blankly on the day her mother lay there dead, finally stared out from a corner next to the bed where Vanessa died. The free self, like the empty room or the white space, might be infinitely desirable but it remains a fantasy, and, like the future, it cannot be lived in.

Servants were part of the furniture. In the 1900s the Stephens' move from South Kensington to the squares of Bloomsbury was a step away from the nineteenth century towards the twentieth, away from stuffy respectability and towards independence. Banishing the horsehair sofas and crimson plush, replacing dark paints with pale distempers, drinking coffee after dinner rather than tea, were all part of being freed from Victorianism. Yet down in the kitchen at Gordon Square, at Fitzroy and at Brunswick, Sophie Farrell and Maud Chart slaved away for the young people as they had for Leslie and Julia Stephen. The outlook in the drawing room might be advanced but in the kitchen it harked back to the past. Those who lived in Bloomsbury felt hampered and irritated by servants, but they could not imagine a life without that division of labour which made housekeeping a female activity, and housework performed, where possible, by women of the lower classes.

In the 1910s, when they were both setting up homes as married ladies, Mrs Woolf and Mrs Bell wrote constantly to each other about 'their' domestics. 'Oh let's not talk about the servants!' they insisted, 'They're too incomprehensible,' devoting page after page to their shenanigans. 'What old wives letters!' Virginia declared. At times they sounded like their mother and their aunts: the servants were feckless and foolish but generally well meaning; like children, they needed a firm hand. But Julia Stephen would never have confided, as Virginia did, that it was 'degrading' to write about them. She never lived, as her daughters were to, almost rubbing shoulders with her domestics. Julia's distance from her servants was too secure for her to be anxious about losing caste; difference did not draw her as it did her daughter.

As long as there were servants, Bloomsbury's interiors were bound to be divided. But this was nothing new. As a feminist looking back at her own upbringing, Woolf knew that even the quietest of rooms, in which the clock ticked and the kettle took an age to boil while the daughters of the house waited to prepare the tea, might be simmering with suppressed emotion. In her biographies and fictions Woolf developed a new method which would illuminate those obscure lives, lighting up the hidden reaches of feeling and memory which lay behind the most humdrum exterior. There was her imaginary 'Mrs Brown', for instance, a random, shabby figure, glimpsed on a train, who was for Woolf a portent of mystery, of unknown, unknowable depths.

Yet when Mrs Brown spoke, she talked about her servant problem in the familiar tones of class condescension. Mrs Brown was not Everywoman, after all, but English, a lady and a snob. Though consciousness might try to soar, it stayed tethered to language, that obstinately social medium. What if the self, another imaginary interior, were also, like domestic life, a social, not a private creation? Such privacy as one found there would always be provisional and temporary, always in relation to others – their presence or absence a comfort or threat.

★

Durbins

When Lottie Hope and Nellie Boxall first walked up to Roger Fry's home, they would have seen a strange, foreign-looking house, glittering with glass, perched at the top of a slope above its terraced garden. Durbins sat square and plain under a slated roof, its bare façade dominated by huge, full-length rectangular windows. The shutters were pinned back and a door from the house into the garden was placed symmetrically in the middle, like in a child's drawing. It looked very odd next to its neighbours, whose Gothic turrets and gables, or mock-Tudor black and white frontages, struck Surrey's squires and stockbrokers as the most appropriate rustic features for new houses. Further up the drive, tucked away at the side, was a low porch and eaves, more like the door into a country cottage. This turned out to be the main entrance used by everyone, family, servants and visitors alike. Lottie Hope and Nellie Boxall would find that life 'at Fry's' was full of such eccentricities.

Inside was equally curious. Durbins was built on two levels, using the slope of the land. From the entrance a short flight of stairs ran down into the main living area at the front of the house, a hall with a very high ceiling, flooded with brilliant light from the enormous, uncurtained windows. The 'houseplace', as it was called, looked startlingly bare. No patterned wallpapers, no portraits of ancestors in oils jostling with random hunting prints and landscapes, but muted grey walls which dramatically displayed a few pots and modern paintings; no carpets, but a scattering of oriental rugs on wooden floors. The comfortable furnishings and knickknacks that usually made a home were missing – all those armchairs and sofas with their antimacassars, nests of tables, potted plants, gilded mirrors, the jugs, figurines, busts, bell-jars and bonbonnières – instead, the bright electric light exposed unpainted woodwork, and a large oak refectory table stood starkly in the centre of the room. Where was the obligatory piano decorously covered with chenille? Even the fireplaces were without grates and were placed offcentre, with simple brick surrounds and plain wooden mantels, without a fringe or tassel in sight. A fire wasn't lit since modern radiators, a continental idea, had done away with the constant need for a glowing hearth. There was little privacy by contemporary standards. No parlour, no drawing room for the ladies, no smoking room, no nursery. The houseplace was overlooked by a wooden balcony or gallery which led off to the bedrooms. Fry's study ran along one side of the house, and his wife's room was on the other, but the effect was of open space, with the houseplace looking

straight into the garden. When Roger's parents visited they were
so disconcerted that he draped and carpeted his study to accommodate them; there was a peat fire and easy chairs. But how odd
it must have seemed to Sir Edward and Lady Fry to hear their
shoes echoing across the floor and to sit at that bare table! Roger
named the house after Durbin's Batch, a favourite field which
belonged to their country property in Gloucestershire, a nostalgic
gesture. It must have seemed to them equally exposed and
draughty.

Fry had designed Durbins himself, though he was no architect,
working closely with the builder (whose name goes unrecorded)
to make a house that suited him and his family. He wanted 'a
town house in the country' with lots of rooms, but couldn't afford
a gentleman's estate, and anyway found such establishments aesthet-
ically and socially displeasing. Fry's background had been in the
Arts and Crafts movement, influenced by William Morris's ideals
for aesthetic reform. Much of Durbins was redolent of the medieval or Elizabethan – the bare wood and open fires, the minstrels'
gallery over the houseplace – but Fry hated the dark, pseudo-
historical interiors, with their leaded lights, cosy inglenooks and
'low snug effect' which had recently become the fashion. In their
turn, his neighbours thought Durbins 'a monstrous eyesore'. The
houseplace reflected his love of the airy, baroque palaces of Italy,
but since he could only afford to have one room of double height,
he had to squeeze Durbins's six bedrooms up under a hipped or
mansard roof. With its south-facing, sun-filled aspect, the house
was primarily intended to be therapeutic, as a retreat for Helen
Fry, whose mental condition was worsening (her room they
jokingly, if poignantly, called the 'boudoir', from the French verb
'to sulk'). From the balcony above the houseplace there were
views right out across the garden into the open downland and
the Wey valley. He hoped that the house would prove 'a real and
lasting home' for his children, but, to Roger's immense distress,
their mother was permanently committed to an asylum at the
end of 1910. Roger's sister, Joan, who kept house, was to look
after the children. These four inhabitants needed a cook and

housemaid, plus 'Tweenie', a nameless maid-of-all-work, a full-time gardener, who stoked the boilers and sometimes polished the floors, and a live-in governess, Madeleine Savary, who was Swiss, followed by Joy King. This was a minimal staff for the scions of the upper-middle class.

Durbins gave more room to the idea of a shared family life. The servants were segregated nonetheless. The kitchen, scullery and cook's sitting room were all on the upper level of the house, above and behind the houseplace. There was no separate staircase for the servants but their quarters were relegated to the gloomy north-east of the building. Lottie's bedroom was the smallest room, smaller than the entrance landing, with only a tiny fireplace, and no radiator since she wasn't expected to sit there. Nellie's kitchen, where the servants ate, and her sitting room, were also built into the hill at the back. Her domain was closed off from the family's living area by a mottled glass door, a more modern version of the green baize. Of course, compared to the dank basements usually on offer it probably felt like heaven. The children, Pamela and Julian, were not allowed in the kitchen or Roger's study, and mostly ate next door in a small breakfast room, where their governess also gave them lessons. Guests in the houseplace could thus be left undisturbed. Nor need they suffer the sight of the coalcart or the fishmonger: deliveries were made discreetly via a lane at the back of the house.

Fry had planned the house very practically and it had the latest conveniences. Thanks to electricity and central heating, both novelties in British homes, Lottie and Nellie's work was cut by half. Fires were occasionally lit, especially in the houseplace, whose windows made it freezing in winter; the rugs would have to be beaten, but the parquet only needed an oiled mop like the 'mop o' Cedar', a great innovation at the time; the oak furniture showed far fewer fingermarks than the rosewood or mahogany of the Victorian home, and there was much less to dust and polish. There were hardly any stairs, though Lottie would need to sweep the carpet on the upper floor and had her usual duties in the bedrooms. Nellie's kitchen housed an old-fashioned range and dresser with a large enamel sink in the scullery next door, but Roger had put in a new contraption, a lift or 'dumb waiter' for the crockery, which ran from outside the cook's room down to the houseplace below. Meals could be served and cleared without the need for waiting at table. The telephone, also a rarity, saved running a number of errands, and a newfangled electric-bell system was used all over the house to summon service, lighting up a panel above the kitchen door. The servants need not hover about the house. Even more impressive were the number of flushing water-closets, though the presence of a 'sloproom', for the emptying and scouring of chamber-pots, allowed guests their privacy at night. Naturally the servants had a separate lavatory.

It was a unique household. Roger and Joan were part of a formidable Quaker family with eight generations of 'Friends' behind them, including the prison reformer, Elizabeth Fry, nonconformists, all imbued with a deep sense of social responsibility. Durbins's austerity may have owed something to the pure white space of the Meeting House, though Roger's relish for the simple life may have been a legacy too of his early friendship with the designer and socialist reformer C. R. Ashbee. Joan was a committed vegetarian, and the household lived on vegetable stews and salads, and Roger's 'Frenchified' additions, including the little-known omelet (he once made an omelet with twenty eggs in a huge pan) and 'cardoons', a kind of artichoke, which he grew in his garden. Roger and Joan's upbringing in the intellectual and scientific climate of the Fry home had been strict, though fair; the Fry children did not go to the theatre and seldom to parties; they did not learn to dance. It left them both with a craving for fun. Roger was an unbuttoned father, taking the children boating or making models with them, as he was a liberal dresser, pioneering a taste for blue shirts and a yellow pullover with Irish tweed in winter, sandals in summer. He was a political Liberal too, actively involved in local politics in the summer of 1910. Like his sister, he was a staunch pacifist.

Lottie and Nellie took their orders from Joan Fry since Roger's commitments meant him frequently staying in town, where he was joint editor of the *Burlington Magazine* and a lecturer at the Slade School of Art. The second oldest of Fry's five sisters, Joan was only four years his senior, but seemed part of an older generation. Like other Victorian daughters at home, she had found her freedom through poor-visiting, early becoming one of the few women Poor Law Guardians. In Guildford she was also involved with the local workhouse and was elected to the Guildford Education Committee. A strong and dynamic presence in the small local community of Quakers, she gave lectures and held philanthropic meetings at Durbins. Joan was more straitlaced than Roger, but like him she knew how to play, singing with the children every day and organizing games of hide-and-seek with Lottie and Nellie in the garden. On Sundays the children wrote letters to their mother, Roger read them poetry and Joan gave them a short Bible lesson before going to Meeting. Joan seems never to have scolded: when Roger's daughter, Pamela, balanced precariously on the roof ledge, Joan put her trust in the Lord. Only Lottie's temper was a trial. According to one story, possibly apocryphal, Joan told Roger after one set-to that either she or Lottie would have to go; apparently Roger chose Lottie. In the event Joan stayed.

Roger Fry first made his name as an art historian of the Italian fifteenth century and as a curator and buyer for galleries and museums in the international art world. By the end of 1910 he had become the man 'who almost overnight radicalized English art'. As the leading advocate in Britain for what he christened 'Post-Impressionism', he mounted two ground-breaking exhibitions in London, bringing the abstract works of Cezanne, Van Gogh, Gauguin and Seurat to a puzzled and sometimes outraged British public. Fry found himself abused by the art establishment and welcomed by the younger generation of British artists, among them Duncan Grant and Vanessa Bell. The Clive Bells had visited Durbins in the summer of 1910 (they too had found its interior rather austere) and had fallen under the spell of Roger's enthusiasm and erudition. They went travelling with Fry, who was a delightful and indefatigable companion, open-minded and endlessly curious about all forms of art. When Vanessa fell ill after a miscarriage, Roger looked after her tenderly and they fell in love. Vanessa found someone with whom she could share the excitements of the new art and of her developing work but who also cared deeply about domestic life. Their letters often discussed the children's lives and illnesses – whether Julian should have his adenoids removed, for instance, a middle-class panic at the time.

At first Roger and Vanessa kept their affair hidden so as to avoid the eye of Joan, whom Vanessa disliked, and who would have been deeply shocked. Roger also advised Vanessa to hide his love-letters, with their sketches of her breasts, from Sophie Farrell, who was temporarily her cook and housekeeper and also of the old school. In Surrey Vanessa took a cottage near Roger's house, and Roger rented in the vicinity when Vanessa went on holiday to Dorset, but anyone who changed the sheets would have known the situation. Vanessa's presence was in any case soon felt in Durbins as its interior came to reflect Roger's new evangelism for modern art. Fry hung her huge canvas *Nativity* or *Mother and Child* in Durbins's houseplace next to a Renaissance madonna and in 1914 invited Vanessa and Duncan Grant to join him in painting Matisse-like murals over the stairway in the entrance: he painted a huge red female nude, Vanessa a yellow male and Grant a red male (versions of their sexual objects of choice, as has been pointed out). A Cubist Picasso and a Russian Vlaminck appeared on the walls; Lottie would have swept her duster over the Brancusi bronze head as well as the sixth-century Chinese sculpture; out in the garden was *The Virgin*, a big statue of a naked standing woman overlooking the pond, by Eric Gill, a carver and sculptor, one of the younger artists whom Fry championed early in his career; a birdbath was designed by Henri Gaudier-Brzeska. Joan, who ran the house and provided meals, found Durbins was invaded by new clever, noisy people who treated her without the usual courtesies and were uninterested, and indeed often frankly disdainful of her attitudes.

Vanessa's sister was an early visitor. She remembered the comfortable eclecticism at Durbins: 'paintings and carvings, Italian cabinets and Chippendale chairs, blue Persian plates, delicately glazed, and rough yellow peasant pottery ... every sort of style seemed to be mixed, but harmoniously'. Although several years their senior, Fry became an intimate part of Bloomsbury. His advocacy of the formal qualities of a work of art over its content influenced Vanessa's move into abstraction as well as Virginia's more formal experiments with the novel – the importance she would give to 'rhythm' in her writing, for instance, and her self-conscious attempts at design. In 1913 Roger, Vanessa and Duncan had founded the Omega Workshops in order, as he told one journalist, to put 'the spirit of fun back into furniture', and the tile-topped tables, gaily painted lampshades and pots, the rugs and screens in gaudy colours (blue sheep on an orange ground), the spindly 'witty' chairs, cushions and crockery, with their vibrant, sketchy designs, soon made their way into all the Bloomsbury homes. Even stodgy old armchairs, the once-loathed symbol of the gentleman's club, could be given new life, decked out in jazzy, geometric covers. The emphasis was on the informal and the fresh. Familiar objects could be given a make-over; new fashions invented and modelled (one of Omega's dressmakers was Joy King, who had been governess to the Fry children). Omega artists were meant to work anonymously, pooling their resources and earnings for the good of the group. Like William Morris, Fry refused to take commissions from big firms but many of Omega's clients them-selves became interior decorators, selling wallpapers, fabrics and paints.

Vanessa often found servants 'tiresome' but she believed she had little option. No one of her generation and class looked after their own children even if they didn't want to paint. When a nursemaid was happy, Vanessa acknowledged her own dependence, writing to Roger that 'my happiness is largely in her hands'. Yet she felt oppressed by old-fashioned servants like those at her in-laws' country house in Wiltshire, who were 'so obsequious – it makes me treat them like slaves which I hate'. It even made her wish for Lottie. With two sons, a husband and a married lover apparently on amicable terms, Vanessa's life was rapidly becoming unorthodox, but she also found herself falling in love with Duncan Grant, who until recently had been having an affair with her younger brother, Adrian. Although the relationship was not yet physical, they spent more and more time painting in each other's company. Much to her relief she found herself 'cut' by South Kensington relations, and in Gordon Square, where all the front doors were a funereal black or respectable dark blue, she painted hers vermilion. Gone were the decorous picture-frame hats, the gauntlet gloves and button-boots: Vanessa wore home-made clothes and peasant head-scarves, going barelegged and barefoot like the other 'Neo-Pagans', as Virginia called them, at a Fabian socialist summer camp where Roger made toasted cheese and wonderful stews on the campfire. Her sons ran about naked and called her by her Christian name; her homes became messy and her guests revelled in the disorderly, congenial atmosphere. Increasingly she needed broad-minded serv-ants who would tolerate her unconventional milieu and help to create this apparently casual, sensual existence.

These she found in the Selwood sisters, who were the mainstay of many Bloomsbury households for several years. They are surely there among the blank-faced figures in Vanessa's paintings of the period – the nursemaids in *Nursery Tea* for instance – but while Vanessa's friends and relatives have been easily recognized, the servants, in keeping with artistic tradition, have been largely condemned to anonymity. The seven Selwood sisters – Elsie, Ada ('Dot'), Beatrice ('Trissie'), Mabel, Marion, Florence ('Flossie') and Daisy – were born at Park View, a Victorian house with three acres, an orchard and a field, in the tiny hamlet of Old Down, near Tockington in Gloucestershire, not far from Bristol. Their father, Arthur Selwood, the son of a blacksmith, worked as a groom and his wife, Ada, was the village dressmaker, working mostly for county folk; she made clothes for the Duchess of Beaufort at Badminton nearby and employed several village girls to work in her sewing room adjoining the house. There were three sons after the seven daughters. Apart from Dot, who suffered poor health and remained at home as the unmarried daughter, all the sisters went into service and worked in the Bloomsbury circles at some point in their lives. The family were introduced to the Bells by George Rylands, whose parents had a place nearby at Elburton. The oldest, Elsie, came to Gordon Square as nurse to Julian Bell in 1908, having first worked for the Stephen cousins, Madge and Will Vaughan, in Yorkshire, where he was headmaster at Giggleswick school. Elsie was joined by her younger sister, Mabel, whom Quentin, Vanessa's second son, adored. On holiday with the Bells at Studland in Dorset, Elsie met her future husband, the local postman, and the next sister, Florence, or Flossie, duly took over. In 1912 Mabel was nineteen and Flossie fifteen. Mabel and Flossie stayed until 1917, when Vanessa's sons needed a firmer hand and Mabel left to get married. Flossie remained in Bloomsbury, working for Faith Henderson, Vanessa's close friend, who had been at the Slade School of Art with her. Another sister, Marion, was the Hendersons' cook. Meanwhile Beatrice, or Trissie, came as cook to the Bells at Charleston. Mabel also went briefly to Adrian and Karin Stephen, whose girls, Ann and Judith, were born during the war, before handing over to Daisy 'Septima' Selwood, after her own son was born. Daisy was nanny in the Stephens' household for eleven years.

Flossie and Mabel Selwood

The Selwoods were lucky in being able to work together. In the peak years of live-in service sisters often followed sisters, hoping to be less lonely and to learn the ropes, but by the 1910s the demand for general servants was growing while households themselves were shrinking. Julia Stephen had seven children; Vanessa and George had three, Adrian two. Though her daughters' lives were eccentric – Virginia remained childless and her sister was to live with a homosexual in 'a left-handed marriage' which also produced a child – their relationships conformed to a general shift away from the old, many-tentacled Victorian family towards the companionate couple with a smaller family. Even childlessness was now becoming an option, rather than a misfortune, in advanced circles. Jobs as nursemaids were over-subscribed and became an early target for professionalization since nannying was considered more genteel and ranked higher in the pecking order than cooking or cleaning. Yet only the very wealthy could afford to keep 'Nanny' on into middle-age and most mistresses, like Vanessa, handed over their offspring to girls in their teens who were used to looking after their own siblings. A nursemaid or a nanny's life was marked by a series of losses which were very bitter to them and their charges: at least one child of Bloomsbury, Faith Henderson's son Nicholas, was devastated when his nurse left. He loved Flossie, he later recalled, more than any other woman in his life. The 'wonderfully supportive, reliable, loveable Selwood sisters, paragons to us of perfection,' he wrote, 'were the central focus of our lives'.

Vanessa soon began looking for her own country place where she might have the peace for her work and freedom for her children. Renting a friend's house one summer, she assured Duncan that 'tidiness can soon be done away with'. Bohemianism had its limits, however. Sitting on the balcony where she would spend the day painting, she noted that 'Flossie, more exquisite than ever, is busy washing my clothes.' Duncan and his new lover, David Garnett, conscientious objectors who were looking for farmwork as the threat of conscription hung over them, found a temporary refuge with Vanessa at Wissett in Suffolk, where they settled into a relatively contented *ménage à trois*; Flossie was there to look after the children and Blanche Payne, who was to be-come a familiar figure in Bloomsbury, to cook and clean. Vanessa set about painting tables and chairs, dyeing chair covers and distempering the walls or covering them with murals which had to be scraped off when they left (including a copy to scale of Fra Angelico's *Visitation* which she and Duncan worked on a bedroom wall). This was a rehearsal for Charleston in Sussex to which they decamped in the autumn of 1916, transporting all that the household had accumulated, including easels, ten bales of canvas, boxes of paints, cases of books, ducks, rabbits and even bees. Vanessa became a fiercesomely efficient managerial mistress: Maynard Keynes took to calling her 'Ludendorf Bell', after the General.

The combination of the decorative with the fine arts became the hallmark of Charleston, which was to be Bell and Grant's home for many decades, an affectionate domesticating of the modern, and the apogee of interior decoration as a form of self-expression. It was also a retreat from the more public, collective projects in art and education which had excited Fry, whose vision of the Omega had been inspired by the ideals of Ruskin and Morris and their passionate, moral reaction against the cheap commercialization of the crafts. Fry was to feel hurt and betrayed when Omega artists, and indeed Vanessa Bell and Duncan Grant, began to accept individual signed commissions. Meanwhile Durbins's heyday proved shortlived. His affair with Vanessa over, his children away at private schools, Roger found the house too expensive to run during the war and decided to let it to the Strachey family. The Omega workshop demanded his resources and energies. In 1916 Joan Fry joined her sisters working behind the lines in France for the Quaker War Victims' Relief Mission, and Roger moved back to London to live with Margery, another of his sisters, at 7 Dalmeny Avenue off the Camden Road. He thought Lottie and Nellie would like working for his friends Leonard and Virginia Woolf, and so he sent them to Richmond, where the Woolfs had recently settled at Hogarth House.

Durbins, as Fry put it in a *Vogue* article of 1918, had tried to express 'the kind of lives we live now'. Arguing against fake and pretentious styles or snobbish domestic architecture, he asked, 'What if people were just to let their houses be the direct outcome of their actual needs, and of their actual way of life, and allow other people to think what they like?' A generous, liberal vision but this laissez-faire perspective had its blindspots. It relied on an assumed freedom of choice, of skill and opportunity, as if housing could be a purely private matter. The live-in servants, who were so crucial to the ease and comfort which Fry and his friends enjoyed, were an archaic, doomed survival, but they were a reminder nonetheless that houses are always part of the wider social environment, a space shared with and serviced by others – be it in a street, a village or on an isolated hilltop. And inside the house the relationships which make up domestic life are often unequal. People who live side by side may just as well be on different planets or living in different dimensions of time. There is never one kind of life 'we live now'. And there could never be a modernist domesticity with servants still in tow.

*

When she became Mrs Leonard Woolf in the summer of 1912, Virginia's homemaking continued to be improvised. Nothing in those early years was secure, except for her private income, and even that must stretch to cover two, since Leonard had resigned from the Indian Civil Service in order to marry her, and was grubbing for work as a writer and political researcher (a trip into the Hoxton slums with Virginia's cousin Marny Vaughan had moved him firmly towards socialism). At first, when they rented rooms in London after their honeymoon, Virginia fantasized as she often did, about the delights of doing without servants altogether, living a nomadic life with 'her Jew', and never having 'a real house'. Shortly before her marriage, though, she had given up Little Talland House in Firle, Sussex, which had always felt too surburban, and had taken the lease of Asheham, a few miles to the west. This was an unpretentious manor house, built by a solicitor in 1820 for his country retreat, with open views across

Virginia Stephen, Julian Bell and Mabel Selwood at Studland Beach

the Ouse Valley to the villages of Rodmell and Itford and the
Sussex Downs. As Virginia finished her novel she imagined herself
living a country life there with horses and children.

Asheham was at first shared with Vanessa (who put up orange
curtains with mauve linings) and was home to lively weekend
gatherings. The habit of removing to the country in the summer
was one which the sisters had grown up with, and it depended
on local help who lit fires, aired houses and beds, supplied the
necessary provisions and even meals when the London servants

had remained in town. Asheham was a lonely house and said to be haunted – even the ultra-rationalist Leonard Woolf heard noises there at night. Forty-odd people lived nearby, though, mostly farmworkers, so a cheap supply of labour was on hand. Asheham had no 'amenities': cold water had to be pumped up and lugged in buckets to the house; outside was an earth-closet which had to be emptied regularly. In a letter at the end of 1911, Virginia had boldly informed Leonard about the relative merits of having earth-closets at Asheham, cleaned out by Mrs Hoper, 'a very old woman', or putting in a drain for a water-closet ('certainly pleasanter in wet weather'), deciding on the former. When Vanessa stayed at Asheham during the Woolfs' honeymoon, the ancient water pump broke down and there was no water, though it was raining hard for days. Mrs Funnell, the local shepherd's wife and new caretaker, refused to empty their pails (which had to be poured, presumably into a cesspit, a rotten job at the best of times). Neither her husband nor her boys were prepared to go on pumping water and Mrs Funnell resented the unnecessary work. Vanessa repeated her complaints to entertain Virginia, 'what *I* say is why dont you put in new WCs at the same time', seemingly unaware that to the hard-pressed Funnells it was inexplicable that these obviously well-heeled folk refused to spend their money. Instead Vanessa worried about keeping face. Sophie Farrell, their old servant, was 'hovering about all the time' and, Vanessa wrote, 'she thinks me very weak'. Eventually the pump was patched up and a farm labourer hired for 5s a week to do both the pumping and the earth-closets. 'I feel we have distinctly scored over the Funnels who have really been very tiresome,' Vanessa concluded. Altercations over the sanitary arrangements were to recur, however.

As her sister's life expanded, Virginia's shrank to a narrow compass. She spent much of her first three and a half years of married life in breakdown or in recovery, being looked after and supervised by nurses and servants, and, of course, Leonard. Asheham became her convalescence home. In the summer of 1913 her symptoms had returned – headaches, sleeplessness, depression, appalling states of anxiety and guilt, and an increasing resistance to food. Another rest cure at the Twickenham nursing-home where she had stayed in 1910 left her even more desperate (her minder there, Jean Thomas, was convinced that finishing her novel, and being afraid of being 'jeered' at about it, had tipped the balance of her mind). That September she survived taking an overdose of the veronal prescribed for her insomnia and was thereafter closely watched. The much-pilloried George Duckworths offered their comfortable country home, Dalingridge Place in Sussex, and she began a slow recuperation. The Woolfs' London lodgings were given up and by Christmas Virginia was at Asheham with two mental nurses in tow. One therapy was to clean the drawing room with nurse – 'Its really rather fun, and makes a wonderful difference, even in the smell of the air,' she wrote to Leonard in December 1913. Leonard continued his political studies when he could – though he had been under an almost intolerable strain – and made journeys to study socialism and the Cooperative Movement in the Midlands and the North, inspired by his friendship with Margaret Llewellyn Davies, who had set up the Women's Cooperative Guild. Virginia sometimes went with him but was frequently left alone at Asheham. Alone, that is, with the servants: Annie Chart, who came as cook, and another local girl, Lily, as housemaid – 'a real servant in the way of brushing ones clothes etc'. Lily was an unmarried mother who had given up her baby to the nuns, thereby earning her the soubriquet of 'the prostitute' from Virginia, who assumed the role of mistress when she could. She wrote to Janet Case that she felt 'the greatest humbug' when she had to 'speak' to Annie about men friends but was amazed by her 'docility': 'in fact I believe they like rules'. Otherwise Virginia lived a carefully regulated life, 'keeping cheerful', taking rests and walking the dogs, drinking her glasses of milk and writing only for an hour or two a day, mostly correspondence. Her novel was held up at the press. Meanwhile Leonard's, *The Village in the Jungle*, was published and he began his second.

When war was declared in August 1914, Virginia was at Asheham but by the autumn was well enough to move to rooms just outside London, in the suburb of Richmond, where they meant to find a house. Leonard could now step up his political activities, becoming deeply involved with the Fabian Society, and he was a popular speaker on the Cooperative Movement and international issues. Virginia went to the society's meetings and became a member. Nursing fees had been a great drain on their finances and Virginia wanted to do her bit as a housewife. That winter she took a course in cookery. 'It's dreadful how we were neglected,' she wrote to Molly MacCarthy in December 1914, 'and yet its not hard to be practical, up to a point, and such an advantage, I hope.' Unfortunately she managed to bake her wedding ring into a suet-pudding in one lesson. She carefully kept the household books at Richmond, itemizing expenditure at the Cooperative stores, the price of soap, tea, 'Keatings' (bug powder), the wash, which was sent out weekly for around 1s 6d a week (7½p), against what she was given for housekeeping – £3 in December. In January 1915 she also began a daily journal, the first since 1905 (the period after her last major breakdown), recording her social life, her jaunts up to town and the novelty of life down among the surburban middle classes – 'the shabby clerks & dressmakers', the women with string bags. Like an anthropologist noting the rituals of a strange people, although without the customary neutrality, she pondered the novelty of shopping for groceries: 'I bought my fish & meat in the High Street – a degrading but rather amusing business. I dislike the sight of women shopping. They take it so seriously.' Nonetheless she experimented with new delicacies, buying 'a mass of pinkish stuff' at the fishmonger's, cod's roe.

She was fascinated too by the comings and goings of the temporary servants who worked for their Belgian landlady: Lizzy, the 'feckless' skivvy, 'only paid £16 a year', Virginia noted sympathetically, who started fires, smashed china – 'since she knows she is going she doesn't mind how many plates she breaks' (Virginia bought her some cheap cups), and left 'carrying a brown paper parcel & whistling loudly – I wonder where she has gone?', and Maud who was 'full of illusions' and whose 'secret obsession is that she is a lady'. When Lily, the girl who had worked for them at Asheham, was in trouble at her new place, Virginia wrote her 'character' or reference, taking her side against a 'tyrannical employer', and remembering 'her charming, stupid, doglike eyes, quite incapable of hurting a fly or thinking a coarse thought'. Later, Lily was found with a soldier in the kitchen at Hogarth House and Leonard, slipping back easily into his role of imperial administrator, gave her a serious talking-to. She stayed on but was apparently so 'miserably contrite' that she decided to leave. Good housekeeping reflected on the mistress's moral character too: when friends rented Asheham and found it dirty, Virginia imagined in her diary that 'Mrs W[aterlow] ran about with a duster, & dabbed her finger under beds' and no doubt 'she cursed that dreadful slut Virginia Woolf'.

Both Virginia's diary and her household accounts break off in February 1915, as she entered what Leonard saw as 'the terrifying second stage' of the breakdown which had begun in the summer of 1913. Sometimes she was delusional, sometimes 'violently' excited and distressed, and again convinced of her own 'badness' and refusing food. Her novel *The Voyage Out* was published in March, a day after her removal to a nursing-home. It was impossible to remain in lodgings. Leonard took on the lease of nearby Hogarth House that spring and Virginia was taken to Richmond with four mental nurses in attendance. There followed another fragile summer at Asheham, another gradual return to sanity. On 4 November the Woolfs finally returned to Richmond. The last nurse left a week later. That Christmas the talk was of conscription, which loomed on the horizon. Nearly all of Virginia's friends and relatives were fiercely anti-war. They became conscientious objectors, applied for agricultural work and faced military tribunals. Leonard, like his brothers, had been willing to fight but eventually gained a medical exemption, partly because of the nervous trembling in his hands and partly because of Virginia's precarious health. 'I am still in a very shaky state,' Virginia wrote to Vanessa in the spring of 1916, '& would very likely have a bad mental breakdown if they took him.' Now, in wartime conditions, the Woolfs could cautiously begin to live a more conventional life in their first proper marital home. They were to stay at Hogarth

House for nine years, the longest Virginia had dwelt in any one place since leaving Hyde Park Gate.

★

When Lottie Hope and Nellie Boxall arrived from Durbins in February 1916, they found a fragile woman in an old dressing-gown, propped up on the sofa. Nellie was twenty-five and Lottie a year younger; their mistress ten years their senior but clearly still needing a great deal of care. They knew that she hadn't been well and that she was a poor eater. The household revolved around the routines which made it possible for her to write and keep her mental equilibrium; regular meals, a rest after lunch, not too many visitors, no late nights. It was odd for servants to have employers who worked at home. Detachment from household duties was usually a male prerogative and the servants would naturally expect their mistress to weather if not welcome interruption as the Victorian matron had; to be available, to instruct or listen, or pour oil on troubled waters. (The poet Charlotte Mew found herself frequently interrupted by her loyal maid-of-all-work, Jane Elnswick, because Jane felt sorry for her mistress and wanted to take her mind off 'scribbling'.) Though Leonard would make beds, light fires and even wash up in a crisis, for the most part housekeeping in Bloomsbury was still a woman's responsibility and the men expected to be looked after, as they always had been, by servants, mothers, sisters and wives. Nor were the old models of womanliness simply overthrown. Vanessa reassured Roger Fry, the least chauvinist of the men, 'Don't think of me as a horrid self-sufficing independent woman for I'm not,' and when she was particularly ground down by domestic chores, her letters to Duncan Grant took on a placatory tone as she apologized for worrying him. Virginia was more angered by this Victorian habit of mollifying the men, but her vulnerable health meant that she frequently had to defer to Leonard even if she chafed, as she often did, under his protective regime.

Hogarth House in Paradise Road, Richmond, was one half of

a grand red-brick Georgian mansion with its own white porch
and 100-foot garden, a few minutes uphill from the shops on the
High Street. The large panelled rooms on the ground and first
floor were light and elegant; there were two bedrooms and a
bathroom with a cast-iron bath and lavatory for the Woolfs, and
four smaller rooms on the top floor, where the panelling ran out
– the servants' bedrooms. But for Lottie and Nellie it must have
been a come-down after 'Fry's' with all its modern conveniences.
Most of their time would be spent underground in the basement
kitchen with its old-fashioned scullery, stone sink and a 'copper'
for boiling water and washing clothes; there was also a larder,
wine and coal cellars, and a servants' water-closet. They shared it
with the usual insect life: at 46 Gordon Square Clive Bell descended
at night into the kitchen with his boots on in order to stamp on
the cockroaches. And from 1917 the hand printing-press which
the Woolfs bought to experiment with as a hobby and as therapy
for Virginia made the servants' lives more difficult. It was installed
in the larder and that meant Leonard and Virginia were continually in and out of the kitchen; type, forms, ink, mounds of paper
and manuscript eventually took over the dining room too. Virginia
was an untidy worker as well as 'an untidy liver', covering her
worktable with an agreeable muddle of paper-clips, ashtrays, pens
and broken cigarette-holders, protective slums of manuscript and
paper, while she wrote in a low armchair with a home-made
writing-board on her lap. In 1916 Nellie and Lottie were paid
about £38 a year each, a decent wage at the time; they had at
least a couple of rises, mentioned in Virginia's diaries in 1919 and
1921, and were probably earning around £40 by then.

The problems really began when the household decamped to
Asheham, which was built in a hollow and always damp. Neither
Nellie nor Lottie found much romance in this chilly house with
its stone floors, where they had to pump water from a well and
lug buckets, work by oil lamps and cook on an ancient oil stove
or primus. Coal also had to be fetched and when it was in short
supply during the war, the servants went wooding for sticks and
branches. They were miles from any shop and deliveries were

irregular; Nellie and Lottie walked or cycled the four miles to Lewes, and then back again, or hitched lifts on carts or the milk float. No wonder they found Asheham lonely and depressing. In the spring of 1916 Nellie gave notice before the Easter holidays – 'can't face 6 weeks at Asheham', Virginia told Vanessa. Behind their backs Virginia tried to get Sophie Farrell to return for good, but Sophie would be expensive and she could not be expected to empty slops. Having been dumped by Adrian Stephen and now settled with the Duckworths, Sophie gave Virginia 'a fearful snubbing'. Bella Wooler, a local girl, refused to help any more with the coal and earth-closets. In the end Lottie and Nellie decided to put up with Asheham once another slopper was taken on. Her work also included emptying the chamber-pots (at the most sociable times at Asheham the volume of such work makes one shudder). The Woolfs presumably refused to countenance the expense of putting in water-closets.

Who emptied the sewage was a serious issue among the servants since it affected their earnings and their self-respect. In wartime, however, these caste distinctions were harder to maintain. During the war, about 400,000 women left domestic service to earn decent pay in the munitions factories, to join the armed forces or the Forestry Commission. After conscription in 1916, the servant shortage became acute. Potential housemaids were found working on the roads or the buses, driving the milk floats and delivering the post, taking over wherever the men had vacated their jobs. A new amalgam, the 'house-parlourmaid', appeared, combining the work of two realms for the same price. Other services performed by 'body-slaves' (as Clive Bell loftily called them), like personal grooming – hair-brushing, shaving and so on – became a thing of the past, except among the very wealthy. Lily was the last of their 'proper' servants, though one of Lottie's jobs, tidying the bedrooms, would have been to pick up and put away the Woolfs' clothes. Nellie occasionally did the mending and delighted Virginia on her thirty-sixth birthday with some hand-knitted red socks, which Virginia found ideal for morning wear. Virginia and Vanessa were often thought scruffy. Vanessa rapidly decided that untidiness and dirt were infinitely preferable to being 'a Town Lady'; the writer Rebecca West thought Virginia always looked as if she had been pulled through a hedge backwards. Virginia's loathing of clothes-shopping meant that she relied on the same skirt and cardigan for years; her undergarments were in a permanent state of disrepair – a source of much hilarity.

Partly through choice, mostly through necessity, both sisters became a little more self-reliant during the war. They made scratch meals when the servants were out, even lighting their own fires (unthinkable for Virginia's parents), and making beds. They learnt about cooking from their own cooks, passing on recipes to each other – 'that egg savoury is made by boiling the semolina in milk not water' – indeed semolina became a staple of Virginia's jokes to friends. 'We eat nothing else for weeks,' she wrote to Margaret Llewellyn Davies, Leonard's old friend and the chief organizer of the Women's Cooperative Guild. 'Try it with a spoonful of lard for supper.' The sisters enjoyed competing over the art of baking bread – 'I have made your rolls, not so good yet as yours, but better than Nellys,' Virginia wrote to Vanessa. She also discussed the setting up of a local bread shop in her meetings of the Guild. Virginia had presided over the monthly meetings of the Richmond branch, held in the drawing room of Hogarth House since the autumn of 1916, and was to do so for the next four years. The Women's Cooperative Guild campaigned for improved conditions for working women, encouraged consumer control, held annual conferences, supported the suffrage and invited speakers to local meetings. Virginia admired the vitality and grit of the working women, though their conventionality, as she saw it, irked her. When Nellie and Lottie continued to be dubious about Asheham, Virginia speculated on a complete change with only one servant and meals from the communal kitchen which the Richmond Guild were proposing for the duration. But, as she relished telling Margaret, at least one of the members, Mrs Langston, was sure it wouldn't work – 'She says "What can you expect of ladies? They dont know anything."' Mrs Langston was apparently right since, after the summer of 1917, the communal kitchen was never mentioned again.

Late in 1916 Vanessa had settled at Charleston, a farmhouse about four miles from Asheham, which was also without gas or electricity; it had only cold water, 'not a very nice w.c.' and a cesspool in the tennis court. Her household included Duncan Grant and his lover, David Garnett, who were working on a nearby farm, her sons, Julian and Quentin; Mabel and Flossie Selwood, and the maids, Jessie and Blanche, though the latter preferred London and soon stayed with Maynard Keynes, who took over 46 Gordon Square. Replacements proved hard to find, partly because Charleston was so isolated. There was also more demand as more families aspired to servant-keeping. Once the school-leaving age was raised to fourteen, the diminutive skivvy began to disappear, just when the majority of mistresses wanted cheap young girls. Those women who hadn't gone into war work were getting older; fewer came from the country to live in. By comparison with the industrial regions and the seaside resorts, London and East Sussex were pretty well off for servants, but still they felt the pinch. Vanessa got hold of a series of fourteen-year-olds, whom she dubbed generically 'the Zanies' and whose 'inconceivable stupidities' frequently infuriated her. One agreed to work for the paltry wage of £8 a year, though this was an exception. There were several occasions when Nellie's sisters or niece looked likely possibilities, but nothing came of it. Virginia spent days scouring the registry offices for Vanessa or writing letters to agencies on her behalf, including 'Mrs Hunt's' of 86 Marylebone High Street: 'a mysterious building, all glass compartments, leading to a space given up to the ironing & washing of pink & blue pinafores, or so it looked'. But, as Virginia noted in her diary, 'Not a parlourmaid to be had.' Mrs Hunt's was where Vanessa had once found nurses for Virginia and now Virginia was able to provide support. 'I want a house-parlourmaid,' Vanessa instructed her in the autumn of 1917, 'but there is practically no parlour work. She need not wait at table, and only bring the courses in when I ring. Otherwise it is all housemaids work. There will be 4 bedrooms to do each morning, except when we have visitors when there would be one or two more. 2 sitting rooms in the winter & 3 in the summer. That is all.' Vanessa was willing to take 'anyone nice, however young & untrained, down to the age of 21' for wages up to £28. One girl seemed ideal: 'fresh from making 40 beds daily at a Y.M.C.A. in Brighton', she 'jumped' at the chance to be near her family and at £22 a year. But she proved another bird of passage.

Both daughters, like their father, worried about extravagance. In February 1917, Vanessa managed to feed nine people and pay for washing and oil lamps (but not coal) for 12s a head (60p in today's money): 'It's really very interesting if one goes into it oneself,' she told Virginia, who was managing rather less well. Her household books stood at 17s (85p) a head and she decided that 'respectable' servants were the problem – 'there's no checking them' – and wished she could get rid of 'the feeling of waste'. Leonard, who kept the accounts, encouraged frugality and Virginia for one always knew the price of eggs, which were growing ever dearer with wartime shortages. By the winter they cost 5d each, so at Christmas they made do with dried eggs, tinned and condensed 'Nestles & Ideal Milk', and a chicken for 6s as opposed to an expensive turkey. Despite their anxieties the Woolfs kept up two establishments for under £700 a year; their servants 'cost' them in wages £76 a year. Vanessa also cut corners, saving on the expense of schooling by elevating Mabel to governess: 'She seems quite competent to teach them at present & I shall teach them French myself.' (At one point she thought of running her own school.) Though Mabel was 'a miracle', and her sister, Trissie, came to join the household, Vanessa lurched from one domestic crisis to another, trying to secure reliable help.

Throughout the war years the letters between the sisters flowed thick and fast, as they wrote almost daily about their domestics. Writing about the servants was a safe topic, a form of attachment between the sisters, whose lives were otherwise very different. It was their way of being mature, married ladies – the more they declared their inferiors irrational, the more sensible their own position seemed. Yet the letters show them in their worst light: accusatory, childish, rivalrous, conspiratorial – there seems little to choose between mistresses and maids. 'Evidently there is a secret society among servants,' Virginia told Vanessa, when Nellie got wind of Virginia's plans to 'give her warning'; sometimes she wrote in French or advised her sister to put the letter down the w.c. 'That is the only safe method, we find.' Mutual suspicion kept real friendship at bay. 'One never knows how much faith to put in these people,' was Virginia's typical response to advice from Nellie. Of course the servants got their own back, maintaining their own confederacies; they bullied and teased each other, sending anonymous notes and setting each other at odds (as when Nellie pretended 'for a joke' that only she and not Lottie had got a rise). They used all the low-down ruses of the powerless. Certainly they read their employers' letters – foolishly, Trissie Selwood quoted a line from one of Virginia's to her – they gave notice and rescinded it, and above all they circulated talk, the ultimate weapon of the servant. 'I see our characters are quite as important as servants',' Vanessa wrote to Virginia in the summer of 1917 when she had effectively 'poached' Trissie Selwood from Clive Bell's mistress, Mary Hutchinson, and caused ill-feeling. Virginia was far from discreet in her letters to Clive, and Vanessa too liked a good gossip. Yet it was Mrs Woolf and Mrs Bell who felt their servants were untrustworthy and always in league with each other.

Secrets and lies were inevitable given the inequalities. Sometimes they were part of the job. 'Mrs Woolf is not at home,' servants frequently lied as they got rid of unwanted guests. Lottie rang the bell 'with meaning' when tradesmen like the 'little printer' Macdermott overstayed their welcome (the diminutive was an often-used put-down). Authority could be capricious. When Vanessa was pregnant and without help, the Woolfs 'lent' her Nellie and Lottie. Privately they planned for the servants to stay on as the Woolfs wanted to economize. Not surprisingly, the servants were upset when they found out. There were more 'telegrams, parleyings, compromises & diplomacies than would have set Europe in flame', Virginia observed in her diary in June 1918, with a reference to the edgy preparations going forward for a new League of Nations. After her daughter, Angelica, was born, Vanessa borrowed Nellie again. She got on 'beautifully' with Nellie, she told Roger, and thought her 'extraordinarily nice'; she enjoyed hearing her gossip – 'most interesting accounts of the Woolf menage' – but feared Nellie would be 'tied for ever to both Lottie & Virginia'. This time Leonard was annoyed. He felt Virginia had an equal need for looking after and Nellie came back after five days. But servants had many ways to revenge themselves: Emily Paton, another temporary housemaid at Charleston, was suspected of stealing and dismissed; on leaving, she flung open her suitcase to reveal a few bars of soap and a pair of Duncan's trousers. Such sad spoils of war.

A sense of 'us' and 'them' was unavoidable. However familiarly they might be treated, servants belonged to another species, who had grown up in a different world, who spoke and behaved differently, and who often looked different too (Virginia frequently commented on the bad teeth of the poor). Politically as well as socially they were at odds. The servants' enthusiastic patriotism embarrassed their employers, who were largely pacifist and loathed jingoism. When Mabel Selwood fell in love with a non-commissioned officer in the Coldstream Guards, the seven-year-old Quentin Bell appalled Leonard by 'bawling out the most atrocious abuse of the enemy'. In the severe winter of 1917–18, the Woolfs joined Lottie and Nellie, sitting out the air-raids on orange boxes or sleeping on matresses with quilts down in the basement kitchen – 'like a picture of slum life'. Talking 'bold & jocular small talk for 4 hours with the servants to ward off hysteria' was boring. 'What an irony,' Virginia wrote to Clive, 'if they should escape and we should be killed.' Lottie kept up 'a general rattle of jokes and comments which almost silenced the guns', but the servants' nervousness seemed inexplicable, though their being a long way from family must surely have added to their anxieties. Virginia, who described the war as 'a preposterous male fiction', was sickened by 'the filthy emotions' which it roused in the populace and found the final outbursts of flags and frenzy at the Armistice particularly depressing after the mindless slaughter. 'Peace Day' – 19 July 1919 – was, she thought, 'a servants' festival, some thing got up to placate & pacify "the people"'. No doubt it would 'play a great part in the history of the Boxall family'.

Class difference reared its ugly head even with the children. Vanessa's boys could be unruly and Vanessa sympathized with Mabel and Flossie. 'I often wonder how nurses do manage day after day,' she wrote to Roger. 'I like it very much, but then they're my own children & I like seeing them so intimately. But even so it's difficult at times not to lose one's temper, they are so utterly idiotic at times.' When Julian pummelled Flossie and pulled her hair, Vanessa confided, somewhat shamefacedly, that 'he is getting old enough to realize that she is uneducated & his "inferior"'. When Mabel decided to marry her soldier and Flossie also moved on, Vanessa hired 'two savage black-haired sloe-eyed women' and a Miss Edwards came as governess but took to meeting soldiers and soon disappeared ('not very well bred or well educated', was Virginia's verdict). Eventually an old flame of Roger's, a Mrs Brereton, arrived with her daughter, Ann. Julian laid into the new governess too but she got the upper hand, and kept stricter order until the boys were sent away to school. Vanessa was 'terrified' of firing her because, despite an external competence, 'La B', as she called her, was 'almost incredibly stupid' and wouldn't find other work easily. When Mrs Brereton left, Vanessa discovered a half-written novel that the governess had drafted about her time at Charleston. Vanessa was amazed by its 'extraordinary bitterness'. Sadly, it hasn't survived.

When five servants living above the shop at Barkers department store in Kensington died in a fire, the Woolfs refused to deal with the shop on principle. Yet under the surface the old attitudes were barely changed. Virginia admitted that at times Lottie 'works like a horse', but when Lottie had the nerve to ask for a rise, saying – rightly – that she could get better wages elsewhere, Virginia lost her temper. She lashed out in her diary (in December 1917): 'The poor have no chance; no manners or self-control to protect themselves with; we have a monopoly of all the generous feelings.' Characteristically, though, she had second thoughts, 'I daresay this isn't quite true; but there's some meaning [in] it. Poverty degrades, as Gissing said.' After another row, Virginia announced her indifference, comparing such domestic squabbles 'to flies in the eye for the discomfort they can produce in spite of being so small'. Yet Virginia also protected Lottie whose temper made her vulnerable, and was second only to Leonard's. Though they might cheerfully 'twit each other about their bad tempers', they were best not left alone together for too long, Virginia felt, since Leonard would surely sack Lottie. When Lottie made up a 'rigmarole' on Nellie's behalf because Nellie didn't like to ask if she could have her relatives to stay at Asheham for Christmas in 1918, Virginia commented in her diary, 'How terrible it is to be in this position to other grown people!' But she was probably referring to the burdens of the mistress rather than to the dependencies of the maid.

There were times when Virginia found herself wishing 'that the old laws of life held good: a husband, a house, servants, establishments'; and others when she dreamt of 'an enchanted world, where I turn a handle and hot mutton chops are shot out on a plate – human agencies entirely ignored'. In 1919, when they found Monk's House, a brick and weather-boarded cottage in the heart of Rodmell village, four miles from Charleston, it was less isolated than Asheham. For the first year the house had no stove or grate and the Woolfs relied on the oven of Mrs Dedman, the village sexton's wife, whose husband, William, was the gardener at Monk's. Rachel Dedman brought over savoury 'stews and mashes & deep many coloured dishes swimming in gravy thick with carrots & onions'; Elsie, a village girl, came in daily to clean. Their relative invisibility made live-in service even less appealing. Though Virginia felt that 'noone could be nicer than Nelly for long stretches', she reflected in her diary that 'the fault is more in the system of keeping two young women chained in a kitchen to laze & work & suck their life from two in the drawing-room than in her character or in mine'. The servants, though in chains, were the bloodsuckers, leeching the lives of more productive people. Nellie had just given notice because in eight days there had been three dinner parties, two tea parties and Angelica Bell, aged eleven months, and her nurse were staying in the house. But Nellie was nonetheless the parasite.

Virginia wrote this at the close of 1919 when the Woolfs were again feeling strapped for cash. Leonard's job with the *International Review* had come to an end and they were thinking, once more, of getting dailies. Yet when their lease ran out on Hogarth House, which had once formed a single property with the adjoining Suffield House, they presumably reached into their capital to buy both houses for £1,950 and then let Suffield House for a year or so; in July that year they had already bought Monk's House outright for £700. They were landlords elsewhere and Leonard had a considerable portfolio of stocks and shares. Eventually, moving from Hogarth House to Tavistock Square in 1924, they let their old house for three years. Like others in their social bracket, when Mr and Mrs Woolf felt they were hard up, they meant there was a risk of touching capital, securities or investments. Even at his most penurious Leonard Woolf received £30 a year unearned income, far more for doing nothing than the woman who scrubbed his floors. Virginia's investments were 'theoretically' worth about £9,000, which gave her an unearned income of around £400 a year. And while Mrs Bell might despise her in-laws for their 'awful rich, foxhunting self-complacency', she firmly kept secret that Angelica was Duncan's child to ensure her daughter's inheritance. Her ménage relied for support on Clive Bell's extensive financial resources from his parents' coal-mining interests.

During the wave of strikes which followed the war, Virginia reported in her diaries and letters that the upper classes were terrified of revolution. At a concert in South Kensington in February 1919 she listened to her titled friends declaring the lower orders to be out of control – '"they're strung up – they're unreasonable – they want higher wages"' and blaming the Jews for fomenting this unrest. 'I almost proclaimed myself a Russian

Jew,' Virginia wrote to Vanessa. Virginia felt at odds with 'the pampered rich' but then equally disliked the hectoring tone of left-wing friends, whose politics she distrusted. No one 'really believes we are in for anything', she decided. 'It will be tided over. Our cellars will be full; our larders too. Nothing is going to upset us.' As a Stephen, Virginia had inherited a social conscience. She always felt that her fire was 'too large for one person'. She analysed her feelings in her diary. 'I'm one of those who are hampered by the psychological hindrance of owning capital,' she observed, reviewing a political discussion among her circle, where she took the Tolstoyan view that they should surrender what they owned. Leonard thought that nonsense: they should keep what they had but do 'good work' for nothing. By now he was a committed socialist, supporting the railwaymen and the miners but under no illusions about the parliamentary Labour Party, which he felt repeatedly caved in on its promises in order to win votes. 'Personally I think the class war and the conflict of class interests are the greatest of curses,' he wrote, and they were 'the first things' one should try to abolish. Yet no one suggested that by paying their char a pittance they were keeping the class system alive and well, or helping to pauperize the poor.

★

In Woolf's second novel *Night and Day*, the heroine, Katharine Hilbery, feels 'so closely attached' to her ancestors that 'she very nearly lost consciousness that she was a separate thing, with a future of her own'. The novel is about Katharine's desire for self-sufficiency and imagines the idea, which is also an ideal, of a new, modern individual, a separate and singular being, who admits the absolute difference of others, and lives freely in a relationship without obligation, without the 'self-abandonment' of a conventional marriage, which is seen as 'degradation'. Set back in the period before the war it restages leaving home, which for Katharine means relinquishing her mother, and the 'slavery to her family

traditions'. In one scene she finds the maids in possession of her
mother's room:

> To Katharine it seemed as if they had brushed away sixty years or so
> with the first flick of their damp dusters. It seemed to her that the
> work she had tried to do in that room was being swept into a very
> insignificant heap of dust   (p. 364)

The uniformed maids are about as unlike Lottie and Nellie as is
possible. They are stable, archaic figures, whose job is to clear the
path for the heroine's future. Yet there is an ambiguity. While
Katharine is relieved, the image suggests an anxiety that the past
is being devalued, even trashed, as it is turned into dust. In order
to create something new, there must be destruction and there is
always the fear that a clean sweep might reduce everything to the
lowest common denominator, an indiscriminate heap.

That fear was very much present during and immediately
after the war when social barriers appeared to be lowered.
Listening to her brother describe the gorilla-like faces of the
crowds on Hampstead Heath in June 1918, Virginia reflected
that 'perhaps the horrible sense of community which the war
produces, as if we all sat in a third-class railway carriage together,
draws one's attention to the animal human being more closely'.
Although much of the fraternizing was only temporary, servants
– in imagination at least – were often seen as potential social
climbers, moving between classes, and liable to be accused of
apeing their betters. In late August Trissie Selwood embarrassed
the Bells by leaving to marry Gerald Stacey, the son of their
landlord. Virginia commented in her diary, 'She is one of the
transition cases – the servant not yet turned lady, but past serv-
anthood.' Perhaps she had Trissie in mind when talking to the
social investigators and Fabians, Beatrice and Sidney Webb, who
came to stay a fortnight later. Virginia asked them one of her
'most fruitful' questions: 'how easy is it for a man to change his
social grade?' Sidney Webb, the son of a shopkeeper, was, after
all, one who had done just that.

It was not the masses coming closer but the expansion of the middle classes, and especially the 'vast, mysterious lower-middle classes' in the period, which was a source of constant fascination to Woolf, as it was to others. *Night and Day* is a cross-caste romance in which the upper-middle-class Katharine Hilbery meets professional-middle-class Ralph Denham, and sits down with him and his suburban family to 'an unpleasant meal under a very bright light'. A reminder that Virginia's own marriage to a scion of Putney villadom (though his family were a cut above Sidney Webb's) was as bold in its way as her marrying a Jew. Leonard shared Virginia's loathing of the suburban and of 'cheap humanity' in 'red villas'; according to Virginia, he thought that the inside of his sister's house in Castello Avenue, Putney was 'the soul of Sylvia in stucco'. But if it was the sign of an intellectual to sneer at the surburban, and the price Leonard had to pay for marrying above him, the surburbanites were equally able to look down on the uneducated or on the 'common', who were in turn bolstered by the jokes and insults aimed at foreigners, which were habitual in all walks of life. The vocabulary of grading and classifying was prolific and pervasive in British society, and the readiest form of put-down was always to demote by class, taking a person down a peg or two (or three) – hence Virginia's calling Princess Elizabeth Bibesco 'a fat housekeeper of a woman' or the writer Edmund Gosse 'that little grocer'. Both Leonard and Virginia were fond of 'housemaid' as an insult (as in, 'what a housemaids [*sic*] mind he has' of Edward Sackville-West, Vita's first cousin).

Night and Day was largely written at Asheham during Virginia's long war-time convalescence. In the autumn of 1917 she also resumed the habit of diary-keeping, which she was to maintain for the rest of her life. Although the diary was to serve many purposes, discriminating between herself and others is one of its most energetic impulses and played a large part in her rehabilitation. Woolf became a writer inspired and excited by difference, though her sense of difference could reach violently alienated proportions, especially when those observed came too close: at its most extreme in her illness, she was terrified of strangers and believed they were laughing at her. Though she was immensely curious about others, her most usual response was to dissociate from the group, a kind of defensive narcissism, by which she anchored her 'self'. Walking through London's Soho, she might be pleased 'to the depths of my heart' by 'the stir & colour & cheapness' but a crowd, with its blurring of individuals, equally produced feelings of disgust: 'the crowd at close quarters is detestable. It smells; it sticks; it has neither vitality nor colour; it is a tepid mass of flesh scarcely organized into human life,' adding, 'I never for a moment felt myself one of "them".' Over the years her diary became a veritable compendium of class and caste distinctions among the British between the wars, including some, now hopefully obscure, such as the crucial differences between an Oxford and a Cambridge man. But by relishing the most hateful, even murderous feelings, she was testing her own resilience. Endlessly drawing and redrawing the lines between herself and others, the diary may also have freed Woolf from the traditional constraints of the Victorian novelist, and encouraged her to take an extraordinary leap in the dark.

Between 1917 and 1921 Virginia wrote a number of sketches and short stories, which were structured by the apparently random flow of thought and feeling, observing how consciousness acts upon the wider 'impersonal world', transforming its objects, and dissolving the separation between inner and outer realities. In 'The Mark on the Wall', a disembodied voice enjoys its own self-absorption, revelling in a great rush of thoughts and images, so that the story becomes an interior space like the mind, exploring its own depths and reflections. Though we discover that the speaker is a woman sitting in an armchair (whose thoughts are rudely interrupted by a man), the body is blissfully forgotten in the great plenitude of consciousness, the vistas of memory and association which continually open up. In 'An Unwritten Novel', the narrator shares with the reader the process by which she invents a story. We listen to her fantasizing about a woman sitting opposite on a train, as the narrator uses her, like the earlier mark on the wall, as a pretext for increasingly elaborated flights of fancy and becomes so merged with her creation that she even shares her subject's involuntary twitch. At times the boundaries between the observer and observed are lost in a helter-skelter, almost perilous moment of negative capability, which borders on unintelligibility, but when, at the end of the story, the 'real' fellow-passenger acts entirely 'out of character', this is but a further stimulus to the writer's appetite. The entire 'adorable world' provides, over and again, a limitless number of objects upon which the writer can project her ego, an endless source of satisfying material, like a good feed. In March 1917 she wrote – with a certain bravado – to Duncan Grant, comparing writing to excretion, 'I wish I could stop writing this letter – it is like an extremely long visit to the W.C. when, do what you will, fresh coils appear, and duty seems to urge you to break off, and then another inch protrudes, which must be the last; and it *isn't* the last – and so on, until – However – I must not tell you about ', as though writing were an endlessly pleasurable source of anal gratification.

Woolf's experimentalism was enabled by the fact that her stories could now – laboriously and sometimes messily – be printed on the small hand press the Woolfs had bought in April 1917. That July 'The Mark on the Wall', together with Leonard's story 'Three Jews', was the Hogarth Press's first publication and the Woolfs sought out other experimental works; their next publications were Katherine Mansfield's *Prelude* and T. S. Eliot's poems. Although Virginia could write about bodily functions in private, her bawdiness was never entirely convincing (unlike her sister's); the body was too much an object of distaste. Famously, in the spring of 1918, when Harriet Weaver, editor of the *Egoist*, encouraged by T. S. Eliot, took the manuscript of Joyce's *Ulysses* to the Woolfs for possible publication, Virginia's first reaction in private was, 'Why does their filth seek exit from her mouth?' (though Leonard looked for a printer who might take it on). 'Why not in fact leave out bodies?' Woolf wondered when she made notes on Joyce's fiction, increasingly admiring his technique but finding his descriptions obscene ('there's a dog that p-s – then there's a man that forths,' she wrote euphemistically to Lytton Strachey). Modern 'indecency' was a reaction, she thought, to Victorian repression, but such irreticence was a cheap 'dodge' and no more a measure of reality in a novel than an exploration of the mind.

Woolf's new technique freed up her 'characters' to move forward and backward in time and memory; it privileged subjective or interior time over that of the clock or the external, public world. And yet when she came to embody those consciousnesses in 'Kew Gardens', a short story in which four couples perambulate the circular flower beds (and a snail marks its own time), the women who are precisely nailed down as 'lower-middle class' are mere caricatures. Unlike the other couples who muse metaphysically, on time and memory, or love and death, their talk is a meaningless chanting of repetitions:

> Nell, Bert, Lot, Cess, Phil, Pa, he says, I says, she says, I says, I says, I
> says –

> My Bert, Sis, Bill, Grandad, the old man, sugar,
> >   Sugar, flour, kipper, greens,
> >   Sugar, sugar, sugar.

They remain brutishly in the present, their talk feeding their bodies, not their minds. Vanessa immediately recognized the scene when she read the story – 'some of the conversation – she says, I says, sugar – I know too well!' (Bert was the name of Nellie Boxall's brother-in law.) Woolf was nonetheless shamefaced when the women of the Cooperative Guild pressed her for copies of the story when it was published in 1919, and didn't want them to read 'the scene of the two women'. 'Is that to the discredit of Kew Gardens?' she asked herself. 'Perhaps a little.' She learnt to be more cautious about ventriloquizing. Trying to imagine the thoughts of an old Cornishwoman for her next novel, *Jacob's Room*, she admitted her own 'ignorance discreditable, indeed disgraceful' and decided to leave her character silent and wise. A deleted passage suggested however that Mrs Pascoe's inner life is like the interior of her cottage, whose cramped dimensions meant 'there would be no escaping the body. [Its functions are detestable]': 'An earth closet out in the rain – sickness – a woman's period – copulation upstairs in the double bed – childbirth' – Mrs Pascoe has no room for thought.

'A servant's life is one long drudgery,' Woolf wrote sympathetically, in a review of a new edition of George Moore's *Esther Waters*, his novel of 1894. Moore's eponymous heroine, a housemaid, is easily pitied, a victim pure and simple – sexual, social and economic; though she rises above circumstances she lives a life of unrelieved toil. The temptation was always to say that servants' lives were ruled by their physical experience, or that their wishes were limited to merely material aspirations: all body and no mind, as it were. But in Bloomsbury the servants were not victims or drudges, and Woolf noted that even her char moved an ornament on the mantelpiece at Monk's House to leave it 'askew' each day, a symptomatic act which, Woolf imagined, showed the desire for ornament and her thirst for art (it might equally have been an assertion of independence). 'Solid Objects', the title of another of Woolf's experimental stories, suggested that in any case 'things' were about far more than the cash invested in them: they became the repository of the immaterial – feelings, obsessions, needs and longings – evidence of a hidden inner life which could not be known or explained.

That servants had souls might have been confirmed by what happened to Mary Wilson, a housemaid who entered Vanessa's service around this time. In February 1920 Vanessa took the top two floors of the Adrian Stephen's house at 50 Gordon Square and travelled with Duncan Grant to Italy and France, leaving the household and children to the care of Sophie Farrell, the old family servant. Vanessa received troubling news of domestic affairs while she was away. Her new housemaid, Mary Wilson, 'had nearly gone off her head', she wrote to Roger Fry, 'owing to the deaths of her mother, father and lover within a fortnight'. Mary's brother was also seriously ill. The bad news had come by telegram or by telephone to Blanche, the maid at 46 Gordon Square, Maynard Keynes's house (the Stephens had as yet no telephone), and relayed to Mary, who had 'terrified Sophie and the 46 servants by raving wildly all night for 3 weeks till it got so bad that [Dr] Moralt had to take her to the infirmary'. Mary was now anxious to come back to work – 'I don't think her state was to be wondered at,' Vanessa added. On her return in mid-May, Vanessa took charge of the situation, corresponding with Mary's friends, in particular a Nurse Gibson and a Mr Bracenbury, mysteriously known by the name of 'Nigger'; the former sent a severe letter to Mary, telling her to 'pull herself together', the latter, now effectively Mary's guardian, wrote, telephoned and set up appointments which he did not keep. Meanwhile Mary's condition had deteriorated; she disappeared on errands, going out of her way to avoid strangers and confessing to 'a strange horror of black men'; despite repeated doses of bromide, she lay sobbing and moaning all night. Eventually, when Blanche took Mary across country to find her guardian, Mary bolted. In the event her parents' home was located and they were found to be alive and well, utterly mystified. Mary's letters and calls had all been impersonations. Meanwhile she was at large in London, sending messages in her various characters, until she was captured and brought to Gordon Square. During the long hours of waiting to be admitted to the infirmary she became more and more incoherent. 'Finally she seemed to know no one' and was led tamely away.

In her diary Virginia decided that it was 'a complete case of servant's hysteria; all coming, I think, from her wishing to act a day dream, & then, poor creature, stepping too far & believing it, & now babbling in St Pancras Infirmary' (the old union workhouse). She found the sight of Mary being taken off 'sinister; & all the servants were looking from all the windows. What horrid people they are!', though presumably she too had watched. After this Virginia had taken a bus across London in a heightened state, feeling it was one of those times when 'everything gets into the same mood'. She found another sight which moved her, though differently, an old beggar woman seen from the top of a London bus, singing shrilly 'for her own amusement' up against a stone wall, and 'holding a brown mongrel in her arms':

There was a recklessness about her; much in the spirit of London. Defiant – almost gay, clasping her dog as if for warmth. How many Junes has she sat there, in the heart of London? How she came to be there, what scenes she can go through, I can't imagine. Oh damn it all, I say, why cant I know all that too?

The inspiring image of the beggar woman was to recur in Woolf's fiction. The romantic figure of the old vagrant, belonging to the eternal caste of the poor, so entirely different from oneself, was far easier to sympathize with than the housemaid, a daydreamer and hysteric, a poor person in the wrong place, who came much too close for comfort.

What, after all, was different about 'servant's hysteria'? Virginia too feared strangers and heard voices; she too made things up, and what she daydreamed turned into her reality; she too had been carted off 'raving', though, like Helen Fry or Vivienne Eliot, to private, expensive nursing-homes rather than to the old union workhouse. And though she lost touch entirely with reality, she could recover, and did. Virginia was always being told – as Helen Fry was – to exercise more self-control, as if her breakdowns were her fault. What if the difference between 'Mad Mary' and 'Mad Virginia' were one of degree and not of kind? Everyone, including Virginia, saw her madness as a sign of her specialness; her friends openly referred to it as a mark of her genius. How could one be a writer and remain in control? In the early 1920s Woolf frequently found metaphors for writing as a process which relied on an active inner life, 'submerged' or working 'in the dark'; her new method of 'tunnelling' or making 'caves' behind her characters, her interior monologues which read like free association, and her advice to herself to cultivate a kind of idle attentiveness, faced with the ebbs and flows of her moods, all seem to chime with the idea of the unconscious life of the mind. Psychoanalysis itself had begun with the interpretation of hysterical symptoms whose origins were believed to lie in forgotten psychical trauma. But the Freudian analysis which Virginia encountered in her circle, and tended to mock in the early 20s (in her essay on 'Freudian

Fiction', for example), was potentially as controlling of the patient as the more conventional treatments she had undergone. Throughout her life Virginia Woolf experienced many intermediate states of illness, of physical and psychological collapse, which she often found fruitful for her writing; the border between madness and sanity, between the life of the mind and of the body, was far more flexible and porous than any opposition or dissociation might suggest. Perhaps that was why, at least at first, she was antagonistic towards psychoanalysis. She wished to keep her interior to herself and to leave the body – which anyone could occupy – out of the account.

In the 1920s hysteria was generally a pejorative label, and in her diary and letters Virginia consistently dismissed the servants' illnesses as mysterious, dubious and a bit of a joke. Nellie, though quiet and thoughtful, was prone 'to work herself up into states' or to 'vapours'; Lottie was cheerful and carefree but she was also lazy and 'volatile', liable to be found 'in a state of hysterics'. 'My private wonder is,' Virginia wrote when Nellie was 'seemingly ill' in July 1920, 'how they contrive to live a week – aren't killed by the thunder, like flies. No root in reality is in them; & as for reason, when the mood's on, as soon might one persuade a runaway horse. And nothing the matter save what one of us would call an upset inside & take a pill for.' Too much time was spent talking about 'the insides of women', wrote Virginia. Though Lottie went into hospital for an operation, leaving the Woolfs to carry the coals themselves, the physical toll of the work seems not to have been discussed. Servants' illnesses were the product of unreason, self-induced or just plain malingering. Certainly this was the view canvassed by Mrs Bell when she entertained Bloomsbury's newly established 'Memoir Club' with the whole 'strange story of Mary Elizabeth Wilson', a shilling-shocker in which the economist Maynard Keynes featured as the arch-detective and ultra-rationalist, able instantly to see through the false 'evidence' of the letters, and pre-empting Vanessa Bell's final verdict on Mary's behaviour – 'There was no word of truth in her story.' Even the servants agreed that Mary was 'an artful hussy and deceiver'. No wonder

Virginia insisted on a clear distance between herself and these other fabricators.

Sooner or later they were all seen as 'temperamental', these girls who cried a lot; who were often frightened and lonely, and a long way from home. Yet their wild insecurity was not unreasonable; they knew they were dispensable, even interchangeable, in the eyes of their employers, and they learnt to live a temporary existence, able to move on at a moment's notice. If they made up stories about themselves, exaggerated and dramatized, just to feel they mattered – to take up more room – what was strange about that? Class was always a matter of fantasy, and 'wishing to act a daydream' the motive-power which underpinned social mobility. Everyone seemed to believe that the upper classes were more important and interesting than the lower orders, and the social hierarchy depended upon that deprivation of self-esteem, which Dickens in *Great Expectations*, with his deep instinct for inferiority feelings, called 'the hurt without a name'. Servant's hysteria might easily have been understood as a veiled, unhappy way of asking for more. But in the early 1920s neither Mary, Nellie nor Lottie could have turned to the budding psychoanalysts for help. Bloomsbury's clients, like Freud's, were from their own milieu. In another life intelligent, inventive, artful 'Mad Mary', doomed to be a housemaid, might well have been a writer. But who knows what she actually was?

*

Lottie and Nellie frequently played their employers off against each other but they never left. In fact many of the Bloomsbury servants stayed for years, becoming old retainers. According to Virginia, her household was 'the easiest place in the world' for servants, and there was some truth in this. In the first place, there was no uniform. Nor were you called by your surname like the aptly named 'Meek', the parlourmaid at Cleeve House in Wiltshire, Clive Bell's family home, where even in the 1930s dinner was served by maids in black alpaca frocks and spotless white caps

and aprons, and no one was allowed to carry 'anything heavier
than a handkerchief'. Virginia and Vanessa were 'Mrs Woolf' and
'Mrs Bell' and not the customary 'Ma'am'; after a row, when
Nellie, in later years, began a letter with 'Dear Madam', Virginia
commented that this was 'significant of much'. These were very
informal households. No one dressed for dinner: hence Virginia's
frequent injunction in her letters to her friends telling them 'to
bring no clothes' for a stay. A bell would still be rung at mealtimes
at both Monk's House and Charleston but, while food had to be
brought in and plates cleared, there was no waiting at meals and
the Omega dining-tables were used without table linen. Other
fetching and carrying was at a minimum. Neither Mrs Woolf nor
Mrs Bell supervised their servants while they worked, and to most
of their class their manners would have appeared unbelievably lax.
Nor were the servants expected to attend church as was still the
norm – and Bloomsbury was sympathetic and decent towards
unmarried mothers in their employ. In 1919, when Flossie Selwood
had an illegitimate daughter, Mary, Vanessa's friend Faith Henderson kept her on and brought Mary up as one of them, saving
them both from disgrace. Mary 'Henderson' went to private school
and played with the other Bloomsbury children. Only when
Flossie married a local man from her Gloucestershire village, and
took Mary home to live with her new husband, did mother and
daughter have to face nastiness and prejudice.

Above all, Bloomsbury was sociable and fun and there were
halcyon times, especially in the early 20s. The servants were in
and out of each other's places in London and in Sussex; weather
permitting, there was much walking and cycling between Charleston and Rodmell, and later to Tilton, the farmhouse near
Charleston which became the Keynes's place. There were many
parties, including fancy dress, to which the servants were often
invited – on one occasion George Harland, who worked for
Keynes, was infuriated because 'Mr' had been left off his invitation, despite his having hired a Napoleon costume. Monk's House
rang with laughter, Virginia told Roger, with Lottie 'in and out
all the time in a transparent white petticoat up to her knees'.

Lottie liked to play practical jokes, and caused much hilarity one Christmas by dropping a marzipan mouse in Virginia's tea. 'The girls' saved up for dancing lessons and practised the foxtrot; Virginia bought a kitten and named it 'Boxall' after Nellie – 'to ingratiate her'. Servants' relatives often came to stay and there were plenty of treats. Daisy Selwood went travelling abroad with the Adrian Stephens and joined them at parties in her flapper frocks. Grace Germany, who came as a housemaid, aged sixteen, to Charleston and took over as Angelica's nurse after Nelly Brittain left, went several times to Cassis, where Vanessa Bell purchased a farmhouse in the 20s. Grace learnt French and enjoyed wine.

Like servants through the ages, those who worked in Bloomsbury saw how the other half lived and it expanded their horizons. If they were sometimes envious and resentful, they were also grateful and appreciative. But these are two sides of the same coin. They rewarded their employers by becoming snobs, enjoying the borrowed glamour of working for famous people, and in a pathetic tribute to Bloomsbury, mirroring the cliquish world in which they moved, the servants called themselves 'the click'. For all its liberalism, Bloomsbury could be possessive and insular; to others the group acted like a gang. Vanessa wanted to exclude Lydia Lopokova from joining their circle when Maynard Keynes married the Russian ballerina; Lydia was often happiest in the kitchen with Grace or Daisy. Adrian and Karin Stephen were outsiders – no one thought Karin, an American, good enough, and Adrian left Charleston in tears after Duncan Grant, who had once been his lover, made his views plain. After forty years, their daughter, Ann, was still angry and had never, she told Leonard Woolf, understood this 'cold feeling'. As a little girl she had sat in the kitchen listening to the servants gossip about 'Mr W' and 'Mrs B', and 'there you all were, larger than life, cracked up by the servants as "great" men and women and played down by my parents as "no more remarkable than anyone else for all they think so highly of themselves"'. Yet Bloomsbury's tribal behaviour was hardly unique to them. Everyone in Britain could find someone to look down on.

Nellie Boxall, Lottie Hope, Nelly Brittain, with Angelica Bell, 1922

No doubt the servants had good times in Bloomsbury. There
they are in Vanessa Bell's remarkably informal photograph, taken
in the early 1920s – Nellie, Lottie and Nelly Brittain, in their
ballerina cardigans and frocks, their hair fashionably bobbed. Lottie
laughs into the camera, her comrades smile; their eyes are hidden
beneath the brim of straw boaters, hands are in pockets. They

could be undergraduates or flappers were it not for the chubby toddler and the custodial pose of Angelica's nurse which suggests that they might all be servants in mufti. (And would young ladies grin quite so much?) There are several more portraits of Grace, 'the Angel of Charleston', whose beauty appealed to her painter mistress. Their number is also testimony to Mrs Bell's affection. Yet there is always one photo missing from the Bloomsbury albums. Though mistresses and maids were constantly in each other's company, they seem never to have been photographed together. They never could appear side by side.

THREE

The Question of Nelly

If my father was a blacksmith and yours was a peer of the realm we must needs be pictures to each other. We cannot possibly break out of the frame of the picture by speaking natural words.

Virginia Woolf, 'Three Pictures', June 1929

She looked out from her writing lodge across to Mount Caburn, already hazy in the August heat. Breakfast, laid on the check tablecloth, was over; there would be coffee and a cigarette at eleven, luncheon at one (rissoles, perhaps, and a chocolate custard). Percy had arrived long ago through the side gate (he never came in the house) and was inspecting the hives. Fresh honeycomb in its wooden box might be cut for tea. Mercifully the church bells were silent and the village children, on their school holidays, scattered. The day stretched ahead. She ought to be working on Wollstonecraft but compressing her thoughts 'was like cutting steps in rock'. She took out her diary instead:

Of course, one is right about Nelly – right that she is, in bad moods almost insufferably mean, selfish & spiteful; but – & this is an interesting psychological remark, she is in a state of nature; untrained; uneducated, to me almost incredibly without the power of analysis or logic; so that one sees a human mind wriggling undressed – which is interesting; & then, in the midst of one's horror at the loathesome spectacle, one is surprised by the goodness of human nature, undressed; & it is more impressive because of its undress.

Two days earlier her mood had been turbulent. She had told Nellie to stay away until October. Rodmell was becoming impossible with her in situ. Privately she and Leonard doubted that they would continue with her after the autumn, and somehow Nellie had divined this. There had been recriminations, supplications, weeping, the usual catalogue of griev-ances, and Virginia had sought refuge in her diary:

This is written to while away one of those stupendous moments – one of those painful, ridiculous, agitating moments which make one half sick & yet I dont know – I'm excited too; & feel free & then sordid; & unsettled; & so on – I've told Nelly to go; after a series of scenes which I wont bore myself to describe.

And in the midst of the usual anger, I looked into her little shifting greedy eyes,
& saw nothing but malice & spite there, & felt that that had come to be the
reality now: she doesn't care for me, or for anything: has been eaten up by her
poor timid servants fears & cares & respectabilities.

Virginia felt confirmed in her wish to have no resident servants ever again.
'That is the evil which rots the relationship.' Then, instead of giving way,
Nellie had cycled to Lewes, four miles and back, to fetch cream for their
dinner. She did not want them to suffer – 'how could she leave us without
a cook?'. This was the goodness, her devotion, and it meant plunging
into more talk. She would find it very difficult to get a place, Nellie
pleaded, it is all the fashion now to engage cooks only who will live out
(Virginia tried to record Nellie's words). But 'Heaven be praised', it was
now all over and calm and settled. Nellie was staying for the summer
and Virginia was 'half pleased to find that it is harder to part after 15
years than I thought'. Already the row had faded and Virginia could
reassure herself ('of course, one is right about Nelly') that she took the
long view. Later in the month she reread what she had written and took
comfort, adding a note in the margins: 'Another scene, Aug. 30th; but
these reflections stood me in good stead – & I laughed. But what a
confounded bore it is.'

Virginia felt 'degraded' by the scenes, brought down to Nellie's level,
yet she felt compelled to repeat them in her diary. She seldom cried, and
witnessing Nellie's display of naked emotions, Virginia too felt exposed.
Being angry might be liberating, even thrilling, but it was a loss of self-
control; such feelings were sickeningly visceral, their ferocity absurdly in
excess of the situation. They brought self-loathing and shame at their
violence, their incontinence. Only writing gave her temporary authority;
in her diary she could at least try to have the last word. Furious at
having made an exhibition of herself by being party to the quarrel, she
retaliated, stripping Nellie bare and displaying her like a specimen on
the page, 'wriggling undressed'. But accusing Nellie of spite and meanness,
she was hoist with her own petard – what could be nastier than 'wriggling'? Ultimately Virginia was left disgusted and empty, feeling 'sordid'.
There were headaches (the strain was 'subterranean', she wrote) and
depressions, and the savage, hateful feelings spoilt everything. All she could

do was to dissect the melancholy which blighted her fertility like 'a curious little spotted fruit': 'whats money,' she wrote, 'compared with Nessa's children?'

Virginia Woolf and Nellie Boxall lived together for eighteen years, and for ten of them Nellie was her sole live-in servant. If the rows between them were proof positive of their social distance, they also testified to their intimacy. Husbands and wives row, friends row and lovers row, but mistresses and maids – at least in theory – do not. Employers might 'have words' with 'Cook' but they did not engage in lengthy argument. Mrs Bell, for instance, adopted the right manner. She began the morning at Charleston like a Victorian matron, sitting at the breakfast table issuing her orders to Grace, who stood waiting, at the ready. 'Gentle, patient and self-controlled', she kept aloof, and seemed to her daughter like a lady 'waving from a train to women working in the fields'. But Virginia couldn't bear the 'kind of measured sweetness' used in talking to servants, children and the elderly, or – as she, of all people, knew – to the sick; she intensely disliked being in any post of authority. Her capacity to row with Nellie was a sign of her unusual openness, that she let down her defences, and allowed unheard-of familiarities.

When Virginia wrote dolefully of Nellie, 'she doesn't care for me, or for anything', she sounded for all the world like a little girl, a lover, or perhaps a mother, rejected and abandoned. The scenes were a measure of reciprocity as well as estrangement, each of them trying to have the last word. 'Me! And me! What about me!' Who was the bully and who the victim? Who was the more dependent?

VIRGINIA WOOLF AND NELLIE BOXALL

Sarah Marden, Nellie's mother, was a village girl from Bramley in Surrey, who married and had her first child by the time she was twenty. Born in the late 1840s she was a contemporary of Julia Stephen, Virginia's mother. Like Julia, like numberless women through the ages, she went on bearing children every eighteen months or so. Six girls and four boys; twenty-odd years of child-bearing. At fifty-four she died, worn out like Julia, perhaps, by maternity. At the turn of the twentieth century the average life-expectancy for a woman was forty-six.

Boxall was an old English name, and probably went back to Boxholte, a village in the next county, Sussex. In fact Boxalls sprang up like dragon's teeth all over Sussex and Surrey. As chance would have it, Henry Boxall, Nellie's father, came from nearby Hambledon, the village where Lottie had grown up. A Boxall had been killed in Hambledon's rotten almshouses, and a Bessie Boxall sat in class with Lottie; Boxalls ran the draper's shop at Chiddingfold which Miss Sichel and Miss Ritchie must have patronized. Sometime in the 1860s Henry and Sarah joined the migrants who left the rural poverty which Surrey's painters found so picturesque. They settled in Farncombe, hard by the bustling town of Godalming, where there were Boxalls working as wheel-wrights and undertakers, and Henry took on labouring jobs to feed his growing family.

Surrounded by hills and woods, with plentiful rivers and streams, Godalming had played a flourishing part in the cloth trades – its bright blue woollen fabric or 'kersey', its hosiery (first wool, then silk, then cotton) were renowned from Elizabethan times. In the nineteenth century, leatherworking and papermaking, which also needed copious water, dotted the town with factories and mills more usual in the industrial north than in the Home Counties. The Boxalls, like most of Farncombe's hardworking poor, lived in the labourers' cottages close to the railway line which ran from Portsmouth on the coast up to London. Farncombe was fast becoming a prosperous suburb of Godalming, rather than a village, and with its brand-new schools and swanky houses, the area was increasing in popularity with the middle classes. (Years later Nellie would serve tea to Aldous Huxley, the writer, whose father taught at Charterhouse, the nearby public school. He'd grown up at the same time as Nellie, a mile or so away, in another universe.) Nellie's own school, Farncombe National School, next to St John's church, was a hundred yards from home, though from there the children could escape along Church Walk down to the river, run along the tow path following the bend of the Wey, past the tannery

and the laundry. When Farncombe opened its own station the
trains stopped right at the bottom of the Boxalls' garden in Somers
Road. Round the corner was the High Street, with its shops and
street lights. Did little Nellie think the world was at her feet?

In 1890 Nellie Boxall was born into a crowded, noisy home,
full of comings and goings. She was the youngest of ten, the baby
of the family. Sarah Boxall was in her early forties when Nellie
was born but might have produced another child if Nellie's father
had survived. Nellie never knew him. He died of a heart-attack
when she was five months old. He was forty-five. His widow
scratched an 'X', her 'mark', on his death certificate as she had
on her marriage lines. She was left to manage and make do. Eliza
Boxall, twenty years older than Nellie, had already gone but Emily
at seventeen was a laundrymaid, while William and James worked
at the paper mill (James was a fifteen-year-old labourer) – they
could all chip in. Then Annie went into service and George into
the tanning yard, lodging at home until the youngest – Alice,
Lizzie, Arthur and Nellie – could earn their keep. The shrinking
family moved into North Street on the other side of the tracks,
a short road of two-up, two-down terrace cottages running uphill
above the station, with long back gardens where people used to
keep pigs. William, now with a wife and daughter of his own,
rented a house there too. At thirty he had risen to be a 'foreman
platelayer', in charge of a gang of men, keeping the railway in
repair. Then just before Nellie's twelfth birthday Sarah Boxall
suffered a stroke, an 'apoplexy', as the doctors put it. She lay for
three and a half days in limbo before she finally died. Nellie's
childhood must be read between these lines.

'We think back through our mothers if we are women,'
Virginia wrote in *A Room of One's Own*. But both Nellie and
Virginia were motherless girls who could only distantly remember
that fading figure. They relied on others for protection and care.
Nellie, with fair hair and a round face, was orphaned at twelve
and out at work at fourteen, and transplanted to other people's
houses from this young age. Not surprisingly, perhaps, she grew
up to be a complicated character, or so they said, inclined to

'nerves' and needing much reassurance and affection. Rather like the woman, in fact, with whom she was to live for nearly two decades.

★

Looking back again to the pre-war world, Virginia Woolf famously declared that 'in or about December, 1910, human character had changed'. In life, she suggested, with her usual mixture of hyperbole and seriousness, the change could best be seen 'in the character of one's cook'. Whereas the Victorian cook, 'formidable, silent, obscure, inscrutable', had lived 'like a leviathan in the lower depths' (a phrase which conjured up the abyss of the slums, and perhaps too a picture of plump Sophie), the modern domestic, 'the Georgian cook', was 'a creature of sunshine and fresh air; in and out of the drawing-room, now to borrow the *Daily Herald*, now to ask advice about a hat'. The walls of the five-storey house and of patriarchal England were tumbling down, the underlings were coming up for air: 'all human relations have shifted', she continued, 'those between masters and servants, husband and wives, parents and children'. Servants were no longer beneath you but working alongside. Cooperation was the new order of the day. The Georgian cook would freely come and go, borrowing hats and reading the radical press; she might appreciate Matisse and even compose music in her spare time. Of course it was all pie in the sky. Barely was the ink on the page dry before Mrs Woolf was at loggerheads with her own Georgian cook.

'I am about to pass sentence of death on Lottie and Nelly,' Virginia proclaimed early in 1924. It was 'a revision of 4 lives' and she felt both guilty and excited. They were returning to Bloomsbury after nine years' sojourn in the suburban wilderness of Richmond, now that her husband and doctors believed she could cope with the stimulus of town life, though Leonard continued to be strict about late nights. For months she had been planning to update her domestic life. She imagined the simplicities of living in a flat with just Nellie 'to do' for them. Then, when they signed the ten-year lease on 52 Tavistock Square, Virginia was elated by the idea of getting rid of both live-in servants. Number 52 was one of the tall terraced houses, built in the early nineteenth century, on the southern side of the square. The ground and first floor were let to a firm of solicitors; the Woolfs had the basement, where the Press was installed, and the old billiard room doubled as the store room and as Virginia's 'studio', where she was to write perched amid the parcels of books and piles of paper; the top two floors housed the living quarters. It was light and airy, and there was no basement kitchen. Their new domestic establishment, she fantasized, would be 'entirely controlled by one woman, a vacuum cleaner, & electric stoves'.

Virginia fully expected 1924 to be 'the most eventful in the whole of our (recorded) career', not least because she was back in the heart of things. Drafting *Mrs Dalloway*, itself a celebration of London, she felt more sure of her new methods for conveying the interior life and its fluctuations; she was reworking the reviews and essays which would become the first volume of *The Common Reader*, including those from the *Times Literary Supplement* which had been published anonymously; she was taking on a more public role as a critic. The Hogarth Press, now a small but flourishing business, relieved her of submitting her work to Gerald Duckworth's firm – the Woolfs had published *Jacob's Room* themselves. 'I'm the only woman in London who can write what she likes,' she declared. She had also negotiated the contract with her American publishers, Harcourt Brace, which was to last her lifetime. Though she often found it amusing, being so grown-up and taking life so seriously, after twenty-odd years of writing, she had finally come of age. Returning to Bloomsbury was a reprise of her first move in 1904 – everything would again be made anew.

When it came to it, Nellie survived the axe by agreeing to stay on alone. Virginia felt responsible for Lottie and was relieved when she was taken on by Adrian and Karin Stephen, round the corner at 50 Gordon Square – 'so keeping Nelly in society'. 'All could not have fallen out better,' she wrote optimistically. Nellie didn't see it that way. With Lottie's departure Nellie became a 'cook-general' or 'general', a term which sounded better to interwar ears than the old-fashioned 'maid-of-all-work', though it might entail the same drudgery. She would have to take on more cleaning and dusting, the bed-making and fire-lighting, clearing and washing-up, some washing (without detergents, of course), though a char would come in occasionally for the really dirty jobs and the larger items of laundry were sent out. And there was all the cooking. Tasks were time-consuming, especially without a deputy: ranges or stoves without 'regulos' moderating the temperatures had to be watched, there were constant interruptions to answer the door or run errands. When she first saw the flat with Virginia in February 1924, Nellie wrote out a timetable of her work, 'to show that by 3 P.M. she would still have to wash up luncheon & do Leonard's boots'. Virginia responded with an ultimatum: 'Very well, I said, find a place with Lottie.'

Lottie had a latchkey to number 52 but now Nellie was alone as never before in her life. The two of them had worked and lived together, sharing a room for eight years. Rodmell was 'the test of poor Nelly's endurance', Woolf noted sympathetically, where the work could be exhausting, especially when performed single-handedly. The kitchen was dark and damp; there was no electricity or gas; no running water or bathroom; the earth privy out in the garden was little more than a cane seat over a bucket. Water had to be pumped, the 'kitchener range', which the Woolfs had installed in 1920, had to be lit and to be kept going with fuel, which had to be fetched before even a cup of tea could be made. Nellie survived the three weeks there at Easter in 1924, 'heroically', helped by Rose Bartholomew, a woman from the village who also stepped in when Nellie was sent back to London to prepare the flat. At Christmas Nellie's work could hardly have been made easier by the 'enormous rats' and the mud at Monk's House. Water flooded the kitchen floor. It was lonely. Nellie was not part of the village and Charleston was too far away for impromptu visits; they were often cut off in winter. 'Moping but loyal,' as Virginia put it, Nellie was thrown more on her own resources in a one-to-one relationship with employers who expected more of her but hoped to feel freer of the service relationship. Monk's House was a very intimate space where every sound was amplified by the uncovered oak floorboards. Leonard and Virginia took their baths in the kitchen behind a curtain; upstairs was a large bedroom which they shared at first, sleeping in their single beds, with a cramped box room adjoining. Then, after Lottie's departure, Leonard moved into one of the two small rooms across the landing; Nellie was in the other. When guests came he sometimes slept in the box room. As Virginia tried to eradicate interruption by having fewer servants, even the presence of a single domestic became intrusive. And that servant craved more intimacy, more company and more attention.

Virginia's vision of a happy coexistence with a Georgian cook was nothing if not wishful thinking. In January 1925 Virginia looked back wistfully on the hopeful 'flourish' with which she had begun 1924. Nellie had given notice 'for the 165th time' – 'Won't be dictated to,' she noted in her diary, 'must do as other girls do.' Virginia felt inclined to let her go, irritated by 'the nuisance of arranging life to suit her fads'. She penned a character sketch of Nellie which oscillated between the familiar portrait of the faithful retainer – an 'honest, crusty old maid' (Nellie was twenty-nine), 'dependable, in the main, affectionate, kindly' – and something more modern and individual and, in a servant, less acceptable: she was 'incurably fussy, nervy, insubstantial'. Though Virginia dismissed 'the servant question', unconvincingly, as no longer worrying her, it grew acute. The next eighteen months were punctuated by more rows.

To Virginia it seemed that Nellie was simply 'playing up'. Mostly she complained about the number of casual callers – 'always people', Virginia quoted Nellie as saying, 'when we have dinner parties', which made it hard to provision. Like most of the English middle classes, the Woolfs contented themselves with plain cooking for many years but mealtimes were regular – breakfast at nine, lunch at one, tea around four, and dinner between seven and eight. Food was substantial if repetitive: a cooked lunch and often three courses at dinner, such as chicken, ices and a 'savoury' (the Woolfs drank little, ordering wine and cigarettes as luxuries). Several people dropping in or staying on meant last-minute baking or shopping, in what was supposed to be a servant's quiet time in the afternoon. Virginia found Nellie 'rather waspish' when 'Mary, Gwen, Julia, Quentin, Geoffrey Keynes, and Roger' called in unannounced. One outburst from Nellie particularly rankled and Virginia fantasized about 'how I might have said, If you have Lottie every day, why should I not have my friends? But one can't – & she is jealous, that is the truth. And next time I will say it – & it was Miss Mayor coming that upset us; And we had Vita, Edith Sitwell, Morgan, Dadie, Kitty Leaf.'

It seems extraordinary that Virginia should think that she and her servant were in the same boat, but the new one-to-one relationship invited this kind of direct comparison without the gradations of hierarchy which could defuse tension in larger households. She tried over and again to devise a new 'methodical system of inviting people' and to unbend, behaving more generously, as if a purely personal solution could move them beyond the inequalities of their situation. Nellie, on the other hand, was bearing the brunt of the work – she might be 'Cook' but she also cleaned boots and swilled out baths. Old habits died hard. Nellie was a conventional servant in many ways, not averse to receiving tips (the young writer, William Plomer, tipped her 5s rather generously, more than a quarter of her weekly earnings), or announcing visitors, especially those with handles to their names. 'You don't treat me like your maid,' she apparently complained to Virginia. Virginia wanted to be 'cordial' and yet she expected Nellie to be 'obedient', a word which harked back to the old days. New freedoms met old expectations; both parties found themselves in a no-man's land between the past and present. It was an emotional minefield.

A cat-and-mouse game developed. Nellie's only weapon was to threaten to leave, immediately withdrawing her notice once it was taken seriously. Virginia in turn schemed to be rid of her, made plans behind her back, and then felt guilty, responsible and equally attached. Nellie refused to make marmalade and they quarrelled; they quarrelled because Virginia told fibs. One minute Virginia dreamt of being 'quit' of all commitments, the next of taking Lottie back since she was getting on badly with Karin Stephen. When Nellie was ill, the Woolfs thought again of poaching Grace Germany from Charleston but nothing came of it. On one occasion, when Nellie gave notice, Virginia wrote six letters in search of replacements, only to have Nellie apologize, blaming the toothache. But would a Mrs Collins and her daughter from the registry office have been any better? 'I am sick of the timid spiteful servant mind,' she wrote, reverting to the generic (yet how incensed she'd been when male authors had patronized 'the female mind'!). Never, never again, she vowed, would she believe Nellie.

They rowed; they made it up. Trips to 'Mrs Hunt's' at Marylebone, searching for servants, left Virginia feeling she was at least 'safe' with Nellie. Nellie also protested that she was too fond of Mrs Woolf to leave her. There were other reasons to stay: she was in her mid-thirties, she had no pension; she was not used to conventional households and she would be cast outside 'the click'. Giving notice was her only sanction – there was no supervisor or trade union overseeing her work or its conditions. Withdrawing her labour also reminded them of how much she was needed; it left the Woolfs pathetically stranded, unable to invite their friends to dinner or even answer the front door. Nellie wanted to be appreciated and valued. After so many years and so much knowledge of each other the quarrels went over old ground and to Virginia it was both painful and 'absurd' or 'ridiculous'. History repeated itself as farce and they were locked into relations which might modify or relax but never change. The relation was familial and they both took turns at playing mother and child. Mrs Woolf gave the orders but Nellie brought Virginia her milk or supper on a tray, ran her bath for her and washed her chemises.

The Woolfs spent hours pacing the Bloomsbury squares discussing Nellie's ultimatums but the responsibility rested with

Virginia. She thought that Leonard took the wrong tone: he was either too authoritarian with servants or too lenient. There were, of course, oases of peace when Nellie was 'as good as gold' – a phrase used of children and babies – and 'in constant spirits & kindness', but such periods of domestic calm were rarely as frequently recorded as those of strife. They feature as absence in the diaries. During the mid-20s Virginia's intimacy with Vita Sackville-West blossomed and it met many of Virginia's emotional needs, not least, as she noted, for mothering. In December 1925 she wrote in her diary that Vita 'lavishes on me the maternal protection, which for some reason, is what I have always most wished from everyone'. In the love letters to Vita, Nellie merely featured as a literary device, elevated to 'my maid' or demoted to 'the domestic', and tapped for amusing low-life scenes. When Lottie fell in love with a dairyman at Thorpe-le-Soken in Essex, near where the Adrian Stephens had a country place, Virginia found it all hilarious; she enjoyed mimicking Nellie's speech to Vita and mocking Nellie's snobbery (a convenient cover for her own). When *Orlando*, which commemorates Virginia's love for Vita, was published in 1928, Virginia put 'Miss Nellie Boxall' (spelt correctly) between Lady Colefax and Mr J. M. Keynes in the long list of spoof acknowledgements, a jokey snub to all three. Yet on a trip to France with Vita, she scribbled 'Love to Nelly' at the bottom of her letter to Leonard. Not many mistresses were so openly affectionate to their cooks.

Good cooks were, of course, hard to find and Nellie was getting to be first-class. As their income grew, the Woolfs began to take holidays abroad and became more sophisticated in their culinary tastes. They were always Francophiles and increasingly so after Vanessa bought a house in Cassis, which they first visited in the spring of 1925, and several times thereafter. Virginia sent Nellie for lessons with the celebrity chef Marcel Boulestin, whose famous Restaurant Français (opened in Leicester Square in 1925) was decorated by Duncan Grant, and popular in Bloomsbury circles. Boulestin ran cookery courses at Fortnum and Mason's in Picca-dilly 'which were eagerly attended by both mistresses and their cooks'. He published a series of books which introduced French cooking to the English, including the mysteries of 'proper' coffee and the use of olive oil for purposes other than ear-ache. Virginia herself avoided having lunch with him but mastered the art of the omelet, for which he was renowned. Returning from visiting friends in Normandy, Virginia regaled them with the horrors of the standard English fare provided by 'emaciated' Mrs Bartholomew, the gardener's wife, 'in the last stages of decrepitude', while Nellie was on her annual holiday: gluey tapioca pudding 'very sticky, yellowish, sweet', potted meat and sardines. Nellie's chocolate creams, schnitzels and sauces were far more welcome.

In the early 20s, with a joint income of around £1,100 a year, the Woolfs were earning relatively little by the standards of their class when, for instance, a barrister might draw at least ten times as much, but it would still have put them into the comfortable end of the middle classes. A general practitioner might earn £700 a year, a male teacher in a council school half that amount, while at the sharp end of the lower-middle class, a clerk averaged between £60 and £200 a year. And the Woolfs could depend on a steady unearned income from capital. In 1919 they bought Monk's House for £700 outright and went on renting in Bloomsbury, but as Virginia's and the Hogarth Press's earnings slowly picked up, they began improving their property. In 1926 the local builders, Philcox Brothers of Lewes, who were to do much of the work on the house, took out the old kitchener and put in 'a Larbert self-setting range with cast iron sides & back' and a 'Number One Open Fire Ideal' hot-water boiler and tank (the house would not go on mains water until 1934). The 'luxury of water running in torrents, boiling hot, for every purpose is inconceivable', wrote Virginia, 'even Nelly had to admit she can cook perfectly there'. Philcox added a bathroom and a lavatory up above the kitchen, and knocked through two rooms downstairs to create 'our large combined drawing eating room, with its 5 windows, its beams down the middle, & flowers & leaves nodding in all around us'. They bought a sofa for £8 10s. After several years of 'the romantic chamber' in the garden, there were now two flushing water-closets, though they did not 'surge & gush' quite sufficiently. Nellie had hers downstairs. The Woolfs were modest payers: by the late 20s Nellie was earning about £50 a year when the average wage for a cook was £56 (though wages might drop as low as £30). They were generous, however, with the new luxuries. Nellie borrowed the gramophone in Tavistock Square and practised the foxtrot; she had a wireless in her bedroom and another in Rodmell, where Virginia would sometimes go to 'listen in'. The Woolfs bought their first car in 1927, a second-hand Singer for £275, which cost about £100 a year to run; they often took Nellie into Lewes for shopping and errands. Yet there would be plenty of long winter's evenings in the Sussex countryside while the Woolfs read and talked or entertained downstairs, and Nellie sat upstairs or a few feet away in the kitchen on her own.

Orlando was Virginia's first substantial success and was into its third edition, selling over 6,000 copies by the end of 1928. For the first time in her life she could look forward to having money to spend, though 'the spending muscle does not work naturally yet'. That year the Stephens also sold their old home, 22 Hyde Park Gate, for nearly £5,000, a large sum at the time. Virginia found 'solace' and pride in the fact that the workers at the Press and 'a great big man like Percy [Bartholomew, the gardener]' 'depend, largely, upon my hand writing on a sheet of paper', that she was 'keeping people fed & housed'. But as the Woolfs' standard of living rose, the improvements which lightened Nellie's load were also making a live-in servant seem less necessary. After five years of tussling, Virginia felt they had reached a stalemate. In the spring of 1929 she examined her conscience in the Puritan fashion. 'I am sordidly debating within myself the question of Nelly; the perennial question,' she complained. 'It is an absurdity, how much time L. & I have wasted in talking about servants. And it can never be done with because the fault lies in the system. How can an uneducated woman let herself in, alone, into our lives? – what happens is that she becomes a mongrel; & has no roots any where.' What Virginia now felt she needed was 'a daily of a civilised kind, who had her baby in Kentish town; & treated me as an employer, not friend'. 'Here is a fine rubbish heap,' she concluded, 'left by our parents to be swept.' No longer 'the servant question', this was a question with a human face, a face with a name. Unlike Pinker, Leonard's spaniel, Nellie was a mongrel, without pedigree, a cultural halfbreed, between the castes (the word had racial overtones too), neither one thing nor the other, belonging nowhere. She was also, by association, part of the rubbish, a byproduct of the system which Virginia blamed on her parents' generation, and which now wasted their time and made the conversations so 'sordid'.

Virginia saw herself as passive in the face of 'the system'; Nellie was 'uneducated', trying to 'let herself in' to a world to which she did not belong. But education was not simply a matter of learning or schooling. Virginia was herself ambivalent about the formal education which she had missed, sometimes attacking the inequalities which had led to her remaining at home while her male peers attended public school and university, at other times deeply scathing about 'schoolmastering', the narrowness of university dons (especially those who taught English literature), and the competitive, prize-winning mentality which struck her as ludicrous and demeaning. She saw it as profoundly masculine, and both *A Room of One's Own* and *Three Guineas* hope that women might create a different model of education. As more people were becoming literate, there were debates across the political spectrum as to what might constitute a vibrant education for the working classes, one which would go beyond the rote-learning and exam-passing which merely pushed people into jobs. Yet when Virginia called herself 'uneducated', as she often did, she was playing down the advantages that growing up in a bookish, articulate home had conferred on her, the cultural confidence or cultural capital she had inherited – and which other people so clearly lacked. 'Culture' was by definition unavailable to *arrivistes*, foreigners – especially Americans – and the lower orders; most of the middle class were also philistine as were the aristocrats (Vita Sackville-West, for instance, had a perfect body but was a 'donkey' when it came to brains). Vanessa put it frankly: alone in Cassis with Angelica and Grace, it seemed silly not to eat together but she missed 'grown up educated companions'. Grace was 'extraordinarily nice', Vanessa wrote to Virginia, but

she is, like all the uneducated, completely empty-headed really, and after a bit gets terribly on one's nerves. She either asks me questions, which it is obvious she could answer as well as I can, or she tells me things she has already told me dozens of times about the Harlands [Keynes's servants]. One has practically no common ground in common. I am rather interested to see what does happen with the lower classes, as Grace is a very good specimen, not only unusually nice, but much more ready than most to try to understand other things, reading all she can get hold of and making desperate efforts towards culture.

Nonetheless Grace's 'desperate efforts' were doomed. Vanessa added, 'there's something I suppose in having educated grandparents, for already Angelica [aged eight] is capable of understanding things in a way one can see Grace never will'. Vanessa looked forward to ending her 'inquiries into the lower class mind' when Duncan Grant arrived and Grace was 'relegated' to the kitchen again. Meanwhile Virginia's solution to Nellie's encroachment on her territory was to opt for a 'complete renovation of domestic life'. She would write her orders for dinner in a book, 'thus putting a glass between' herself and Nellie. It's hard to see how this would help.

*

Virginia blamed the liberal attitudes of her set for Nellie's discontent: it was 'the fruit of Bloomsbury'. But attitudes were changing everywhere, and Nellie was well aware that plenty of 'other girls' had different expectations, and were no longer prepared as she and Lottie had been to sleep in one room without proper heating and ventilation. Live-in service appealed less and less to younger women who, as the 20s wore on, increasingly had other options:

clerical, shop or factory work, work as a waitress or a chamber-maid, receptionist, florist, beautician, anything that gave them their evenings or weekends off, the freedom to meet friends, or simply to stay at home. Service was more and more seen as 'Victorian', anachronistic and demeaning. If the mistress was a tartar or the position particularly isolated, the maid was 'expected to belong body and soul' to the job, according to a Ministry of Labour report in 1923, the first of many anxious studies of the 'service problem'. Shop-girls, they said, looked down on factory girls, but everyone now looked down on servants. The very term was derogatory – 'domestic' or 'domestic worker' being preferred. Meanwhile Nellie's generation was growing old in the job.

In fact the total number of servants had been declining since the 1890s. Although there was a surge during the industrial recession of the early 1930s, only a quarter of the total female labour force worked in indoor domestic service between the wars, as opposed to a third at the turn of the century. The appeal of live-in service was definitely on the wane. Nonetheless the number of women, in 'personal service' was still greater than in any other occupational group: giving or taking orders was the most common relationship between women. After the First World War the apparent shortage of servants led to a number of laments about the fecklessness of young working-class women 'stealing' men's jobs. In the wake of working-class militancy, the government made stringent efforts to maintain continuity with the past, pressurizing those women, who lost their wartime occupations when the men returned, to don apron and cap once more. The *Saturday Review* put it succinctly: 'Abolish the dole for unmarried women and you abolish the servant problem.' Class distinctions still obtained, however. Munitions workers were offered domestic work while their former lady supervisors found similar posts in 'management' – training and placing working-class women for the domestic sector.

In the early 1920s the right-wing press stirred up indignation at the 'Scandals of the Dole', the existence of 'the thousands upon thousands of women' drawing benefits who 'ought' to be in domestic service, though thousands in the textile or mining areas of Britain had never been servants. The more genteel of the women's magazines editorialized on the way in which the 'refined and educated housewife of the middle-classes' who couldn't find domestic help was being needlessly worn out and 'crushed with work that is far beyond their physical strength'. The health of the nation was felt to be at stake and such discussions often had a eugenicist tinge: 'the women who are really the most valuable to the community' were being exhausted while poorer 'specimens' were receiving the dole and 'literally undermining the health of the race'. One outraged young wife wrote to the papers that women like herself were 'not going to undertake the responsibilities of motherhood when they cannot get servants on reasonable terms and conditions'. The assumption that girls from poor homes ought automatically to go into service as their 'station' in life was difficult to budge. In 1920 the Ministry of Labour's Central Committee on Women's Training and Employment (CCWTE) had assessed women's work and the prospects for the future. It concluded that 'domestic service is the only occupation under existing conditions for which training would show an immediate return and in which there was a shortage of workers'.

Part of the problem of the 'missing maids' lay in the ever-increasing demand from the ever-expanding middle class, which now included a high proportion of salaried 'white-collar workers', as well as professionals and businessmen. Many of the accountants, managers, civil servants, teachers and solicitors, or the skilled workers in engineering or the light industries who now made up 'the salariat' were buying (or mortgaging) the four million new houses built between the wars. In the bigger detached properties on the edges of towns, accommodation existed for perhaps one or even two servants living in, but there was little of the physical separation between mistress and maid, the old spatial divisions of the five-storey house with its servants tucked away below stairs or behind the green baize door. In the new semis and flats, the servant was often in the next room, in a cubbyhole

off the kitchen or 'lounge'. If solitary servants were more prone
to their mistress's scrutiny, mistresses also felt their activities (or
lack of them) were more on show. The thinness of walls was
often literal but it was felt psychologically and emotionally. What
Virginia had experienced as uncomfortably close quarters in their
cottage at Rodmell was becoming the norm in a number of town
residences.

Plenty of servants joined Nellie in complaining of loneliness.
Between the wars British households went on shrinking and there
were fewer confederacies in the kitchen or in 'the area' outside
the kitchen door. Gradually too, the regular callers, the hawkers
and pedlars, who had been so much a part of the Victorian street,
began to diminish: telephones still meant deliveries for the more
affluent, but in the new suburbs, domestics could become
marooned.

Of course many of the new lower-middle class could not afford
a resident servant, though they might manage a daily or a char.
The ideal modern housewife in her new airy kitchen overlooking
the garden, with electricity and 'hot and cold' laid on, was expected
to perform her chores cheerfully and effortlessly, oscillating between
her roles as a skilled 'technician' wielding appliances, manager and
consumer in the ideal home. In fact the much fabled 'labour-saving
devices' were initially rather humble improvements, like the introduction of stainless steel cutlery that could be soaked in vinegar as
opposed to silver, which required constant cleaning. Vacuum
cleaners, electric cookers and water-heaters were beyond most
pockets; washing machines and fridges an unthought-of luxury.
Even by 1945 only 20 per cent of British homes had an electric
cooker, 15 per cent had a water-heater, 4 per cent a washing machine
and a mere 2 per cent a fridge. If fewer servants were immured in
dark and dingy basements staring at the chocolate brown or sickly
green paint, British kitchen design nonetheless changed very little
in the majority of homes: some might have a fitted cabinet with
a fold-down flap but most kitchens still had a table in the centre
and a dusty dresser for the crocks. Equipment mostly dated back
to the last century. There might be aluminium pans rather than

those hefty iron or copper ones, and a sink that was white enamel rather than cement, with a few white tiles for a splashback behind if you were lucky – but the eternal kitchen pail would be lodged underneath.

An increasing number of households were obliged to deal with servants on a one-to-one basis and were finding it difficult. In a time of expanding social mobility it was both harder and more crucial to signal your distance from the class below. Servants had long been given inferior accommodation with 'suitable' furniture, and they went on receiving different food, sleeping in different beds (shops sold 'servants' beds' of 2' 6" not 3'), using separate lavatories and bathrooms, or making do with a 'toilet set' in their room and a poorer brand of soap. Mistresses continued setting tests for their honesty – coins deliberately left lying about was a common one; they went on counting the number of biscuits in the barrel or, literally, cheeseparing. New equipment could be jealously guarded: at least one mistress wouldn't let her 'general' use the electric iron in case she fused it, and had her heat up an old iron on the gas instead. Distinctions were resented far more in smaller households. Handing a newspaper or the post to one's employer on a platter was standard parlourmaid practice; in a large household it might feel bearable but when there were only two at home it was humiliating. Most mistresses insisted on uniform, which girls were usually expected to buy from their pay; they wanted to be 'Ma'am' or 'Madam', and some still gave permission to sit and the order to stand when the maid was in their presence; employers felt entitled to go through a maid's room, to comment on her clothes, to ban cosmetics, long hair, sheer or 'nude' stockings and to monitor how time off was spent. Nonetheless it baffled the mistresses that girls who would have been living in far worse conditions at home were not more grateful.

According to the upper classes, the 'wrong' people were employing servants and did not know how to deal with them. The new suburbanites were an easy marque, yet the well-to-do could be every bit as mean or rude. Working for Lady Cranborne in the 1920s her lady's maid, Rosina Harrison, was still earning

£24 a year after five years, and when her requests for an increase were flatly, 'almost rudely', turned down she decided to leave. 'I don't know whether there was a conspiracy among the upper classes to keep servants' wages down,' she later recalled, 'but everyone I knew in service at that time met with the same brick-wall attitude.' Frequently those who had the money refused to modernize their homes. Why bother buying a vacuum cleaner or installing hot water for the top of the house? (At Eaton Hall in Cheshire, for instance, the Duke of Westminster had fifty indoor servants and forty gardeners; 'a ratio of three to four to each member of the family was quite normal' in the wealthiest houses.) Visiting the bathroom in the Bells' country house in Wiltshire in the late 1920s, Vanessa's small daughter, Angelica, enjoyed covering 'her excrement like a cat' using a tiny shovel and pan for the ashes. The well-to-do Bells presumably didn't see the point of flush toilets when there were servants to do the emptying. The USA had water-heaters, vacuum cleaners, toasters, kettles, fridges long before the British, whose need to go on being served was as much emotional as economic. 'Let electricity be your servant' became the slogan of the Electricity Board and many of the 'labour-saving devices', such as vacuum cleaners, were marketed with snob appeal as mechanical servants. Gradually the better-off began buying the goods which helped reduce the time spent on domestic labour in the home. Ironically, such goods were being produced in the factories and on the assembly lines by the very same girls and women who might otherwise have been laying fires and baking biscuits in their mistresses' kitchens. The difference was that more working-class women were leaving older forms of deference behind.

The idea of more equal relations with one's cook was frequently canvassed but breaking ranks was still deemed full of dangers. Popular magazines, newspapers, cartoons all made short shrift of any pretensions on the Georgian cook's part. A 1923 Ministry of Labour report noted that a reference to the domestic worker's lack of opportunity 'to cultivate a talent for music aroused only ridicule and sarcasm in the daily press'. Employers routinely discouraged aspirations on the part of their domestics which they thought 'inappropriate' – tennis, for instance. Reading was often frowned upon. Servants themselves were less interested in higher wages than in time off and self-respect. They began to want what other workers had and what their mistresses had too: personal freedom and to be treated like individuals, to be called Miss or Mr, and not by surname or Christian name; not to wear uniform (especially the hated cap). 'Recreations' were considered paramount; one maid contributing to a BBC's symposium on domestic service in 1930 maintained, 'I think the wireless must come first.' There were stories of employers who forbad their domestics from 'listening in'; one told her charge that she could listen through the closed drawing-room door, another confiscated the wireless for a punishment when her servant overslept. The more liberal took the view that the answer lay in improving personal relations: service was a moral problem issue left over from the more servile traditions of the past and could be solved, as Violet Markham, the chair of the CCWTE put it, summing up for the BBC symposium, by 'mutual respect, goodwill, and consideration'.

Many older servants were affronted by change. Stripped of paternalism and deference, or of the Christian ideal of self-sacrifice, service looked cheapened in their eyes and they missed their old privileges and the borrowed esteem. Many found it hard to adjust to new equipment which could be intimidating and felt like 'de-skilling'; there were plenty who insisted that a stiff old brush did the job better than the new-fangled carpet-sweeper or vacuum cleaner. Others maintained that the advantages of a job in service always outweighed the temporary freedoms of factory or shop work. Becoming a skilled cook, for instance, could lead to a job for life, and be taken up after marriage, or indeed widowhood; ex-servants were considered quieter and more refined than factory girls. It was also easier to save, and the old arguments were reiterated that such girls made better wives and were more able to 'settle down' after marriage. Those servants who worked in the 'big houses' were especially likely to vote Conservative with their employers, and *The Times* liked to carry obituaries throughout the period extolling the virtues of 'Faithful Servants', a response, perhaps, to the fact that at the start of the 30s over a third of London servants moved on within the year.

In the 1920s and 30s there were endless attempts to bully or coax girls into service. Most revolved around the idea of raising the status of the work. Training schools sporting new certificates and badges, charitable agencies that offered clubs and socials for girls on their own, the new language of domestic 'science' in schools, all hoped to keep service buoyant. None of them ultimately worked. No one suggested that housework or childcare would be valued more highly, or at least reorganized, if shared with men: the shift was towards the middle-class mistress taking on more housewifely duties. The new women's magazines, like the government reports and committees, subscribed to the notion that the home was essentially a woman's responsibility and pleasure and therefore that no girl could be better employed than in helping another woman to bring up her children and make home comfortable for the breadwinner. The domesticated husband of the interwar years might roll back his shirtsleeves to potter in the garden or tinker with the car but only the very rare or eccentric man would learn to cook. When the servants were ill or away, considerate husbands like Leonard Woolf and Adrian Stephen mucked in and made beds or even, at a pinch, helped with the washing-up; impossible, though, to expect them to mop floors or wring out 'smalls'.

Of course there have been unhappy servants as long as there has been domestic service. Nellie Boxall was one of a majority throughout history who have made their presence felt through surliness or tears, downright disobedience, petty acts of revenge (like spitting in the soup) or vicious talk. Between the wars, however, those who remained in service started to draw on the new vocabularies of trade unionism, feminism and popular psychology, however inappropriate, to articulate a sense of grievance and an expectation of rights, a language which took their complaints out of what had been deemed the purely private sphere. Scruples, anxieties and alarms about service were responding to the slow democratization of Britain. When women finally gained the franchise on equal terms in 1928, maids became able to vote alongside their mistresses. It now seemed distinctly possible that 'the bad spirit', which Violet Markham identified on the BBC and which she feared 'may seize on a house', was another instance of 'the class war'.

Although feminists and socialists might campaign for the poor, few were strictly egalitarian and plenty assumed that housework was beneath them or that others were more suited to it. In the early 20s the feminist journal *Time and Tide* had taken issue with the Hulton and Rothermere presses, reminding its readers that the majority of people in Britain did not have servants, and arguing that the modern young woman did not want to be a domestic, printing the views of one ex-housemaid in support. Yet middle-class feminists rarely did without servants themselves. Vera Brittain, feminist campaigner and frequent contributor to *Time and Tide*, whose unconventional household was shared with her husband and her close friend, Winifred Holtby, depended utterly on two devoted servants, Amy and Charles Burnett. This didn't prevent her from bemoaning the lot of 'the creative woman perpetually at the mercy of the "Fifth Column" below stairs'. Brittain argued for a better developed system of domestic service, while sharing the general consensus that such activities were 'a waste' of time for more educated or intelligent women. In *The Cause*, her history of the Women's Movement published in 1928, Ray Strachey cheered her readers with the news that service was now 'a less dreary and dismal trade', thanks to the disappearance of basements and flights of stairs, and the fact that tobacco – 'the great comforter of small woes' – had made its way into every scullery.

Labour Party commentators saw the issue as belonging outside the sphere of industrial relations: service could never be fully politicized since conditions could not be standardized. The language of class antagonism, however, began to filter into discussions in the press and elsewhere. In 1930, when the Charity Organization Society reviewed the subject, it protested so much that domestic service 'is not a class question' or a matter of 'hostile camps' that it helped ensure it was seen as such. Young girls were apparently 'growing daily more "class conscious"', thought the liberal and well-meaning novelist Leonora Eyles (Mrs D. M. Murray), writing in 1931, putting the awkward term into inverted commas. Eyles agreed that personal service like valeting had to go but argued, like others, that service had the social good of the community at stake: girls 'have not yet learnt to serve us from the ethical point of view', she wrote – but, with encouragement, they would. A number of ladies tried swapping places with servants in order to investigate conditions in the kitchen, in much the same spirit as George Orwell when he went 'down and out' amongst the tramps in London and Paris. They all suggested that class was equally a matter of feeling ('inferiority complex' was a handy phrase), so that while conditions might be improved and payment raised, the basic problem might go unaddressed. According to Violet Firth, one of those who experimented with life below stairs and published her findings, being better friends with your servants, understanding 'the servant psychology', employing women as equals or training specialized assistants would alleviate matters.

In May 1929 when the Labour Party looked set for victory, the British public had the novelty of hearing the election results on the wireless. Politics was becoming a shared national experience. At Monk's House Virginia was 'shocked' when Nellie said at tea, 'We are winning,' shocked to think that both she and Nellie wanted the Labour Party to win. 'Why?' Virginia asked herself, characteristically probing the sore spot, 'partly that I dont want to be ruled by Nelly. I think to be ruled by Nelly and Lottie would be a disaster.' It hadn't occurred to her that while Leonard talked to miners, there might be a common political cause between mistress and maid. Had Nellie deliberately enjoyed shocking her or just assumed that they were on the same side? Perhaps she had simply voted with her employers as the servants in the country houses were prone to do. Driving home from the polls in Lewes, Virginia noticed there were no lights on – no celebration or crowds or shouts – only a man 'pumpshipping' against a wall, and three black cats 'out on business with the mice', images of the sordid and the predatory. 'So we shall be ruled by labour,' she concluded. Government meant being ruled and, for Virginia, being ruled in any form always meant tyranny.

Lottie and Nellie

*

The year in which Virginia Woolf began to draft *The Waves*, her most experimental and inward work – 1929 – was also the year when a revolution took place in Monk's House kitchen: Mrs Woolf began to cook dinner. The Woolfs replaced the old solid fuel kitchen-range, which ate up wood or coal and needed plenty of manual labour to stoke it and nurture it, with a modern oil stove. Anyone could cook sausages or stews in glass dishes 'without smell, waste or confusion', those bugbears of the bourgeois home:

one turns the handles; there is a thermometer. And so I see myself freer, more independent – & all one's life is a struggle for freedom – able to come down here with a chop in a bag & live on my own. I go over the dishes I shall cook – the rich stews, the sauces. The adventurous strange dishes with dashes of wine in them.

She wrote gaily to Vita that it made her 'free forever of cooks. I cooked veal cutlets and cake today. I assure you it is better than writing these idiotic books.' Without children, without a large household to run, with increasing income, new gadgets and regular help, Mrs Woolf, like other middle-class women, could afford to enjoy domesticity. Unlike many of them, her ultimate fantasy of freedom was to live on her own; to be able at last, in her late forties, to fend for herself.

Independence was the keynote of that summer. In June, the month of the oil stove, she finished revising *A Room of One's Own*, and noted that 'this last half year I made over £1800; almost at the rate of £4000 a year; the salary almost of a Cabinet minister; & time was, two years ago, when I toiled to make £200'. The Woolfs had long planned an extension to Monk's House and now, thanks to *Orlando*, Mr Philcox was adding on a bedroom and writing room for Virginia, overlooking the garden and downs. The attic became Leonard's study. Virginia still wrote in the garden 'lodge' in warm weather but she was at last to have the room of her own which her earnings had afforded her. Brought up without extravagance she could now enjoy buying things, including 'desks, tables, sideboards, crockery for Rodmell', corner cupboards, beds from Heal's; she commissioned Vanessa and friends to design fireplace tiles, armchair covers or table tops and curtains, drawing on her 'hoard', the excess of income which was left to her after Leonard had worked out the year's joint expenses. She warned herself, however, about becoming too attached to property, disliking the display of possessions in a friend's plush home: 'Can one really be in love with a house? Is there not something sterile, so that one's mind becomes stringy in these passions?' Her goal was freedom, though that too could become 'a fetish', but it remained the justification for comfort or trying out new gadgets, or even experimenting with her appearance. In 1927 Virginia was 'bingled' and bobbed, feeling hugely liberated from long hair and hairpins: 'In front there is no change; behind I'm like the rump of a partridge' (she later grew it back). In the late 30s she even wore trousers, finding them liberating.

The Woolfs had long slept separately, but separate beds were frequently welcomed in the period among the middle classes as a sign of the 'companionate' marriage and an advance on the invasive intimacies of Victorian life. It was also thought more aristocratic. Only the poor had to tumble together willy-nilly. With eight siblings, Leonard too was the child of a crowded nursery. The garden became very much his territory, growing into a vegetable empire to which he added substantial glasshouses and exotic plants reminiscent of Ceylon. Leonard spent his 'hoard' on a new oak gate, on embedding millstones for a path to the front of the house, and, in 1931, a garage. Three years earlier the Woolfs had bought a field, adding an acre to the garden and putting up a fence to keep the cottage children out – 'my first act as a land-owner', Virginia noted uneasily. Monk's House was a much more bourgeois version of the country-house life; it allowed for far more autonomy and individual privacy than the obligations towards a network of dependants which usually characterized a patrician existence. But it was not a matter of doing without servants altogether. Leonard purchased a cottage for his gardener in the village – rent-free but tied to the job. Writing to the owner, a Captain Byng-Stamper, he sounded like a landed gentleman as he offered to 'make arrangements for my man to go into the cottage'. Virginia, however, joked about this quasi-feudalism in her diary – 'Percy is our man!' Percy Bartholomew, his wife, Lydia, and three children, moved into 1 Park Cottages, a two-up, two-down flint-faced terraced house with a privy in the yard and a patch of rough grass at the front; water was drawn from a well by bucket; summer and winter alike they relied on an old solid fuel range for heating and cooking. In 1929 Percy earnt £2 a week and was seldom to get a day off: Leonard's greenhouse heaters needed stoking at dawn and checking again last thing at night.

Virginia certainly wanted to be free of giving orders. The summer of 1929 was also the summer of the most violent, explosive rows with Nellie, those 'painful, ridiculous, agitating' scenes which drove Virginia constantly to her diary to anatomize the 'loathesome spectacle' of human nature 'undressed'. Nellie's presence felt all the more oppressive at the beginning of a new book when Virginia, like many artists, needed to submerge everything – 'to be thinking, feeling or seeing' only the embryonic work. She had begun drafting *The Waves*. Constant domestic interruptions from Nellie, visiting Leonard's querulous mother or entertaining a string of visitors, all jerked her out of that inner world into which she needed to disappear. It was a hectic summer which took its toll in headaches and melancholy. When Nellie's niece Gladys came to stay, they all drove over to Charleston. 'Having Nelly in the car is to me a strain,' she noted, 'imposes another forced atmosphere.' Like Dickens, who felt refreshed and rejuvenated after his 'confidential interviews with himself', when she was immersed in writing, Virginia felt 'everything is green and revivified in me'. Otherwise she could be 'psychologically tired'. Such changes of gear wrenched her out of her 'premonitions' of the next book. Illness might provide the necessary insulation and 'fertilise' her mind, and she had imagined earlier in the summer how 'six weeks in bed now would make a masterpiece of Moths' (an early title for *The Waves*). When she wasn't working she might lose her moorings, 'sinking down, down' to the bottom of what she saw as the solemn truth of life: 'the fact that there is nothing – nothing for any of us. Work, reading, writing, are all disguises; & relations with people. Yes, even having children would be useless.'

That year – 1929 – was to be the last summer with Nellie in residence. Virginia found it very wearing, though she tried to understand Nellie's position. When Nellie picked seven pounds of blackberries to make jam, Woolf noted that it was 'her way of thanking me for having Lottie – after all, she has no other. And one tends to forget it.' (Lottie had been dismissed by the Stephens in May but was taken back on eventually.) Nellie was especially redundant in Rodmell where there were always women wanting to help and whose need for a little cash was desperate. Virginia was well aware of the 'incubus of injustice' which weighed down the village women: 'Annie Thompsett and her baby live on 15/-

a week. I throw away 13/- on cigarettes, chocolates, & bus fares. She was eating rice pudding by the baby's cradle when I came in.' Thinking of her own privileged life she noted that 'if I were Mrs Bartholomew [Percy's wife] I should certainly do something violent'. When Annie, 'up against this terrific high black prison-wall of poverty', came asking to work for them as their permanent 'daily', Woolf grabbed at the chance. They could leave 'poor, dear Nelly' in London and help someone whose need was much greater. Meanwhile Nellie continued to dig her own grave: she had just given notice again 'over Leonard's coal scuttle', presumably at having to fill and carry it too often.

With Annie in mind the Woolfs had bought 2 Park Cottages, the one next door to the Bartholomews, for another £350, quite a bargain since pairs of cottages were selling for £1,200 a couple, Virginia noted in her diary in 1927, and village property was a good investment. Leonard saw no more contradiction between socialism and landlordism than he did in arguing trenchantly for Indian Independence while investing in Ceylon Para Rubber or Burmah Oil, United Dairies or Great Southern Railways. The tied cottage was a familiar way of life to farmworkers used to the nineteenth-century estates and Leonard, who had been accustomed to a huge staff of clerks and servants in Ceylon, combined a strict paternalism with strenuous work for the village's self-improvement. The cottage was certainly a godsend for Annie, while a good economy for the Woolfs. Young, willing and grateful, Annie was far more appealing to Virginia. With Nellie away, Annie came in the mornings and made lunch, often leaving a pie for Virginia to cook for dinner. By three o'clock the Woolfs were alone – a complete and utter novelty. It is worth emphasizing. They had never been alone before in their own home. Thus the life of the British modern couple was inaugurated.

Back in London that autumn there were more scenes at Tavistock Square, culminating in the ultimate reversal of roles: Nellie ordered Virginia out of her room. The irony of Nellie feeling able to dismiss Virginia – a measure of Nellie's independence – when Virginia had just published *A Room of One's Own* went unremarked. Nellie had got above herself; in reality the room was not 'hers'. Being treated like a servant was so painful and humiliating that Virginia went straight to Leonard and determined to sack Nellie by Christmas. The 'famous scene' was relived in her imagination many times. She found herself muttering and rehearsing arguments, unable to work, sick and shivery, trembling with anticipation at the forthcoming day – 17 November – when she would give Nellie a month's notice. She wrote her diary as if possessed, copying out replies to Nellie, speaking their parts. Yet Nellie took her notice calmly, saving face by claiming she had already given it. Virginia therefore suspected that she had no more intention of going than she, Virginia, had of sailing to Siberia.

Nonetheless Virginia excitedly imagined doing without her. The oil stove, Annie, new rooms at Rodmell and Leonard giving up the literary editorship of the *Nation*, would all be part of that 'great advance towards freedom which is the ideal state of the soul'. As if she were the servant, she reassured her imaginary reader that she hadn't really suffered from 'servitude' but threw off any chain 'directly she felt it' (rather an overstatement). It wasn't to be that simple. With fewer chances in life and limited prospects now that live-in servants were less in demand, what choice had Nellie but to 'weaken', as Virginia put it, in the battle of wills? She had far more to lose.

After the outburst Nellie softened and, though Virginia tried to remain stiff and angry, Leonard advised another talk, and they 'were landed; not emotionally, rather wearatedly & disillusionedly on my part' in a compromise from January. They would try out a char for a month to help Nellie. Mrs Mansfield, the caretaker who lived in the basement of 37 Gordon Square, where Duncan and Vanessa had rooms, would come in to do more of the rough (cleaning steps, floors and lavatories, washing-up were the usual requirements).

Virginia kept her misery largely to herself. The days of writing regularly to her sister about the servants were over now that Vanessa was settled with Grace Germany. Diary-writing helped her survive her own demons but it was not to be trusted: 'whom do I tell when I tell a blank page?' she wondered, knowing that while she might appear to be confiding, 'something was always suppressed'. 'Certainly it is true that if one writes a thing down one has done with it,' she maintained; yet the opposite was the case. The diary never worked as exorcism. Always she meant to 'get nearer feelings' and 'have them out', but it was 'boring' to write down what was so 'acutely exciting' at the time. Virginia blamed her lack of narrative power – she couldn't tell stories, liked to enter minds, but she imagined how much the story might inspire a random reader like herself. In December 1929 she wrote, 'If I were reading this diary, if it were a book that came my way, I think I should seize with greed on the portrait of Nelly, and make a story – perhaps make the whole story revolve around that – it would amuse me. Her character – our efforts to get rid of her – our reconciliations.' The trouble was that there was no development in the scenes with Nellie; they merely repeated. Woolf never found a way to ironize or make light of their relations, to impersonate 'Cook' as others were cheerfully doing in novels or on the stage. When she wrote 'living portraits' or 'lives of the obscure', she always feared turning character into caricature as she felt some of the new biographies did. In the end the diary could not be edited nor the attachment cut down to size. And, of course, any 'Portrait of Nelly' would have to be a 'Portrait of Virginia'.

Woolf distrusted her tendency in the diary to make her feelings 'more creditable' to herself. She rarely, for instance, recorded the actual nature of Nellie's complaints. There were veiled references to 'accusations' and to the Woolfs' not giving Nellie extra help when she was ill. Nellie suffered from swollen ankles and a bad back, but her ailments appeared vaguely comical or a nuisance. Then, in May 1930 she was taken seriously ill, was hospitalized and had a kidney removed. She was liable to be off for months. Virginia set to writing letters to registries, interviewing potential domestics, as well as provisioning, and for once had a glimpse of what it might actually mean to be a housewife, though Annie came up to London and Mrs Mansfield went on cleaning: 'How

any woman with a family ever put pen to paper I cannot fathom.'
Virginia took Nellie to the hospital and what with doctors, planning and cooking dinner, found she had lost a fortnight's work.
Leonard ploughed on regardless. There was a series of temporary
dailies – an elderly Frenchwoman, Mrs Taupin, who couldn't cope;
then Mrs Margaret Walter, an American journalist, whose son was
at King's, Cambridge, and who moved in socialist circles. Her
no-nonsense approach made Virginia dread all the more having
Nellie 'in control again'. On her way to convalesce for the summer,
Nellie appeared briefly – 'obliging friendly affectionate'. Virginia
was barely civil. 'I cannot bring myself to talk to her as I should.
I am always seeing myself told to "leave my room".' The quiet
evenings in London – 'the absence of lower classes' – was a 'divine
relief'.

In the spring of 1930 the Woolfs had decided to live rather
more at Rodmell; they were eventually to spend about a third of
the year in Sussex. The extension to the house was finished and
Virginia had a writing room and bedroom, rooms of her own at
last – 'what I've always hoped for'. As she hoped, the summer of
1930 was blissful, the happiest since they had bought the house,
even 'occasionally sublime' because of the absence of servants, 'the
groundwork and bedrock' on which this 'expansion' rested. It was
like taking off boots when one had swollen feet (an analogy which
put her in Nellie's shoes). Over and again she declared, not without
a certain bravado, to Vita, to 'Dadie' Rylands (neither, one imagines, a dab hand in the kitchen): 'our happiness is being without
a cook'. There was more produce to be had from the garden –
asparagus, raspberries – and one evening she served up 'two chops,
broiled in gravy with green peas'. Without Nellie's presence 'at a
different angle' from theirs, with only 'nice bright Annie', they
were free from lunch till breakfast. Virginia found both cooking
and being able to wander into any of the rooms in the house a
huge liberation and resource. She was living 'without terrors &
constrictions' and felt 'more & more attracted by looseness, freedom
& eating one's dinner off a table anywhere, having cooked it
previously'.

The interregnum increased Virginia's resolve. In September she placed an advertisement in *Time and Tide*, the feminist journal: 'Woman of intelligence and initiative wanted to do entire work of flat, WC1, for two writers. Live out. Good cooking essential. Might suit two friends half-day each. Wages by arrangement. Long summer holidays, also at Easter and Christmas.' Meanwhile they 'played a game of diplomacy' with Nellie's doctor, Alan McGlashan, paying her wages but asking not to have her back till she was well. He wrote praising their generosity and decency, quite ignorant of their plotting. That autumn the Woolfs employed Mary Rivett-Carnac, a daughter of the Anglo-Indian middle classes, a perfect lady (that is, 'enough to be careless of being one', Virginia observed in her diary). In her mid-thirties, she had 'been through a good deal: social work; hostels; running clubs' and Virginia imagined a sad life, fleshing out her character, 'perhaps, vengeful, acid, worn, trusty, starved of happiness'. There were problems employing the more genteel. Mrs Walters had proved too expensive in her upmarket tastes, and giving orders to a lady with a double-barrelled name was tricky: did one call her 'Rivett' or 'Carnac', Woolf wondered, trailing off after 'Miss . . .'? Dailies were paid a higher wage, £1 a week, though checking her 'books', Virginia found that without Nellie she could save that much on weekly groceries. In 1930 their weekly accounts came out at around £5 a week (bills included the butcher, the milk and 'the wash', which was sent out). Rivett was a poor cook (too keen on tapioca) and a little too refined for cleaning and scrubbing. Leonard took against her, though Virginia considered her a nice woman. Privately she thought 'Annie – forever'. Annie Thompsett, Woolf reported, had been reluctant to give up helping in London: 'how can I put up with Rodmell now, she says', but having a small child made it impossible to work full-time. Perhaps, in any case, Woolf mused, it would be for the best: 'livers out' were preferable.

The temporizing had to end. Early in October, Nellie reappeared, wanting her job back, very much 'the old & trusted servant'. Virginia boasted about her lovability to her new admirer, the composer Ethel Smyth: all her domestics became impossibly attached to her, 'nothing I can do will prevent their loving me! hahhah!' (a flirtatious warning to Ethel, who had declared herself smitten with Virginia). She wrote a long, frank and friendly letter of dismissal to Nellie, whose 'good humour, sense and niceness' she could now acknowledge, fooling herself that Nellie wouldn't mind much, and would anyway expect it. Surely Nellie knew that relations between them had changed since 'the famous scene last November' and that they were already doing without her? Nellie was furious and refused to be turned off. She outmanoeuvred the Woolfs, appealing to Dr McGlashan, who innocently wrote that there must have been 'a misunderstanding': Nellie was now perfectly able to come back to work. Virginia felt 'Nelly's pistol' at her head and dreaded an interview – 'we're in for a visit and a tempest of rage'. There were two hours of exhausting and affectionate talk on a November evening, but it was this 'dependence & intimacy' which Woolf found 'a psychological strain'. Nevertheless her diary recorded their exchanges in the same kind of 'infinite minuteness' she so loathed:

> Still I can't understand why you won't have me back …
> But Nelly, you gave me notice 10 times in the past 6 years – & more …
> But I always took it back.
> Yes, but that sort of thing gets on the nerves.
> Oh ma'am I never meant to tire you – dont go on talking now if it tires you – but you wouldn't give me any help. Now Grace [at Charleston] has all the help she wants – Well, I says, this is long service.
> But then Nelly you forgot that when you were with us.
> But then for 3 years I've been ill. And I shall never like any mistress as much as I like you …

The 'senseless reiteration of grievances' drove Woolf frantic, like the endless gossip which ricocheted between servants and employers. But their stories were their territory and each stuck to her guns. Having one's affairs inspected by servants, Virginia wrote, was like 'frying in greasy pans'. Nellie must go: that was the diary's final word as she enjoyed pitying 'poor old Nelly'. But by the start of 1931, she had again relented. Nellie was back – but only for three months. She stayed another three years.

★

At the height of her most bitter rows with Nellie, Virginia had been thinking about the room a woman needed if she was to write, the psychological, emotional space as well as the literal, physical separation from others. The ideal author with both money and leisure would be impersonal and detached. She would write novels which would no longer be 'the dumping ground for the personal emotions' (another image of feelings as bodily waste) and she would avoid 'pleading and protesting'. In *A Room of One's Own*, she imagined such a writer would be creatively androgynous, like Shakespeare or Jane Austen, with a mind which 'had consumed all impediments' and was 'woman-manly, man-womanly'. The 'one' of her title underscored the sexlessness or rather, the both-sexedness of this ideal state of mind: singular, complete and self-contained. 'One' was also, of course, polite usage and firmly placed both writer and reader within the middle classes (a room of 'your' own would have been unthinkable), like the £500 a year, the amount which Virginia suggested as a putative income. Very few women could expect that level of income in 1929, unless, like Virginia, from invested capital, and a full-time job at this salary would hardly provide the freedom to write. But this was the point: denied education, unable to own property after marriage until the 1880s, unable to enter any of the professions until Woolf's own time, 'women have always been poor', she argued, and 'intellectual freedom depends upon material things', like health and money, and the houses we live in.

That summer and autumn of 1929, the last summer with Nellie in residence, Virginia returned again and again to the question of material things and to the nature of the differences between people: the social and cultural but also the physical differences.

How had such differences come about and how critical was the history of our bodies in shaping our mental lives? In both the drafting of *The Waves* and in her polemical writing she pushed hard against her own prejudices, her instinctive, perhaps instinctual reactions to getting closer to the poor; she wrestled with the problem of how to represent those who could not yet – or so it seemed – represent themselves, either in writing or in politics. Was it possible, or indeed desirable, ever to speak for others? The impasse with Nellie, her glimpses of the lives of women like Annie Thompsett, eating rice pudding by her child's cradle, were part of an inquiry into the ways in which human beings made sense of themselves and formed their identities, through their relations of love and hate: 'how curiously one is changed by the addition, even at a distance, of a friend,' says Neville, one of the voices in *The Waves*, and how incessantly 'one's self' is 'adulterated, mixed up, become part of another'.

A Room of One's Own was prompted by the silences in conventional accounts of the past, the absence of women and of women's history. It was one of many works by women in the period which tried to address their exclusion. 'This book is chiefly concerned with the kitchens of history,' wrote the medievalist Eileen Power, introducing her bestselling *Medieval People*, whose work Virginia certainly knew (Power was a close friend of Karin Stephen). In an eloquent passage, Woolf wrote of the 'infinitely obscure lives' of women which 'remained to be recorded', meaning not only the shabby genteel 'Mrs Browns', or the ladies whose often thwarted existences she had already limned in her own 'Lives of the Obscure', but working women, poor women. Encountering the denizens of the London streets she imagined feeling 'the pressure of dumbness, the accumulation of unrecorded life'

whether from the women at the street corners with their arms akimbo, and the rings embedded in their fat swollen fingers, talking with a gesticulation like the swing of Shakespeare's words; or from the violet-sellers and match-sellers and old crones stationed under doorways; or from drifting girls whose faces, like waves in sun and cloud, signal the coming of men and women and the flickering lights of shop windows. (p. 81)

These figures, though, were safely removed from her private life. They were 'the poor', the eternal poor, the violet-sellers and match-sellers, who would have been equally at home in Mayhew or Booth's surveys, or peopling Shakespeare's London or Defoe's, as much as the London of the 1930s. They could become figures of romance, like the old woman clutching a brown mongrel, who surfaces in *Jacob's Room* and, in similar guise, the female derelict outside Regent's Park tube station in *Mrs Dalloway*, 'a rusty pump', whose song is 'the voice of an ancient spring spouting from the earth', reiterating, 'love which has lasted a million years', and rendered by Woolf as pure sound and rhythmic impulse, thus:

ee um fah um so
foo swee too eem oo

Though her song issues 'from so rude a mouth, a mere hole in the earth', it replenishes the city, 'all along the Marylebone Road and down toward Euston, fertilising, leaving a damp stain' (p. 89). Of the same archetypal species is Mrs McNab (and her friend Mrs Bast), the charwoman who comes 'lurching and leering', in the 'Time Passes' section of *To the Lighthouse*. Singing her tuneless song, Mrs McNab cleans the decaying house of the upper classes, sweeping out the dirt and detritus of the patriarchal past, ushering in the future. Not to inherit it herself, only to stave off destruction and open the doors to her betters. Her song is also wordless, 'robbed of meaning, like the voice of witlessness, humour, persistency itself, trodden down but springing up again' (p. 142). Mrs McNab, working against death, is mythicized as a care-taking woman but, like the exotic tramps of Woolf's imagination, her presence does little to challenge the reassuring stereotype of the inarticulate lower orders – 'she was witless, she knew it'.

Far from dumb, working women were usually represented as

blabbermouths, a version of the garrulous female. Virginia was frequently irritated by her servants' voices and found their talk invasive, a mere babble – like that of foreigners – too close and intimate, especially at Monk's House where every word, every sound echoed across the uncarpeted oak boards. Furious with Lottie for interrupting her, Woolf quoted her 'going on' in her diary, 'Talk-talk- talk- wonder expressed-loud laughter-agreement.' 'Talk with them a muscular activity,' she wrote. 'The difficulty about these people is their flow of language; personal history must be told at length. I believe it is a form of good manners.' This was a version of the Victorian adage 'servants talk about people; gentlefolk discuss things'. The more they talk, in other words, the less they have to say. But Virginia herself was renowned as an incontinent talker, whose conversation took off on flights of fancy, often punctuated by her wild hoots of laughter. These flights made her sister uneasy and Virginia often found herself apologizing for talking too much, yet like the laughter, they seem one of her few ways of letting herself go. At her most manic Virginia talked non-stop, pouring out words for days; talking prevented her from eating, from taking anything in. She always feared being thought a 'ladylike prattler'; that she might write gibberish. Garrulity was associated with the lower orders, like the 'garrulous' nurses who had looked after her father; it was insulating, protecting too; a kind of verbal reverie as it is in her children's story, 'Nurse Lugton's Curtain', but it always risked disparagement as childish and irrational.

Usually working women were depicted as objects of pathos or comedy. Mrs McNab is not quite a comedy-turn (though she leans towards it), nor is she a victim, like the simple-minded char, Elsie, in Arnold Bennett's novel *Riceyman Steps*, whose over-whelming passion is 'the desire to serve' ('such dishwater', Woolf wrote, when she read it, just before inventing her own fantasy of the Georgian cook); or like Katherine Mansfield's 'Life of Ma Parker', another story of 1922, of an elderly cleaning lady, also a long-suffering victim, who 'does' for a selfish literary gentleman. Like them, Mrs McNab is an idealized maternal presence, but

Woolf's life-force is a modernist one: unstoppable, amoral, thoughtless and directionless. The time-bound, personal histories which make up the book's minimal sequence of events are put into parentheses (to convey simultaneity but also their irrelevance to the larger scheme of things).

How to get beyond these 'pictures' of the poor as exotic or mythic or pathetic? When Virginia returned to drafting the first version of *The Waves* after the scenes with Nellie, she decided to include lives from across the social spectrum, a group who would be connected by being alive in the same place and time (like the random individuals who watch the sky-writing aeroplane in *Mrs Dalloway*). This was to be 'the life of anybody', concerned not with 'the single life, but with lives together', and how they differentiated themselves. In a surreal fantasy she imagined a scene of heterogeneous, mindless regeneration, 'waves succeeding waves; endlessly sinking & falling: waves that were many mothers, & again many mothers, & behind them many more, endlessly sinking & falling, & lying prostrate, each holding up, as the wave pass[ed] its crest, a child'. Her vision of fecundity was tinged also with disgust. The mothers go on spawning 'little bald naked purplish rolling balls' of 'twisting' babies, 'little more than animals' (the word 'brats' was deleted), until, in a sinister image, 'the beach was black with them'. 'And how discriminate?' the narrator asks. One answer is apocalyptic: the 'sad mind' might feel 'the strong desire' to obliterate the 'whole mass of pullulating life', these 'pinkish rings of flesh', so that 'whether that was a cottage child, or that a lace-cradled child, it would not matter'. Another, looking on, wants only to leave 'the feebler' – 'field labourers, factory workers, miners' – to give them their place in the sun. Yet 'even the most violent & sanguine of partisans' is fazed by the persistence of nature, which again puts human life in perspective. Hardly a celebration of maternal creativity, the scene conjures a prehistoric, precultural moment, a utopian vision of birth without origins or social markers.

In her draft Woolf tried to juxtapose 'Albert', whose father is a cowman, and 'Roger', the son of a civil servant. There were also

'Flora & Dorothy' who 'would be going to schools in Switzerland about the same time that "Florrie" [another character] went out for the first time as kitchenmaid'. But their 'paths branched off as soon as they could take a step in any direction'. Within a few lines the narrator declared that following these diverging lives produced a kind of 'squint'. The lower-class characters would become 'fragments merely' rather than 'rounded & entire': 'No single person could follow two lives so opposite; could speak two languages so different.' In one scene she imagined Florrie, lonely and scolded by the cook for kissing 'the knife-boy', making herself sick by eating 'a great lump of greasy white heavenly fat' stolen from a ham in her employers' larder. This is Florrie's dubious compensation for an 'extraordinarily opulent world' where 'gold watches were curled up on dressing tables'. Florrie eats to make herself important in an unequal world but is unable to digest what she has taken in. But like the whistling Irish cook in an early draft of *Mrs Dalloway*, and others who are pencilled into the drafts of *To the Lighthouse*, these working-class characters faded out to be replaced by more conventional props. Did Virginia realize how much her characterization was tinged with revulsion? The slippage always occurs: the steamy 'sordid eating house' with its sweaty scullions in *The Waves*, Florrie's association with fat and grease, like Florinda's animality in *Jacob's Room*, the flesh of these others is always distasteful as if too much physical appetite turns the stomach. Florrie's alter ego in *The Waves* is 'Jinny' (the anorexic to Florrie's bulimic?). With her streamlined figure and svelte appearance, Jinny represents a fantasy of complete sexual control, 'I open my body, I shut my body at will.' Florrie, on the other hand – 'half a savage; but she was all the same very affectionate' – had to be eliminated from the body of the text.

Virginia's public sympathy with the lives of poor women was always at odds with private recoil. During the rewriting of *The Waves*, Virginia was persuaded by Leonard's old friend Margaret Llewellyn Davies to supply an 'introductory letter' to a collection of testimonies by women of the Women's Cooperative Guild, *Life As We Have Known It*. The women had been asked to write about the conditions of their lives, their poverty, their hopes and fears. Virginia was sceptical about the introduction and thought herself a bad choice. It was written 'with great plodding'. 'I have to write about working women all morning,' she told Vanessa, 'which is as if you had to sew canopies round chamber pots' (like a child being deliberately naughty, she could usually rely on her sister to countenance her most offensive statements). Her introduction is impressively honest and uneasy, frankly expressing her ambivalence towards middle-class observers like herself, whose sympathy with poor women was bound to be 'fictitious', because 'we pay our bills with cheques and our clothes are washed for us': 'The imagination is largely the child of the flesh. One could not be Mrs Giles of Durham because one's body had never stood at the wash-tub; one's hands had never wrung and scrubbed and chopped up whatever the meat may be that makes a miner's supper.' Yet 'whatever the meat may be' seems excessively distancing. Virginia's own body could stoop and suffer but the idea of a shared physical experience or the vicissitudes of female biology roused resistance. It was not possible to identify with those women because such sympathy 'is not based upon sharing the same emotions unconsciously'. It was an 'aesthetic' sympathy. It seems an odd thing for a writer to say. In her drafts of *The Waves*, she was concurrently imagining the lives of three different men – one homosexual – relying, presumably, on aesthetic sympathy.

Instead she emphasized the physical differences between ladies and working women with their muscular bodies and 'enormous arms', offending the Guild women. An unhappy correspondence with Margaret followed, which led to revisions, with Virginia insisting that she was only telling the truth: ladies' arms were flabby because they never lifted anything, but, she wrote, 'if you want me to make them sylphs I will'. Irritated by what she saw as working-class propriety, she couldn't see that working women might hate being depicted so much in terms of their bodies, or that they understood how much the stress on their physicality implied a kind of mindlessness, as if their lives were dominated only by material needs. Virginia's own text suggested this. The

working women were 'humorous, vigorous, and thoroughly independent,' she wrote, but 'at the same time, it is much better to
be a lady; ladies desire Mozart and Einstein — that is they desire
things that are ends, not things that are means'. In other words,
'not merely money and hot water laid on'. Wanting material things
(as if ladies never did) meant an impoverished inner life. Though
Virginia toned down her first version and replaced her harsh
judgement that 'It is not from the ranks of working-class women
that the next great poet or novelist will be drawn' with 'Poetry
and fiction seem far beyond their horizons', these were mere
tinkerings. The overall drift remained the same. Despite having
often felt moved by the women's testimonies, with their 'restless
wishing and dreaming', she needed to keep her distance, to insist
that these inner lives were framed differently from her own.

Virginia wrote in her introduction that if 'every reform' the
Guild women demanded 'this instant was granted, it would not
touch one hair of my comfortable capitalistic head'. Her fierceness
was impressive but self-deceived: how could society not change
once such women became equal citizens? 'The question of Nelly',
as Virginia had already suggested, was a question of social mobility,
and Nellie was far from alone — many of the Guild women had
been servants. In fact the encroachment of the poor, unsettling
her own position, provoked her most exorbitant feelings. In the
midst of revising her piece in October 1930 she wrote to Ethel
Smyth that faced with servants, 'one sees their poor fluttering
lives as one talks'. Their 'dependence and defencelessness' left her
feeling 'hopeless, helpless', 'have I ever felt such wild misery as
when talking to servants? — partly caused by rage at our general
ineptitude — we the governors — at having laden ourselves with
such a burden, at having let grow on our shoulders such a cancer,
such a growth, such a disease as the poor are.' The visceral responses,
the squeamish, queasy language which compared servants or 'the
poor' to 'flies' or a rubbish heap, the imagery of animality, or of
corruption and waste, read like violent attempts to gain control
as the writing touched on the ungovernable. 'Again, enough,' she
insisted as she tried to staunch the flow.

Early in 1931, when Nellie finally returned to work, Virginia was too excited by the idea of a new book to finish off the last pages of *The Waves*. She was imagining a sequel to *A Room of One's Own*, which would be about 'the sexual life of women' and had its origins in a talk she had just given to the National Society for Women's Service. In it she tackled head-on the inhibitions which faced a woman of her generation who wanted to write. In an often-cited passage she described how she had had to kill 'the Angel in the House', the 'phantom' of the Victorian lady who haunted her writing, conciliating a male readership whose sensibilities would otherwise be shocked, and always subordinating her own wishes to those of others (an image, of course, of her mother). That obstacle, she wrote, had been overcome. But there remained another, more powerful inhibition: 'telling the truth about my own experiences as a body', which she believed no woman writer of that time had so far managed to do. Woolf blamed the male reader for this block but since she also tended to associate physical or bodily experiences with the degraded lower orders, it was clear that the angel in the house was far from dead.

In the published version of her speech, 'Professions for Women', Virginia returned to her earlier conceit: 'you are earning your five hundred pounds a year ... the room is your own but it is still bare'. 'How are you going to furnish it?' she asked her imaginary female listener. 'With whom are you going to share it?' She did not ask who would clean it. In *The Waves* the empty rooms which shimmer in the sunlight are miraculously free of dust. The ideal room, like the ideal body, would be free of dirt and waste.

★

The last chapter in the saga of Nellie and Virginia was a series of recapitulations mounting, at last, to a final climax. In London Virginia felt infuriated then depressed; she hated their resuming the life of a solid middle-class household with 'overcooked meat'; she was irritated by Nellie's whispered conspiracies with Lottie, who was in and out of places, and the servants' constant presence added to her feelings of dejection. 'I toss among empty bottles & bits of toilet paper,' she wrote in her diary. There were the usual intimacies of a shared domestic life, Nellie exaggerating Virginia's illnesses to keep visitors at bay, or their bailing out the bath together down the wc when the pipes were frozen; the coping with fleas, black beetles and mice in Sussex; huffs and minor skirmishes. Virginia learnt more in the kitchen from Annie, who was far less territorial. Apart from baking bread, at which she was adept, Virginia was now cooking mushrooms, preparing fruit for stewing, paring cold mutton for a hotpot. There were anxieties, nonetheless, about 'livers out'. 'Was Percy stealing their anthracite?' they wondered. 'Why is there always this relationship between master and servant?' Woolf asked, bewildered. 'Always deceit & distrust. Our Transition Age perhaps.' Accusing Nellie or Percy of 'servant meanness', the Woolfs, like millions of other employers, continued to pay their servant £40 a year while they earnt £4,000. Yet during a peaceful time, in April 1933, when Nellie was 'touchingly friendly', Virginia reflected that 'Age is like lichen on roofs – knowing people I mean – gives our relationship some yellow red glow.' The old loyalties could be comforting, if also clinging.

There were further house improvements – the end of 'Aladdin' oil lamps, the arrival of electric light, electric fires and a fridge at Monk's House; electricity was installed at Tavistock Square and an electric boiler gave hot water for the bath – all of which meant more independence for the Woolfs and less need for Nellie. Arriving at Rodmell in the dead of winter in 1933 Virginia observed that it was 'no longer the great transition that it used to be'. Nellie's one weapon of giving notice was all but losing force; Virginia and Leonard were learning how to do without constant attendance. Virginia saw herself as disengaging, refusing to meet claim with counterclaim, yet she remained furious. If Nellie wanted more money or more appreciation she was being self-centred, so powerful was the belief that a servant's devotion should be selfless. On Nellie's part, the longer she stayed, the more uncertain her future. Unemployment at her age was to be dreaded:

it usually meant eking out an existence cleaning or accepting much worse conditions. In the past, after such long service, a servant might well expect to be looked after. When Nellie, feeling vulnerable and defenceless, resorted to tears and temper, Virginia, like a Victorian husband, called it 'hysteria'. She slowly learnt to steel herself, to become cold and angry and withdrawn. Yet she could not quite relinquish the fantasy of all masters: she wanted her servant to love her.

For Virginia 'the most disagreeable six weeks of my life' began in mid-February 1934. It started with 'a great Nelly row'. Tavistock Square was undergoing redecoration and presumably – but Virginia doesn't give details – Nellie refused to give up time off or found she couldn't work around the decorators. It culminated in the Woolfs being left with 'only eggs for lunch' and 'forced to dine' at the local pub 'expensively & badly'. This time Virginia decided she would not give notice and then live for a month with Nellie's trying to regain ground, wearing down Virginia's defences. She would sack Nellie the day before they left for Sussex at the end of March, simply present her with a *fait accompli*, and then disappear to Monk's House. They would leave Nellie even if she wouldn't leave them. It would be a strategic campaign which Virginia would wage in silence, biding her time.

March was spent in a state of acute anxiety, not helped by the flat being in a chaos of builders and painters. Virginia fell ill with influenza and had the shivers; she was utterly unsettled, abandoning 'Here and Now' (an early version of *The Years*). Her hours were dominated by the prospect of the fatal day: 'Can I do it? I must. I must.' Nellie, oblivious to her fate, was 'gay & garrulous as a lark'. As Virginia warded off any intimacies, Nellie advanced. 'You show no confidence in me; you dont treat me like a maid,' Virginia reported. Whenever Nellie offered to dust books or make tea, Virginia's guilt oppressed her – 'How human beings torture each other!' On the eve of the dreaded day, she reassured herself that 'by this time – 3.30 – tomorrow it will be over. And then there'll only be the one dreadful day & we shall be off.' She felt 'executioner & the executed in one', but 'this has to be lived I say to myself'. Virginia battled it out with herself, determined not to discuss it all with Leonard but to take charge. On 27 March she gave Nellie notice and then went straight to her diary to write about it; she had left Nellie standing 'by the drawing-room door in the full light, white & pink, with her funny rather foolish mulish face puckered up'. Virginia had tried to give her a cheque for £25 and £1 for her mending. Nellie refused – 'but you dont owe me anything', she had apparently cried. Like a proper mistress Virginia had cut short any argument and acted her part convincingly. 'I made my speech correctly,' she wrote approvingly in her diary. It was relatively painless, though there was still a day to go before their departure to Sussex.

The full account of her 'long drawn out struggle with a poor drudge', who only a month before had been like an old friend, went immediately into a letter to Ethel Smyth after the Woolfs arrived in Sussex. No mention was made of the row over the workmen or days off but only of Nellie's hidebound refusal to try an electric oven when Virginia was ill, her 'tempers and glooms', and the Woolfs' realization that they would soon be lumbered with a dependent old retainer – 'she will grow on us and wither and decay,' Virginia wrote to Ethel. The letter was both confession and vindication. Nellie's violent behaviour utterly exonerated the Woolfs: 'all Tuesday and yesterday we lived in a storm of abuse and apology, and hysterics and appeals and maniacal threats'. Nellie refused to go, refused the cheque – 'a handsome one', Virginia couldn't resist adding – till her mistress 'was driven in the cold wind' to 'parade' Oxford Street in order to avoid her. The 'final battle' ensued before Leonard and Virginia drove off to Sussex. In the end they had to abandon Nellie in the kitchen 'grasping a wet cloth at the sink and glaring', refusing to shake hands, which seemed to surprise Virginia, and refusing to accept her dismissal. 'No, no, no, I will not leave you,' she cried, to which Virginia had answered, 'Ah but you must.' 'And so,' she wrote, 'we slammed the door.' It was a scene worthy of Victorian melodrama.

Woolf rarely divulged such private miseries in letters and apologized for her 'egotism' in a postscript, but to Ethel Smyth she wrote some of her frankest and angriest letters. In 1930 the 72-year-old composer and suffragette, a major-general's daughter, had barged her way into Virginia's life, striking up a passionate friendship and declaring herself in love. Virginia was mildly alarmed and somewhat flattered. She hugely admired Ethel's indefatigable energy and youthful vitality, though she was less impressed by her music – here was a woman refusing to wither and decay, 'a game old bird', 'an uncastrated tom cat'. Ethel was a strenuous friend, however; she took to turning up uninvited and staying for hours, talking endlessly about herself, demanding instant responses to her autobiographical manuscripts, shows of affection and – worst of all – staging scenes. The more Ethel, like Nellie, took umbrage, the more she exhibited her hurt feelings, the more she was likely to alienate. It was the kind of domineering behaviour Virginia associated with her father, his temper tantrums and emotional blackmail. Ethel, she felt, also had 'a lust for emotion' and Woolf had long before let her know that 'scenes' were odious to her; they left her demoralized and horrified. Remembering one such occasion, she told Ethel that 'it makes me feel so degraded – so humiliated – as I used to feel after a scene with Nelly'. It might be her 'peculiarity', she admitted, but she must be honest about her limits. Ethel's aggressive egotism was part of her attraction but Virginia was no longer the clinging, shy, gawky girl who had overflowed into her journals and letters; she would stand up to Ethel's bullying. With Ethel, as, to some extent with Nellie, she was battling with her own tendency towards submission; the passivity which she so often felt to be abject.

Sending Ethel her account of Nellie's dismissal was another way of giving Ethel notice: she too could be dropped. During the final month with Nellie Virginia rowed with Ethel and wrote furiously to her, condemning her as 'selfseeking' and 'attitudinising', 'living in a mid-Victorian dentist's waiting room of emotional falsity', working up quarrels and dramatizing herself. Feeling intense relief at the separation from Nellie, she announced to Ethel 'I shall make no attachments ever again.' Perhaps testing her resilience with Ethel made it easier to break with Nellie. Virginia's firm stance towards the 'bragging' and 'brawling' Ethel certainly made it more likely that their friendship would survive.

Two weeks after the showdown, Woolf resumed her diary, at Monk's House with a final version of the last scene in the drama, having reread the whole episode again (the door hadn't quite slammed shut). She congratulated herself for keeping to her resolution, relishing the freedom: 'no more brooding; no more possessiveness; no more sense of being part of Nelly's world'. As if she needed still to absolve herself, she drew one more picture of Nellie, half-bully, half-victim, 'whimpering' and holding a wet cloth ('grasping' was again Virginia's word), and saying, 'they'll blame me'. She was, Virginia wrote, 'thinking of herself as usual', ignoring the fact that Nellie's getting another job would indeed depend on what people said about her. Virginia thought her ungrateful and that taking the cookery books and a chair cover was 'a last spasm of possessive spite', though the same might be said of the diary entry. For a while, Virginia told Vanessa, Nellie continued to 'bombard' her with letters through her sister Lizzie (none survives), but the Woolfs were off to Ireland for a fortnight and that was the end of communications. A couple of months later, in July 1934, Virginia wrote a final single sentence about her ex-cook, 'After eighteen years I at last got rid of an affectionate domestic tyrant.' It was meant as an epitaph for Nellie but Virginia was, after all, executed as well as executioner. Had she finally despatched the helpless and friendly, but ultimately despotic mistress?

*

The godlike power of a diary! After 1934 Nellie Boxall was expunged, as if she had indeed been murdered on that last day. No more references, no more fleeting glimpses of her as there are of Lottie Hope or Sophie Farrell, only a blank, after eighteen years of intimacy. No letters or reminders were kept. Perhaps Virginia still felt guilty, or furious and ashamed of her own terrors too; perhaps she needed to believe she was all-important to Nellie – much more preferable to believing that she wasn't. In fact she must have known that far from being dead to the world, Nellie had landed triumphantly on her feet and moved into far more glamorous circles. For Nellie stayed in Bloomsbury. She went to work for Charles Laughton and Elsa Lanchester, the most famous British stage and screen couple of the day, who lived at 34 Gordon Square.

The job was ideal. In the first place, Nellie stayed in 'the click'. Lottie was now at number 50 Gordon Square working as cook-housekeeper for Clive Bell. Bell's secretary and companion for most of the 1930s, Benita Jaeger, was Lanchester's closest friend. Nellie had found another unconventional place. Her new mistress was a true radical and Bohemian. Born into a pacifist, feminist, vegetarian and socialist family, Elsa Sullivan Lanchester had trained as a girl at Isadora Duncan's school in Paris, taught dance at the age of thirteen in exchange for education at a coeducational progressive school, organized a children's theatre, posed nude for 'artistic' photographs and run an unlicensed nightclub, The Cave of Harmony, in Gower Street, where she sang and performed in cabaret and one-act plays, before making her film debut as a comedienne. Lanchester found security with Laughton, whom she'd married in 1929, and when she later discovered that he was a homosexual, she made very little fuss about it. Nellie too was used to such left-handed marriages and to a lifestyle which was relaxed and extremely sociable. Laughton appreciated good food and by now Nellie was a top-flight cook; there were plenty of first-night parties and impromptu suppers. In the late 30s London's theatreland was at its zenith. Laughton was also one of the mainstays of Alex Korda's London Films, founded in 1932, together with Vivien Leigh, Merle Oberon (Korda's wife) and Ralph Richardson. In 1933 Laughton was voted outstanding actor of the year for his *Henry VIII* and won an Oscar for the film version with Katharine Hepburn (the film was hugely popular and inspired a fashion for 'tudor-halo' hats). Both the Laughtons were fresh from Hollywood successes when Nellie went to work for them and they lived a transatlantic and cosmopolitan life at Gordon Square, welcoming actors such as Douglas Fairbanks Jnr and Marlene Dietrich to London, and those Europeans in the industry who were increasingly at odds with Hitler and Goebbels's propaganda machine. Nellie would have seen, if not met, some of the most dazzling of the stars. There was plenty of prestige in the job.

The apparently hidebound Nellie was now ensconced in a thoroughly up-to-date flat. In 1932 the Laughtons had hired Wells Coates, the Canadian architect and engineer, to convert their apartment and design furniture for it. Coates was deeply committed to the modern movement in art and architecture, and to 'a servantless society' where people might learn to live in a more mobile, freer way, without the old values of 'stability, security and individuality' exemplified by the bourgeois trappings of the Victorian house and also the interwar suburb. In Lawn Road, Hampstead, he was to create 'the minimum flat', as part of his vision of housing for the cosmopolitan, modern person who travelled light (a fantasy which would have appealed to Virginia) – Walter Gropius and Agatha Christie were among the first tenants – though a communal servants' quarters existed on the ground floor. Wells Coates gutted and stripped the Laughtons' flat in Gordon Square, which was on

The Laughtons' living room at Gordon Square

the top three floors of the building and originally dark and cluttered in the Victorian manner. He knocked down interior walls to create a huge living room and added enormous windows. With white walls, sliding glass doors, parquet floors, flush bookcases and built-in cupboards, central heating and integral gas-fires, it was extremely light and airy. The furniture was mostly 'pale-finished modern pieces of the most advanced design' – brand new, no heirlooms – though made of wood, which the Laughtons preferred, rather than the tubular steel which Coates favoured. The partition sliding doors were decorated with animal and tropical motifs by the surrealist John Armstrong. 'Feminine touches', as they were called in the new 'interior decorating' magazines, were added by Lanchester's arrangements of dried flowers brought back from the country. Laughton bought contemporary pottery and found old pieces in junk shops and markets. Aside from the spacious open-plan living room, there were bedrooms for Lanchester and Laughton, an office for their secretary, Hope Chenhalls, a separate room for Nellie and one for the maid. There was also a gym where the portly Laughton could keep fit. Nellie found herself in a small but efficiently planned and fitted kitchen with all mod cons. Divisions existed but were minimized. There were two bathrooms and three modern flush lavatories (one, no doubt, for the staff). This really was a modernist attempt at a new domesticity.

In the late 30s Elsa Lanchester wrote an account of her life with Laughton, describing their 'modernized' flat and, briefly, their household. She was frank about the demands which the theatre life made on Nellie (not 'Nelly'), her 'housekeeper and cook' – overcooked dinners, late nights, 'casseroles and stews at any hour (diet ones if necessary)', and decided that Nellie 'would have my sympathy' if she gave them up. A younger generation than Virginia and ten years younger than Nellie, Lanchester wrote combatively about having servants. She was the child of Irish Marxist parents who had been active members of the Social Democratic Foundation and, though her breezy tone covers some uneasiness, she stressed that she and Laughton argued about 'art, politics, publicity, food, morals, economics and trade unionism' with their servants in their off-duty moments. Their maid was a Communist and kept her end up in discussions about 'the worker' in such a way as to make the film stars 'shiver': '[the servants] have been known to call us "the idle rich", and we call them "slave" or "serf" in the same spirit'. Lanchester polished off her bright account with a witty drawing of a cook throwing pots at her mistress.

As it happens, their maid also recorded her recollections. Happy Powley (her first name was a family one) was barely twenty when she came to London, and considered herself very fortunate to find the Laughtons after her first grim jobs in Suffolk where she'd grown up. Her days in Bloomsbury were great fun – 'No caps, no aprons, or anything. No Sir or Madam; and this was marvellous!' There was no waiting at table, and she remembered Dietrich bringing out the dirty plates to a cupboard on the landing where they were left. The servants in Gordon Square were very sociable; she and Nellie frequently went over to number 50, where Lottie 'did everything' for Clive Bell, or to Mrs Bell's studio in Fitzroy Street; they often helped with luncheons and dinner parties. Mrs Bell's crowd, 'they treated you like one of themselves'. The guests spoke to the servants using Christian names. 'And they would talk to you – you know, as if you could read and write,' she added dryly. Lottie even had 'the old boy' – the philosopher Bertrand Russell – 'in stitches while she was taking his coat'. Happy remembered Virginia Woolf very well – 'oh, she was lovely – she was always sort of the grand lady'. Nellie, she knew, had worked for her for eighteen years, but 'had to leave because she was a bit highly strung'. And, Happy added, 'of course you know Virginia Woolf was'.

So Virginia and Nellie saw each other often. What did they say to each other in those brief encounters over the hors d'oeuvres or at the studio when 'the girls' donned little pinnies, unpacked food from Fortnum's, and later joined in the party? No doubt, being Englishwomen, they kept up appearances. Perhaps Mrs Woolf knew about Nellie's moment of celebrity, the advertisement in the papers headed 'Mr. and Mrs. Charles Laughton's cook'. By courtesy of her employers, 'Miss Nellie Boxall', interviewed 'in her spotless little kitchen', now gave the nation advice on how to cook roast beef to perfection, thanks to her 'New World' cooker (gas not electric) with its 'modern miracle of labour saving', a 'regulo'. She was an authority at last.

And Virginia? For all the protestations, the insistence on the unworkability of 'the system', she was interviewing another live-in servant even before Nellie's notice was up. The room was there after all. Roger Fry's sister, Margery, offered them Mabel Haskins, 'a treasure', and Virginia was sure Mabel would be perfect, 'steady silent unselfish'. Nellie may have been given the *coup de grâce* but the fantasy of the ideal servant was alive and well.

*

The years when Nellie Boxall was Virginia Woolf's sole resident servant were Virginia's most fruitful years, and among her gayest and happiest. Her major novels – *Mrs Dalloway*, *To the Lighthouse*, *The Waves* – as well as the playful *Orlando* and *Flush* were all written, and she published a huge panoply of reviews and essays, including *A Room of One's Own* and the literary criticism which she shaped into *The Common Reader*. While their rows were happening offstage, Virginia's reputation and her social world expanded; she became wealthy for the first time in her life; she began her love-affair with Vita Sackville-West; her marriage to Leonard still delighted and invigorated her. The idea of independence was central to this life, to her feminism and her aesthetics, to a celebration of the republic of consciousness that might transcend the material needs of the individual life, the distinctions and discriminations of personal relationships, and the narrow confines of a personal history. But these were also years when Virginia continued to need looking after and it was Nellie who drew the curtains, brought the lemonade and the trays, who tempted Virginia's appetite with invalid foods, and presumably emptied the chamber-pot which continued to reside under the bed at Monk's House.

Virginia was always very susceptible to physical strain and shook

off illness slowly; influenza or a cold might prostrate her, her headaches, which sound like migraines, with blinding lights and nausea, might continue on and off for days. Drugs had a powerful effect too. In 1929 travelling back from a holiday with Leonard she took part of one of Vanessa's sedatives to ward off travel sickness on the boat and was knocked out by it, and then ill for three weeks with a headache, backache, pain and a racing heart. There was also the beginning of the menopause ('T[ime] of L[ife]' in her diary). During all these times Nellie and Leonard were her caretakers. Though Virginia was never to break down as she had in the years 1913–15, her mental stability was always closely connected to the stages of writing, and was frequently in jeopardy, especially during the depressions which followed on from finishing a book. After the drafting of *To the Lighthouse* in the summer of 1926, for instance, she felt she suffered 'a whole nervous breakdown in miniature'. Virginia was robust, even tough, about her mental and physical fragility, and certainly far from valetudinarian, but she nevertheless frequently found herself in the hands of others. If the servant mirrored back to her a loathing of dependence, which her feminism associated with 'the clinging doll heroine' or the submissiveness of the angel in the house, the need to be dependent and to tolerate dependence in oneself and others could not be simply banished.

While Virginia Woolf had her own history of being looked after, the fury felt at dependence, the depressive feelings it provoked, and the depletion which followed the rage are hardly unique to her. Such times seemed to evoke primal feelings which belong to the earliest states of existence, when the infant has no control over its body and cannot meet its own needs, the absolute terror that those who look after it will abandon it in the dark horror of helplessness, annihilated. Equally, in adulthood, dependence can feel like being infantilized and conjure up the fear that carers will exploit the other's vulnerability. Who is more helpless than a baby and more powerful than the mother? In her closest relationships – with Vanessa, Leonard, Nellie, Vita and Ethel – Virginia knew she wanted mothering and protection but she also distrusted 'the maternal passion'. She disliked 'maternal partiality' and possessiveness, the preferring of one's own child to others, and in a hostile vein she wrote to Vanessa: 'what you feel about marriage I feel about motherhood, except that of the two relations motherhood seems to me the more destructive and limiting'. Characteristically, she modified her view, 'But no doubt I'm merely trying to make out a case for myself: there's some truth in it though; I dont like profound instincts – not in human relationships.' Visiting Marie Woolf, Leonard's mother, reminded her of 'the horror of family life', as she put it in her diary, and the emotional vampirism of parents who drained the life's blood from their children, asserting their own needs over those of their offspring. Fathers were guilty, of course, but there were also 'thousands of women' dying of the 'tyranny of mother over daughter' – 'Short of killing Mrs W. nothing could be done. Day after day one's life would be crumpled up like a bill for 10 pen[ce] 3 farthings. Nothing has ever been said of this.' In a long, long letter to Vanessa, giving her mother-in-law's talk almost word for word, she tried to milk some comedy from the visit. She said nothing of her outraged feelings but when Virginia returned to writing about her childhood in her memoirs in her fifties she was able to be more critical of her own mother, noting that Julia had almost eclipsed her oldest daughter's life. Stella's devotion to her mother was 'almost canine,' Virginia wrote. Woolf's fiction, which is so often fuelled by a desire to merge, to enter other people's minds, also expresses the equally powerful need to disconnect, to separate and differentiate our selves and our lives from others'. The soliloquies in *The Waves* are full of gleeful hatreds as well as varieties of love.

Must all attachment mean dependence and was intimacy always a form of invasion? This too was 'the question of Nelly'. In her writings about servants Virginia was drawn towards a nostalgic representation of a lost union, idealizing the Victorian servant as the good mother, the mother who gave everything and asked nothing, the antithesis of the greedy, sordid working woman who was always wanting things. Both representations were to be resisted. In the midst of her scenes with Nellie, Virginia had visited Sophie

Farrell, the Stephen family cook, now retired, and written the affectionate, sentimental portrait of 'Biddy Brien'. But she did not try to publish it. Usually in Woolf's published fiction and essays maids and mistresses form a neutral alliance, the maid as willing co-worker, presenting a united front when faced with the demands or whims of despotic men. Visiting the house of Thomas Carlyle, a famously tyrannical husband, Virginia wrote sympathetically about the load of work which the insanitary, inconvenient Victorian home entailed. Yet she implied that this burden was shared equally. The house was 'a battlefield' where 'mistress and maid fought against dirt and cold for cleanliness and warmth'. In *Flush*, her spoof-biography of Elizabeth Barrett Browning's spaniel, Woolf drew attention to the marginal presence of that other 'dog's body' in the story, Mrs Browning's servant, Lily Wilson. In an absurdly long endnote, illustrating 'the extreme precariousness of a servant's life', she described Lily as 'typical of the great army of her kind – the inscrutable, the all-but-silent, the all-but-invisible servant maids of history'. But she too consigned Lily to silence ('all-but silence'?), if knowingly and ironically: the last words on Lily's life go to her mistress, whose trite praises 'may serve her for epitaph'. Regretting the absence of the lives of maids in the *Dictionary of National Biography*, her father's *magnum opus*, in another endnote, this time to *Three Guineas*, Virginia stressed the importance of the maid 'in English upper class life from the earliest times until the year 1914', seemingly ignoring the present day. Yet what she emphasized was the maid's unwitting collusion with patriarchy: as helpmeet and chaperone, her main task was to protect her mistress's chastity in order to deliver her safely to her master. The Victorian retainer, 'the glory of the British basement', who deserved a life (in both the literal and biographical sense), was always a far safer topic than the quarrelsome Georgian cook. What could not be written about publicly were the divisions between women, the hatreds and tears, the frenzied misunderstandings, the bossing and placating, the exercise of power and the attempts at control on both sides. In 'Women and Fiction', an essay written in the spring of 1929 as relations with Nellie deteriorated, Virginia looked forward to a time when women might meet each other as 'fellow beings' and not 'as masters and mistresses with counters between us or kitchen tables'. That time had not yet come.

★

Long after Virginia died, Nellie Boxall got the chance to have the last word. In 1956 she was part of a BBC programme on the wireless and, in a quiet, meditative voice with a slight country burr, she recalled first seeing Virginia forty years before: 'She hadn't been well' and 'She was so sweet that I knew I should like working for her.' All the memories were rosy. Nellie had soon coaxed Mrs Woolf's poor appetite with treats and fresh puddings like home-made ice cream with chocolate sauce and crème brûlée; all was harmony in the kitchen (except that Mrs Woolf, being a lady, always used up all the saucepans when she tried to cook). 'She' always liked Nellie's cooking and 'She' was 'always very nice' to Nellie's relatives, having Nellie's niece, Dorothy, to stay every year. Then Nellie added, almost as an afterthought, 'I had to go to hospital and She was very kind. She came to see me in the ward carrying a huge pineapple and came straight up to the bed and cuddled me up.' This was the spontaneous, affectionate Virginia, with her idiosyncratic gifts, who sought love and protection from all her women friends; Sophie's 'Miss Genia', who was trusting and childlike and demonstrative. Not many mistresses would cuddle their maids in public. Nellie wanted Virginia's goodness remembered but also, in this memory of her own neediness, Virginia's need of her.

FOUR

Memoirs of a Lavatory Attendant

Consider what immense forces society brings to play on each of us, how that society changes from decade to decade; and also from class to class; well, if we cannot analyse these invisible presences, we know very little of the subject of the memoir; and again how futile life-writing becomes. I see myself as a fish in a stream; deflected; held in place; but cannot describe the stream.

Virginia Woolf, 'Sketch of the Past' (1939)

Always she was tempted to make that reversal: the inner life, the writing life, was 'the real life'. The outer life, what people called 'real life' – ordering dinner from Mabel, mending, going for walks, seeing people – this was unreality, the neutral ground in the carpet which made the figures in its pattern more intense. It was the unconsciousness of the humdrum, the dailiness of marriage, for example, which might crystallize, now and then, into a pure bead of happiness or moment of vision, an epiphany, like a fin glimpsed far out in the water.

The outer life, the unreal life, was the life of the body. Bodies were obstacles in the way of what mattered – the flight of the mind – they were matter in the way. And yet (there was always an 'and yet') the body played its part, cradled and nurtured the mind, held it safe in its keeping, allowed it, in illness for example, to give up control so that one soared or plunged, and offered so many delights of eye and ear, taste and touch. But the life of the body alone, without the mind in command – a veil should be drawn over it, surely?

Servants were part of the so-called real life, the prose rather than the poetry. She couldn't write about this relationship because she couldn't make it beautiful. It could not be pared down or put into her pot. And yet one should try to combine, as she put it, the two worlds, 'outer' and 'inner'. As she grew older she wanted to work against this dissociation, to have no wrench or disjunction, trying mixed forms: a prose-poem or an elegy, not a novel; an 'essay-novel'; a novel with a drama enacted between its pages. She no longer thought of herself as a novelist and would write no more novels – had she ever written them? That old business, that faith in narrative, had long given way to the present moment, the moment inside which one lived, variously, in other dimensions of time; the space, as she conceived it, of an interior. Individuality was interiority; narrative, with its random plots, was a group experience. But 'we' belonged to different groups: how could there ever be, she wondered, a story to connect these different lives, a language which spoke to all?

Was it possible to be one's self without aggression, the ramparts of hatefulness which drew lines and found differences? She vowed to 'have no screens' but the habit of shutting others off from our sympathies was so universal, without it 'we might dissolve utterly'. Separateness would be impossible. But the screens, she felt, were in the excess not the sympathy. Democracy meant letting others in. And if we were, as she believed, 'splinters & mosaics; not, as they used to hold, immaculate, monolithic, consistent wholes', how did we keep disintegration at bay? Could one protect oneself against invasion?

One went on generating life, 'that decoction of illusion', as if one were the author of it. But what was a life? Not biography, those torn bits of stuff tacked together, those 'phrases laid like Roman roads across the tumult of our lives', as she'd written in The Waves. *She was fifty-eight. Reflecting on her unfinished memoirs, which spluttered like a candle, she knew that a real life had no crisis, nothing to tighten its threads. 'It must lack centre. It must amble on.' Nonetheless she would weave a very thick pattern, make a selvedge. And yet a history of one's self was always the history of others, was not in one's possession but fashioned by all those invisible presences, so many long gone – mother, father, Stella – and a multitude of the nameless, unknown, unmourned. Sometimes the veil of appearances was lifted and light shone through the fabric: 'The whole world is a work of art,' she wrote, 'we are parts of the work of art.' A life was always wonderfully prolific.*

It was this moment, it was already the past, a gloomy winter's evening in Sussex. Even the weather was political (would there be a raid tonight? Rain might delay the invasion). The only place to go was into the cathedral space of the past, where there might be sanctuary. And all this time the walls were wearing thin, the containing and reflecting walls, inner and outer. In Bloomsbury the house where they had once lived was blasted and now stood wide open, exposed to the air; other people would come to sweep up the broken glass and the smashed furniture. She could just make out her studio and her ghost still scribbling as the women arrived – Mrs Gape, was it, Mrs McNab or Mrs Moffat? – brushing away the years, the work the writer had tried to do in that room swept into a handful of dust. One's life no more than a pool of water in a charwoman's bucket.

And if she had looked back, old Virginia, as she so often imagined herself doing, she might have thought that in, or about, December 1940 human character changed again. Or rather, it changed in one of its local, provincial varieties, on a small island in a backwater of the North Sea. It didn't happen overnight, of course, but the signs were there. She herself had sat in the village hall with the other excellent women, learning what to do if 'Jerry' invaded, discussing Hitler with the butcher when she brought home her bacon (but when a soldier came to play chess with Leonard, he still called him 'Sir'). Meanwhile Mrs Ebbs at the vicarage put on A Midsummer Night's Dream *and the gardener's daughter, who sometimes came in to grub up weeds from their path with a blunt kitchen knife, bruising her knuckles, pranced to and fro as Puck. Later that evening the little girl leant out of the bedroom window at Park Cottages to watch the ladies and the gentlemen at Monk's House play bowls in their lovely clothes. They would stay in her mind. She would not be a cleaner like her mother.*

All over Britain, as the bombs were coming down, the girls and women who should have been maids went to do their bit, as they had in the first war. But this time there would be no return to service, or so they reckoned. When Britain emerged phoenix-like from the ashes, there would be a new world, they imagined, and someone else would have to do the dirty work.

MRS WOOLF AND 'MRS GAPE'

Despite a brief resurgence in the number of girls and women who became live-in servants – put down to the Depression – the trends of the 20s continued into the 1930s: the demand for servants rose with a greater number of households employing a single servant and yet, whenever there was any other work available, women went elsewhere. Service was still the biggest employer of Britain's women but it was becoming the least desired occupation and residential service was the least preferable option. Given the opportunity, women went into the light industries, or became shop assistants or elementary school teachers (both positions losing their status once they became perceived as suitable jobs for women), anything other than service. Servants got older. Around a third of all maids were over thirty-five. After 1928 they were eligible for a pension at sixty-five, not seventy as previously, if they had contributed to National Health Insurance, which meant that mistresses could keep on elderly maids without having to worry about supporting them in their old age, either by leaving a legacy or providing a yearly stipend as Virginia did for Sophie Farrell. Younger servants still tended to come from the villages, especially in the south and west of England, where they had fewer options than in industrial areas. Most domestics still thought of the work as temporary; marriage was assumed to be the next step, though they might have to return to cleaning or charring in later life. Poverty made most girls and women servants in the 1930s as it did in Sophie Farrell's day. A servant usually had enough to eat, especially if she were a cook, and she would be warm in winter. There were still general maids who left school at fourteen and found themselves working an eighty- or even hundred-hour week. For many even this drudgery seemed at least 'respectable' and better than any other.

At a time when more and more of the British middle classes were beginning to do without resident servants, the Woolfs straddled the old and new worlds: they found a young local woman in Sussex who worked as their daily but lived in a cottage tied to the job in a semi-feudal fashion; and an unmarried, ageing live-in servant in London who had nowhere else to go and acted as caretaker when they were away. After Nellie's departure Virginia toyed with the idea of poaching Grace Germany from Vanessa. Then, in May 1934, Grace married a Sussex man, Walter Higgens, and since the cottage he had found for his wife was apparently too gloomy, they moved into a large bedsitting room at the top of Charleston, reached by stairs from the kitchen – was it too hard for Grace to leave or for her mistress to relinquish her, one wonders? She certainly wrote gratefully to Clive Bell thanking

him for the money he sent as a wedding present, 'it is very kind
of Mrs Bell & yourself to allow me to stay on'. In this room their
son, John Peter, was born the following year. Grace was later
afforded a small sitting room off the kitchen but no bathroom:
the Higgenses had to take their baths once a week between eight
and ten p.m. on a Friday, while the Bells were eating dinner.
Otherwise they washed at the kitchen sink. Meanwhile the Woolfs
were offered Mabel Haskins, who occasionally came down to
Rodmell, until they advertised, and took on Louie Everest, who
started at Monk's House in the summer of 1934.

Mabel was used to Bloomsbury and its ways. She and her sister,
Florence, had worked for years, cleaning and cooking for Margery
Fry, Roger's sister, at 7 Dalmeny Avenue in Camden, where Roger
had moved after he gave up Durbins. The house had welcomed
many artists and writers. Picasso had visited Dalmeny Avenue, as
had Derain, Sickert, the Sitwells, T. S. Eliot, as well as the Bells,
Stracheys and Woolfs. The sisters had prepared many impromptu
meals, mostly the salads of fruit and vegetables – 'a protest against
Mrs Beeton' – which Margery preferred, though Flossie could
also cope with pheasant and the *boeuf en daube* so favoured in
Bloomsbury circles. In the late 20s Florence had married George
Riley, who had worked with the Fry sisters for the relief of
Belgian refugees and had suffered imprisonment as a conscientious
objector. George had helped find the house and do it up; he
found Roger the powdered paints which he needed to decorate
the walls 'artistic colours', and was all-purpose handyman and
decorator to Bloomsbury. When Roger left the house in 1926 to
set up home with Helen Anrep, he presented Flossie with a
painting of the ornamental garden in its memory: Holloway, best
known for the looming women's prison where Margery
campaigned, managed to look like Provence in the Cezanne-like
blocks of ochre and gamboge. That year Margery returned to
Somerville College, her alma mater, to become its principal; Florence settled her in and then married George. It seems likely that
both Flossie and Mabel went on to work for Roger and Helen
at Bernard Street in Bloomsbury until Roger's death in 1934.

Thereafter 'tall and gaunt' Florence was shared between Helen, who moved to Charlotte Street, WC1, and Vanessa Bell, at 8 Fitzroy Street, a short walk away, where she and Duncan Grant had a studio. Vanessa now made her own breakfast and lunch so Flossie went first to clean and cook for Helen, then arrived with shopping at Vanessa's around six o'clock, where she made supper for Vanessa and her friends and cleared up, suitably screened behind appliqué curtains in a tiny area of her own. Presumably Flossie went home in-between her ladies, somehow managed to do her own housework and squeezed in meals with her husband early or late. Mabel, meanwhile, went to live in with the Woolfs in London. Both sisters were in their forties, the same generation as Nellie and Lottie.

Leonard never took to 'strange, silent, melancholy Mabel', as he called her in his autobiography. He found Mabel's old-fashioned ways and appearance depressing: she wore long black stockings and her shoes were cut down on one side, presumably because of bunions; she often felt 'low', especially in Rodmell, away from her sister and her London life. She was 'a dump', they decided, though Virginia got on rather better with her and didn't mind her glooms. (Virginia also refers in her diary to 'Mabel's lugubrious sister' who copied dresses cheaply, but whether this was Florence is unclear.) Mabel was slow and ruminative; she may have been 'low' because she suffered from neuritis and sciatica, which made her lame at times. The Woolfs called her 'the Cow', not entirely kindly, though it had been Stella Duckworth's nickname too; very quickly they decided she wouldn't do. Within a few days of her arrival, however, such is the fickleness of employers, Virginia deemed her 'a treasure'. They were never to be as dependent upon Mabel as they had been upon Nellie. She was to stay six years until the worst of the bombing hit London in the autumn of 1940.

The Woolfs were much happier with Louie Everest. Their new daily in Sussex was a bright, lively person, a local girl from the nearby village of Southease, who had two sons by the age of twenty-two. In August 1934 she and her family moved into

2 Park Cottages, one of the pair owned by Leonard, next door
to the Bartholomews, after Annie Thompsett got married. Virginia
thought her 'a merry little brown mongrel'. Louie came in at
eight, called 'Mr Woolf' if he wasn't up, prepared the breakfast
trays, though making coffee was Leonard's special province, took
breakfast to Virginia in bed, washed up the dinner things from
the night before and began the house. She rang the bell for lunch
at one, and cleared up after it, and usually left supper prepared;
sometimes she mended clothes. She and Virginia managed the
provisioning between them, using as much of Monk's House
garden produce as they could. Though it was a long day for Louie,
beginning with her husband's early breakfast, and with only a
little free time in the afternoon before starting on her own chores,
many of her friends were doing similar jobs and, she later recalled,
'did not think of [their] day in terms of hours'. Interviewed in
the 1970s she remembered what a lifesaver the job had been: '7s
6d a week and a cottage rent-free was really a big wage'. Eighteen
pounds a year was in turn a saving for the Woolfs: a daily from
the agency had cost them £1 a week in the early 1930s and
would now be much dearer.

Leonard had made almost no changes to 'Monk's House
Cottages', as he liked to call them in his correspondence with
Philcox and Co., the builders from Lewes. Rodmell went on
mains water in October of 1934, but Leonard's properties were
not refurbished until after the war. Until then the Everests and
Bartholomews, with their two and three children apiece, lived in
the damp cottages without hot water, bathrooms or water-closets.
They had an outside privy. Marie Bartholomew, Percy's daughter,
recalled how bitterly cold it was inside the cottage with its brick
floors and bare flint walls, which were 'all knobbly' under the
distemper; she often used to pop next door as a child to get warm
since Louie had more fuel. When anyone fell ill they used Mrs
Avis from the village as a nurse; the doctor was too expensive.
Yet recollecting the period Louie Everest knew herself to be well
off: her two boys spent much of their time at Monk's House; she
had a roof over her head; they would not starve. Born just before

the First World War she was a generation younger than Nellie and Lottie and was not living in; but her home depended on her job. Louie might have been surprised at how often Mrs Woolf worried that she was cheating on the bills.

Throughout the 1930s the Woolfs got steadily richer from Virginia's earnings and the Hogarth Press. They continued to improve their home and garden. The proceeds from *Flush* paid for a new pond, regrouted the old one, and paved the front garden. A summer studio for Virginia was built, Leonard had two fountains installed in the garden, the verandah opened out, and added a 'new Crystal Palace greenhouse in the orchard', plus new boilers. His aggrandizing led to some squabbles between them. Vita Sackville-West, scion of Knole country estate, thought his garden statuary pretentious, like a miniature Versailles (Virginia gently mocked Leonard's penchant for buying 'leaden' Cupids for a new water-garden). Inside the house the boards were stained and a pair of fluted wooden columns formed a decorative feature in the dining room; there were mantelpieces, new fireplaces, and in the summer of 1937 they had the kitchen improved at last, with new cupboards and a decent three-foot square window. The following year the builders, now P. R. Wicks and Sons of Lewes, made a room in the roof with two dormers for a library. Virginia liked to distemper the walls in her favourite sea-blue green which always gave the house an 'underwater' look. Even so Monk's House remained messy, dusty and smelly – their marmoset, Mitzi, had erratic bladder control; there were platters on the floor for the cats and dogs, piles of books, ashtrays and general clutter, and open fires (central heating didn't arrive until 1959, though this was early by British standards). Despite her pleasure in their comforts, Virginia's Puritanism continued to make her anxious about having too many gadgets and possessions, much as she enjoyed her Heal's chairbed, the new radio and car, the delights of electricity. She disliked the idea of 'the complete English Gentleman's home' with its 'endless clean, well prepared rooms', its choice objects, and maid in cap and apron. Her fantasy remained that of a house which one could leave at will, like the Romany caravan that caught her eye as a girl: 'a house should be portable like a snail shell. In future perhaps, people will flirt [*sic*] out houses like little fans; and go on. There'll be no settled life within walls.' In fact they were 'digging themselves in' at Monk's House, as she knew.

Having a daily meant that Virginia took on more of the cooking. She liberally sprinkled her letters with references to her culinary achievements and often signed off like a busy housewife, in the 'I must just go and put the dinner on' vein. Over the years she graduated to making soups, pies and roasts, rice pudding, curry; sometimes she'd rustle up a scratch supper – 'macaroni cheese and bacon fry' – baked haddock was a favourite standby, though often she'd find a 'nice dinner put away in the corner of the fridge', as if by magic. She was turning the sausages 'delicately' with a penholder, she wrote to Ethel, enjoying the image of the writer-cook, and was about to serve them up, in the meat-rich diet of the time, with chicken and oatcake. She enjoyed her competence and her range now went far beyond her first attempts at bread-making. She might become bored by housekeeping but she never underestimated its importance. She watched how Mabel topped and tailed blackcurrants; when Louie told her lamb's liver was more tender than calf's, she wrote it down in her diary, 'thus filling up a blank in my knowledge of the world'.

Cooking, perhaps; cleaning, no. In the 30s thousands of British housewives were learning to do without live-in servants, feeling rather plucky as they donned an apron, cleared the table and set to on the washing-up. But this was unheard of in the upper-middle classes, except among the truly Bohemian or impoverished. On a rare occasion when Virginia found herself doing the dishes, she was amazed at the effort: 'I've been washing up lunch – how servants preserve either sanity or sobriety if that is nine 10ths of their lives – greasy ham – God knows.' Others were utterly at a loss as their servants withdrew, not knowing how to feed themselves or how to keep clean. After Mabel and Flossie left, Margery Fry gradually gave up on housekeeping. Never having cooked she couldn't imagine why one should wish ever to replace a saucepan; used to her meals being fetched, she was baffled as to why servants found basements inconvenient. Many of the well-to-do would rather live in mild squalor than learn how to housekeep in old age. Others were simply ignorant: Katherine Mansfield wept when the congealed fat from a leg of mutton could not be washed away with cold water, blocking the sink and coating the cutlery; Lytton Strachey's sisters couldn't boil an egg and had to wait on the servant's day off for one of their younger relatives to come in and light the stove before they could put a kettle on. Others tried pathetically to keep up appearances, like the poet Siegfried Sassoon, who refused to see visitors rather than open the front door himself. When Angelica Bell, Virginia's niece, at nineteen was considered old enough to stay at Tavistock Square on her own, she nonetheless borrowed Mabel to cook and clean for her. Men were naturally not expected to help – throughout the 30s Grace continued to take up jugs of hot water to Clive Bell when he stayed at Charleston and to draw his bedroom curtains. Virginia noted all the changes as the next generation, or some of them at least, began to see servants as human beings. When Christopher Strachey worried that in his aunt Marjorie's house there was only a little box room for the servant, 'how very unlike Lytton!' Virginia commented. In this context she felt adventurous buying cakes from the bakers in Lewes (shop-bought cakes were considered vulgar), and arranging them on little plates for guests.

'We do without a char!' as Virginia once claimed, was never strictly true. It was one of the fibs they told themselves, like Leonard's insistence in his autobiography that they were 'servant-less' while employing both Percy and Louie, who lived in 'his' cottages. For him the 'prehistoric' times were when they had resident servants. There was a string of casual helpers in London and Sussex who came in 'to do the rough' – scrub floors and sinks, clean lavatories; when laundry wasn't sent out there were local washerwomen who took in washing (in 1938 only 4 per cent of British households had washing machines of any kind). Bloomsbury's chars are occasionally mentioned in diaries and letters (usually as a joke), like Mrs Mansfield, who charred at Tavistock Square and lived in the basement of 37 Gordon Square; Mrs Uppington ('Upp'), who worked at Rodmell and Charleston, and sometimes got rooms ready in London – 'Old Uppington has had all her savings stolen & can't get any work,' Virginia reported to Vanessa in 1931, wondering if they might help; and Mrs Langford, who cleaned for the artists in Fitzroy Street. But as live-in service was gradually whittled away, and as servants got older, the line between the daily and the more ignominious char was fast disappearing. For many people a daily cleaning woman became the only servant available. Louie was expected to clean floors and Grace had to scrub the bare boards and quarry tiles at Charleston with a hard brush and a bar of soap where clay from the pottery was trodden into them; the kitchen got so dusty and dirty from the Aga that she periodically whitewashed the ceiling and walls herself. Once she came back from her annual holiday in Norfolk to find a week's washing-up piled in the sink waiting for her. Mabel and Flossie would also have mopped, vacuumed and polished. Virginia used the word 'char' indiscriminately, often as a put-down, which showed how much caste distinctions still mattered. Louie Everest would not have thanked her for being called 'my charwoman' and preferred to be known, in later years, as 'cook-housekeeper'. After the war Vanessa would ask Mrs Bessie West, who came in occasionally to help with the cleaning, to watch her grandchildren for her. Mr West helped with the car. Such childminding and chauffeuring came cheap.

Servants, as ever, were Virginia's window on the world, the chinks of light glimpsed through the thick hedges of class feeling which boxed her in. She listened to Mabel's stories and, however impatiently she might call them interruptions, transcribed odd bits and pieces into her diary as future copy, perhaps: that 'Mabel had a chicken that lived with her fourteen years & was called old George', that she sat for two hours in London in the Lyons Corner House at Piccadilly watching people and listening to the band. 'Many people do this, she said,' though Virginia made no comment on the picture of loneliness or poverty which might prompt them to do so. When Percy's wife, Lydia, inherited a legacy, Virginia discussed it with her outside Park Cottages. Lydia gave Annie Thompsett a cheque on her marriage and was helping out Mrs Grey, a very elderly resident in the village. Virginia thought Mrs Bartholomew 'an uneducated spray' though 'rather a nice sharp kind woman'. She seems not to have discovered that Lydia Bartholomew had grown up with servants, been to boarding school and learnt French, but at least Mrs Bartholomew was no longer just 'the emaciated char'. (According to her daughter, Lydia's painful thinness was due to going without food for her children's sake.) Virginia noted that Mabel thought a party at Helen Anrep's 'crowded noisy drunk' and that Mabel had washed up until two thirty in the morning: 'This is a jaundiced pantry view,' Virginia wrote, adding, 'but so would mine have been I daresay had I gone.' In some ways she had moved on since Nellie.

Leonard, however, remained a stickler for proper service. Mabel's indifferent cooking – all those soups and salads for vegetarians, perhaps – occasioned argument, only this time between the Woolfs. Weak coffee, 'a badly cleaned fish' at lunch; then Mabel broke the gramophone, a 'terrible faux pas'. Leonard, resentful, called her 'your cook' to Virginia, which annoyed her, and he reduced Mabel to tears, which Virginia put down to his 'despotic' temperament and 'extreme rigidity of mind'. His severity with everyone was partly, she thought, due to his not being 'a gentleman': 'uneasiness in the presence of the lower classes; always suspects them, is never genial with them'. She seemed to have forgotten her own attacks on the suspicious 'servant mind' of Nellie. The row provided a good excuse for sacking Mabel but Virginia sided with her against Leonard. Eventually the coffee and the cooking improved: Mabel was sent, as Nellie Boxall had been, to Marcel Boulestin for cookery lessons. Virginia suggested that Louie go locally to classes organized by Brighton Corporation and in 1936 Louie achieved a Diploma in Advanced Cooking. Both became adept at the French additions to English cookery, the crèmes, soufflés and fresh sauces, which the Woolfs favoured. Then Mabel irritated Leonard again by asking for a rise.

Virginia concluded that Leonard's dislike of Mabel was instinctive and physical, therefore not rational or likely to change. At
the same time she saw his autocratic behaviour as an inevitable
by-product of his masculinity and his class. His brothers were the
same, she wrote. 'His desire, I suppose, to dominate. Love of power,'
though she noted, 'And then he writes against it.' In the mid-30s
domestic despotism was much on her mind. She was gathering
material for 'The Next War', one of several early titles for what
was to become her anti-fascist pamphlet, *Three Guineas*, in which
she would make connections between the authoritarian personality
abroad and 'Hitlerism' at home.

★

On a hot June evening in 1931 the Woolfs attended a gala opera
performance at the Lyceum Theatre, off the Strand, and sat in the
stalls among the grandees. They were invited by the smart society
hostess Christabel McLaren (later Lady Aberconway). Leonard was
ill at ease and Virginia listened to Lady Abingdon, a fellow-guest,
rather critically, noting later in her diary that 'She has only a thin
rigid trickle of a mind, & no play, range, or more than an inch of
depth.' Their hostess sought common ground by gossiping about
the royal family in the usual English way – how Princess Mary
was short and clumsy, 'dressed like the upper housemaid in peacock
blue'. Virginia felt her familiar ambivalence towards the aristocracy,
a mix of snobbish pleasure and satirical distance. The well-
upholstered matrons and the wand-like girls conveyed 'traditional
English life, its garden like quality; flowers all in beds & rows; &
the ceremony that has been in being so many years'. 'Between
the acts', Virginia wrote, the ladies in their long dresses and 'large
clear-stoned necklaces' went outside on to the street, opening
their cloaks: 'then came dribbling through us a draggled proces-
sion of poor women wheeling perambulators & carrying small,
white haired dazed children; going across Waterloo bridge'. Virginia
watched Lady Abingdon's expression – 'to see if she had children'
– but gathered only 'a momentary schoolboyish compunction' at

the sight of such poverty. 'The women involved in this garish feathered crowd,' Virginia added, shifting her point of view, 'pushed on stolidly.' Keeping her distance from both groups, as she composed it in her diary, the scene is suggestive: ancestral continuity and English tradition, that romance of origins, interrupted and disrupted by the sight of the poor.

In the 30s it became increasingly hard for the comfortable classes to turn a blind eye. Of course the poor had always been visible, and in London, at least, they always lived cheek by jowl with the wealthy. Since the Chartist demonstrations the poor had marched on London and had gone on strike, but they now had a differently militant presence; they had their own flourishing press and they were represented by a parliamentary party, the Labour Party, the political arm of the organized working class, whose membership rose fourfold between the wars, and by the trade unions. The phrase 'Labour Movement' became a political usage in this period and these newly mobilized poor were not the mob, even if some hidebound Tories still saw them as riff-raff, they were the working classes, asserting their rights as citizens and voters. The Hunger Marches in the early 1930s, led by the National Unemployed Workers' Movement, were organized and disciplined (though this was in large measure due to the Communists from whom the Labour Party rapidly dissociated itself). Together with the Jarrow Crusade in 1936, when 2,000 people marched the 300 miles to present Parliament with a petition calling for government action on unemployment and the nation's desperate poverty, they are only the best-known examples of many displays and parades of group solidarity or unity.

Communal activities, from fundraisers and 'drives', mass rallies and demonstrations, to hiking, rambling, group singing; the crowds at football matches and cinemas – all give a new public presence to the 'lower orders'. Group identity found its icons in the image of the miner, the man in the flat cap at the Labour Exchange or the mother with her arms folded over her apron and, like the figure of the irrepressible cockney, these were disseminated, vocalized and animated in a far wider variety of media and on a much larger scale than ever before. In photography, documentary film, newsreels, in the press and magazine journalism, advertising, through the loudspeaker and the gramophone (the monologues of a Stanley Holloway or the songs of a Gracie Fields), the image and the sound of a working class was reproduced across Britain, for information and entertainment. Photography took viewers inside the interiors of slum dwellings; it showed them the damp, the cracks in the walls full of bugs, the newspaper spread on the table as a cloth. Importantly, the extent of their poverty was made ever plainer to the working classes themselves, even as 'the distressed areas' or 'the housing problem' became the objects of government studies and commissions, local and national inquiries of all kinds.

For Virginia class politics was literally coming closer to home. Leonard had long been involved in the Labour Party and they both attended Party conferences, but from December 1931 a Rodmell branch had begun to meet monthly in Monk's House. It was only ever a tiny group with at most a dozen members, and sometimes as few as five, including the Woolfs. At first Leonard took the chair and Mrs L. Thompsett was secretary (Annie's first husband, Leslie, had died young); the local candidate for Lewes, F. R. Hancock, and his wife were naturally regulars, as were Mr and Mrs Fears, the postman and his wife, and Mr Hubbard, a farm-worker. Louie Everest replaced Annie as secretary at the beginning of 1935, and her husband, Bert, attended (Percy Bartholomew was an original member but soon ceased to come, perhaps because he was of a more combative nature). Annie and her new husband, Bert Penfold, often came. The bare bones of the minutes say little about the tenor of the discussions, which aired the political issues of the day. In 1936, for instance, Leonard addressed the meeting on the Colonial Question – '& a very good discussion followed'; Hancock talked about Palestine and, in August of that year, Quentin Bell, Vanessa's younger son, who had joined, introduced a discussion on the Popular Front; Louie remained secretary and was re-elected to the post when the meeting canvassed views on the situation in Spain early the following year.

In Rodmell there were few of the organized, self-taught working men of the kind to be found in the industrial constituencies or in the cities, and the old habits of deference were more likely to be ingrained: one of Hancock's earliest talks was on 'the Agricultural Worker', a term which was unpopular among men who still called themselves 'labourers' (though not 'peasants', as Virginia did, half-jokingly). The meetings frequently functioned as an adult education class and the Woolfs could hardly be on an equal footing with the villagers, any more than the bustling ladies who ran the Women's Institute. They had the habits of command and they were the employers of half the membership. Louie Everest, for instance, would never be able to call Mr and Mrs Woolf by their Christian names. There was likely to be far less of the openly politicized language of class antagonism, of 'class against class', or 'bosses and workers', which characterized argument elsewhere, especially among those touched by Communism. Leonard's socialism, with its roots in Fabianism and Cooperation, and in the public-service ethic of the nineteenth century was in any case far less agitational and tended to emphasize managerial efficiency and fairness. His vision was of a socialist society based on organizing consumers' control of the production and distribution of goods; he disliked and distrusted more radical views which put the emphasis upon promoting state ownership and, in his opinion, locked the workers into an endless struggle with capitalists. The villagers could have found a far larger, more mixed membership at Lewes and Brighton, but travel in the evenings was out of the question. For Louie, at least, branch meetings boosted confidence. When it was decided to discuss education and the school-leaving age, Louie read a paper. The details have not survived, but she remembered being frightened and how much time it took to prepare a speech. Being asked for an opinion was a new thing; this was a world in which the uneducated knew they were 'disadvantaged' and were grateful for advice. Leonard, for instance, often helped villagers with legal matters. Even so, change was in the air.

In 1931 the national conference of Labour women had proposed a charter for Domestic Workers, reiterating the need for training, the regulation of hours of work, rates of pay, food and accommodation standards, and holiday entitlement. A 'domestic worker' was not a servant; uniform was not necessary, and should only ever be provided by an employer, but no 'badge of servility, such as a cap which serves no purpose or utility'. Although, like other attempts at organizing servants, this too never really gathered up a head of steam, once women began to think of themselves as 'workers' with rights then much of the idea of service made little sense. The language of labour relations, of employer and employee, crept into popular parlance, though very patchily, across the political spectrum: the liberal, left-leaning *Adelphi*, for instance, saw the Trade Union Movement as inevitably creating more of 'a class war mentality' in the home yet, in an issue of September 1936, it blamed lazy mistresses for exploiting servants when they should be doing much of the work themselves; an article in *The Times* the following spring on 'Why Workers Do Not Enter Domestic Service' felt able to report that 'there is a strong feeling among many workers that they should be allowed a complete day off, say, once a month' – a sentence in which paternalism and the language of industry sit uneasily side by side. Only the most militant stressed the link between poverty at home and domestic service: Joan Beauchamp, in her survey of British poverty in 1937, *Women Who Work*, deemed domestic servants as 'perhaps, of all classes of workers, the most liable to oppression'. Her book included photographs of miners' homes, factory workers in mills, details of working-class budgets and housing conditions, emphasizing the double burden of domestic work which women undertook, and pointing up the advantages of crèches in the Soviet Union. Fellow Communist John Gollan, however, who was to be come General Secretary of the Party after the war, seemed to miss the point in *Youth in British Industry* (1937), his own survey of labour conditions, which borrowed from her work. He attacked service as a feudal remnant of serfdom, creating 'flunkeydom'. Like 'lackey', another conventional insult, the term conjured up the male servant, and neatly evaded the larger question of the division of labour in the home. Male chauvinism among socialists of every hue frequently impeded discussions.

Most women went on cooking and cleaning at work and at home as their husbands became more active politically. George Riley, the husband of Flossie Haskins, Vanessa's char in London, was a Labour man. In 1934 he became an alderman and a member of Islington Borough Council, and he was president of the North Islington Labour Party for nine years. When he came down to mend Virginia's windows in the studio at Rodmell, Virginia remarked that he was 'a nice honest eyed false toothed man who shines in the Labour world', noting down the technical terms he used – 'Theres the force, the push & the fit' – for later use in her novel. She was unable to resist a sneer at his displaying his 'intellectual eminence' and got his name wrong, calling him 'Mr Shine'. But there is no sign of any political conversation with either Flossie or her sister or that live-in service was felt to be demeaning by the sisters themselves. On the contrary, deference and loyalty were more likely to be expressed by women who had so few choices (what they thought in private was another matter). When Virginia asked herself, after attending the Labour Party conference in 1935, 'how far does anybodies single mind or work matter? Ought we all to be engaged in altering the structure of society?', she was thinking of domestic service. 'Louie said this morning she had quite enjoyed doing for us, was sorry we were going [back to London]. Thats a piece of work too in its way.'

Virginia thought it 'very good for my conceit and ignorance to have to pass the time of day' with people whom she never normally met, though naturally she relished the opportunity for satire at the expense of her fellow Party members. She was always alert to the self-deception and to the unspoken assumptions which characterized attempts at fraternization between classes, telling a French acquaintance how usually the middle classes talked at meetings while the villagers sat silent. (She also commented on finding the locals smelly when they all gathered in the village hall.) At times she seemed to wash her hands of politics altogether, reminding herself that 'happily, voteless and uneducated I am not responsible for the state of society'. She was referring to the powerlessness of her generation of women, 'the daughters of educated men', who had not been able to earn a living or take up public office, let alone influence foreign policy, thoughts which were to make their way into *Three Guineas*. At times she liked to send herself up as completely empty-headed about politics, preferring, say, gossip with the Labour Party member over the abdication of King Edward and his affair with Mrs Simpson, than political discussion. Throughout the 30s, however, she began keeping scrapbooks into which she pasted clippings from the three newspapers which the Woolfs took, extracts from her reading, photographs and articles – 'history in the raw' – charting, among other things, the rise of fascism and fascist policy about women.

What concerned her was whether and how 'altering the structure of society' was possible or desirable. Was all politics a kind of violence or dogma, interfering with the souls of others? How *did* people change? And what might a writer best do in a politically charged time? In 'Why Art Today Follows Politics', an article for the Communist *Daily Worker* in December 1936, Virginia took her usual line, arguing that to mix art and politics was to 'adulterate' the former. Today's artist, she maintained, felt 'forced' to engage and was 'besieged by voices', hectoring, censoring, preaching. That did not mean, however, that Woolf herself was unaffected by the pressure to write differently. On the contrary, after *The Waves*, she was searching in her major work for a way to write far more deliberately about history and the effect of the external world or public events on the inner life of the individual. In both *The Years* and *Between the Acts* she tried to curb the novelistic instinct to individualize by staging the experience of the group against a backdrop of change and continuity.

By the late 1920s the Hogarth Press was increasingly publishing books by and about the working classes, and especially those by a new, more overtly left-wing younger generation. Thanks in part to John Lehmann, who was to become a partner at the Press and was a great friend of her nephew, Julian Bell, the Woolfs were introduced to that group of public school Oxbridge poets – W. H. Auden, Stephen Spender, Louis MacNeice, Cecil Day-Lewis – who were to set the tone of much of the poetry of the 30s (the Press published Day-Lewis's *From Feathers to Iron* in 1931). In 1932 Lehmann persuaded the Woolfs to publish Christopher Isherwood's second novel, *The Memorial*, and launched a poetry anthology, *New Signatures*, edited by Michael Roberts, which included work by William Empson, Auden, Spender, Day-Lewis and Lehmann himself. Roberts's Preface nailed his colours to the mast, distancing itself from modernism in robustly masculine terms, declaring that 'as the writer sees more and more that his interests are bound up with those of the working class, so will his writing clear itself from the complexity and introspection, the doubt and cynicism of recent years'. Lehmann's other project, the 'Hogarth Letters', was a series of pamphlets on 'topics of the day' and in her own contribution, 'A Letter to a Young Poet', Virginia took up the cudgels, exposing some of the clumsier examples of the political poetry of the new generation which risked being caught 'between realism and beauty'. It was her old argument, in part with the Edwardian 'materialists', in part with preachers like Lawrence, that art should be free of teaching. Now that she was famous and 'an old stager', she inevitably came under attack and found herself regarded, especially by the younger generation, as redundant, mandarin or elitist. Despite some troughs, she could usually convert this to her own advantage; she would uphold a new philosophy of anonymity that would allow her to stand outside the fray. Mostly she felt braced, even liberated, and enjoyed meeting and arguing with the young. Until her death, however, she too was preoccupied with the search for a new kind of form which would take the novel and poetry, in Spender's phrase, 'forward from liberalism'.

★

Virginia had long felt the need to include more 'low life scenes' though, like the proletarian voices in the drafts of *The Waves* or the Whitechapel interlude in *Flush*, they always caused her trouble. She was always clear about her limitations and dubious about 'the glamour' of slumming, writing to Margaret Llewellyn Davies, that

old warhorse of the Cooperative Movement, that 'the young are
all on the side of the workers, but naturally know nothing whatever about them'. Throughout her writing in the 1930s, and
especially in her diaries, Woolf experimented with a kind of
reportage, of the 'I am a camera' or documentary variety, trying
to be a neutral observer of the working classes. Noting her own
'nice lunch', for instance, on a September day in 1935, she watched
the workmen in Tavistock Square: 'They are having the road up
with a drill. They eat with the point of the knife. They have lunch
wrapped in newspaper. They warm some drink in a bucket. They
have at least an hour off.' Visiting Trent Park, at the far end of
the Piccadilly line, Virginia observed the tramps among the litter,
'the middle aged woman was trying to make a fire: a man in
townish clothes was lying on his side in the grass. Both had stupid
coarse broad rather truculent faces, as if they wd fire off oaths if
one spoke or even looked too long.' It was a wet cold day and
they were eating a loaf of bread without butter. These were the
antitheses of the romanticized vagrants in her fiction. Sometimes
she 'saw', her word for 'the sudden state when something moves
one', an epiphanic moment which helped to compose a scene: 'a
man lying on the grass in Hyde Park. Newspapers spread round
him to keep off the damp. A cheap attache case; & half a roll of
bread.' One evening in March 1936 a girl, an out-of-work Jewish
seamstress from the East End, more or less collapsed from hunger
on the doorstep at Tavistock Square. Virginia was stunned by her
condition. They got the girl soup and listened to her story; she
was apologetic and pathetically grateful when they gave her
'tongue, 2 eggs, & 5/-'. Virginia's guilt was acute: 'Never saw
unhappiness, poverty so tangible. And felt its our fault.' She felt
helpless at 'the horror' of this suffering. 'Think of one of our
"class",' she wrote in her diary, the inverted commas suggesting
how awkward it still was to think in these terms: 'this is what we
exact'. Yet what she saw vividly became 'stylized' when she wrote
about it. 'What a system,' she concluded. For Virginia, at least,
such glimpses inside a working-class life were rare; most of her
encounters were out of doors. Like many other writers and artists,

she could juxtapose or contrast 'scenes' but she could not find a narrative or plot which might link these different points of view.

'Seeing' may have been her visionary form of 'Mass Observation' but it also allowed her to keep at arm's length those old feelings of physical revulsion which were stimulated by intimacy. Despite her efforts, her depiction of the working classes en masse barely changed. On a visit to the London docks she noted the 'sinister dwarf city of workmen's houses', an underworld image which belonged to the emotional geography of her youth. The draft of a mock-heroic ode about a butcher in Pentonville, the area adjacent to King's Cross railway station, described the dark streets where the poor were living like 'nocturnal animals' in houses with 'meat smells everywhere': 'semblances of human faces seen in passing, translated from a foreign language'. Pubs were equally alien and fearsome places (she can't ever have set foot in one) and corner-shops too – in *The Years* little Rose is accosted on the way back from buying sweets at one. Any depiction of physical habits such as eating and drinking, or of the body, was likely to slide into familiar feelings of disgust. Of course, she was not alone in this but absolutely typical – think of Orwell's insistence on 'the strong, bacon-like reek' of the villagers' clothing or the 'dirty subworld' of the tramps in *The Clergyman's Daughter*, and his frank discussion of smell as a trigger for prejudice in *The Road to Wigan Pier*.

Sweating always provoked loathing, perhaps because it is a physical process that cannot be controlled, a common denominator. 'Mabel sweats when she is making jam,' Virginia observed in her diary, and 'clammy' was another favourite register of distaste, signalling those contamination fears which were so often part, too, of anti-Semitism and English xenophobia. One example at random: in November 1933, meeting the author Michael Arlen, Virginia described him to her nephew, Quentin, as 'a rubber faced little sweaty Armenian monkey'. The conventional association of the Jew with grease or the glutinous – a substance which threatens to blur or dissolve distinctions – vitiates a story written in 1932,

'The Duchess and the Jeweller', which has 'Oliver Bacon' compared to 'a giant hog'. It relies on the conventional sick joke within anti-Semitic writing which inverts Jewish food taboos. Those prejudices remained a fall-back position, however much her fiction grappled with them. As late as February 1940, when Virginia had written sympathetically in her diary of Jewish persecution abroad, she found common ground in social snobbery while talking with the South African Dr Rita Hinden (formerly Rebecca Gesundheit) of the Fabian Colonial Bureau:'we discussed how nice ordinary people are. Then why are they so repulsive in the mass?' She was interested to hear that Dr Hinden found the African natives smelt, but their shared disgust didn't prevent Virginia from finding her a 'cheap hard Jewess'. Contamination fears permeate Woolf's diary, her most defensive, paranoid feelings often roused when others were no longer safely exotic or able to be individualized as victims – like Virginia's rant against the shoppers off Oxford Street, 'deformed & stunted & vicious & sweating & ugly hooligans & harridans', a crowd who, like her, was feeling 'the sticky heat'. This was class consciousness boiled down to gut reactions. At such times hatred became a violent shield against the feelings of invasion by the group or 'the herd'.

When Virginia wrote that she didn't want to be part of Nellie's world, she was echoing the sentiments of millions of British citizens who felt that the boundaries between themselves and the lower orders were being eroded. Many were fiercely defensive of their privileges or their way of life, though few went as far as the householders in a leafy Oxford suburb who literally erected a wall in the middle of their tree-lined avenue to serve as barricade between themselves and the newly built council houses. 'Every middle-class person', so George Orwell argued in *The Road to Wigan Pier* in 1937, had 'a dormant class prejudice', feeling himself actually to be worse off than the working man: 'in his eyes the workers are not a submerged race of slaves, they are a sinister flood creeping upwards to engulf himself and his friends and family and all decency out of existence'. Hostility to the working class was taken for granted across the social board and a working-class way of life was assumed to be inferior or disadvantaged. In particular, to be uninhibited about the body in public: to whistle or sing, blow your nose, comb your hair, eat in the street, be physically demonstrative – all these were firmly stigmatized as 'common'. Servants were expected to respect such taboos – one popular guide, Mrs Peel's *Waiting at Table* (1929), was typical in making her second 'general rule': 'Do not breathe heavily' (her first was 'Do not speak unless necessary'). 'Is that Tom?' asked Virginia, waiting for the poet T. S. Eliot to arrive, only to decide 'no, only the lower classes run upstairs'. To have a cockney accent was universally seen as a disability. Rosamund Lehmann's *Invitation to the Waltz* (1932) has her bourgeois heroine taunted by the sweep's children in their broken cockney. The narrator describes the family as 'from another world', with their 'sharp, bright, hard, rats' eyes', their dirty faces and their new baby spawned every year, 'another weevil' taken out for an airing in the pram 'as ants convey an egg'.

When she wanted to evoke the invasion fears of class Woolf staged a scene in which they could make no sense of working-class speech. At the close of *The Years* the gathered family of Pargiters listen to the cockney caretaker's children 'sing a song for sixpence'. It is a deliberately uncomfortable, evasive scene. Commanded by the gentry to perform for them like seals, their tuneless song is almost 'a shriek ... their voices were so harsh; the accent was so hideous', the narrator comments. 'Etho passo tanno hai/Fai donk to tu do/Mai to, kai to, lai to see/Toh dom to tuh do. That was what it sounded like.' Though it sounds 'meaningless', Eleanor, the most openminded of the older generation, asks whether the song is not beautiful and reserves judgement. The song – like a nursery rhyme in ancient Greek – remains to be interpreted and the children are an ominous chorus speaking to a world which hears but cannot listen. Though it echoes the bubbling, wordless songs of Woolf's vagrants and charwomen, that of the urchins is unrecognizable, sheer noise by comparison, like the 'mumbo-jumbo' or babble of foreigners when heard by those outside their own group. As the dawn breaks over the grim present-day world of the late

1930s at the end of *The Years*, the scene is of a piece with the novel's repeated emphasis on the limits of language, the failure of communication not only between the classes but within them. Yet what else was there if not these attempts at communication? What else indeed for a writer?

'We have nothing to lose but our aitches,' Orwell told his readers at the end of *The Road to Wigan Pier*, adapting the Communist rallying-cry, and reassuring those at the shabbier end of the middle classes who feared 'sinking' lower. Woolf's novel, published in the same spring of 1937, captures the disorientation and loss felt by those at the other end of the spectrum, the upper echelons of the British ruling classes and the professions. 'Why not down barriers and simplify?' asks a young Pargiter, only to fear that it would make 'a rice pudding world', a world that was 'all one jelly, one mass'. 'Brown jelly' was also the term Woolf had used for Hitler's followers, a vision of an amorphous mass waiting for their leader to mould them. As Virginia saw 'the man in uniform exalted' in these years, many within her milieu would seek to appease him, or even to flirt with fascism. Her next work, *Between the Acts*, like *Three Guineas*, would probe the attraction of violence as an antidote to feelings of personal and social impotence. It would bravely express the wish that women as the 'outsiders' within a patriarchal culture might continue to be denied 'the full stigma of nationality'.

The Years sold better than any of Virginia's novels to date. In America it became a bestseller, with nearly 38,000 copies sold in the first six months; it was taken up by the monthly bookclubs and Virginia's face appeared on the cover of *Time* magazine. 'Virginia Woolf' was now very marketable, one of the literary 'stars' of England. Virginia disliked this intensely; she found celebrity vulgar and degrading (her metaphors for commercial success or for popularity were all drawn from a disdain for the body), and her hatred of publicity inspired some of her most rancorous outbursts. Like suburban villadom or the bungalows which had invaded Sussex, where 'all aesthetic quality' was destroyed, she associated publicity with the culture of the 'middlebrow', which she pictured as a kind of fungus or cabbage-blight infecting every-thing. Virginia, like Leonard, might look forward to an equalizing up, but what would be the place of literary culture in a world where everyone was a 'betwixt and between'? This was Virginia's phrase for the BBC, but also for the working men she lectured to at the Workers' Education Association in Brighton, in a talk which nonetheless looked forward to a classless society. Though she claimed to be an outsider like them, since she had not attended public school or a university, the phrase implied her social distance and her cultural confidence. One model of a mongrel nation was the USA, both worse and better for being more mixed. It was a place, as she put it ambiguously to the novelist Hugh Walpole, who was visiting Hollywood in February 1936, 'utterly uncon-taminated by civilisation'. Two years later, when *Cosmopolitan* magazine in New York offered her £1,500 for 200 words, however, she produced a flattering piece which airily compared the English 'marooned on their island' and tethered to their hidebound tradi-tions with the freedoms of America, 'a primeval country; a country before there were countries'. With her tongue only slightly in her cheek she imagined that there were no servants in America: 'Every-body is equal.' The Americans, she wrote, 'face the future, not the past'.

Arguments about social democracy partly explain why, even in the late 1930s, as international politics worsened month by month, the British were still exercised about domestic service. 'Good Domestic Service is the foundation of National Health and Happi-ness,' the Domestic Services Exhibition held in London in January 1938 declared on its banners. The need for service was at the heart of discussions about the 'decline of deference' and the move towards a society no longer based on rank and place. Young working women with their new ideas about independence and enjoying themselves (the 'cheap dance hall' was usually invoked here) were the focus of considerable moral alarm. When one of the experts in the new field of 'occupational psychology', the eminent British psychologist Charles Myers, tackled 'The Servant Problem' in 1939, he linked the private and public in a way which would have spoken to Virginia: just as the old paternalist relation of 'master to men' had disappeared, so too had 'the old maternal relation' in the home. The mistress was no longer 'the strict disciplinarian and dictator of former days', he wrote, 'but assumes the role rather of the elder sister'. His conclusions were far from feminist, however: 'If democracy is to endure', he argued, girls would need to surrender individual liberty for the sake of social obligations, and cease to try 'to get all they can out of the community'. Since these were the same people who had long been excluded from equality, let alone privilege, it was effectively an argument for the status quo. One former servant, broadcasting in yet another BBC forum on the topic in 1938, put it succinctly: 'I wanted to live my own life – not a life through someone else.' She wanted to be 'her own mistress'. That year a National Union of Domestic Workers was finally established, which aimed at raising 'the status of the industry'. Though it had few enough members, it found a source of unity by hardening its ranks against the influx of foreign refugees from Europe wanting domestic work, including Jewish women from Austria and Germany fleeing persecution. It absolutely refused to accept foreign entrants for membership. A large proportion of these working-class women didn't want a mixed society either.

The Years, as ever, avoids representing contemporary servants, relying on the old retainer, Crosby, to carry the weight of the 'abominable system' of the old patriarchal house and family. By the '1917' section of the novel, resident servants have disappeared, and the cheap-lodging plates and undercooked mutton are the signs of the dirt and disorder in which the characters now live. In less experimental novels of the day the servant continued to be the conventional scapegoat for anxieties about social mobility or the poor encroaching too near. Writing about one's servant usually relieved one of the larger questions of social inequality. In Noël Coward's patriotic revue of 1931, *Cavalcade*, the Tory imagination was reassured by the sight of a demobbed butler going up in the world only to be ruined by drink, while the coffee-break and commuter classes could be comforted by P. G. Wodehouse's

'Jeeves' novels, in which Bertie Wooster, an asinine toff, relies on his superior manservant, or by E. M. Delafield's *Provincial Lady* series, which was equally flattering to its readers, making social comedy of the inept, genteel mistress at the mercy of her rebellious staff. Domestic novels written by women often agonized about class consciousness. In *The New House* (1936), for example, Lettice Cooper's heroine, Rhoda, feels troubled, and therefore appears likeable and sensitive, when faced with the family cook, a woman a few years older than herself, 'and as far apart from her as a foreigner who did not speak English', while her mother, more of the old school, prefers to assume that servants are 'automatons'. At the end of the decade, Daphne du Maurier's *Rebecca* lets her readers have it both ways, welcoming and mourning the demise of her corrupt, glamorous upper-class heroine. The sinister housekeeper, Mrs Danvers, is the figure on to which envy and desire, as well as fear, are displaced. As ever, class and caste distinctions were the lingua franca of insult and comedy. The mousey nameless heroine in du Maurier's novel, overwhelmed by her new life, feels 'like a between-maid' (and when she is flirted with by Rebecca's louche cousin Jack, he makes her feel 'like a barmaid'). Enid Bagnold's novel of 1938, *The Squire*, is more patrician: an applicant wanting the post of cook is dismissed unapologetically by the narrator as having the character of 'a born lavatory attendant'.

Now that live-in servants were disappearing or becoming 'bolshie', only the charwoman remained intact as the last 'treasure'. An icon of long-suffering motherliness and of the passive, manageable poor, she was the eternal good mother, who never took off her apron or her overall, like the relentlessly cheerful 'Mrs Burchett' in Jan Struther's 'Mrs Miniver' columns, which ran on the woman's page of *The Times* from 1937 to 1939. The char wasn't a social climber, she wasn't sexually titillating or desirable like the 'saucy' or 'pert' maid, and was a popular figure of fun in the period. At The Cave of Harmony nightclub in the 1920s, Elsa Lanchester and Hermione Baddeley had camped it up as two chars soaking their feet in a bucket, discussing the headlines of the day; twenty years later BBC radio's popular comedy *ITMA* ('It's That Man Again') featured the office char, 'Mrs Mopp', with her mildly lubricious catchphrase, 'Can I do you now, Sir?' Why was the voluble char so funny? The number of chars increased in this period and it was usually the oldest women, unmarried or widowed, among society's most vulnerable members, who took on the most gruelling jobs in homes, hospitals, hotels and offices – scrubbing floors and sinks, cleaning lavatories. Like her ageing, complaining body, the char's job was, perhaps, a source of social embarrassment, shame and disgust, so among the guilt-ridden anal English, she was bound to become the butt of jokes.

When Virginia Woolf wanted to put her finger on what she disliked most about the overtly polemical writing of the younger generation of political poets, she invented another of her char-women and called her 'Mrs Gape'. ('I must go and see what that poor gaping imbecile my charwoman is doing about dinner,' she had once written about Rose Bartholomew, when she wanted to impress a snooty friend.) Poets such as MacNeice, Day-Lewis or Auden, she wrote in 'A Letter to a Young Poet', hadn't swallowed 'Mrs Gape'. 'Something has worked in,' she wrote, 'which cannot be made into poetry; some foreign body; angular, sharp-edged, gritty.' 'This foreign body' was a favourite phrase of hers for the raw material upon which one worked. In writing everything conscious must become unconscious, automatic, invisible, so that one might go down into the depths and retrieve it again from formlessness into words. She often described the irritating but necessary presence of friends as well as strangers as putting 'gross material in one's fire', material which nonetheless fuelled one's art. Yet if Mrs Gape was 'real life', the outer rather than the inner world, lodged in the throat or stuck in the eye like a speck of dust or a splinter, she was also, as her gormless name suggested, an opening, something missing, that gap or rupture from which the new emerged. Once 'swallowed' or digested the formless became the embryonic, waiting to be born.

Now that Virginia was in her fifties, facing her own ageing as she went through the menopause, the char was her opposite

number. She observed her women friends as they grew older and
disliked any signs of their letting themselves go. The char or the
washerwoman was a favourite image of shrunken old age, 'the
ugly poor woman look', or friends who aged 'shapelessly' and
became little better than a bundle of old clothes. Like all the
servants who kept the upper orders clean by getting filthy themselves, the char was an ambiguous figure. Sexless and ageless, she
might be pictured as the life force in Woolf's writing, but with
her 'fingernails clotted with dirt', wringing out the 'hot pitted
damp cloths' which Virginia found so unwholesome, she was also
close to decay and death, her body spilling over like her garrulous,
formless talk. A wrung-out dishrag was one of Virginia's favourite,
semi-comic metaphors for her own depletion and exhaustion. A
care-taking woman, the char is also an abject portrait of the artist
whose work is both crucial and worthless, as she handles the
detestable, down there in the primeval mud. Out of the mess
something might perhaps, momentarily, be made whole: *Between
the Acts* opens on a beautiful summer's evening in an English
country house but the talk is all of cesspools. And 'Miss La Trobe',
directing the village pageant, creates her illusion of real silk by
winding a dishcloth round the actor's head.

★

In July 1937 Virginia had another of her field days and made an
outing to the family tomb of her ancestors in a little churchyard
in Stoke Newington, a suburb of North London, far off her usual
beat. She read the inscription put up by her great-grandfather
James Stephen, to his friend and brother-in-law William Wilberforce, who had fought for the abolition of slavery, and then she
wandered into the public park, Clissold Park, which abutted the
ancient church. There too was the elegant, white-pillared house
to which the Stephens had moved from the noisome city in the
late eighteenth century. For a moment she imagined James Stephen
studying *The Times* and his wife cutting roses: 'now it smelt', she
wrote the next day in her diary, 'of Clissold Park mothers; & cakes

& tea; the smell – unpleasant to the nose – of democracy'. Virginia had stopped to look at the deer in the park – some said there was a kangaroo – before she went home, despite, or perhaps because of, her observations, 'much refreshed by all this'. Smelling democracy might be unpleasant and yet it took one out of oneself.

That same evening after her churchyard visit she sat with her sister in the studio at Fitzroy Street, gingerly discussing politics. Vanessa's beloved eldest son, Julian, had gone to Madrid to join the Republicans in the fight against Franco in the Spanish civil war. Virginia was sure he would be killed: 'Always I feel the immeasurable despair just on tother [*sic*] side of the grass plot on wh. we walk.' A week after their conversation Julian was hit by fragments of a shell and died of his wounds, aged twenty-nine. His death, which seemed such a waste to Virginia, strengthened her polemic against war, but it also, in a savage, horrible way, was yet another example of politics forcing itself into daily life. Like the park surrounding her great-grandfather's house, what was once protected and private now seemed exposed and public. This feeling of the erosion, or dissolution, of the boundaries surfaces time and again in these last years. Writing and rewriting *The Years* had brought Virginia to the edge of breakdown in the early summer of 1936. The imminence of war invaded her dreams: 'its rather like sitting in a sick room, quite helpless', she wrote, as if Europe were her father dying. 'Politics go on all day,' she wrote to Ethel Smyth during her collapse, 'everyday L. is entirely submerged,' adding characteristically, 'I might be the charwoman of a Prime Minister.' All she could do was to go on 'like a doomed mouse, nibbling at my daily page'. At home, democracy populated one's head like a constant argument, while political ideologies from abroad, which elevated the needs of the group above those of the individual, threatened the very idea of the private or separate inner life which was so essential to her idea of art and culture.

Like the first war, the second brought new intimacies, but it would be a war on the home front on a different scale, one in which national unity would be constantly evoked and the nation rallied and exhorted on the wireless and on newsreels. During the Munich crisis in September 1938, Virginia noted in her diary that 'poor Louie missed the PM's broadcast' ('"We dont want war." Thats Louie's verdict') and 'listening in' together became a regular part of all their lives, the day now punctuated by news bulletins. Although hostilities were held off for another year by Chamberlain's parleying with Hitler, the British had entered the anteroom to war in which the country was to remain until the spring of 1940. Like Leonard, Virginia believed war to be inevitable and shared with millions of her fellow citizens the unnerving feelings of suspense as the fascist dictators gained ascendancy over Europe: 'Its like being in a temporary shelter with a violent storm raging outside.' 'Immunity' was her word for the desirable condition of detachment from which it was possible to write, but she felt she could not remain aloof and took on journalism again. It was as if 'all the surroundings of the mind have come much closer,' she wrote, and books were surrounded by 'invisible censors', a continual feeling of 'ought' which broke into any contemplation. In one sense the threat of war simply exacerbated the strange disjuncture of a writing life where so much that is significant goes on 'inside'. At other times it seemed to Virginia to wrench that separation out of joint as the outside reality constantly invaded the inner world. The feeling of incongruity, between the seriousness and force of public events and the need to go on with everyday life, created a sense of unreality, no doubt, for everyone; for a writer who needed to retreat into herself it was acutely disabling.

In March 1939 Hitler and his troops marched into Prague and declared that 'Czecho-Slovakia has ceased to exist'; Franco's forces were in Madrid ('And Julian killed for this,' Virginia commented in her diary). Like everyone else Virginia listened to the news that Chamberlain had guaranteed to support Poland's independence and felt 'the severance' which war made: 'everything becomes meaningless; cant plan: then comes too the community feeling: all England thinking the same thing – this horror of war – at the same moment'. 'Private peace is not accessible,' she wrote in her diary that April. As it happened, she found cooking a useful sedative at such times, but domestic life was also precarious since the lease on Tavistock Square was up and the Woolfs needed to move house after fifteen years of stability. 'Shall we ever live a real life again?' Virginia asked Leonard as they packed up their old home ('at Monk's House', he reassured her).

In April she had also begun writing her memoirs, perhaps looking for a kind of sanctuary. Their rhythm, slow and meditative, took her inward. Nonetheless this 'Sketch of the Past' meant going over old, painful ground and, typically, what interested her was her apartness from others: 'I do not know how I am different from other people,' she began, trying to understand how it was that she had become a writer, what part her individuality, a separate sense of self, had played. She wrote coolly – seemingly for the first time – about the resentment and dislike she had experienced as a girl – 'what is the word for so dumb and mixed a feeling?' – when her step-brother Gerald had molested her, trying to objectify her feelings, where she had once felt like an object. The despair which overcame her when she had given up during a fight with her older brother, Thoby, and let him hit her, confirmed her belief that she had become a writer thanks to her 'shock receiving capacity'. It led her to 'create wholes', 'to put the severed parts back together again', as if being passive 'under a sledge-hammer blow', however wretched it felt, and however risky, was the place from which to write, releasing 'a whole avalanche of meaning'. She wrote again about her mother and her mother's death but this time noted how unreliable memory was, how it changed as one grew older. She was unravelling the premises of life-writing, the idea of plotting a life when a life has no plot, and the piling up of 'events', which so often, she believed, left out the person to whom things happen. Though ostensibly about her 'self', the memoirs recognized that this was an illusion: the inner life was crowded with others. Writing about these 'invisible presences', she moved from memories of her mother to the larger questions of the group, how classes and other forces shape the world inside. She saw herself as a fish caught in the stream of history but could not describe the stream. As war came ever nearer she meditated upon the afterlife we have in the minds of others: 'How many people are there still able to think about Stella on the 20th June 1939?' she asked herself, conjuring the ghost of her half-sister. How long do any of us survive?

In August the Woolfs and the Hogarth Press moved across Bloomsbury to 37 Mecklenburgh Square. Looking over the property Virginia was struck by the grim thought, 'wh. of these rooms shall I die in?' They were not to get the chance to settle there. Germany invaded Poland and on 3 September war was finally declared. The circumference around their lives tightened. Virginia's diary noted that when Mabel came down to Rodmell, 'Atmosphere at once stiff and prickly. Mustn't mind, says L.' Percy Bartholomew gave notice after another row with Leonard ('Something about leaving lilies in the shed did the trick,' wrote Virginia – had Leonard castigated him again?) but in the end stayed on. Virginia looked forward to Mabel leaving: 'old Mabel who is like one of the clammy kitchen flies goes back on Tuesday. London no worse, she says, than anywhere. An opinion I encourage.' In Rodmell they savoured their 'happy obscurity with Louie'. Where Nellie had been a bully, Mabel appeared as the quintessential victim – 'pathetic to me in her dumb acceptance of snubs & all her life is a snub to her'. Yet it emerged that 'old Mabel' had a fancy-man, Charles, a Yorkshireman, whom she saw often in London – 'her lover', as Virginia called him. Mabel went to the dog races with him and to the Old Vic to plays.

There was more to-ing and fro-ing with Mabel during the winter of 1939–40, which was a severe one. When there was no electric light at Monk's House, Virginia managed to cook break-fast on the dining-room fire; she took up knitting, which helped her get through the long nights, and she made rugs. She sympa-thized when the Rodmell butcher said he'd had enough of the bitter cold – 'as he has to be in the shop cutting joints at 6, I can follow'. Mabel was 'suavity & capacity itself' when she appeared but there were strains with Leonard and with Louie, not surpris-ingly since they had to share the work. As the weather improved and spring came on, the two servants went out picking currants and went to church together at Southease, Louie's home village. Lottie Hope, now settled at Charleston with Clive Bell, came over with Grace and there was, according to Virginia, a 'great flirt with Percy & presents of tomatoes & plants'. Like British house-wives everywhere, Virginia found it harder to juggle meals now that rationing had returned: 'Dinner in the oven. Meat bad & scarce. Eggs for dinner. Fish for L. Macaroni.' She found herself worrying at the cost of the knife-grinder or when visitors greedily consumed the ration of sugar and cream: 'so the housekeeper in me rises into being, in this miserable life of detail & bombast', she wrote in her diary in early May, the last a reference to war rhetoric. There was a 'little triumph' when the grocers gave her extra tea but it was all so petty. 'Now margarine is rationed & I have a horrid skinflint morning ordering dinner, suspecting Louie who of course helps herself to this & that' (Percy she suspected of swindling them on honey and stealing wood). She felt harassed by thinking about economizing and wondered about giving up Mabel altogether. The great adventure of housekeeping could soon pall – 'And now dinner to cook. A role.'

In Rodmell the war brought the classes even closer together. The Labour Party ('that fat timid sheep') went on meeting at Monk's House: Annie Penfold opened a discussion on the war budget – the food control and prices which were hitting them all hard (Leonard wrote at the top of the minutes for 10 May: 'the day on which Hitler invaded Holland & Belgium', as if he too must bring the realities together). Virginia found it mildly ridiculous when Leonard proposed to undertake fire-watching and air-raid precautions duties in the village. She continued her irritable relationship with the 'tweed wearing sterling dull women' of the Women's Institute, though admiring what Leonard called 'the English genius for unofficial organisation'. Annoyingly, Leonard donated their saucepans to Mrs Ebbs, the parson's wife, as part of the war effort towards aeroplane manufacture. Virginia missed the intellectual stimulus of her friends and felt bored by 'the readymade commonplaceness' of the plays which the WI chose to put on, resenting, as she expressed it in her diary, 'being

smeared with the village mind'. (She would put her own drama,
a village pageant, into the centre of *Between the Acts*.) When Annie
tried to persuade her to stand for the WI committee as treasurer,
Virginia cried 'No' rather too violently and felt guilty later, taking
the old tone in her diary: 'The poor dont understand humour.'
Characteristically she went round to Annie's afterwards and agreed,
offering to nominate Annie too for the committee – 'she takes
this infernal dull bore seriously: its an excitement'. Worst of all
was the constant cheery falseness of wartime propaganda, which
she thought promoted 'sentimental & emotional parodies of our
real feelings'. Though she could be intensely moved by a vision
of London streets or the Sussex countryside, she loathed any
patriotic feeling being whipped up into nationalism, writing to
Ethel Smyth that one must 'enlarge the imagination and take
stock of the emotion', rather than be subsumed by it.

Virginia carefully recorded what Louie Everest's older brother,
Harry West, had to say on his return from France, harrowed and
disillusioned by the evacuation of Dunkirk. He'd seen his cousin
dead on the beach and other men shoot themselves as the German
planes swooped over; the man he was talking to was bombed to
bits: 'Harry has had eno' of war,' Virginia recorded bleakly, '& is
certain of our defeat' (though he later rejoined his regiment and
saw the war out overseas). 'We pour to the edge of a precipice,'
she wrote in her diary, 'and then? I cant conceive that there will
be a 27th June 1941.' In Sussex they were a mere three miles
away from Newhaven, where Hitler's forces were now expected
to land. These were the months in which Leonard and Virginia
calmly discussed gassing themselves in the garage and whether
Mabel should go with them; invasion was expected any day and
Jews or 'Jew-lovers' could not hope to survive: 'capitulation will
mean all Jews given up. Concentration camps. So to garage.' This
was 'behind' Virginia's correcting of the proofs of her biography
of Roger Fry – 'a kind of growl behind the cuckoo and t'other
birds; a furnace behind the sky'. Again it was impossible to inte-
grate the two realities. 'Its the vastness & the smallness,' she wrote,
noting that her most intense feelings had been while writing

Roger's life and yet how absurdly unimportant this seemed in the face of possible obliteration. Or was it more important? In such times what else was there but to maintain the fabric of life, whatever that was? 'One old woman putting on a hat' was more meaningful than the distant terrors. 'I dont want to go to bed at midday,' she added, thinking of their suicide. 'I've a wish for 10 years more.'

The problem was to fight paralysis of the will; to keep on going when one was merely 'a gnat on a blade of grass'. Although she was now working on 'Pointz Hall', her title for *Between the Acts*, it felt as if 'the writing "I" had vanished'. 'No room of my own', she wrote in her diary in July 1940, harassed by callers but also by a feeling of insubstantiality. Her identity needed 'thickening': 'All the walls, the protecting & reflecting walls, wear so terribly thin in this war. There's no standard to write for: no public to echo back.' She had resumed her memoirs, left off for a year, finding them by chance in a wastepaper basket (where one put one's emotions?). Their density, the weaving of threads at a leisurely pace, was utterly different from the random violence of the war. They are written as if the author had all the time in the world; yet she knew that she might die at any moment. This was not fanciful. During the Battle of Britain in the summer of 1940, they found themselves in the eye of the storm as the German planes strafed South East England. Bombs came close enough to shake the windows of the house and to make the pen jump from Virginia's hand as she sat writing in her garden lodge; daily raids threatened her walks (haystacks came in handy). She imagined a peaceful 'matter of fact' death being 'popped off' on the terrace, where they had been playing bowls one cool sunny evening when a plane with a German 'black cross' had flown low over them and let off a volley of machine-gun fire. Death was an affront, nonetheless, to the writer: 'The one experience I shall never describe.'

When Louie's father died in August (she must have had a hard summer), and Mabel was away visiting Charles in hospital, Virginia became almost a complete housewife. She told Vita that she had

had to 'descend to the sink' but boasted like a child, 'I did all
the peas; potatoes; and made a pie,' something neither Mrs
Nicolson nor Leonard Woolf could have managed. Elsewhere the
upper classes were hanging on for dear life to their old ways.
Virginia visited the establishment of Philip Morrell, widower of
Lady Ottoline, and was taken aside by the old servant, Milly, who
spent her life fussing over him, geeing him up to play bridge,
and putting him to bed. In her diary Virginia noted a tribute in
the newspapers to someone 'for sixteen years housekeeper &
faithful friend' (almost the length of time that Nellie had been
in the Woolf's employment) – 'Note the doglike attribute,' Virginia
added. Nonetheless the Woolfs felt responsible for Mabel, especially
when the bombing of London began with renewed fury in the
autumn, and staying in the country became their best option. But
Leonard lost his rag with Mabel again and Mabel was in tears
'about L. & the electricity', Virginia's diary notes mysteriously.
Mabel felt that she could never give Leonard 'satisfaction' and was
too nervous to speak to him. 'The poor tallow fleshed almost
petrified woman; who can smile tho', & is unselfish (to me) but
its no good.' They had 'a friendly cool talk' about her plans. Mabel
thought of going to Flossie and perhaps setting up outside the
raid area. Everyone wanted to be with their own sort. Just as
Virginia dreaded finding herself 'prisoned here with Mabel', Mabel
preferred death in a Holloway shelter playing cards with her family.
On the eve of Mabel's departure – 15 September – Virginia wrote
that 'now we go to our last Cook cooked dinner for I dont know
how long. Could it be the end of resident servants for ever? This
I pray this lovely fitful evening, as well as the usual Damn Hitler
prayer.' Mabel's leaving was rather different from Nellie's: 'thank
you for all your kindness', Mabel said to both of them, and would
they give a reference? 'I hope we meet again,' Virginia replied
cordially, reflecting that '5 years uneasy mute but very passive &
calm relation' was now over.

   With Mabel gone, life contracted to 'the village radius' now
that petrol was rationed and trains were uncertain. Mostly Virginia
felt relieved to be 'on our lovely free autumn island', but she

knew they were hunkering down for a grim winter. Housekeeping was more erratic: 'Fish forgotten. I must invent a dinner. But its all so heavenly free & easy – L. and I alone.' She bottled honey and watched Louie make butter – a process which provided an analogy for the new method of her book, 'The Pageant – or Pointz Hall', whose draft she had finished rather triumphantly in November: 'More milk skimmed off. A richer pat.' War impinged most on domestic life. 'If I could take today, Thursday, & say exactly how the war changes it,' she reflected, 'it changes it when I order dinner' – little margarine, no sugar, milk rationed, few visitors, infrequent post – 'Economy on Mabel means less variety in food, more dusting & L. tidying.' But these she knew were inconveniences rather than hardships. In fact rationing could be a stimulus: 'How one enjoys food now,' she observed at the end of the year, 'I make up imaginary meals.' Nonetheless she felt the need to jot down a brief summary of public and private events since the bombing began, recording deaths and raids, and their moves from house to house, as if writing might still provide the security which was now missing from their lives.

From September to November 1940 London was bombed every night. Over three million homes were damaged or destroyed, but half a million fewer people left the capital during the Blitz than had at the outbreak of war. So Mabel was one of the thousands who took to the shelters or spent the night in the tube. Over 30,000 people were killed during the bombing. Bloomsbury was hit and Mabel was to be found loyally caretaking for the Woolfs, nailing up curtains to protect what remained of Mecklenburgh Square. She had herself been close to death in a raid when the local flats fell on top of the shelter. When the Woolfs made a trip up to London, Virginia walked round to her old home at Tavistock Square and could 'just see a piece of my studio wall standing: otherwise rubble where I wrote so many books'. Mecklenburgh Square was equally smashed up: a mess of glass and plaster, litter and 'soft black dust', a grim fulfilment of her fantasy of the temporary house with 'no settled life within walls'. Mabel arrived to help and Virginia found her 'as discreet & matronly as ever.

Rather finer & sadder' after the Blitz and 'almost, in her very trained servant way, overcome'. Mabel's own home in Holloway was, she said, 'like a monkeys house. Hadn't had her clothes off since she left.' Death was on Mabel's mind as much as it was on her mistress's: 'You hear them whistling round you, you wonder is it our turn next?' Mabel struck her as 'a stormy petrel, only happy in a gale'. They worked together in a very friendly fashion at Vanessa's studio packing glasses and crockery. Despite the earlier dismissal, Virginia arranged for Mabel to come for a fortnight to Rodmell to escape the nightly raids but was glad when she didn't immediately turn up. Mabel appeared at Monk's House for a few days at the end of October; her friend Charles had died after an operation in Tooting hospital. 'I could envy him,' Virginia reported her as saying, 'they say I've grown fatter – sitting doing nothing.' The old fears resurfaced: that Mabel would be 'passive, dependant' and Virginia felt 'the old weight of respectable damp despair'. Then Mabel trod on Leonard's spectacles. But in the end she was passed on to Isabel Fry, another of Roger's sisters, and Mrs Woolf bade her a chill early-morning goodbye, this time for good.

Pondering Mabel's history, Virginia wondered, 'Could I write it, how profoundly succulent it wd be. The cold pear shaped woman: her suppressed country childhood' (why suppressed isn't clear), but she still couldn't write it. Faced with Mabel's deference she saw only 'the bloodless servitude of the domestic poor'. Charles she thought 'a typical underworld card'. It was Mabel's life with Charles that interested her, 'a queer relationship' which she couldn't fathom, though she thought Mabel maternally proud of him as if he were 'a small impetuous boy'. 'Now his life is over; & no one will know more than I do about Charles & Mabel' – an extraordinary claim. But when she cast her portrait of Mabel it became 'something like an Arnold Bennett novel' in her mind: 'the life of the bastard woman; her subterranean London life'. Reading Arnold Bennett was the nearest she had come to such lives.

In any case she had probably had her last word about servants in a dog story in 1939, which she had palmed off on an American

Vanessa Bell, Interior with Housemaid, *1939*

magazine to make some cash. In 'Gypsy, the Mongrel', Virginia again compared two dogs to two maids, one of whom was not 'everybody's money' (was she thinking of Lottie Hope, that wild but admirable character, who was often compared to a gypsy, and was now ensconced again at Charleston?). A trite tale but it returned to the question of how history might look from below: 'what was she thinking of us – down there among all the boots and old matches on the hearthrug? What was her world? Do dogs see what we see or is it something different?' In the end the question was left open. Gypsy runs off and is never seen again, as if the author had finally to admit that she had no idea what would become of history's dogsbodies. Virginia wisely left the future blank, like the face of the housemaid staring over at the artist's desk in the picture her sister had painted that same year.

*

In *Three Guineas*, Virginia had written that 'the public and the private worlds are inseparably connected; that the tyrannies and servilities of the one are the tyrannies and servilities of the other'. She was describing the Victorian household ruled by the pater-familias but she was also exploring the dialectic of master and slave more generally, of power and fear, which she believed was at the heart of sexual politics. In Woolf's account the tinpot dictator in the home was always male; aggression a masculine attribute. She thought her own caste, 'the daughters of educated men', the least powerful in history, unable even to take up paid work. They were dependent, vulnerable and sometimes servile, but their exclusion from power might also be a freedom. As non-participants in the 'great patriarchal machine' they could refuse its values and remain indifferent to its rituals; as outsiders who had once been victims they could refuse mastery over others.

At least one working woman had been 'irked' by Virginia's class-blindness in *Three Guineas* and had taken her to task for it: 'your book would make some people think that you consider working women, and the daughters of educated men as a race apart. Do you think we enjoy being "hewers of wood and drawers of water", that we do menial tasks from choice and are fitted for nothing else?' In a nine-page letter Agnes Smith, an unemployed weaver from Huddersfield, expressed her indignation. Though she was in deep sympathy with Woolf's pacifism, she argued that Virginia ignored the economic and emotional dependence of women like herself, which she deemed far worse. Family dominated and directed her life just as much, if not more, since wages were so low – 'a working woman who refuses to work will starve', as she put it succinctly. Agnes had looked after her sister and her mother for years, doing the same skilled work as her male peers but earning 10 per cent less, living barely above the poverty line. Now in her forties, she had attended Hillcroft adult education college for a year, had stood briefly as a Labour candidate, but was left without work, not quite destitute but living a 'death-in-life', sometimes staying in bed to save the money on cooking a meal. From the age of twelve she had known the 'sick hopelessness' of being doomed to work when she wanted to stay on at school and learn.

Virginia was writing generically about war and the sexes, looking for the grand narrative, an account of the desire to dominate and its psychological structures; Agnes wrote from the political specificity of her situation, from experiencing, in her words, the injustice of 'an economic system which is run for profit instead of service, and which holds both men and women in subjection, though it holds women in greater servitude than men'. Virginia wanted to change the fantasy life of her peers; work from the inside out. Agnes wanted to address local and national issues, to have proper housing and heating, to raise the school-leaving age and to provide universal school libraries, equal wages, and all the conditions in which her inner life would be recognized. She insisted that she was not to be classed by her job, 'to hear some people talk you would think that a weaver was born of a cross between a loom and a spinning frame, and a kitchen maid of a union between the cooking stove and the kitchen sink'. 'There is only one Agnes Smith,' she wrote proudly. 'I am an individual as unique in my way as you are in yours.'

More letters were exchanged, and photographs of their homes, and some warmth grew between them, though they were never on first-name terms. Virginia asked her to come and visit; Agnes returned the invitation. Agnes's letters are touching and generous, Virginia's haven't survived. Agnes deferred to Virginia's talent and she restrained herself from pointing out her privilege, but she also wanted to educate Virginia. She saw that the Mrs Woolfs of this world couldn't help their ignorance. They didn't even know their own country. Agnes gently ticked Virginia off for thinking Yorkshire somewhere near Birmingham, 'We're the North, love, not Midland.' In the autumn of 1940, Agnes imagined a reversal of roles with Virginia staying a week in her workman's cottage, writing during the day, since Agnes now had war work, and then getting the meal ready for the worker's return: 'It would be very nice to find you waiting when I got in at night.' There were very few times in her life when Virginia looked after others, although after Julian's death Vanessa had relied utterly on her sister's constant care. In these dark months, as Virginia felt increasingly useless, it is a pleasing fancy to imagine that cooking Agnes's dinner, feeling wanted and appreciated, might have saved her sanity. In November Agnes signed off affectionately, 'Cheerio, my dear,' hoping that Virginia wasn't too tired and worried by the bombing, 'But dont stop writing so long as you have anything to say.'

'Hitlers are bred by slaves,' Virginia wrote in her 'Thoughts on Peace in an Air Raid', which she had been working on over the summer of 1940. She canvassed her ideas at a Labour Party meeting in Monk's House in a discussion on 'women and war' at which Annie and Louie were present, though not with much success. The woman's task, she maintained, was to eschew the slavish womanliness which bred manliness and help to imagine peace in ways which would 'compensate the man for the loss of his gun'. Servility, and the shame which accompanies it, was in her mind, drawing her back to a feeling of guilty complicity. When she returned to her memoirs in mid-November to draft a portrait of her father, she depicted his melodramatic displays of emotion, his dependence on female relatives and friends for sympathy and support, and the supplicating role of the available woman, 'part slave part angel', in pacifying or mollifying the male. Yet she had also tried to see him in the round, as a young man whom she had never met. Reading Freud she found his concept of 'ambivalence' fitted her own mixed feelings towards 'the alternately loved and hated father'. She told Octavia Wilberforce, her doctor and herself a robust feminist, that Leslie Stephen had made 'too great emotional claims' on his children after Julia's death, which accounted for 'many of the wrong things' in her life. She could never remember any enjoyment from her body. She left off the memoirs, writing to Ethel Smyth in January 1941, that 'as so much of life is sexual – or so they say – it rather limits autobiography if this is blacked out'. Women were especially likely to be reticent: 'I still shiver with shame,' she told Ethel, at the memory of Gerald Duckworth exploring her 'private parts'. In her memoirs she wrote that she responded to the 'mutilations' of the past by creating what she called her 'good friend', that part of herself which split off. 'There was a spectator in me,' she wrote, 'even while I squirmed and obeyed.'

'It seems as if there were no progress in the human race, but only repetition,' Woolf had written in *Three Guineas*, a fear that surfaces over and again in her writing at this time. By 1941 it was harder for liberal intellectuals to believe that modernity had simply moved the culture forward. There were those in her circle, including her own husband, who saw now only barbarism, regression rather than evolution – it would be 'downhill all the way' from here; and to the older generation the second European war seemed at its start a meaningless rather than meaningful repetition: '1914 but without even the illusion of 1914'. In her memoirs Virginia was making peace with the past – or at least a truce – trying to see it in its own terms and less as the product of her own rebellion and reaction. It was no longer possible to assume that Europeans in the mid-twentieth century were an advance on their parents or grandparents; that the liberal philosophy with its emphasis upon individual self-fulfilment had worked. In an audacious moment, almost of heresy, she even wondered whether it might not have been better to remain 'family surrounded', and not to be ejected into individuality by those traumas which made her take herself and life so seriously. Nonetheless, she left off the memoirs with a wistful 'childs vision': how 'beautiful they were, those old people – I mean father & mother – how simple, how clear, how untroubled', she wrote in her diary at the end of 1940, 'no mud; no whirlpools'. An idealization or nostalgic longing, perhaps as dangerous as despair.

In times of extreme violence and threat the intellectual's capacity to doubt and question could be a double-edged sword. 'We do represent the last utterances of the civilised,' her friend Morgan Forster had written to her. This was hardly a view Virginia could espouse, knowing, as she did, that 'civilization' had shut out women for centuries. *The Years* had offered its own critique of the idea of progress, seeing her own class as 'crippled'. When she wrote a pageant of English history and put it as an intermezzo, another interval, in *Between the Acts*, it was not a display of national glory, no Canterbury pilgrimage, or continuous story of our island past. It was broken and farcical, a series of stagey scenes parodying the history of England through its literature, and if the villagers spoke in chorus they were only acting their unanimity. Faced with fascism and war, would it be enough, this temporary performance of community? It was hard to imagine any forms of common life that would be possible after the war; hard to imagine a 'post-war' at all.

In the past English literature had provided her with the possibility of common ground. 'Literature', Woolf had written in *A Room of One's Own*, 'is no man's territory,' and, taking her cue from Dr Johnson, her essays and journalism had aimed at 'the common reader', ranging across the variety of writing in English, relishing especially the lowly genres of memoir and biography, and reinstating forgotten figures, especially women. Now she went back to the oral traditions of song and minstrelsy, to what she saw as a shared culture and an organic connection between singer and audience. In those last months she launched an ambitious new project, a 'Common History book' to be called 'Reading at Random', or 'Turning the Page', beginning with a chapter on the 'nameless vitality' of 'Anon', and moving on to the arrival of print with its proprietorial author and more self-conscious relations between writer and reader. Understanding her own position at the end of this tradition, she also evacuated it: the literary was only one instance of 'the universality of the creative instinct'. 'Only when we put two and two together – two pencil strokes, two words, two bricks,' she wrote in draft, 'do we overcome dissolution.' Creativity was life, was self-preservation, a 'stake against oblivion'.

In her letters of this time Virginia's most frequent image was of Rodmell as an island, a retreat that could become marooned and was vulnerable to attack. Barbed wire curtailed her walks on the cliffs; searchlights set up surveillance across the downs. A bomb had burst the riverbanks of the Ouse and flooded the watermeadows at the end of the lane – 'the Park', which gave Park Cottages their name, had become a beautiful strange sea, and animals could no longer graze there. Rodmell was even more cut off and yet socially the barriers were coming down. She used the image of a 'breach in the bank of class manners' when the local policeman gave her 'a dressing down' for showing light during the blackout. To her he was 'the official bully'. 'So "rude": so rasping; the working man male dressed up.' He took no notice of her being 'a lady'. In December 1940 the papers said a German landing was likely in February; in late January they said before Easter, 'say in three weeks'; on 7 February Virginia noted in her diary that 'the third week in March is fixed for the invasion'. All her life the desire for independence and autonomy as a writer and a woman had been paramount. Yet such freedom might turn out to be socially meaningless, not a splendid isolation, but solipsism or autarchy, the individual in a world of one. The words of a 'half-forgotten' woman writer, George Sand, had given Woolf her own last words in *Three Guineas*: 'Individuality has by itself alone no meaning or importance at all. It takes on meaning only in becoming a part of the general life.' If 'Virginia Woolf' did not write what was the point of her existence? And yet would English literature matter in a year, let alone fifty years' time?

At the end of February 1941 Virginia finished her drama-novel, now called *Between the Acts*, though she clawed it back from the publisher, disparaging and disowning it. She was fifty-nine. She had lost, she told her doctor, her power over words. There was no audience; the illusion failed. She felt 'no echo in Rodmell – only waste air'. She was afraid of the past coming back, she said. For the first time in her life she had no home in London: 'all that completeness ravished & demolished'. It was bitterly cold. She ceased to eat properly. She began to hear voices. But she determined to avoid introspection and to rely on the spectator within herself, to become her own analyst: 'Observe perpetually. Observe the oncome of age. Observe greed. Observe my own despondency. By that means it becomes serviceable. Or so I hope.' She went to cook dinner having anchored the unreal world of things in words: 'Haddock & sausage meat. I think it is true that one gains a certain hold on sausage & haddock by writing them down.'

'Who do we speak to when we speak to ourselves?' she had asked twenty years before in 'An Unwritten Novel'. Solitude is never empty but full. Angels and demons, friends and lovers, caretakers and bullies, invisible presences who soothe or torture, who quarrel and make it up, skirmishing and embracing, over the borders of our being. 'Each is part of the whole', according to the benign discourse of the priest in *Between the Acts*, even the village idiot gibbering like a long-lost relative – he is ourselves too – and all the village and their betters, acting their parts. All England had become a medley, polyphony or cacophony, Demos become Legion. At the end of the novel, which is set in a hiatus, the summer of 1939, the protagonists become cave-dwellers, fighting and making love, acting out the endless drama of their humanity. Yet even here, 'in the heart of darkness', as the curtain rises on the theatre of war, in the interstices something new might be born. 'Love. Hate. Peace. Three emotions made the ply of human life,' she wrote, ready for it all to begin again.

The plane interrupts. Always that fear of invasion, outside and in. One must be immune, like Antigone, Woolf's pacifist heroine in *Three Guineas*, passively resisting the dictator, the voice of power and the law. How to preserve one's self against psychological annihilation; how to keep one's identity, one's interiority, intact? One might be bounded in a nutshell, find infinite space, and still have bad dreams, or float freely, the mind adrift, transforming weeds into flowers. It was 'Anon', featureless and nameless, with whom she identified. But no such person has ever lived.

★

Whom does the suicide kill? Among Virginia's manuscripts is a sketch for a story, based on an outing the Woolfs made to Brighton about a month before her death. On 25 February they had lunched at the Sussex Grill, where Virginia paid a visit, as they say, to the cramped lavatory on the first-floor landing. She was of the generation of Edwardian ladies for whom using 'public necessaries', as they had first been called, in department stores, at railway stations or in restaurants was a novelty, a measure of their emancipation. On this occasion, though, as she sat 'p-ing' as quietly as she could, and eavesdropping on the conversation of the women outside, her reactions were visceral and violent. 'They were powdering & painting, these common little tarts,' as she put it vindictively in her diary. She recorded their apparently mindless talk, banal exchanges of the 'he said, she said' variety, like that she had given to the lower-class women all those years ago in 'Kew Gardens', and most recently to the nursemaids in *Between the Acts*. Her disgust at finding herself closeted with them slid into a loathing of the other women she encountered later that same day in Fuller's teashop – a fat smart woman 'consuming rich cakes' with a 'large white muffin face' and her shabby dependant 'also stuffing'. 'Something scented, shoddy parasitic about them,' she wrote. 'Where does the money come to feed these fat white slugs?' The incontinent talk and self-display in the lavatory, the middle-aged women 'eating and eating', provoked familiar spasms of recoil from female physicality. Though her hatreds remained consistent throughout her life, they became acute in times of crisis, usually acted out in the privacy of her diary. Hatred was always a last-ditch defence against disintegration and in these last months the villagers, the local gentry, even her own doctor, were vampires and leeches, battening upon her and sucking her blood.

Yet writing was not the same as hating. It was a way of being mindful of those feelings. Characteristically, not long after this trip, Woolf tried to transmute what she had heard and seen, to turn the ugly into the aesthetic. She included the conversations and an image of Brighton in a fragmentary draft entitled, no doubt ironically, 'The Ladies Lavatory', imagining the seaside resort, translated into 'a fairy town by night', its 'gross body' sunk down, its skeleton 'picked out by little lamps'. But the seachange does not work; the town cannot escape its corruption and is daily 'born again in all its grossness', like gold which obstinately turns back to lead. Rankness is distilled in smell, the fishy smell 'of brine, of lubricity', which pervades the streets but especially the restaurant and – she repeats – 'this savour, this lubricity' seems more 'concentrated' at lunchtime where it smells too in the ladies lavatory. Fish, urine, female sexuality all mingle in the images of disgust which make the restaurant so unsavoury and in the little smelly room of the lavatory, where an 'emetic' gush of water drowns the voices of these ladies who are not ladies, as they answer the calls of nature and then apply cosmetics, as rotten as their words, which 'had a strong savour of decaying fish'. The 'scent of the rubbish heap', of the putrid, hangs about the female body with its unwholesome spaces, never entirely flushed away, identifying the women with the waste they produce.

Only when she notices the lavatory attendant – 'one of those women who are forever opening doors' – does curiosity surface and the miasma lift: 'of their private lives nothing is known'. Such lives, the narrator reflects, would surely be utterly strange: 'when, in old age, they look back through the corridors of memory, their past must be different from any other. It must be cut off: disconnected. The door must be always opening and shutting. They can have no settled relations with their kind.' In a leap of imaginative sympathy she notes, 'The memoirs of a lavatory attendant have never been written.' Her life cannot be incorporated in the record since she is severed from history: 'The woman who lives in this room has the look of someone without any past.' Partly mythicized – she has heard and seen such things since time immemorial – the attendant remains silent, an observer, a medium or conduit, who watches with the eye of eternity as the transitory people, like fish floating through a cave, are 'always passing through'. An alter ego, perhaps, she is also buffeted and helpless, 'like a piece of seaweed that floats the waves'. 'She inhabits a fluctuating world' and is 'constantly forced up and down'. Nurse, cook, maid, char – and now lavatory attendant – Virginia imagined a woman further and further down the social scale, abjectly dependent on the fluctuations and functions of others, and yet also detached from them. Perhaps some memory of violation surfaced in the phrase, 'constantly forced up & down'. Her room is open to all comers, like a self or a body, or a nation, at the mercy of others. Such a room cannot be lived in. Cleaning up the draft, Virginia deleted the lavatory attendant.

In these last months Octavia Wilberforce, Virginia's doctor, saw her many times. When Octavia came to Monk's House in the third week of March, Virginia told her that 'she had taken to scrubbing floors when she couldn't write – it "took her mind off".' Octavia, who was a second cousin of sorts, took a brisk view of her depression, urging her to keep busy with practical activity, thinking Virginia too much immersed in the past, and noting privately that it would do her 'the world of good to harrow a field or play a game'. Monk's House was dirty and chaotic, crowded out with piles of books and relics of their London furniture, salvaged from the bombsite. Virginia spent two hours carpet-beating, then watched as the flakes of dust continued to flock down on to the books she had just dusted. 'I'd no notion,' she wrote to Ethel, 'having always a servant, of the horror of dirt.' That she would get down on her hands and knees to scrub a floor was itself extraordinary. Vanessa, not realizing, perhaps,

Virginia's desperate need to feel useful, wrote saying 'don't go scrubbing floors', assuming it to be a degrading business. Anxious about her sister's fragile state, she chided her, presumably to buck her up, 'what shall we do when we're invaded if you are a helpless invalid' – not 'if' but 'when'. She added, with an unusual show of feeling, 'what should I have done all these last 3 years if you hadn't been able to keep me alive and cheerful? You don't know how much I depend on you.' As Virginia's mental state deteriorated Leonard himself suggested that she help Louie with the housework. Dusting had been good therapy at Asheham, all those years ago. But then, at Asheham, she had been in recovery, not breakdown. Louie, looking back years later, thought it very strange: 'I had never known her want to do any housework with me before.' And so Virginia spent her last morning dusting alongside Louie. After a while she put down her duster and went away.

Women, apparently, are more likely to choose a suicide which leaves the body whole. Men shoot themselves, die spectacularly; women take pills or drown. Death by drowning, so often the fate of the fallen woman in the nineteenth century, so often idealized as a purgation and a rebirth after the dissolution of the body. Water, like dirt, does not differentiate. To be submerged, 'going under', was also Virginia's metaphor for that mysterious process which made writing possible. Did she make a work of art of her body and abandon it, at once treasure and litter? No more putting on flesh. She was a nobody at last. She would not return to dust.

Who drowned in the Ouse on that March morning? Perhaps it was the woman who lived in that room, now floating up and down, flotsam but also jetsam, gross material flushed away, leaving only clean bone, pearls not eyes, pocketfuls of words at last turned into stones.

*

In 1945, as Clive Bell fulminated against the Labour victory and his son delighted in it, Grace and Walter Higgens found they'd stayed too long at Charleston and could no longer afford a Sussex cottage. It would have to wait now. Mrs Bell, mixing with the locals at the pig club, felt moved to write to her daughter with surprise, 'these rustics can hardly read or write' but they were 'sharp' – 'it's curious to have got into such society, for one is on quite different terms with them than one is as a rule'. And that man who fixed the windows – was it Shine?, no, Riley – the husband of Flossie, 'Nessa's char', actually became Lord Mayor of Islington, the leading figure in Labour politics at the town hall in one of London's key boroughs. One of his campaigns was to tackle the problem of refuse and the smells on the Islington streets – 'Riley's white elephant', his scheme was called, but it worked. Meanwhile, his sister-in-law, Mabel Haskins, poor dumpy Mabel – that 'unsunned pear' – was married a week before Christmas in 1948, twenty years after Flossie. At the age of fifty-four she stood up in the Baptist church off the Holloway Road and became Mrs Arthur Tierney. If her husband, a widower, was nearer seventy than sixty, what of it – she was no spring chicken; and who's to say that it wasn't a romance? After years of lodging with the Rileys, Mabel found a room of her own. And Louie Everest? She stayed on at Monk's House to see the next chapter. Within a year of Virginia's death Leonard Woolf had fallen deeply in love. Time and tide, as they say, wait for no man.

FIVE

Afterlives

*God, how cheap, to have nothing worth having except your money,
and your address; fancy being proud of that. And where would you
be today if the two of us thought that was all you were worth? You'd
be in a mess, that's where you'd be.*

One of the servants, a maid, in *The Island of Slaves* (1725) by
Pierre Marivaux (translated Neil Bartlett)

When they looked back in old age the girls who had gone into service were often mystified, sometimes furious or appalled, that they had emptied those earth-closets, scrubbed the stone flags, washed their employers' clothes. They felt like collaborators – 'how could I have done it?' the old ladies asked, as if it had all been their fault. And they tried to remember how they had felt: 'Haven't we been awful, going out cleaning all our lives?' they said, proud and apologetic all at once.

Years later it was possible to break ranks, to have opinions. At the time nobody was much interested but years later there was an audience for these tales of bygone days, the old days. And they told their stories. 'I shan't be sorry,' they remembered parents saying, 'when young So & So gets her knees under someone else's table.' When Winifred Foley looked back on leaving her mining village in Gloucestershire at fourteen for a job in London, she believed she had been 'cut in half'. But it was the common lot and parents' word was law. 'I felt I was in jail,' said Margaret Powell when she recalled her first post. She told her mother, 'but she had decided that the job would do for me. So that was that.' Margaret didn't feel ill-used: 'It was just the thing', nothing to write home about. Looking back, though, was different. 'My childhood was dead: now I was the skivvy,' wrote Winifred reflectively. 'I was in mourning for my lost self.'

In retrospect they found the words for the emotions. And sometimes they found the emotions too. They remembered how they had learnt how to be servants at home, minding the babies, running errands and sharing the chores, helping Mother, making the midday meal, fetching the little ones from school. 'When I was thirteen I was like a little old woman,' said one, who had taken on all the baking and washing for the family after her mother died. They learnt early to do what they were told and not to answer back. Like charity, obedience began at home; a girl already knew her place long before she went into service. Another remembered what she was told by her step-mother, now that she was going to mix

with a different sort of people: 'Got your eyes to see, your nose to breathe
– keep your mouth shut.' It proved good advice, she thought.

Minnie Cowley, sent away at thirteen, was miserable in sumptuous
surroundings: 'It doesn't seem right,' she remembered thinking, 'that this
big room should be just for one person.' Sleeping alone was frightening,
the hush of the house with its carpets and drapes like a death-pall after
the liveliness of home. How to survive the homesickness, week after week?
Happy Powley, who had worked with Nellie at the Laughtons, recalled
her first job in Suffolk and thought she had been frightened all the time
– 'truly' – 'we were always tired; always unhappy; we really were, because
you could never keep up with the work'. She was always worried – there
were so many rules, timetables and rigmarole, so much to get wrong. Two
girls of fourteen served two grown-ups from silver entrée dishes, and had
to behave (and work) as if they were a staff of twenty. 'She' was always
telling them off and they felt guilty – 'you really had that feeling, how
wicked you were not to be grateful'.

Memory made them rebels, though they'd usually been good girls at
the time. Always in by ten, just like Madam said. Jennie Owen and her
sisters, from Wales, knew they were well off in London – 'we were very
happy and we were well fed and we had a comfortable bed and to us
that meant a lot'. They had money in their pockets and could send a
parcel home, 'bedding, a blouse for mother – or an apron', 'we practically
furnished my mother's home'. Some were left cowed by years of service,
unable to say boo to a goose; others seethed quietly, waiting to boil over.
Even after fifty years, insults still rankled. The humiliations taken for
granted: not eating with your employers, the permission to sit, the order
to stand, never being trusted. 'You were just a servant: that was it';
listening always to that tone of voice, whether kindly or hectoring, which
assumed superiority: you had to keep 'strong-faced'. Some took revenge
by patronizing their mistresses and mimicking their accents, as their own
had once been mocked. Poor creatures, who didn't know which end of a
broom was which. 'They' didn't know how to enjoy life. 'They' didn't
know they were born.

Health suffered – all those ailments which British comedy found so
amusing – bunions, housemaid's knee, lumbago, rheumatic joints – and
sometimes mothers fetched their girls home after a couple of months lest

it all got too much for them. Mrs Woodburn, for instance, remembered how she broke down as a skivvy at thirteen in a house with forty rooms; she was up at four in the morning, washing and scrubbing till midnight. They sent her home for a spell but she returned to be promoted to housemaid. Yet she remembered the kindness of the mistress, who gave them all new uniforms: 'we were all dressed in grey, lovely silver grey'. The house had been so elegant. At the big houses they were never isolated and the food was plentiful (though many were shocked by the waste). 'I acquired an appreciation of quality furniture, china and pictures,' said Eileen Balderson, looking back fondly. Happy Powley, too, felt life at the Laughtons had been an education: 'he'd got a marvellous Utrillo in his room', and she saw lovely things, 'really lovely things': 'And you don't know what lovely things are till you see them like that, do you? Till you see them every day?'

What looked like sameness under the cap and apron hid a world of difference, of personalities, of histories. One girl was not like another. Even the poverty they had in common was different, though the hunger had felt the same. And sometimes those who listened and interviewed and recorded, those who went in search of anger or resentment, found laughter and were baffled. The past came back not as nightmare but as farce, a hilarious fugue of anecdotes. But you had to laugh, the old ladies said. If you didn't laugh, you'd cry.

In 1956, when Nellie Boxall and Lottie Hope were interviewed by BBC radio, it was a set-up. This much was obvious when the narrator of the programme, the Woolfs' old friend George ('Dadie') Rylands, introduced them as the 'faithful cook and parlourmaid' who would supply 'cheerful domestic details'. Of course all the memories were rosy from the days at Monk's House, which Rylands coyly described as a 'humble and rustic cottage'. Nellie remembered how sweet and frail Mrs Woolf was, her love of nice china, the way she rolled her own cigarettes; Lottie, as excitable as ever, laughed as she recalled the early days there, how physically cramped they'd been with no running water or bathroom. She gave a lively account of the four of them starting the day in the kitchen, she having to clean while Mr Woolf took his bath behind a curtain, then breakfasted, and the same performance all over again while Mrs Woolf took hers. 'Yes, it was bread one end and bath the other!' Nellie put in, as they laughed. It was a picture of absurdity, these people giving their orders from behind the curtain, but needing feeding and cleaning like children – bread one end and bath the other. Both the laughter and the comments were edited down in the broadcast. Too much like saying, perhaps, that the Emperor had no clothes.

In his autobiography, which he spent his last years writing, Leonard Woolf mentioned Nellie and Lottie only briefly: they belonged, he wrote, to 'the pre-historic days'. Yet he reprinted in full in a footnote one of Sophie Farrell's letters to Virginia, as a strange nineteenth-century phenomenon, an example of 'the curious psychology of these devoted female servants' who worked 'sometimes without exorbitant recognition'. Neither Sophie, Nellie nor Lottie was granted surnames in his index; nor was Percy Bartholomew, 'my gardener', who, Leonard wrote, lived in 'my cottage' and 'cultivated my garden for twenty-five years'. Percy received the dubious accolade of 'the most pig-headed man I had ever known' – a case, surely, of pot calling kettle black. (Mabel Haskins disappears between the pages in Leonard's account of what he calls the 'servantless' days.) Only 'Louie Everest' appears in full, as if only she had become a whole person to him. Leonard wrote warmly about Louie and took pride in her long service; he kept in his papers the first note she had ever sent them, applying for work. Thanks to Louie and Percy, he added paradoxically, they were able 'to live in comfort without servants'. Leonard paid tribute to Louie's 'native intelligence', her cheerfulness and her 'rare impersonal curiosity which the Greeks recognised as the basis of philosophy and wisdom'.

Louie stayed on to keep house for Leonard until he died in 1969. She continued to come in at eight o'clock in the morning, making Leonard his bacon and eggs in separate pans (a weird half-nod, perhaps, towards his Jewish upbringing, despite the pork, separating dairy and meat). She went on washing his clothes in pure soap-flakes because of his skin condition, and her mother did Leonard's ironing and put the creases in his trousers (though he 'neither noticed nor cared'). After the war, the old boiler and stove at Monk's House finally went and a brand-new Rayburn, complete with oven thermometer, plate rack and hand rail, appeared. Louie and Bert, meanwhile, went on living at 2 Park Cottages, which was at last refurbished by Wicks and Sons in 1949, after twenty years of tenancy. The windows were repaired, the rooms redecorated and a bathroom put in, though Leonard haggled for six months over the costs until he broke off with the builders altogether. In fact Leonard still owed them money on an earlier bill for repairing Virginia's studio, since by now he was in love with an artist, Trekkie Ritchie, and she was coming down to Monk's House to paint there each week. When Vanessa learnt about this 'young woman', who had appeared on the scene at Rodmell during the fly-bombing of London in June 1944, and now seemed a fixture, she merely commented that Leonard looked 'far happier and better', 'more rested than he has done for years'. No words of condemnation or jealousy. This surely was the best of Bloomsbury.

Trekkie Ritchie was born Marjorie Tulip Ritchie in Durban, Natal, but she preferred her South African nickname. She was also Mrs Ian Parsons, the wife of a director of the publishing firm Chatto and Windus. A Slade-trained painter, she had designed book-jackets for the Hogarth Press in the 30s; her sister Alice had sold books for them and the Press published two of Alice's novels. Death and wartime brought Trekkie and Leonard together; he visited when Alice was gravely ill, before she died of cancer in October 1941, six months after Virginia's suicide. Leonard fell in love as recklessly as only the recently bereaved and adolescents can; in his early sixties, perhaps he also felt that he had no time to waste before turning his face to the sun. He certainly knew himself to be a relentless, obdurate personality in love as in every-thing else. Trekkie was touched and wrote tenderly, but was more moderate. She was twenty years younger than Leonard, approaching forty when they met (not so much a young woman, after all).

Somehow a loving friendship was managed and Trekkie kept her marriage alive. Leonard wanted Trekkie to divorce Ian and marry him but she resisted: 'I want you to love me, you see, but not as an epidemic disease.' He offered her three-quarters of Monk's House to live in and half the garden – she refused; he offered, only half in jest, to give her it entirely and move to Northumberland if she'd come for regular, agreed visits; she refused. Eventually she persuaded him to live next door in London and spent the weekends with him in Rodmell. After the war the Parsons bought a house near Leonard in Sussex; they shared Leonard's flat in London; Ian became Leonard's colleague when he took over John Lehmann's shares, and effectively the partnership at the Hogarth Press. Their complex domestic arrangements worked for twenty-five years and were kept firmly private, though not secret. Trekkie was a keen botanist and gardener; she travelled the world with Leonard and went back to Sri Lanka, the former Ceylon, with him. She was his 'Dearest Tiger' but he soon grew out of the baby-language he had used with Virginia, writing more freely and openly of his affections, 'To know you & love you has been the best thing in life.'

In his second volume of autobiography Leonard printed photographs of Louie and Trekkie, the anchors of his life, on the same page. These two women, so different and yet equally devoted to Leonard, got on well with each other. What, though, had Louie thought when Trekkie first appeared in October 1945 and opened a debate on feminism in the Labour Party branch meeting at Monk's House? Louie had carried on as secretary throughout the war, and never missed a meeting, though they were always tiny gatherings with never more than a dozen or so members attending. When Louie in turn launched a discussion of 'Is Woman's Place in the Home?' a couple of years later, Quentin Bell's minutes simply record that, while there was 'considerable division of opinion', the meeting was 'generally favourable to the principle of equal pay'.

Traditionally the loyal servant watches over the deathbed and her testimony frames the stories of others. After Leonard's death,

Louie's importance as witness grew, and Nellie and Lottie faded further into the mists. In 1970, when Louie's memories of Virginia were recorded for a BBC television *Omnibus* programme, she was able for the first time to give her own account of the day of Virginia's death. At this time all the main sources for a life of Virginia Woolf were still unpublished – diaries, letters, memoirs – and the programme served in part to herald Quentin Bell's biography and showed him working on it. It was a bold, demo-cratic move, to include Louie, giving her equal place with the other interviewees. With her bright eyes and 1920s bob, she appeared a relaxed and fluent storyteller, rather a natural for TV. She described her job and her intimate knowledge of Virginia's working habits and made up the chorus of female voices, including Angelica Garnett and Elizabeth Bowen, whose last memories of Virginia closed the programme. Looking at the script of Louie's interview, her own experience emerges a little in the out-takes – how she remained an active member of the Labour Party, that she had gained a diploma, how she had a nervous collapse after Virginia's death – but what the interviewer really wanted to know about were all the famous people who had visited, that Tom Eliot went to church and the Woolfs didn't.

When these recollections were published, Louie added her own account of Leonard's death and of their care for each other. It is a touching portrait of the vigorous widower in his eighties visiting Louie every day in the Brighton hospital where she had an operation (she had cancer), and then being looked after in turn when he was helpless after a stroke. It was Louie who protected him, telling the ambulance driver, '"You are not going to take Mr Woolf to hospital. I know it would not be his wish." The driver knew that I meant what I said.' She tended him day and night for months: 'I stayed with him every day until the end.' The Tolstoyan image of the old man cared for by the devoted servant is not, of course, the whole story. Louie mentions 'a neighbour' helping and Trekkie Ritchie was also there, though her presence is kept veiled. Trekkie was aided in turn by her own housekeeper, Anneliese West, from Pomerania, who had met and married Harry,

*Louie Everest and
Trekkie Parsons*

Louie's brother, when he was part of the army of occupation in Germany after the war. When Louie became ill, Anneliese came in to Monk's House, and at the last there was also a nurse. Leonard died alone in the middle of the night. The night nurse woke up Trekkie to tell her. No matter. When Louie said that she was with him right until the end, so she was. After thirty-six years this was the story she wanted to tell and which made sense of her life: 'They were very happy years, I had loved my work, and become very fond of Mr and Mrs Woolf.'

*

But what became of Nellie and Lottie? Talking on the BBC, Nellie had said little about leaving the Woolfs, adding only a slightly triumphant note: 'I was sorry to leave but I wasn't out of a job for long.' But in 1939 the Laughtons joined the exodus to the USA, and, though they asked her, Nellie didn't go with them. Coming up to fifty, with war looming, she preferred to be near her own family. She went back to Farncombe, where she had grown up, to live with her brother Arthur at 30 North Street, the street where her mother had died, a stone's throw from where she was born. Lottie Hope, meanwhile, was in hot water again. She was working in Charleston, where Clive Bell had retreated, but the kitchen wasn't big enough for both her and Grace. There were 'terrific domestic upheavals', as Vanessa Bell described them: 'Lottie got at odds with the Higgens family (Grace and the Dolt) and our sympathies were divided. But when it came to the point of loud shrieks during dinner and terror lest a carving knife should be brought into play something had to be done.' 'The Dolt' was Vanessa's nickname for Walter Higgens, Grace Germany's husband, of whom Vanessa seems to have been jealous – she was always rude about him. During the war, Vanessa had to cook the evening meal but found herself well off for local produce and luxuries from London. 'With unlimited quantities of milk, potatoes, bread, vegetables, apples, coffee etc. . . . one can do without Lottie's spate of iced cakes, and not starve.' So Lottie was dismissed without a pension after twenty-five years in Bloomsbury. Where could she go except to join Nellie, her old comrade? Down in Surrey, with no telephone, no *Times*, they probably didn't get to hear the news about Mrs Woolf for a while. Nellie wrote belatedly in June, brief notes of condolence to Leonard and Vanessa, on behalf of them both: 'Lottie & I are very sorry indeed to hear of the sad news about Mrs Woolf. We both feel extremely sorry for you.' These are the only letters from Nellie in the archive and suggest the pattern of their lives: Nellie took the lead and Lottie fell in with her.

Number 30 North Street was, and is, a terraced house, with a passageway at the back running between it and number 32. It was two-up, two-down, the front door opening straight into the sitting room, mostly kept for visitors, and a kitchen and scullery at the back; upstairs Nellie and Lottie shared a bedroom, while Arthur had the other (he had his spot downstairs, 'his' chair just near the scullery door). They had an outside lavatory and a decent length of garden where they grew their own veg. During the war Nellie took a job at Farncombe Manor, where St Thomas's hospital had been evacuated from London. She worked as a cook in the canteen. Lottie went to work with Arthur and his daughter, Grace, in the local laundry in Farncombe High Street. Did they see it as a come-down? Nellie, who had trained under Boulestin and rubbed shoulders with writers and actors, who could cook Wiener schnitzel and crème brûlée, whom even a food inspector, dining with the Laughtons, had thought a very good cook, now turning out sausage and mash and spotted dick for the doctors and nurses? Lottie, who had slaved for a fortnight to cook a cordon bleu dinner for Angelica Bell's twenty-first, now that lady at the laundry with dyed hair? Did they ever mention the people they had seen – Marlene Dietrich, Douglas Fairbanks Jnr, Tyrone Guthrie – and were they believed by those in the queue passing their plate to the stout dinner lady, or picking up their sheets? Probably Nellie and Lottie didn't talk much about the past. It would hardly make them popular. Maybe they followed the fortunes of the stars when they went to the Farncombe Odeon.

All the houses in North Street were let by the same landlord and at first Nellie and Lottie shared the rent with Arthur. In the early 1950s he reached his retirement and moved out to live with Grace and her husband, in a house attached to the laundry where they worked. Nellie bought number 30. She was the first in the road to do so. She had a fair bit put by and, while the bequest from Virginia was minimal, the Laughtons had been generous to her. The girl from the family of ten got her own house; she was – according to family and neighbours – the first to have an extension built, and a bathroom and indoor toilet put in; the first to have a television in the 50s (a smart one in a cabinet), which her great-niece, Wendy, who called her Auntie Nellie, watched of a Saturday afternoon. There were a lot of children in the close community of North Street and number 30 was welcoming to them. Wendy became a favourite of the two old ladies. Her own mother, Dorothy, had often visited Monk's House as a girl and, with her father away in the RAF, Auntie Nellie's house became a second home. Wendy remembered its luxuries – the let-down bed patterned with fawn velveteen, the soft fitted carpet in the front room and up the stairs, the 'very nice china, napkins, home-made cakes', though she maintained proudly that Lizzie, her grandmother, Nellie's sister, had been a better cake-maker. The Laughtons had given Nellie some furniture – a 'beautiful three piece suite' and an elegant screen; a wooden statue of Laughton as Henry VIII, in reds, greens and yellow and, most fascinating of all to a little girl, a hexagonal biblioterre with its revolving shelves of books. There was a solid oak bureau from Waring and Gillow, the fabled cabinet-making firm, and a wind-up gramophone, perhaps the one Nellie had danced foxtrots to upstairs at Tavistock Square. In time it made its way to Nellie's great-nephew, John, who loved listening to the 78s, the wartime dance bands of Ambrose or Roy Fox. Margaret MacDavitt, the little girl from number 28 came in sometimes too; she remembered the music-box which played the music hall favourite 'Daisy, Daisy, Give Me Your Answer, Do'. Her brother Roger thought the house gloomy, overshadowed by the solid, plain 30s pieces of 'sit-up and beg furniture' which had once been avant-garde (what he remembered with a child's vision was the sight of the old ladies' pink bloomers hanging on the line). Nellie was always 'Miss Boxall' to the neighbours and the local children, though Lottie was either 'Lot' or 'Auntie'. Nellie seemed 'a lady', thought Margaret, not posh but 'a notch higher in her manner'; whereas Lottie 'was one of us', her brother reckoned. Thinking of 'Miss Boxall's', their own house was just 'normal poverty' by comparison.

Everyone was clear on one point, even fifty years on: Nellie 'was the boss'. At number 30 they were cook and parlourmaid. Lottie did all the cleaning; Nellie, the cooking (the children remembered pork pies and sponge cakes) and Nellie was in charge. She'd hated Rodmell, she told Mrs MacDavitt, for its lack of facilities. But they didn't talk much about the past. As far as everyone knew, Lottie couldn't cook, or Nellie didn't let her. She was an awful cook, according to Nellie's niece, Grace, who often went to stay in Tavistock Square in the early 30s, and sometimes helped Lottie too, taking Mr Bell his breakfast and tidying up for him. Yet according to Quentin Bell, Lottie was 'a gifted cook' producing 'rich and elegant meals' for his father, who was something of a gourmet, and had been known to order a butler from Fortnum and Mason's when entertaining at home. If Lottie was annoyed at being demoted and having to do the donkey-work, she didn't show it. Nellie told her off but she didn't take any notice. It was all water off a duck's back. She went on drinking and smoking, and sending little Roger MacDavitt to put 6d bets on Lester Piggott's horses down at the woolshop which doubled as a bookie's. If Nellie was a saver, Lottie was a spender; she almost got a Boxall nephew into trouble, encouraging him in bad habits at the Duke of Wellington pub.

As for Nellie, 'she was a forceful character. Forceful,' was Wendy's verdict, 'She bossed everyone, bossed me.' 'Terribly bossy', said Vanessa, Wendy's cousin, who'd been named after Mrs Bell, whereas 'Lottie always used to have a smile.' Was it her servant-training or frustrated mothering? Was it temperament or training or both? Wendy, according to her cousin, was 'the child Nellie never had',

but in many ways Lottie was the child. She was always 'an innocent', they said, 'a sweet soul' but a bit wanting. Nellie had to
keep an eye on Lottie and sometimes calm her down, sending
her to the shop for one thing at a time. If Lottie tried not to
upset Nellie, Nellie was always protective. The children in North
Street used to run in and out of open doorways and passages but
the little boy at number 32, Bob Atkins, remembered he would
always knock at number 30 'out of respect'. He was a foster-child,
abandoned by his mother. He didn't think Miss Boxall was at all
a disciplinarian: Nellie gave him cake and lemonade because she
felt sorry for him.

Lottie had known Nellie's family for years and was completely
adopted by the Boxalls who were scattered around the area. Lizzie,
the older sister who had looked after Nellie, moved to Peasmarsh
when she married (not 'Peaslake', as Virginia once mistakenly
wrote in her diary) and now the family ran the village shop. Every
Sunday Lottie and Nellie went to tea there. Lottie was 'always on
the go', always game for a laugh. Nellie was more reserved; she
hardly drank and wouldn't play cards at the Christmas gatherings
where Lottie joined in with the men. Everyone still thought
Lottie a bit of a gypsy – 'not of English extraction – Balkan?
Maltese?' a neighbour thought – a romantic identity Lottie encouraged with her increasingly unconvincing jet-black hair; she liked
to 'tell' the tea leaves at parties. In the photos Lottie stands boldly,
hand on hip; Nellie is more decorous, often in formal outfits,
wearing her spectacles, her hands folded in front of her in the
pose of the respectable servant. As Nellie grew stouter, Lottie
stayed pencil-thin, still dressing glamorously, with the scarlet slash
of lipstick, her hair swept up into a feathery turban, a cerise scarf
or hat against a bright green sweater, a frock of pillar-box red.
They did everything together: weddings and funerals, holidays at
the seaside. They treated Wendy to trips, taking the little girl to
the coast or up to town on the milk train, to buy shell-pink
boned corsets at Marshall and Snelgrove (where Virginia had once
shopped), or visiting their old friend Dora Harland, the cook who
had worked for Maynard Keynes, and who now worked for the

critic Raymond Mortimer and the architect Paul Hislop at 5A Canonbury Place. They always travelled on buses as nervous Nellie wouldn't use the underground; they had lunch or tea at the Lyons Corner House at the Strand and went to the London Palladium. When Dorothy and her family moved back to Farncombe in the late 50s, Wendy went to supper with the old ladies every Thursday evening before her shorthand classes. There they were, still cook and parlourmaid. They made rag rugs (a local Godalming craft). They were, as Wendy said, 'an item'.

But not lovers. At least, it seems not. Upstairs in North Street were two single beds in two separate bedrooms, though that is hardly conclusive. It was certainly a relationship as intimate as a love-affair, and no doubt in the old days when they had shared the same bed, as maids did, they had given each other a good cuddle. Lottie, however, was popular with the blokes and had several men friends in London and Essex. Sometimes Nellie and she fell out over it, and on one occasion Nellie confiscated Lottie's key until she behaved herself. In the Sapphist-conscious world of Bloomsbury, an ongoing affair between Nellie and Lottie would not have gone unremarked. It's more likely that Nellie was intensely attached to Lottie as she was to Virginia. She was protective of Lottie and wouldn't want her to get pregnant. Whether the two were lovers or not, Nellie took revenge for her dismissal from the Woolfs. When asked why she left, she told her relatives that she couldn't keep Mr Woolf out of her bed. Yet, if this were true, why would Lizzie in 1934 write desperate letters asking for Nellie to be reinstated and why would Nellie plead to return? Of course such things happened and there was tittle-tattle about Leonard in Bloomsbury, since Bloomsbury couldn't imagine any man managing his life without sex. At least one friend, however, looking back forty years to the mid-20s, remembered Leonard being prepared to give up on 'ever having any sort of sexual satisfaction' in his marriage because his wife was a genius, and never even flirting lest it upset Virginia. A rumour had apparently done the rounds that 'he had an affair with a parlourmaid', but years later, Leonard, who was scrupulously honest, told Trekkie that he never had been involved with another woman, since, had Virginia learnt of it, 'it would have sent her mad'. It's far more likely that Nellie was saving face and resorting to the one weapon all servants have had through the ages – gossip. After eighteen years with Mrs Woolf, what reason could she give for her dismissal which wouldn't reflect badly on herself? It was easier to blame Leonard than admit relations with Mrs Woolf had broken down. Years later, Grace, Nellie's niece, gave a more restrained account: 'Virginia and Nell were the best of friends, she was always sorry to have left there. But Mr Wolfe [*sic*] wasn't one of the best to work for.' Mabel Haskins had also found Leonard difficult; he was quick to anger and he could be authoritarian, as Virginia had observed.

Like many live-in servants who stayed too long with their employers, Nellie Boxall didn't marry; she didn't have children; she saved. But unlike Sophie Farrell, she didn't end her days in a rented room. She bought her own house and had an inside bath-room; she moved very slightly up the social scale and had her own ideas of what was proper. She was like those women her mistress had found so disappointing, who wanted baths and money. She was conservative; she probably voted Labour. She died in 1965, aged seventy-five, not far from where she was born. She hardly moved at all; she had come a long way. Depends how you look at it.

Lottie remained faithful to Nellie and looked after her in her last illness, till Nellie fell out of bed one day and never recovered. Nellie hadn't made a will and nothing belonged to Lottie, but the Boxall family let her stay on. Without Nellie, they said, Lottie couldn't cope. She went to pieces; she kept coals in the bath (which would have been easier than lugging a scuttle up from the coal-shed in her seventies), she turned the fridge off overnight and got even scattier. She needed the organizing, fussing Nellie to keep her going. But she was also getting very old. Eventually she went into a home, run by the council, the Hambledon Homes for the Aged. For the first time in decades she wasn't able to colour her hair and she went white. She didn't look like Lottie any more. Many of the carers there were Hambledon residents,

Lizzie, Nellie, Lottie, with Wendy

local, like Lottie herself. They would all have known that this comfortable home for '80 non-sick aged people' was the old Union workhouse. If Lottie had sat outside amid its trees and lawns she would have seen the old plaque on the wall reminding her that it had been erected 200 years earlier 'for the better relief and employment of the poor'. The institutional child finally ended up in the institution she had so narrowly avoided as a girl. She probably thought herself lucky. She died in 1973 in her early eighties, a mile or so from where she had grown up in Miss Sichel's Home.

Lottie never knew where she came from; she'd had no family but those of her employers and Nellie's, no house, no savings – she was the ultimate hanger-on. She came into this world with nothing and she took nothing out. Like Virginia Woolf's imaginary mongrel, 'Gypsy', she really was a nobody. 'Bless her', one relative of Nellie's said, slightly unctuously, and with a mixture of affection and pity, like the adult's pat on the child's head or the tipping of a nod to an aged parent. Well, maybe; maybe she always was a child; maybe she became more so. Real grown-up people, after all,

have children, own property, make money. That's how they
know they're grown up. Yet she was always remembered with
affection. Everyone who talked about Lottie lit up and laughed
at the thought of her. If a life should be judged by what it gener-
ates rather than what it accumulates, then maybe Lottie Hope
knew the secret of success.

In the 1970s Hambledon Homes was sold off by Surrey council
to the Institute for Oceanographic Sciences, who then sold the
site on for private development in 1995. Hambledon Park as it
now is, retains the workhouse buildings as luxury flats and smart
executive homes amid the extensive grounds. The plaque is still
there.

★

In 1973, the year that Lottie died, Happy Powley, now Mrs Happy
Sturgeon, who had been maid to Nellie's cook at the Laughtons,
was recorded by George Ewart Evans. Ewart Evans had been
collecting testimonies of 'folk life' in Suffolk since the mid-50s.
Most of his previous informants had been male agricultural
workers, born before the turn of the century, who'd worked on
farms prior to mechanization, and spoke the old dialect, rich in
proverb and folklore – horsemen, blacksmiths, shepherds, wheel-
wrights – and many others whose skills and crafts were fast
disappearing. The son of a grocer from Wales, Ewart Evans was
a pioneer in listening to others and in documenting rural life and
language, the memories and experience of working people. He
began to tune in on the words and customs of Suffolk when his
wife took a job as school mistress in a remote village in East
Anglia and, extraordinarily, when he himself began to go deaf.
Deafness made him listen more intently. When he talked to the
older women of East Anglia, he found they had usually been
domestic servants and, although their testimony sometimes sat
uneasily with his emphasis upon the rural, he ploughed on,
including them in his collection of 1976, almost his last, *Of Mouths
of Men*.

No matter how patient the transcriber, a voice cannot be written down. Inevitably its flavour and richness is lost and editing is also inevitable, as the free flow of memory and talk is channelled into a convincing narrative. On the page, Happy's memories of her past read a little flatly and sound like many others': the familiar tale of going into service at thirteen or fourteen, with its hardships and loneliness, and its endless round of drudgery. The taped interview, however, is a different story. Happy laughs throughout, a rich, throaty laugh, which often overcomes her, and stops her from talking. The laughter conveys her warmth and personality and was accompanied no doubt with gestures and facial expressions, which only film or video would do justice to. (Ewart Evans rather bossily tidied up Happy's grammar and syntax, translating her slang terms into 'proper' English, editing out her asides to her listener, 'you see', 'you know', and those exclamations – 'now this is really true!' – which are also a part of her friendliness.) Far from being simply a victim, Happy is clearly an entertainer with an ear for the right anecdote; she is obviously enjoying having her say.

Mrs Sturgeon also laughs every time she mentions a terrible experience. Her laughter ironizes much of what she recalls: 'oh it was the most marvellous door!' she says, tongue in cheek, when she remembers the almost sacred ritual of cleaning the oak front door and the brass door knocker. There is her story of 'The Day of the Flues': 'Saturday afternoon was a very *enjoyable* time,' when she was expected to clean the flues in the kitchen-range, covering herself with soot and mess. She had then to clean the kitchen thoroughly too, scrubbing and polishing the dresser, table and tiles, and next start on the scullery, heating water in saucepans – 'but you were only allowed to do so much of the floor with the same water, you know, so that the water mustn't be dirty'; then 'scrub the back yard on your hands and knees. And then it was time to start on Saturday evening's dinner.' Sometimes – she is laughing throughout – 'Ma'am' appeared in a long mac, wearing rubber gloves and her hair tied up. She'd poke into the flues and bring out more soot – so the whole thing had to be done all over again.'I'd have gone mad!' Happy exclaimed, if that had happened every week. 'I used to say it never would have worried me if I'd joined a concentration camp!' In retrospect her first mistress seemed a sadist, and Happy's reference to the concentration camp, which she was very unlikely to know about in 1931 as a fourteen-year-old in Suffolk, came out of her unconscious as a measure of how absolutely vulnerable she'd felt. Her laughter was also that of a survivor. A defence against the painful feelings these memories might stir, it covered her embarrassment, her disbelief that she had been that fourteen-year-old, covered in soot. And that she had stood it. She laughed with relief, but anyone who wanted to understand what it was like to be in service might listen to the laughter as much as the words. The laughter was a built-in commentary, a distillation of many responses and feelings – an escape from shyness, for instance – why should you share the worst experiences of your life with someone you hardly know? Sometimes the laughter prevented any further discussion. And do only the English laugh like this?

Happy Sturgeon was born in 1917 and, like Louie Everest, belonged to that last generation of English girls and women who went into residential service as a matter of course. When he published extracts from the interview, Ewart Evans wanted to show a shift, between the 1900s and the 1930s, and to illustrate the backwardness of provincial employers compared to the London progressives Happy Powley had encountered in Bloomsbury, where her life had been so much better. Yet in the midst of these later memories of Bloomsbury she broke out, 'You think when you're in service, you think why am I doing this? Why should I do this? Why? Why? Why?' She knew her upbringing had prepared her for it. 'I had the kindest mother; but, you see, she said: "This is what it is to work for your living! All the others had to do it. This is just what you have to do."' Both she and Ewart Evans agreed on the humanity of the employers in Bloomsbury circles. Her gratitude was heartfelt. Yet neither of them noticed how much she made them sound like her mother, encouraging her, however nicely, to resign herself to her lot: 'Their attitude was: "We get paid a lot of money for doing what we do: you don't get paid as much for what you do. But that's just how it is. It doesn't mean that we are better than you.'" Since she couldn't blame her parents or her employers, then the laughter was also a holding operation – there was no way of moving on.

Looking back at his early interviews Evans criticized his tendency to weigh in too often, rather than let his informant speak. He had to learn how to listen and leave space for others. Thirty years on, 'oral historians' now take their models from both anthropology and psychoanalysis as they try to understand how life-stories so often become 'the myths we live by'. They are as likely to comment on the manner in which the story has been told, and the language we use when we 're-present' it to others, as on its content. They try to be attentive to the hesitations, the digressions and the insistences; the repetitions and the gaps. And they assume that the interviewer has his or her preoccupations, that the reaction they might want from their subjects – 'weren't you angry, weren't you unhappy?' – tells them as much about themselves and their own needs as those of their informants.

Nonetheless, after centuries of domestic service in Britain, what it meant to be a servant – and to have servants – is still a remarkably undiscovered country, perhaps, because the history of service is so peculiarly bound up with our relation to maternal or paternal care, to what happens at home as well as in the wider world of economic relations. Servants, especially girls, learnt to be obedient and deferential as children, and those childhoods need to be better understood. What did it mean for them when they became mothers and housewives in turn? How did they treat their own children and grandchildren? Experiences both at work and in their own homes need investigating, as part of a whole life, and not only those years spent in service. As servants, some of them became second mothers to strangers but found themselves infantilized for their pains. How to distinguish dependence from dependency, being abandoned from being independent; how to differentiate between protectiveness and bullying; how to value the capacity to put our own needs second and how best to be mutually responsible for each other – the history of service raises all these questions. 'The question of Nelly' has always reminded us of the strange human habit of kindness beyond the call of duty or the power of coercion, which, like the baby splashing happily in the bathwater, ought not to be thrown away.

★

George Ewart Evans's interviews with women servants proved to be of their time. In the 1970s the lives of British servants began to register with the public and capture the popular imagination. As live-in domestic service now seemed a thing of the past, it was recognized and sometimes romanticized as part of British history. It became acceptable to talk about being in service and to reminisce. Popular novels, like those of Catherine Cookson, whose autobiography also included her time in service, *Our Kate* (1969), and media interest, notably, the hugely popular television series *Upstairs, Downstairs*, which was first broadcast in 1971, brought servants to the fore, as did the National Trust's opening of the kitchens and servants' quarters for public viewing in several historic houses. Autobiographies were published or republished which put the experiences of women who had been in service on the literary map – Margaret Powell's books, *Below Stairs* (1968) and *Climbing the Stairs* (1969), Winifred Foley's *A Child in the Forest* (1974) or Jean Rennie's *Every Other Sunday* (reprinted in 1975) among them; their voices were heard on the radio – Rosina Harrison, whose *Rose: My Life in Service* (1975) described her time as maid to Lady Nancy Astor, found herself the subject for the BBC's *Desert Island Discs*. In the universities, 'history from below' – labour history, local history, regional history, as well as the new oral history – highlighted the lives of working people, drawing on their life stories. And a number of radical or alternative presses flourished in the 70s, such as that under the umbrella of such as the Workers Federation of Writers and Community Publishers, encouraging local people to write. Many who did had been domestic servants. At the same time the collecting of spoken testimonies and the setting up of sound archives was under way in local and national museums, and many of those recorded were ex-servants.

Naturally when Quentin Bell, at Leonard Woolf's invitation, took on the biography of Virginia Woolf in the late 1960s, consulting or including the servants must have been the least of his worries. There was an excess of unpublished materials, a veritable mountain of written sources, of diaries, letters and memoirs to decipher, sort and sift – a biographer's dream or nightmare. In the event Bell wrote sympathetically about Nellie and Lottie, though he introduced the subject of service as a 'digression', seeing it largely as a problem of a time before mechanical appliances: 'no very serious effort is needed of you' these days, he argued, with a certain masculine blitheness, when a meal needs cooking or the house cleaning. Nigel Nicolson, Vita Sackville-West's son, was rather more dismissive of a subject he found 'tedious', when he edited Virginia's letters, casually muddling up the chars and marrying Annie Thompsett to her own father in a footnote. Quentin Bell acknowledged Louie, though she disappeared again from the last scenes of Virginia's life; twenty-five years later Hermione Lee put her and the other villagers back in. By the late 1960s Nellie Boxall was dead, though not Lottie; Annie Thompsett still lived in Rodmell; Percy Bartholomew died in 1956 but his wife and daughter were up the road in Lewes; Elsie, Trissie, Flossie, Mabel and Marion Selwood lived till into their eighties – all might have shed their own light on Bloomsbury. Publishing a selection of his mother's photographs in 1981, Bell observed, coming to the servants, that 'their testimony if known would be intriguing'. By then it really was too late, though Daisy Selwood, like Annie Thompsett, lived to be a hundred.

Biographies must also edit. Life is always in excess of the stories we tell about it – to others, to ourselves. Always the awkward relation is a sign of more to come; the stories which don't fit; the lives lived in parallel universes, intersecting, overlapping, together and apart. A real life includes conflict, anger, mistakes; it spills over into the next generation, the generation after that.

Memories are passed on. Jim Bartholomew, Percy's son, had been able to move back to Rodmell after the war thanks to a loan from Leonard, who also helped him find work as a printer. Jim bought number 2 Stile Cottages, next door to where his father had been born and where his Uncle Bill and Auntie Rose lived (William lived there till he was ninety-seven; saving water, he never took a bath, but had a strip-down wash in full view of the world in his back-scullery every day). Yet even in the 1990s Jim was still furious that his father got so little acknowledgement in Leonard's autobiography, and was just 'Percy (gardener)' in the index. Jim was at pains to point out how much Percy had been the mainstay of the garden, with its considerable crop of fruit and vegetables. He resented not being consulted by Quentin Bell either. No matter how generous Leonard had been, it was, in the end, a kind of patronage, and not a friendship after all. Both sides – servants, as well as masters – could feel disillusioned when the limits of the relationship were exposed.

At Charleston, Grace Higgens had also stayed on. She cared for Vanessa Bell in her final illness, shocked that after all this time, her mistress was just as reserved. After forty years, Grace still didn't know her; she was still 'Mrs Bell', never in a million years 'Vanessa'. Everyone knew of Vanessa's 'parsimony' and that, while there might be mutual respect, Vanessa drew the line at paying Grace more. With Duncan Grant and Vanessa's children, Grace was one of the few who followed the coffin after Vanessa died one rainy April morning in 1961. She then looked after Duncan Grant until she finally retired in 1970, still only earning £5 a week plus her board. Quentin Bell put a ceramic plaque to 'Amazing Grace' above the stove in Charleston's kitchen. In a volume of Grace's recipes, her daughter-in-law, Diana Higgens, tactfully hinted at another history and at the inequalities in her life, adding carefully, 'Grace loved Charleston I am sure, or she would never have stayed for fifty-two years.' Virginia Nicolson, one of Vanessa's granddaughters, was blunter, calling it 'exploitation'. A new tour of Charleston now includes 'Grace's day', but the bedsitting room in which she and Walter and her son Peter lived is not on show. The guide refers to it as her 'flat'.

Like furniture, houses inherit us. In 1963 Leonard learnt that 'Monk's House' had never seen hide nor hair of a monk. Jim Bartholomew had done the research for him and it turned out that the house was called Glazebrooks in the nineteenth century until 1919, when the estate agent must have invented the new name to add picturesqueness to the place (Virginia had certainly been delighted by it, imagining niches for holy water). Leonard took some pleasure in the discovery, hating – as he did – anything sham. A couple of years later, answering an inquiry from an American who offered to buy Monk's House and manage it 'as a literary shrine', Leonard wrote robustly that there was 'no question' of Monk's House being used in this way 'as I shall leave it to someone else after my death'. When he died in 1969 most of his estate, including the house, went to Trekkie. His relatives contested the will, claiming 'undue influence' and she was forced to declare in court that there had never been a sexual relationship, only love between them. Her affidavit reads like a Victorian novel. After years of legal wrangling, she donated the house to the University of Sussex, glad to be relieved of the burden. The university was meant to look after the house and its contents, and Leonard's two cottages. In fact they cashed in quickly, sold the cottages off, and put the furniture in store so that much of it was stolen. Visiting academics and writers staying at Monk's House then came and bashed the Omega plates about, scrubbing them in the sink (the novelist Saul Bellow left after discovering how freezing the house was). Eventually the university sold it to the National Trust, who now manage it as a literary shrine. (Meanwhile the Stephen family home at 22 Hyde Park Gate has had an unexpected lease of life: it is now a guest-house offering bed and breakfast.)

Park Cottages had gone with the estate to Trekkie. Percy's had long been let. He had developed cataracts in the late 1940s, and, refusing an operation, eventually went blind. The Bartholomews had moved to Lewes. Louie had to move on when Leonard died. He left her £8,000 to buy a cottage, having upped the amount after consulting Trekkie (Quentin and Angelica received £10,000 apiece).

In 1962 Louie had married Konrad Mayer, eleven years her junior, who was working at Itford farm (but that's another story). They retired to Seaford on the Sussex coast, where she died in 1977, at only sixty-five. Her portrait, painted by Trekkie, hangs in Monk's House. Trekkie Ritchie Parsons was universally remembered as a warm, 'bubbly' person. The more conventional obituaries, stoutly calling her 'Trekkie Parsons', protested that her husband remained the great love of her life (though no one mentioned, of course, the misery and torment she had suffered during Ian's long love-affair with another director of Chatto). They all paid tribute to the love and care devoted to her in her own old age by Anneliese West, her 'help' and housekeeper for forty years. Anneliese protected Trekkie's independence until the last weeks of her life. It's a good job water is often thicker than blood. Who will care for you when your turn comes?

Not being much of a one for literary pilgrimages, I put off visiting Monk's House for as long as I could. One of the volunteers who oversees the spruce interior – no smelly dishes of cat and dog food now, no clutter of ashtrays and books – is Marie Bartholomew, Percy and Lydia's daughter, who used to come there as a little girl to grub up the weeds and scrub flowerpots in the cold-water butt, a job she hated. She took me around the house and garden and on a tour of the village. Out in 'the lodge', Virginia's writing-shed now double its original size since Leonard converted it for Trekkie, there was an array of photographs but not one of the servants; the guide – in 2002 at least – made no mention of Percy Bartholomew in its section on the garden. Marie was philosophical. She remembered her father's astonishment at all the ornamental plants and flowers Leonard began to plant (his garden became even more exotic after he met Trekkie). 'If you can't eat it, don't grow it,' was Percy's harsh motto (they used to laugh at home when Virginia gave the children an apple: that was the one thing they had bags of). Her brother, Jim, she said, fed and clothed four children on the produce he grew and took to market. Even dahlias and chrysanthemums are historical documents.

Percy named his daughter Marie Louise, after the pear tree which used to grow outside their house. Park Cottages are now knocked into one and worth a small fortune. Marie Bartholomew's front door no longer exists. As I walked around Rodmell village with her, we met one of its oldest inhabitants, who told me, 'if they didn't get their hands dirty we didn't think much of them'; the gentry were 'a dozy bunch', another added, mingling hostility with pity, and reversing the legacy of forelock-touching. Their lives – the gentry's – were largely irrelevant to the farm-workers. Jim had been writing a history of the village before he died and now Marie had it piled up somewhere and was worried that no one would finish it. Perhaps it would put the cat among the pigeons, revealing how unharmonious the past was. Marie wasn't angry but calm. Her mother had looked after her father for eight years after he had gone blind and then Marie had looked after her mother for nearly twenty ('I was the girl, you see'). She remembered Trekkie and Leonard's generosity, how they had taken Percy to the hospital, and sat with him. Marie had been the only girl of the twenty in her class at Rodmell village school to pass the exam for the grammar school: Leonard had given her £1, an enormous sum for an eleven-year-old. He had written her references when she went away to teachers' training college – 'which didn't do any harm'. She became headmistress of a village school nearby at Wivelsfield and remained twenty-four years until retirement. In her talk her father emerged a little from the shadows – a Rodmell boy who found himself in the trenches as a gunner, watching in horror as his beloved horses were maimed and blown up. No wonder he took to growing things for the rest of his life. His parents are buried in the churchyard next to Monk's House: Thomas and Jemima Bartholomew; under a stone like a Bible. Harry James (Jim) Bartholomew is buried there too.

Louie must have kept – or been given – Virginia's walking-stick, which was found lying on the riverbank that day in March where she went into the water. It was eventually sold at auction in Lewes by Louie's widower. For a while solid objects acquire talismanic status but soon it needs magic words to bring their histories back to life, like spirits released from imprisonment in wood or stone. Who will know the 'Miss Florence Haskins' to whom Roger Fry dedicated his painting of the garden at Dalmeny Avenue? Her husband omitted to give his wife's name when he chose to donate it to the library, where it is now stored in some upstairs attic, like Lily Briscoe's painting in *To the Lighthouse*. There again, interviewing the servants' descendants and turning the pages of their old photograph albums, only I recognized the young Virginia Stephen on the beach with the nannies and their charges, women who were far more important to the family. Objects, like stories, do their best to stave off oblivion; 'orts, scraps and fragments', as Virginia would say.

Even Nellie Boxall now has a literary afterlife of which this book is part. A French novelist has imagined her looking back on her life on the night before the Laughtons go to America: a Spanish author directs our sympathies entirely to Nellie, inventing her diaries to show the snobbish goings-on in Bloomsbury, but the truth often turns out to be less clear-cut than the melodrama of heroine or victim. In *The Hours*, a film of Michael Cunningham's novel which draws on Woolf's life in the 1920s, the British director

Rodmell churchyard

trundled out the old comic stereotypes which are the traditional
inverse of pathos. While a great deal of fuss was made about the
Hollywood actress Nicole Kidman, who had to wear a false nose
to play Virginia, no one bothered much about the 'authenticity'
of the servants, who were also real, historical people. The film
turns them into 'character parts' as if in an old British 'B' movie,
a version of comic relief. Nellie, the highly strung, quiet girl from
Surrey, appears as a mutinous middle-aged cockney, a battleaxe in
the kitchen, older than Virginia, while her sidekick is a silly young
girl, nothing like Lottie. Both are in grey uniforms with starched
white cap and apron. Nellie is seen chopping an unlikely mountain of raw meat for some gargantuan steak and kidney pie, her
apron smeared with blood, while her sensitive mistress hovers
queasily on the threshold. The message is clear: working women
are all flesh and no mind; Mrs Gape, all over again.

★

Fragments shored against ruin. In September 1940 Virginia Woolf
ventured back to Mecklenburgh Square and met Mabel clearing up
after the bomb which had taken out the windows and brought
down the ceilings. She salvaged twenty-four volumes of her old
diaries – 'a great mass for my memoirs' – and took them back to
Rodmell. Her memoirs were left unfinished but Quentin Bell
consulted them for his biography, and their revelations of Virginia's
sexual abuse as a child brought much publicity. In 1976 some
drafts of her last memoir, 'Sketch of the Past', were printed in a
volume of her autobiographical writings, *Moments of Being*. Four
years later, it was Trekkie Ritchie, now executrix of the Woolfs'
estate, who found the seventy-seven continuous typescript pages,
including a portrait of Leslie Stephen, which confirmed how
constantly and coolly Virginia revised her own version of her past
and her self, and would have gone on revising, if she had lived.

Woolf's memoirs and diaries have been the key texts for all
the biographical writing that has since appeared about her
(including my own). In the end, though, no biography can cope

with Virginia Woolf's extreme scepticism about the form, her urge to unravel the fabric of the past, to relinquish the idea of authority of both the biographer and her subject, her view that there is no story to tell about 'a self', and no self to tell it about. 'My God, how does one write a biography?' she asked Vita Sackville-West, as she struggled writing the life of Roger Fry. 'And what is a life?' Life is not susceptible to treatment, as her character Bernard puts it in *The Waves*. In 'Sketch of the Past' she insists that a real life has no crisis, though it may have many; that our capacity to create and recreate ourselves endlessly through the activity of memory is a sustaining fiction; that we do not necessarily get wiser as we get older, and, perhaps most unacceptably of all, there are times – in all lives – when meaninglessness predominates. The effort of making meaning is for many of us, much of the time, not a single act but a continuous struggle ('Fight, fight', Woolf would say to herself when she woke agonized in the night). A real life needs the capacity to bear that meaninglessness, those times out of time when it is all 'pure loss'. Lives may be most real when they lose the plot.

Virginia Woolf loved to read biography, memoir and auto-biography and she set a high value on all forms of life-writing, genres which in her day were considered the poor relations in the literary family. Like Freud, however, who was far more hostile to both biography and autobiography, Woolf saw memory as 'selective amnesia', thinking that what we forget is probably as important as what we remember – if not more. The past was only ever sketchy, memory leapt and jolted, confused and sometimes invented; it changed its mind, depending on 'the platform of time' from which it was viewed. Approaching old age she gave a new, more ambivalent account of her parents, allowing for change in her views of them: 'As a child condemning; as a woman of 58 understanding – I shd say tolerating.' Crucially she asked herself, 'Both views true?' Her memoirs resist determinism and romance, including the romance of trauma, as if that were the only signi-ficant way in which modern individuals know themselves to be special and real. If a life is shaped by the events of childhood, her memoirs imply, it is not railroaded by them. Fixed stars need not govern a life.

When Virginia Woolf imagined the lavatory attendant, she thought that 'the woman who lives in this room' would have no settled relations: 'She has the look of someone without a past', but what would such a person look like? To be entirely without a past was to be wiped clean of memory, the continuous thread woven into one's being that confers a sense of self; to be so disconnected was for Virginia a kind of death. Yet, at other times and in other places, Woolf found the idea of the discontinuous, heartening and necessary: to be unsettled was to be capable of change and experiment. The past clung to one's skirts and to be free of its grip meant being able to move. The memoirs of a lavatory attendant might offer a different history, of comings and goings, certainly, but a history nonetheless. Hers might be an inner life differently organized, less tethered to place, less in love with origins; the chatelaine of a floating world. But in 1941 there was only a gap in the records, the sign of doubt and possibility.

Virginia Woolf's memoirs, like her diaries, are her most transient, temporary work. Yet they have staying power, they satisfy, they compose. Like a dream, 'Sketch of the Past' feels both fragmentary and complete, partial and full, marked by breaks and pauses, like the intake of breath, the punctuation employed to give shape to a real life, 'by way of making an end', as she wrote, 'where there is no such thing'.

★

Who should have the last word? No one really. There are only three emotions which make 'the ply of human life', Virginia wrote in *Between the Acts*: 'Love. Hate. Peace.' Left out of the published interview with Happy Sturgeon were the many comments she made on her enjoyment of the present. Her contentment was probably harder to take than her irony and, anyway, her interviewer was interested in the past. Maybe too her pleasures – a comfortable home, package holidays in Romania and Italy – seemed too materialist or commercial. For her, travelling was evidence of an expansive, resilient life: 'we go on a local bus inland – we're not a bit afraid!' (laughs). The little girl who was told by her mother 'this is just how it is; this is what it is to work for a living', was now a woman in her mid-fifties, for whom another story was just beginning. When she looked back in her eighties, service – even in Bloomsbury – would mean what? 'It's a new life,' she told Ewart Evans several times, though he omitted her final fanfare,

And now I'm as happy as I've ever been. My husband and I, I will say now, that really this is a lovely time for us. You know there's a dignity in living, we've got all the material things we want and we've got the family – 'cause he had the same sort of experience – poor little boy on the farm – 'open that gate, boy, or you get the riding crop across your shoulders', you know – [she laughs].

Postscript

Between 1939 and 1941 the number of private domestic servants declined as women took on shop and office work, went into light industry, hotels and catering, elementary teaching or other occupations. In 1941 women were required to register for war service at the age of sixteen and only those households which could prove a special need were allowed to retain a servant. Though the Second World War saw the demand for women clerks and typists rise dramatically, the most significant decline in domestic service came after 1945. In 1945 the Labour government put the school-leaving age up to fifteen (sixteen was thought too expensive a measure), and there was free milk for all school children; these two things ensured the end of the British skivvy, though the woman who fought for both of them, Ellen Wilkinson, 'red Ellen', the first British woman to become a Minister of Education, took a lethal overdose, depressed by the lack of more radical reforms. Significantly, by 1952 Barnardo's ceased to train their charges for household employment, and, though cultural commentators were still anxiously discussing the need for service, the live-in maid or cook-general had largely disappeared from the vast majority of middle-class British households. The number of dailies or chars, on the other hand, rose dramatically in the 50s, but many signed on for office-cleaning, preferring to avoid personal service.

Of course, 'the question of Nelly' wasn't settled. It was simply displaced elsewhere. Gradually those who felt beached up on the shores of their own gentility looked to 'foreign help' for their dailies. Those who a century before would have shuddered at the thought of an Irish 'savage' in the house, were now only too glad to welcome a girl from Mayo or Kerry; or in the 70s, from the Philippines, from Spain and Portugal, and the Caribbean. In the last decades of the twentieth century, despite, or because of, feminism, 'cash rich, time poor' professional couples on dual incomes began to employ other women to do their cleaning and bought in other kinds of help from childcare to catering, from laundry to dog-walking.

Even personal domestic service became a growth industry again: new training schools for butlers and other staff are now regularly advertised on the internet. And in the new century domestic work in hotels, hospitals, schools, offices and homes remains the chief employer of thousands of low-paid casual workers, including many immigrants. Cleaning is still the lowest-status job. And cleaners are predominantly women.

All of us begin our lives helpless in the hands of others and most of us will end so. How we tolerate our inevitable dependence, especially upon those who feed and clean and care for us, or take away our waste, is not a private or domestic question but one which goes to the heart of social structures and their inequalities. We rely constantly on others to do our dirty work for us and what used to be called 'the servant question' has not gone away: how could it? The figure of the servant takes us inside history but also inside our selves.

Appendix: Biographical Notes
on the Servants

These brief notes summarize what I have managed to find out about the servants' lives. I have kept the details for Sophie Farrell, Lottie Hope and Nellie Boxall to a minimum as they receive fuller attention in the main text. I would be delighted to receive more information or any corrections via the publisher.

BARTHOLOMEW, Percy (1887–1956), gardener at Monk's House from 1928 until the late 1940s. Born Rodmell, Sussex, eldest of three followed by Will and Rose, he grew up at Stile Cottage. He served as a gunner in the artillery in the Great War; after demob he was a hotel porter in Brighton, where he met and married Lydia Green on 13 November 1918; he trained at Cheale's Nurseries, Sussex. Percy and his family lived in tied accommodation owned by Leonard Woolf, 1 Park Cottages. In the late 40s Percy developed glaucoma, refused an operation and went blind; he and Lydia moved to Lewes. His recollections were not recorded.

BARTHOLOMEW, Rose (1894–1968), occasional cook and char at Monk's House. Born Rodmell, Percy's younger sister. According to her niece Marie, Rose worked in Seaford as an assistant matron to boys at a boarding school while helping out at the Woolfs' from the mid-20s; a very good dressmaker. She looked after her brother Will, who lived to ninety-seven, at Stile Cottages, until she died.

BARTHOLOMEW, Lydia, née GREEN (1896–1975), 'Mrs Bartholomew' in Virginia Woolf's diaries, occasional cook and char at Monk's House. Born Aldham, Essex, daughter of James Green, Master Miller (and not the exotic 'illegitimate child of a circus manager' which VW fancied her to be: *D*, III, 25 November 1928); she worked as a children's nurse in Brighton before marriage; after marriage to Percy, they moved first to 3 Poor Cottages, Rodmell, where their first son, Tom, was born; son Jim and daughter Marie were born at 1 Park Cottages. According to her daughter, Lydia was an appalling cook, as Virginia Woolf maintained in her diaries, because she had herself never learnt, having been used to servants. Lydia's inheritance made it possible for the Bartholomews to move to Lewes after Percy's blindness.

BOXALL, Nellie (1890–1965), cook and 'cook-general'. Born Farncombe, Surrey, youngest of ten children and orphaned by the age of twelve; worked for Roger Fry from *c.* 1912 until February 1916, when she joined the Woolf household at Hogarth House, Richmond, as cook, with Lottie Hope as maid; they worked together until 1924. Nellie then became general servant to the Woolfs at Tavistock Square and Rodmell until March 1934, when she was dismissed. She next worked for the actors Charles Laughton and Elsa Lanchester in Gordon Square, Bloomsbury, until the war, when she returned to Farncombe, and lived at 30 North Street with her brother, Arthur, and Lottie Hope. During the war she worked as a cook in the canteen for nurses and medical staff at St Thomas's hospital, which was evacuated to Surrey. She never married or had children but shared her home with Lottie Hope until her death. Nellie was recorded with Lottie by the BBC Home Service, in *Portrait of Virginia Woolf*, 29 August 1956, which can be heard in the National Sound Archive at the British Library. No other recollections recorded.

CHART, Annie – from Sussex, cook to the Woolfs at Asheham and at Hogarth House during Virginia's illness in 1915–16; she then stayed on to work for the Waterlows at Hogarth House, and was subsequently cook to Maynard Keynes at 46 Gordon Square, working with Blanche Payne.

CHART, Maud Annie (1881–1962), housemaid; no relation to Annie Chart above. Born at 219 East Street, Walworth, in the heart of London's poverty, in the parish of St Saviour's, where Stella Duckworth volunteered at the local workhouse. Her father worked on the railways as an engine stoker. Maud appears in a photograph of the Stephen servants in 1899 and is given in the census for the Leslie Stephen household at Hyde Park Gate in 1901; she subsequently moved with Sophie Farrell to the Bloomsbury households in the 1900s, Gordon Square, Fitzroy Square and Brunswick Square, until at least 1914 (and went with Virginia Stephen to Little Talland House in Firle before Virginia's marriage), so she worked for the family for fifteen years or more. Aged thirty-eight, she married John Edwards, a widower some twenty years older, in 1919, and moved into his house, 43 Tintern Street, Brixton, taking lodgers, including Sophie Farrell, from 1926, though the latter was not to retire there permanently until 1930. Maud died at the age of eighty-one in South Norwood, close to Brixton (John Edwards is given as a 'club steward' on her death certificate). No recollections recorded.

DEDMAN, Rachel Ann (1867–1941), cooked and helped out at Monk's House in the first year, bringing hot food over to the Woolfs from Pear Tree Cottage where she lived. Wife of William Thomas, who was the sexton of Rodmell village church and the gardener at Monk's House, working for Jacob Verrall, its former owner, for twenty-one years. William worked for Leonard Woolf until Percy Bartholomew took over. According to Virginia Woolf, the Dedmans had eleven children (*L*, II, 1109). She died at Briar Cottage, Rodmell.

EVEREST, Louisa Annie, née WEST (1912–77), cook and house-keeper to Leonard and Virginia Woolf. Louie's life deserves a book in itself. She was born in Eastdean, Sussex, and then lived at Burwash, where her father, Jesse Solomon West, worked on the Rudyard Kipling estate, before moving to Southease, near Rodmell. She married Albert Everest in 1929, when she was seventeen and he twenty-one. On the marriage certificate Bert's 'rank or profession' was entered as a labourer at a cement works, where his father was also a foreman (Louie's father was given as a 'carter on farm'). According to Virginia Woolf, Louie was a mother at fourteen, but I can find no record of this. Louie came to work as a daily cook-general for the Woolfs, moving into 2 Park Cottages with her two boys after Annie Thompsett's marriage in August 1934. In Rodmell her mother acted as the village's 'layer-out and night-watcher', and also looked after a mentally disabled son. Louie obtained her Diploma in Advanced Cooking in 1936 and stayed working as a daily at Monk's House until Leonard's death in 1969. An active member of the local Labour Party, she was secretary of the Rodmell branch, which met at Monk's House for many years. Bert Everest died in October 1961 in his early fifties. Six months later, in March 1962, Louie married Konrad Wilhelm Mayer, who had apparently been a German prisoner-of-war in the camp outside Rodmell and stayed on after the war. Louie was forty-nine and Konrad thirty-eight and it would be interesting to know their story. He gave his profession as 'dairyman' but there is no entry for his father's name or rank. When Leonard died, Louie was recovering from cancer. She and Konrad retired to Seaford in Sussex, buying a house with the money Leonard had left her. For her memories (mostly of VW), see Noble, *Recollections*; Stape, *Virginia Woolf: Interviews*. She also appeared on the BBC *Omnibus* programme of January 1970, 'A Night's Darkness, A Day's Sail', the script, in MHP, Sussex, has more details of her life. She is fondly remembered by LW in his autobiography. See also Glendinning, *Leonard Woolf*.

FARRELL, Sophia (1861–1941), cook to the Stephen and Duck-worth families for most of her working life. Born Ranby, Lincolnshire, one of nine children; her father was a gardener and groom, later also parish clerk and sexton in the nearby village of West Barkwith, where Sophie grew up; her mother was a laundress. Where she first worked is unknown but in 1886 she went as cook to Leslie and Julia Stephen at 22 Hyde Park Gate;

she then moved with the Stephen siblings to their various Bloomsbury homes until Virginia married in 1912, when she worked for Adrian Stephen until his marriage two years later. After twenty-eight years she was obliged to move to the Duckworth side of the family: first to 'Aunt' Minna (Sarah Emily, Herbert Duckworth's sister), who also lived at Hyde Park Gate, until her death in 1918, and then on to Lady Victoria Herbert, George Duckworth's sister-in-law. Sometimes she also helped out in the Bell household in London in the early 20s. From 1926 she can be found renting a room at 43 Tintern Street, Brixton, the home of Maud Chart, now Edwards, the former housemaid with whom she had worked, though she also occasionally worked for George Duckworth and his wife, Lady Margaret. Virginia Woolf sent Sophie £10 a year pension after her retirement in 1931. Sophie died in Brixton just before her eightieth birthday. No recollections recorded.

HASKINS, Florence (1891–?), cook and daily to Vanessa Bell. Born Portbury, Bedminster, in Somerset (later a part of the area of Bristol), to Abraham and Clara Haskins, close to Roger Fry's family home in Failand. Her father is given as a railway labourer. With her sister, Mabel, as housemaid, she worked first as Margery Fry's cook and at 7 Dalmeny Avenue, Holloway, London, which Margery shared with Roger Fry; then, after settling Margery in as principal of Somerville College in 1926, she married George Riley in 1927, and moved to 43 Alexander Road in Holloway. From 1934 she was shared as a daily, working for Vanessa Bell in her studio at Fitzroy Square and for Roger Fry's partner, Helen Anrep. During the 30s George Riley was a Labour councillor and alderman in Islington and became Lord Mayor of Islington in 1945–6; he was a Justice of the Peace and chairman of the North Islington Labour Party for ten years. The Rileys left Holloway in 1949 for George to take up a senior post with the Ministry of Pensions and National Insurance in Coventry; he was in the Amalgamated Engineering Union for forty-nine years. In 1926 Roger Fry presented Flossie with a painting of the back garden at 7 Dalmeny Avenue – donated by the Rileys, and now in the Islington Local History Library, London – inscribed to her. George Riley died in Cambridge in 1979, aged eighty-six, but there are no details about Flossie or any children of the marriage. George Riley's recollections of old Holloway, plus a letter about Roger Fry and Dalmeny Avenue are also in Islington Local History Library.

HASKINS, Mabel (1894–?), cook and housekeeper to Leonard and Virginia Woolf. Born Portbury, Bedminster, in Somerset. With her sister, Flossie, Mabel worked for Margery Fry; and as housemaid from 1919 for Margery Fry and Roger Fry at 7 Dalmeny Avenue. From 1934 to 1940 she went as the last live-in servant to Leonard and Virginia Woolf at Tavistock Square. During the war she lived with her sister at 43 Alexander Road, in Holloway, and then worked in a canteen; later she went to Isabel Fry but no further details are known except that, tracking her from the electoral rolls, I discovered that she had left her sister's house and in 1948 married Arthur Tierney, a widower of sixty-eight. Where she then lived and later died remains a mystery.

HIGGENS, Grace, née GERMANY (1904–83), 'the Angel of Charleston', who worked there for more than fifty years, came from a Norfolk smallholding in Banham to work as housemaid to Vanessa Bell in May 1920. She was rapidly promoted to nursemaid to Angelica Bell when her nurse, Nellie Brittain, left; then finally to housekeeper and cook in 1935. She married Walter Higgens in 1934 and they both moved into a large bedsitting room over the kitchen at Charleston (which she enjoyed referring to as 'High Holborn' because, like the street in London, it 'looked down on Bloomsbury'); their son, John Peter, was born there the following year. Although Grace bought her parents' house in Banham in 1959, she never moved there but remained at Charleston looking after Vanessa and then Duncan Grant, and frequently visiting France with them, often for two or three months at a time. She eventually retired with her husband to Ringmer, near Lewes, in Sussex in 1970. A copy of a taped interview between

Grace and the art historian Isabel Anscombe can be found in the archive at Charleston. Her son, John Higgens, also recorded his recollections for the British Library National Sound Archive as part of their 'Artists' Lives' series. An obituary of Grace, written by Quentin Bell, can be found in the *Charleston Newsletter* no. 4, May 1983. See also, Diana Higgens, *Grace at Charleston: Memories and Recipes*, Lockholt and Co., 1994.

HOPE, Lottie (1890?–1973), housemaid and cook. Lottie was a foundling, adopted by Miss Edith Sichel, and grew up in her Home for Deserted Children at Hambledon in Surrey. The school admissions register gives her date of birth as 6 May 1890 but I could find no birth certificate. How she spent the years after leaving school at fourteen is unknown, until she is mentioned as housemaid to Nellie Boxall's cook at Durbins, the home of Roger Fry in Surrey, from 1911 until 1916; then she worked, again with Nellie, for the Woolfs at Hogarth House in Richmond and at Asheham and Monk's House in Sussex until 1924. Her next place was with Adrian and Karin Stephen at 50 Gordon Square until 1930; she suffered a period of insecurity until she became cook-housekeeper for Clive Bell early in 1932; in 1939 she went with him to live at Charleston, joining Vanessa Bell's household. Lottie left in 1941 although, according to Adrian Stephen's biographer, she helped him move house during the war. She then lived with Nellie Boxall in Farncombe, working at the local laundry, and died at Hambledon Homes for the Aged. Like Nellie, she never married or had children. She too can be heard on the BBC radio programme *Portrait of Virginia Woolf* (1956), in the National Sound Archive at the British Library.

LANGFORD, Mrs, char at 8 Fitzroy Street, the studio of Duncan Grant and Vanessa Bell. She 'did' for many of the artists in the area. Painted by Grant – *Portrait of Mrs Langford* – in 1930.

MANSFIELD, Mrs, char for the Woolfs in Tavistock Square. She lived in the basement of 37 Gordon Square and was caretaker there.

SELWOOD, Elsie (1888–1973), nanny. The oldest of the sisters to be born at Old Down, near the village of Tockington in Gloucestershire, not far from Bristol. Their father, Arthur Selwood, worked as a groom, and his wife, Ada, was the village dressmaker, who made clothes for the gentry and the Duchess of Beaufort at Badminton nearby. Elsie went as nanny to Julian and Quentin Bell from 1908, having first worked for the Stephen cousins, Madge and Will Vaughan, in Yorkshire. She married Robert Bessant, the postman from Studland, Dorset, whom she met while on holiday with the Bells, in 1916; she worked later for the Villiers family in London. Robert became a gardener after the war, and in 1921 they moved to Sudbury, Derbyshire, where he worked for Lord Vernon at Sudbury Hall; three of their five children also worked at Sudbury Hall.

SELWOOD, Beatrice or 'Trissie' (1891–1973), cook to Vanessa Bell, who 'poached' her from Mary Hutchinson in 1917. She married Gerald Stacey, son of a wealthy farmer from the Charleston estate, in 1918. The Staceys moved to Nailsea, Somerset; three children.

SELWOOD, (Caroline) Mabel (1893–1989), nurse to Quentin Bell from about 1910 to 1917, when she married Richard Leakey from her home village in Gloucestershire. Mabel went briefly to Adrian and Karin Stephen, whose girls, Ann and Judith, were born during the war. She had three children. Mabel Selwood's family have loaned to Charleston two paintings by Duncan Grant which were gifts to her – a portrait of Vanessa Bell, *c.* 1917, and a painting of Bosham Church, *c.* 1918 (Mabel's wedding present). The family has also donated some photographic material to the archive at Charleston.

SELWOOD, Marion Alice (1894–1974), briefly cook to Vanessa Bell's close friend Faith Henderson and her family. Married Sidney Ward, smallholder from Norfolk; no children.

SELWOOD, Florence Emmeline or 'Flossie' (1887–1978), took over from Elsie Selwood as nanny to Julian and Quentin, and was, like Mabel, 'adored' by her charges, accompanying the Bells and settling with them at Charleston. She left in 1917 or thereabouts to work for Faith Henderson, as nanny to the Henderson children. Flossie's daughter, born in 1919, was brought up as Mary Henderson; she features in Vanessa Bell's photograph albums and remained close to the Henderson family all her life. In 1926 Flossie married Edward Weeks, a chauffeur from her home village in Gloucestershire; their son, Peter, died young. Mary's daughter, Carolyn, thought Flossie saw his death as a punishment for her earlier lapse with Mary.

SELWOOD, Daisy Septima (1899–1999), nanny to the Stephen family. During the war she worked in a munitions factory before going in 1919 to Adrian and Karin Stephen and their two girls, Ann and Judith, at Tanza Road, Hampstead. She then worked for them (with Lottie Hope as cook-housekeeper) at 50 Gordon Square and their country home near Harwich in the 20s. Daisy learnt to drive a car, went with them two or three times to Italy, travelling sometimes with just the girls and a maid and staying with Lady and Sir Bernard Berenson, Karin Stephen's mother and stepfather in Florence. She waited until the Stephen girls, aged fourteen and twelve, no longer needed her before she married George Davis in 1930, and until George had saved the substantial sum of £1,000. George Davis's family ran a grocery business in Knightsbridge, then Gower Place, Euston, where they probably met. It was Daisy who kept the sisters in touch with each other. She died at the age of a hundred in December 1999 in a substantial house in Queens Drive near Finsbury Park, London. Daisy had apparently saved her flapper dance dresses from that era which she had worn to various house-parties to show her descendants. She was 'treated more as family member than a servant,' she told her family. Sadly, her frocks, letters and memorabilia were all thrown away. She had two children.

No recollections of any of the Selwood sisters were recorded, though Mabel and Flossie are warmly remembered by Henderson

in 'Child of Bloomsbury', *Charleston Magazine*, 13, 1996, and in
Old Friends, and in Bell, *Elders and Betters*.

THOMPSETT, Ann Louisa, née WATERER (1901–2001), cook
and daily help to the Woolfs in the late 1920s and 30s. Annie's
mother had already helped out when the Woolfs first moved into
Rodmell in 1919, cleaning and cooking dinner. Annie's first
husband, Leslie Thompsett, died young. In 1929 Annie moved
with her daughter, Joyce, into 2 Park Cottages, owned by Leonard
Woolf, next door to the Bartholomews; she worked as a daily for
the Woolfs and left to marry Albert Penfold, a painter-decorator,
in July 1934. The Penfolds moved to Rose Cottage, Rodmell,
where they had two children. Annie lived to see her hundredth
birthday. No recollections were recorded but Oldfield's *Afterwords*
gives her brief condolence note to Leonard on Virginia's disappearance, together with a photograph of her. It reports that she
was 'a fantastic cook', captain of Rodmell village team of the
(Elizabethan) Sussex game of stoolball and an 'outstanding' member
of the Women's Institute.

WALTER, Margaret née HARDY, (1879–1953), temporary daily
help to the Woolfs in 1930. Born Minerva Lucrezia, the daughter
of a Louisiana farmer, she was secretary to the translator and author
Helen Zimmern, and then worked at the *New York Times* in the
1900s. She married Karl Walter, a journalist, poet and anarchist in
Kansas, where they both wrote for the *Kansas City Star*. Their only
son, William Grey, mentioned by Woolf as being at King's, became
an eminent neuroscientist (see *DNB*). As a postgraduate student,
duly dubbed 'the son of our old cook', he came to tea with Virginia
(*D*, IV, 21 July 1934). Margaret Walter died in Bordighera, Italy.

Notes

Abbreviations

Archives and Collections

Berg   The Henry W. and Albert A. Berg Collection at the New York Public Library

King's   Modern Archive, King's College, Cambridge: CHA: Charleston Papers; REF: Papers of Roger Eliot Fry

LA   Lincolnshire Archives, Lincoln

LMA   London Metropolitan Archives

LRO   Lincolnshire Records Office, Lincoln

NSA   National Sound Archive, British Library

SHC   Surrey History Centre, Woking

Sussex   University of Sussex Library, Manuscript Collections: CP: Charleston Papers; LWP: Leonard Woolf Papers; MHP: Monk's House Papers

Tate   Charleston Trust Papers, Modern Collection, Tate Gallery Archive

People

CB	Clive Bell	MLD	Margaret Llewellyn Davies
VB	Vanessa Bell	AVS	Virginia Stephen
QB	Quentin Bell	ES	Ethel Smyth
VD	Violet Dickinson	VSW	Vita Sackville-West
RF	Roger Fry	LW	Leonard Woolf
		VW	Virginia Woolf

Works frequently cited in the Notes

D: *The Diary of Virginia Woolf*, ed. Anne Olivier Bell and Andrew McNeillie, 5 vols., Hogarth Press, 1977–84

E: *The Essays of Virginia Woolf*, ed. Andrew McNeillie, 6 vols., Hogarth Press, 1986

HPGN: *Hyde Park Gate News: The Stephen Family Newspaper*, ed. Gill Lowe, Hesperus, 2005

L: *The Letters of Virginia Woolf*, ed. Nigel Nicolson and Joanne Trautmann, 6 vols., Hogarth Press, 1975–80

LLW: *Letters of Leonard Woolf*, ed. Frederic Spotts, Bloomsbury, 1992

PA: *A Passionate Apprentice: The Early Journals of Virginia Woolf*, ed. Mitchell A. Leaska, Hogarth Press, 1990

SF: *The Collected Shorter Fiction of Virginia Woolf*, ed. Susan Dick, Hogarth Press, 1985

SP, MB: 'Sketch of the Past' in *Moments of Being*, ed. Jeanne Schulkind, Sussex University Press, 1976, revised 1985; Pimlico, 2002

VBL: *Selected Letters of Vanessa Bell*, ed. Regina Marler, Bloomsbury, 1993

Sources and Notes

Full details of all works cited are given in the Bibliography. The primary sources for this book are Virginia Woolf's diaries and letters, where references to the servants can usually be tracked through editors' indexes. At the beginning of each section I have indicated which volumes of diaries and letters have been used and contented myself with giving references only for those quotations where the context isn't clear, where there is some inaccuracy, or where the quotation falls out of chronological sequence or belongs to another period. References are given for any unpublished letters which are not in the public domain. I have used the 1992 Penguin edition of Virginia Woolf's fiction and essays unless otherwise stated. My policy has always been to use the most accessible edition.

One. The Family Treasure

Quotations from VW's diaries and letters throughout this entire chapter are from *PA* and *L*, I, unless otherwise given. The opening description of Hyde Park Gate draws on Virginia Woolf's memoirs of her childhood gathered together in *MB*, and in *HPGN*, the newspaper produced by the Stephen children. Virginia's remarks on the servants can be found in *PA*, and her memory of her oceanic feelings of ecstasy and of Sophie Farrell's basket, in SP, *MB*, together with her retrospective guilt about the conditions at Hyde Park Gate.

9 **the greatest disaster:** AVS, 'Reminiscences', *MB*, p. 11.

SOPHIE FARRELL AND JULIA STEPHEN

The letters from Sophie are in MHP at Sussex. I tracked Sophie and the Farrell family through the LRO in Lincoln. For Lincolnshire local history, I relied on Rawding, *The Lincolnshire Wolds in the Nineteenth Century*; Olney, *Rural Society in Nineteenth-Century Lincolnshire* and Russell, *A History of Schools and the Education Provision in Lindsey, Lincolnshire 1800–1902*.

For mid-nineteenth-century service, Horn, *Rise and Fall of the Victorian Servant* and Gerard, *Country House Life*; the managerial mistress emerges in Davidoff and Hall, *Family Fortunes*; Waterson, *The Servants' Hall* has many histories of frustrated and ambitious servants; Waterfield and French, *Below Stairs*, has essays on several aspects of service and its history.

For the early lives of Julia Jackson and Leslie Stephen, and their life in Hyde Park Gate and at Talland House in Cornwall, Woolf's biographers, Bell and especially Lee, and Spalding, *Vanessa Bell*; Leslie Stephen's *Mausoleum Book* for his memoir of Julia and their marriage; Boyd, *Bloomsbury Heritage* and Curtis, *Hidden Houses* for many helpful details. Henrietta Garnett's *Anny* is a lively account of old Kensington and Dakers, *The Holland Park Circle* expands on the Duckworth/Stephen milieu; Dell and Whybrow give more on the family's Cornish summers in *Remembering St Ives*.

For the changes to London houses and domestic life, Cruickshank and Burton, *Life in the Georgian City*, Porter, *London: A Social History*, Harrison, *The Kitchen in History*; Briggs, *Victorian Things* is invaluable. The photograph albums of Vanessa Bell and Virginia Woolf are now handsomely reproduced in, and discussed by, Humm, *Snapshots of Bloomsbury*.

12 **to spray an atmosphere:** VW, *L*, III, 4 September 1924.
13 **400,000 single-servant households:** Longmate, *Workhouse*, p. 186.
15 **later sketch of a family cook:** VW, 'The Cook', MPH/A.13d/e, Sussex.

18 **the diary of the Reverend Francis Kilvert:** Kilvert was renowned
for his generosity to his parishioners. Horn, *Labouring Life*, p. 170.

18–19 **the children of the lower orders … should go to school:**
Russell, *History of Schools*, pp. 10–11.

22 **Their headstone is one:** *Louth Cemetery Monumental Inscriptions*, p.
251 in LA; Charles Farrell was seventy-one; Ann, sixty-eight, died in
Longford, Nottinghamshire, before being buried with her husband.
So at least one of Sophie's siblings had also left the county.

22 **thorough country gentleman:** Stephen, *Mausoleum Book*, p. 35.

25 **practised, not very seriously:** VW, SP, *MB*, p. 100.

25 **the place of Peace:** John Ruskin, *Sesame and Lilies* (1864).

25 **Angel in the House:** Coventry Patmore, whose poem by that name
was published in 1854, was a close friend of Maria Jackson, Julia's own
mother. It became a bestseller in the cheap edition of 1887.

26–7 **moral shock:** for the story of Mary and the Carlyles' fraught
relations with servants, Holme, *Carlyles at Home*.

27 **A servant is not to be seated:** Harrison, *Kitchen*, p. 108.

28 **One estimate in 1876:** May, *Victorian Domestic Servant*, p. 8.

28 **that's the best:** Stanley, Introduction to *Diaries of Hannah Cullwick*,
p. 16. Hannah Cullwick was the most extraordinary of ordinary servants, a 'pot girl' or kitchenmaid who began a secret romance of
eighteen years with Arthur Munby, an upper-class man of letters,
whom she eventually married. Munby was obsessed with working
women and liked to see Hannah 'in her dirt' or blacked up as a slave.
See also Davidoff, *Worlds Between*.

29 **She was as unhappy:** VW, SP, *MB*, p. 100.

30 **little backwater of a street:** Leslie to Charles Eliot Norton, 6
October 1876, quoted in Maitland, *Life*, p. 293.

31 **under the influence … shrined in crimson velvet:** VW, '22
Hyde Park Gate', *MB*, p. 31.

32 **no longer considered suitable:** Mrs Beeton, for instance, recommended 'deodorizing' cabbage by boiling it with bicarbonate of soda
for three-quarters of an hour.

32 **incredible gloom:** the details here are from VW, SP, *MB*.

33 **makes but very little work:** Harrison, *Kitchen*, p. 110.

33 **almost complete darkness:** VB, *Sketches*, p. 71.

35 **all the water through spouts:** Garnett, *Anny*, p. 108.

36 **mixture of absolute compliance:** ibid., p. 228.

36 **Suzette, her Swiss maid:** Stephen, *Mausoleum Book*, p. 97.

36–7 **darling dog . . . he is long-haired:** *HPGN*, 11 July 1892.

37 **She was moved to write:** Julia Stephen's writings are collected in Gillespie and Steele, *Julia Duckworth Stephen.*

39 **like the Master:** VB to VW, presumably reproducing Sophie's accent, *VBL*, 23 August 1912.

40 **One summer's day:** *HPGN*, 25 July 1892.

40 **Mrs Stephen in her spiritualized portraits:** her future son-in-law, Leonard Woolf, found something 'insipid' and 'too feminine' in Julia's 'saintly dying duck loveliness', which he thought improved in her daughters by the masculine good looks of the Stephens: LW, *Autobiography*, I, p. 119.

MISS GENIA AND SOPHIE FARRELL

Sophie in the 1900s is remembered by Vanessa Bell in her, 'Life at Hyde Park Gate after 1897', in *Sketches*; for 'Miss Jan' and the terrible year of 1897, *PA*. Together with *L, I,* this is the main source for the descriptions of Virginia's thoughts on reading and writing. For the vexed question of Virginia Stephen's breakdowns and how they might be interpreted, here and elsewhere I have relied on Lee's scrutiny of the evidence and her analysis of the accounts given by Leonard Woolf in his autobiography and by Quentin Bell in his biography. I find it hard to agree with her view, however, that Virginia's reluctance to eat had little to do with an obsession with the body. It seems to me that a fraught relation to physicality and to bodily experience is central to Woolf's life and work, which is not to say that it was not a creative tension, as well as a potentially disabling one. But see also Lee's chapter, 'Reading', especially pp. 409–11.

The obituary of Shag (1892–1904), 'On a Faithful Friend', appeared in the clerical newspaper the *Guardian* on 18 January 1905; reprinted in *E, I,* ed. Andrew McNeillie. 'Reminiscences', begun in 1907, is in *MB*. For the discussion of Virginia's first novel, see DeSalvo, *Virginia Woolf's First Voyage,* and *Melymbrosia,* which is the source for the later discussion of 'Chailey'. For Edwardian service, Gardiner, *Edwardian Country House,* Horn, *Life below Stairs.* 'Old Bloomsbury' in *MB* gives the details for Gordon Square and Thoby's Thursday evenings. In this memoir of the 1920s Virginia made light of the past, telling a circle of

friends of George Duckworth's unwanted embraces; not until she wrote
her memoirs in her late fifties did she contemplate publishing her
memories of being six years old and being molested by Gerald Duckworth, who, she wrote, explored her 'private parts'. I have tried to
respect this time-lapse.

Details for Sophie Farrell and Maud Chart were found by trawling
the Family Records Centre and the Lambeth Archives in London. The
letter from Margaret Duckworth is in MHP as are Sophie Farrell's condolence letters; these are reproduced in Oldfield's *Afterwords*, but she gives
Bristol rather than Brixton as Sophie's home.

42 **A house that is rooted:** 'Wilton Fair' (1903), VW, *PA*, p. 208.

43 **the extraordinary increase:** VW, 'Old Bloomsbury', *MB*, p. 46.

43 **the whole world:** VW, SP, *MB*, p. 90.

43 **Much thinking:** AVS to VD, *L*, I, March 1904.

44 **one gradually sees shapes:** *L*, I, to CB, 26 December 1909.

46 **vivid, ebullient, attentive:** Lee, introduction to *HPGN*.

48 **to do all kinds of wild things:** *L*, I, 22 September 1904. Notoriously, describing this period, Quentin Bell used the phrase 'all that
summer she was mad' in his biography of his aunt; Lee challenges
this and gives a judicious account of how drugs may have exacerbated
her symptoms.

49 **My own monkey:** VB to AVS, 4 November 1904, Berg.

49 **Do write his life:** ibid., 6 December 1904, Berg.

50 **unthinkable:** Maitland, *Life*, p. 364.

50 **that extraordinarily ubiquitous dog:** VW, *PA*, p. 243.

50 **the private side of life:** VW to ES, *L*, V, 2 June 1935.

50 **How seldom I have:** *D*, III, 18 December 1928.

52 **I love writing:** VW, *PA*, 7 August 1899.

52 **like one rolled at the bottom:** AVS to Lady Robert Cecil, *L*, I,
16 August 1907.

53 **a Fabian couple:** Marjorie Davidson, for instance, told George
Bernard Shaw that she didn't think 'the ideal Socialist home' should
have servants but as a school teacher felt it would be impossible for
her to do all the housework: MacKenzie, *First Fabians*, p. 195.

55 **completely independent young women:** Bell, *Old Friends*,
p. 129.

59 **shape infinite strange shapes:** AVS to CB, *L*, I, 19 August 1908.

61 **women's own domain:** Horn, *Life below Stairs*, pp. 17–18.

61 **free to go ... The more I think:** VB to AVS, 9 August 1909, Berg.

62 **The poor old thing ... Is Sophy away now ... The servants all radiate ... Sophy is keeping us:** VB to AVS, 18 August 1909; 4 September 1909; 16, 10 August 1909; Berg. VB wrote most days.

63 **you mustnt simply retreat:** VB to AVS, 5 August 1910, Berg.

64 **My brains are becoming:** ibid., 12 October 1910, Berg.

69 **when she made her will:** the cash legacies totalled only £260, with the bequest of £100 to Vanessa, the largest; my thanks to Stephen Barkway for sending me a copy of the will made on 27 July 1930.

69 **dashed off a cook's talk:** VW, *D*, IV, 14 October 1931; 'The Cook', MHP A13d/e.

71 **to float ... all a lie:** VW to Lady Robert Cecil, *L*, II, 25 October 1915.

73 **What you give me:** VW to ES, *L*, IV, 1 April 1931.

Two. Housemaids' Souls

My italicized paragraphs draw on Virginia Stephen's 1897 entries in *PA*, where she refers to Miss Octavia Hill's legs and to her family's philanthropic work. For the picture of Kensington as the most divided of the London boroughs, see White, *London in the Twentieth Century*. Virginia's image of the rat-eyed feral poor occurs in a story of 1906, 'Journal of Mistress Joan Martyn', ostensibly set in the 1580s but emotionally located in South Kensington, reprinted *SF*. All other quotations are from *PA*.

81 **foul and itch wards:** Curtis quotes Stella Duckworth's diary where she refers to using this powder, *Hidden Houses*, p. 23.

81 **Hogsden:** AVS to Emma Vaughan, *L*, I, 1 November 1904.

82 *animaux farouches*: LW, describing the slum-dwellers in the South Kensington of his childhood, *Autobiography*, I, p. 34.

82 **Slopers Sall:** a prostitute (pimped, presumably by Sloper) in the novel read by the heroine in an early draft of *Voyage Out*, DeSalvo, *First Voyage*, p. 97.

EDITH SICHEL AND LOTTIE HOPE

Apart from the scattered references indexed in Woolf's diaries and letters, Lottie is remembered briefly but vividly by Vanessa Bell's daughter, Angelica Garnett, in her memoir, 'Life in the Kitchen and Elsewhere', and in *Deceived with Kindness*; she is also mentioned in MacGibbon's biography of Adrian Stephen. Virginia's reference to her, in a letter of March 1922, as 'my parlourmaid, Lottie Hope, a Miss Sichel's foundling' sent me in search of Edith Sichel and her home for orphans. Two volumes gave some biographical evidence: the private collection edited by Emily Marion Ritche, *Letters, Verses & Other Writings*, in the British Library, the main source for Edith's correspondence, and Bradley's anthology of Sichel's work, *New and Old*, which includes her photograph. I met Nellie Boxall's great-niece, Wendy Court, who attended Lottie's funeral, and from her death certificate I could hunt for Lottie's birth, fruitlessly as it turned out, in the registers and minute-books of London's workhouses, housed in the LMA – though I found the evidence of Sichel's other adoptions. In Surrey, local historians, who were immensely helpful, had not heard of Edith Sichel or her Home. I eventually turned it up in the 1891 census for Chiddingfold. The register and school log books, which finally gave proof positive of both Miss Sichel's Home and Lottie, are at the SHC.

For foundlings, orphans and adoption generally, I have drawn on Boswell, *The Kindness of Strangers* and Davies, *Relative Strangers*. Fishman, *East End 1888* and Longmate's *The Workhouse* are among the most vivid in the extensive literature on London's poor. For the schooling of poor girls, Davin, *Growing up Poor* and the essays in Hunt's collection, *Lessons for Life*, in particular. For slummers and the charity world, I have relied especially on Prochaska, *Women and Philanthropy*; Vicinus, *Independent Women*; Koven, *Slumming* and Darley's *Octavia Hill*. Garnett's *Anny* adds to the South Kensington dimension and gives glimpses of Pinkie Ritchie's life. Full records of the MABYS disappeared in the Blitz and only a handful of annual reports are lodged in the British Library.

For 'Old West Surrey', I also mined the Local Studies Library at Godalming Museum, a veritable hive of material about the county's history and its residents; the Hambledon Village Scrapbook is deposited there. The connection between Roger Fry and Edith Sichel is my own discovery.

84 **dancing energetically:** Garnett, *Cezanne in the Hedge*, p. 158.

84 **always unseats her:** *D*, II, 12 January 1924.

84 **loud shrieks:** VB to Jane Bussy, *VBL*, 13 June 1941.

84 **wild but in some ways:** VW to MLD, *L*, V, 18 October 1931.

84 **left in a cradle:** Garnett, *Cezanne in the Hedge*, p. 158.

85 **Lottie should have:** *D*, I, 23 September 1918.

87 **Naomi Lambeth:** her details and those of the other children in this paragraph are taken from the Whitechapel Union Registers for Deserted Children, St.B.G./Wh/140/1 for 10 December 1889–27 March 1906, LMA.

87 **A census on New Year's Day:** Longmate, *Workhouse*, p. 166.

88 **Billy O'Connor ... Jane Hall ... Daniel Gibb:** St.B.G./ Wh/141/1, Register of Children Boarded Out, 27 April 1882–6 February 1908, LMA.

89 **Scores of children:** see Parr, *Labouring Children*.

89 **Nothing to Nobody! ... the poor girls:** MABYS Annual Report, 1880, 1879.

90 **some 800 visitors:** Prochaska, *Women and Philanthropy*, p. 150.

91 **We seemed destined:** Ritchie, *Letters*, p. 16.

91 **total numbers:** Davin, *Growing up Poor*, p. 256.

93 **Nellie Tipples:** Whitechapel Union Board of Guardians Board Minutes, 10 January 1899, LMA; individuals can be found via the index under 'Servants' Association'.

93 **One of her MABYS reports:** a fragment quoted in Bradley, *New and Old*, pp. 10–11.

95 **the inconsistencies:** 14 October 1887, Ritchie, *Letters*, p. 35.

95 **Marx's daughter Eleanor:** for this incident, Kapp, *Eleanor Marx*, p. 222.

96 **the poison of the East End ... a small home:** Ritchie, *Letters*, p. 44.

96 **one amongst them:** Ritchie does not name Lottie but the phrase recurs several times in accounts of Lottie and there were unlikely to be others.

97 **Mary Ryan ... little girl called Ellen:** Olsen, *From Life*, gives the full story of Mrs Cameron's maid; Garnett, *Anny*, p. 37 for the Thackeray daughters.

97 **As the minutes of the Board:** St.B.G./WH/74, LMA.

99 **her mother-instinct:** F. Warre Cornish, 'Edith Sichel, A Study in Friendship', *Cornhill Magazine*, vol. 39, August 1915, p. 228. Provost of Eton, he was married to Emily Ritchie's sister Blanche; their daughter, Molly, married Desmond McCarthy who became close friends of the Woolfs.

99 **a regular simple Susan . . . joy of a moral grandchild:** Bradley, *New and Old*, p. 35.

100 **taking my normal:** ibid., pp. 185–91.

101 **Lottie Hope is there:** Hambledon School Admission Register, CC616/3/4, SHC; there is no surviving register for Chiddingfold School for that period.

101 **with high banks:** extract from M. R. Parker, *Natural History of Hambledon* in the Hambledon Village Scrapbook, Godalming Museum.

102 **a charming, conservative vision:** Spalding, in *Landscape in Britain 1850–1950*; also for Foster and Allingham locally, Monk and Mabley, *Hambledon*.

104 **When Lottie Hope joined:** all the details that follow are from the Hambledon School Log Books, CC616/3/1; CC616/3/2, SHC.

107 **at reasonable prices:** these details are from the Hambledon Village Scrapbook.

107 **You will like:** to Helen Fry, 11 September 1908; he had met Edith in January according to his appointments diary, and dined with her shortly after moving into Durbins, on 6 January 1910; perhaps she offered Lottie then: REF 3/58/9, King's.

109 **Edith's praise:** VW to VD, late May 1913.

110 **of obtrusive, and medicinal morality:** AVS to Lady Robert Cecil, 13 April 1909.

110 **nice enthusiastic working women:** AVS, *PA*, 7 January 1905; 'Report on Teaching at Morley College', Appendix B, Bell, *Virginia Woolf*, vol. I, p. 203.

112 **Imperial tread:** VW to Katherine Cox, *L*, II, 18 March 1913.

112 **lowest class . . . the protoplasm:** an address to prison-visitors at Holloway prison, probably in 1914, quoted in Ritchie, *Letters*, pp. 184ff.

113 **a bit of salvage:** Cornish, 'Edith Sichel', p. 228.

MRS WOOLF, MRS BELL AND 'THE CLICK'

The main sources for this section, which covers the period of roughly 1912–24, are VW's *D*, I and II, and her *L*, II. I also refer to a number of unpublished letters which editors leave out for reasons of space but also for fear of boring the readers (Nicolson refers to 'the tedious climax' of Virginia's 'servant-juggling'). The quotations from Vanessa Bell's letters are from *VBL*, unless otherwise given. Marler's selection also necessarily omits many of VB's letters about domestic life but this has the unfortunate effect of making her appear far more independent than she actually was. Information about the Selwoods has mainly come from their descendants, especially Carolyn Phillips.

For Durbins, Fry's retrospective article in *Vogue*, 'A Possible Domestic Architecture', and Reed's *Durbins*; Powers, 'Roger Fry and the Making of Durbins'; other details from Spalding, *Fry*, and my own visit to the house and discussion with Erica Lukas. The Fry sisters cry out for a collective biography; for Joan, see Fawell, *Joan Mary Fry* and the memoir 'Durbins' by Pamela Diamand, Fry's daughter. For Omega and Bloomsbury, Naylor, ed., *Bloomsbury* and Anscombe, *Omega and After*; Reed's *Bloomsbury Rooms* and Todd, *Bloomsbury at Home*, were differently helpful. For Asheham House, LW's autobiography, Shone, 'Asheham House', and Garnett's *Flowers of the Forest*. VW's unpublished 'Asheham Diary' is in the Berg but reprinted by Olivier Bell. According to Wright's *Clean and Decent*, earth-closets were invented by Rev. Henry Moule in 1860. Usually a wooden seat with a bucket beneath, and a hopper at the back generally filled with earth or ashes: 'When the handle is pulled, a layer of earth falls into the bucket, which is emptied at intervals.' Of course rural ecs would often be less sophisticated – though ecologically sound.

This is not the place for a lengthy discussion of Leonard Woolf's politics; I relied in the main on the helpful brief analysis offered by Leventhal in *After the Victorians*, though Glendinning's biography now adds much more. For the impact of the war on domestic service, Horn, *Life below Stairs*. 'The Mark on the Wall' and the other sketches written between 1917 and 1921 can be found in *SF*. A number of Woolf's 'holographs' or manuscript versions of her novels have now been published (see Bibliography); Briggs, *Virginia Woolf* is the best account of the evolution of the works. For Hogarth House, see Lee, pp.351–2.

Bell's talk on Mary Elizabeth Wilson, given to the Bloomsbury Memoir Club in the early 1920s was reprinted in *Charleston Magazine*. The subject of psychoanalysis and Bloomsbury deserves a book in itself and is only glanced at here: Meisel and Kendrick's *Bloomsbury/Freud* gives the evidence of Virginia's ferocious hostility to psychoanalysis. LW was more open-minded and in September 1924 ran a debate on psycho-analysis when he was literary editor of the *Nation*. Clive Bell took the opportunity to snub Freud in the most withering way he could think of: 'in matters of art he has the taste of a housemaid'.

114 **the very hearth:** VW, SP, *MB*, p. 125.

115 **They're too incomprehensible:** VB to VW, 27 June 1918, Berg.

118 **a monstrous eyesore:** RF, *Vision and Design*, p. 224.

118 **a real and lasting home:** RF to his father, 14 December 1909: REF 3/57/36 King's. Helen Fry was sent to the Retreat in York where she remained for twenty-seven years and died in 1937. She appears to have suffered from 'chronic paranoid schizophrenia' but Spalding later learnt that her condition was due to inherited syphilis: Introduction to VW, *Roger Fry*, p. xiv.

121 **According to one story:** Nellie Boxall to VW, who passed it to VB, 22 December 1922, *L*, II.

121 **who almost overnight:** Spalding, introduction to VW, *Roger Fry*, p. xii.

122 **Julian should have:** VB to RF, 3 July 1911, Tate.

122 **Eric Gill:** this replaced an earlier version which Roger had turned down because it might offend Joan and her visitors. Gill was nasty about this, blaming Roger, 'I think he's frightened of it and ... it hardly goes with strawberries and cream and tea on the lawn', MacCarthy, *Eric Gill*, p. 107.

122–3 **paintings and carvings ... the spirit of fun:** VW, *Roger Fry*, p. 163.

123 **the spirit of fun:** ibid., p. 194.

123 **my happiness is largely ... so obsequious:** VB to RF, 19 August 1912; 27 December 1913[?], Tate.

126 **wonderfully supportive:** Nicholas Henderson, 24 April 2003, private communication.

126 **Flossie, more exquisite:** VB to AVS, 12 October 1915, Berg.

127 **Ludendorf Bell:** Spalding, *Vanessa Bell*, p. 183.

130 **what *I* say ... hovering about ... I feel we have:** VB to VW, 2 September 1912, Berg.

130–31 **increasing resistance to food:** according to Bell's biography, VW saw food 'as repulsive matter which must be then excreted in a disgusting fashion', vol. 2, p. 15.

132 **the household books:** LWP, II R 65, Sussex.

133 **miserably contrite:** LW, *Autobiography*, II, p. 124. Leonard tells this story at some length and his biographer suggests that he may have sought 'sexual solace' with Lily, or another maid (Glendinning, p. 193). This strikes me as most unlikely – not least because of the close quarters at which servants and employers lived and the likelihood of gossip. It would have been impossible to keep it from Virginia and, as Glendinning writes, any hint of infidelity would have been 'catastrophic' for her mental health. If Leonard's account carries a stronger charge than it seems to merit, perhaps Leonard still felt guilty about chastising Lily whom he saw as one of life's innocents. She was, he wrote, 'one of those persons for whom I feel the same kind of affection as I do for cats and dogs', not quite as patronizing as it sounds, given his intense feelings about animals. He thought Lily, like Virginia, a 'silly', at once 'terribly simple' and 'tragically complicated'. We never learn Lily's surname and her fate remains unknown.

134 **The poet Charlotte Mew:** Fitzgerald, *Charlotte Mew*, p. 91. In the 1900s Mew lived in genteel poverty near Gordon Square.

134 **Don't think of me:** VB to RF, [20?] October 1913, Tate.

135 **an untidy liver:** LW, *Autobiography*, II, p. 222.

135 **Nellie and Lottie were paid:** ibid., p. 168. Wages are notoriously difficult to fix since for live-in servants they include food and board: a parlourmaid at a minor country house in Wales was earning £24 a year in 1916; another, working for a clergyman's wife in Essex, still only earnt £25 in 1918: see Waterson, *Servants' Hall*, and Horn, *Life below Stairs*, for more examples.

138 **the Zanies ... inconceivable stupidities:** VB to RF, early 1917 and *passim*, Tate; to Saxon Sydney-Turner, 19 January 1917, *VBL*, though the American editor can't quite believe that the fourteen-year-olds are really servants.

138–9 **I want a house parlourmaid ... anyone nice ... fresh from making 40 beds:** VB to VW, 24 September 1917, Berg; to RF, 17 October 1917, Tate; to RF, n.d., Tate.

139 **It's really very interesting:** VB to VW, 1 February 1917, Berg.

139 **the price of eggs:** details from VW, 'Asheham Diary'.

139 **She seems quite competent:** VB to VW, January 1917, Berg.

140 **I see our characters:** ibid., 4 July 1917, Berg.

141 **extraordinarily nice:** VB to RF, 18 February 1919, Tate.

141 **bawling out:** Bell, *Elders and Betters*, p. 3.

142 **I often wonder ... he is getting old enough:** VB to RF, 1 January 1917, Tate; VB to RF, n.d., 233, Tate.

142 **two savage black-haired:** Garnett, *Flowers*, p. 180.

142 **almost incredibly stupid:** VB to RF, 19 February 1919, Tate.

144 **Virginia's investments:** LW's *Autobiography*, II, pp. 62–3.

144 **awful rich, foxhunting:** VB to RF, 18 December 1913. When Clive Bell's father died in 1927 he left more than £250,000; his mother left an estate worth £100,000 in 1942 (£1 was worth about £40 in 1930; £35 in 1940). Rudikoff discusses Virginia and Vanessa's inheritances in *Ancestral Houses*.

145 **Personally I think:** LW to Lord Robert Cecil, 11 April 1921, MHP, Sussex.

147 **vast, mysterious lower-middle classes:** how her biographer describes the new and exciting world ventured into by Roger Fry's sister, Margery, in the period, Huws Jones, *Margery Fry*, p. 57.

147 **The vocabulary of grading:** a taxonomy of insults between the wars would be fascinating. Among Virginia favourites aimed at establishing pecking order were: 'underbred', 'philistine', 'parochial', 'average' and, of course, 'vulgar'. A person might be 'nondescript', a 'non-entity', 'flashy' or 'mediocre'; everything from a meal to a mind could be classified on a scale from 'first-rate' to 'tenth-rate'.

147 **what a housemaids mind:** VW to VSW, *L*, III, 22 November 1928.

148 **the crowd at close quarters:** *D*, I, 24 April 1919.

149 **Why not in fact:** reading notes for 'Modern Novels' (1919), reprinted Kime Scott, *Gender of Modernism*.

150 **A deleted passage:** holograph of *Jacob's Room*, July 1920; Appendix to World's Classics edition, ed. Kate Flint, 1992, pp. 254–5.

151 **noted that even her char:** 'The Char', MHP A13f, Sussex, a fragment dated as 'probably 1930s', but the deleted passage in *Jacob's
Room* has Mrs Pascoe take 'down the gaudy box placed askew on
the mantlepiece', so it may be earlier.

154 **an artful hussy:** David Garnett, who had known Mary Wilson as
a pretty 'English rosebud' of a maid, decided thirty years later that
it was a case of 'split personality' and says she later recovered, *Flowers*,
p. 214.

155 **budding psychoanalysts:** including Adrian Stephen and his wife,
Karin; Lytton Strachey's brother James and his wife, Alix, who were
analysed by Freud. They translated his complete works for the Hogarth
Press. Alix thought it right that Virginia was never psychoanalysed
as it might have 'stopped' her creativeness, which 'was so interwoven
with her fantasies – and indeed with her madness': Noble, *Recollections*, p. 143.

156 **anything heavier than:** Garnett, *Deceived*, p. 57.

157 **she told Leonard Woolf:** 3 June 1964, *LLW*. A typo in the tran-
scription of this letter turns Daisy Selwood into Lottie Hope's sister;
the mistake is repeated in MacGibbon's life of Adrian Stephen.

Three. The Question of Nelly

The italicized paragraphs draw on VW's diary entries for August 1929
and this chapter as a whole closely follows the chronology of the relationship between Virginia and Nellie during Nellie's employment as
'cook-general', 1924–34. I only reference those quotations which cannot
be found easily via the index of *D*, II, III and IV, and in the corresponding
volumes of the letters. Where possible, the rough dates are indicated in
the text. Nellie's family history I pieced together from the census records,
with the help of local historian Clive Downes at the SHC and Nellie's
relatives. For the improvements at Monk's House, the Woolfs' household
finances and other domestic matters, the main source is LWP at Sussex
and LW, *Autobiography*; I also relied on Spater and Parsons, *Marriage*, and
Lee's chapter on 'Money and Fame' in her biography of Woolf. Bell's
discussion of the servants is acute and helpful, as is Lee's; Glendinning's
Leonard Woolf has little to say about Lottie or Nellie (whom she muddles
with Annie and houses in Park Cottages). For the overall picture of

women's lives and service between the wars, and for many servants' stories and memories, Horn's invaluable *Life below Stairs*; Lewis, *Labour and Love*, and Giles, *The Parlour and the Suburb*. Among the many works on the middle classes and living standards between the wars: McKibbin, *Classes and Cultures* and Lewis, *Women in England*.

Xavier Marcel Boulestin was probably the source of the *boeuf en daube* (hotly debated by Woolfians), which makes its way, somewhat anachronistically, into the dinner party of the Ramsay family in the 1880s scenes of Woolf's *To the Lighthouse*. Virginia was actually drafting this in March 1926. Boulestin has two recipes for this beef stew in his 1925 cookbook, *A Second Helping or More Dishes for English Homes*, so perhaps Nellie, who took lessons with him, cooked it for the Woolfs.

Life as We Have Known It is an extraordinary book which deserves to be reprinted. Virginia's introductory letter to the volume was much reworked but a version can be found in Bowlby, ed., *Crowded Dance*.

Nellie herself mentioned her employment after leaving the Woolfs in the BBC radio interview she gave in 1956. There is no decent biography of Lanchester. For the debate about modernist domesticity and for Wells Coates, who had many connections with Bloomsbury (not least via the surrealist John Armstrong, who married Clive Bell's mistress, and McKnight Kauffer, who designed the wolf's head colophon for the Hogarth Press), Cantacuzino, *Wells Coates*. I return to Happy Powley in Part Five.

165 **Gentle, patient**: Garnett, *Deceived*, p. 91; QB remembered his mother issuing orders 'quite in the manner of Hyde Park Gate': *Family Album*, p. 12.

VIRGINIA WOOLF AND NELLIE BOXALL

167 **with its shops**: local historians maintain that in 1881 Godalming was the first place in the world to try out a public electricity supply, Janaway, *Godalming*, p. 53.

168 **in or about December:** 'Mr Bennett and Mrs Brown', July 1924, *E*, III. The Georgian cook isn't there in the original version printed in the *New York Evening Post* in November 1923; nor in the version given as a talk the following May. So an idealized Nellie-figure was on her mind when they settled into Tavistock Square.

168 **she might appreciate:** in *Vision and Design* (1920), Fry argued that

'the revolutionary anarchism' of the Post-Impressionists was a blow to the art establishment because their work needed only 'a certain sensibility' to appreciate it, which 'one's maid' might possess as readily as a connoisseur or art historian. For Virginia's composer-cook, see Leaska, ed., *Pargiters*, p. xxxviii.

173 **I am sick of the timid:** *D*, III, 11 July 1927.

174 **which were eagerly attended:** Boulestin, *Myself*, p. 98. Boulestin wrote columns for the national press and was the first cook – in 1937 – to give 'culinary demonstrations' on British television.

175 **in the last stages:** this is Lydia Bartholomew, Percy's wife, who has 'several children', and not his sister, Rose, with whom she is confused in VW's *L*, 1 August 1927.

175 **a Larbert self-setting range:** LWP, II/I/3c, Sussex.

176 **Nellie was earning:** Horn, *Life below Stairs*, p. 154.

178 **Grace was 'extraordinarily nice':** *VBL*, 22 February 1927.

179 **the thousands upon thousands:** Horn, *Life below Stairs*, p. 30.

180 **refined and educated . . . health of the race:** *Girls' Own Paper*, vol. 46, March 1925.

183 **almost rudely . . . I don't know:** Harrison, *Rose*, p. 35.

183 **a ratio of three to four:** Lambert, *Unquiet Souls*, p. 143.

183 **her excrement like a cat:** Garnett, *Deceived*, p. 60.

184 **I think the wireless:** Lizzie Willsden, symposium on domestic service, *The Listener*, 2 April 1930.

186 **the creative woman perpetually:** Berry and Bostridge, *Vera Brittain*, p. 242.

190 **make arrangements:** LWP II/I/3g, Sussex. Until he bought it, LW rented the cottage for 5s a week.

190 **seldom to get a day off:** in 1944 Percy's wages were £2 7s 6d a week.

196 **their generosity:** the Woolfs also paid for Annie Thompsett to see the optician; she tried to repay them with all she could spare, a paperweight from Scotland, *D*, III, 28 August 1930.

196 **their weekly accounts:** this was unluxurious living: LWP/II/R65, Sussex.

197 **her diary recorded:** *D*, III, 12 November 1930; I have punctuated the dialogue to make the parts clearer.

198 **the dumping ground:** 'Women and Fiction' (1929), in Barrett, ed., *Virginia Woolf*, p. 51.

201 **Talk–talk– talk … Talk with them:** *D*, II, 14 February 1922; *D*, I, 19 November 1917.

201 **'Nurse Lugton's Curtain':** Dick, *SF* prints a version of this manuscript; a mention of Nurse Lugton in the diaries suggests she was a real person in the Stephen household, *D*, V, 12 November 1939.

201 **'Life of Ma Parker':** Mansfield's violent feelings about her own cook, which she expresses in her letters and journal of 1919, suggest that the story's rage is deflected rather too conveniently upon the British upper classes.

202 **the first version of *The Waves*:** Graham, *The Waves*, gives the evolution of the text.

203 **the anorexic:** one current psychoanalytic view sees eating disorders, the refusal to put on flesh, as a rebellion against womanhood and the biological order which puts a woman at the mercy of her body's capacity for motherhood: anorexia and bulimia represent 'the desire to escape the mastery of the mother, who has eternally imprisoned her within her own body', Chasseguet-Smirgel, *Body as Mirror*, p. 111.

204 **I have to write:** VW to VB, *L*, IV, 7 June 1930.

204 **if you want me:** VW to MLD, *L*, IV, 10 October 1930 where a footnote confuses VW's reference to 'the size of the Guilders' with the size of the membership.

206 **telling the truth:** 'Professions for Women', in Bowlby (ed.), *Crowded Dance*, p. 102.

210 **it makes me feel:** VW to ES, *L*, V, 28 July 1932.

212 **Elsa Sullivan Lanchester:** VW had liked 'little Lanchester' when she met her, *D*, II, March 1922. In 1927 Lanchester made three short films, written by H. G. Wells, in which she played a slightly dim maidservant. She was hailed as the 'female Charlie Chaplin'.

212 **a fashion for 'tudor–halo' hats:** Graves and Hodge, *Long Weekend*, p. 355.

213 **a servantless society:** the details are from a 1931 BBC broadcast, cited in Oliver, *Dunroamin*, pp. 38–40.

215 **their maid also recorded:** Ewart Evans, *From Mouths of Men*.

219 **maternal partiality ... she wrote to Vanessa:** *D*, IV, 27 November 1934; *L*, III, 21 April 1927.

219 **the horror of family life ... thousands of women ... tyranny of mother:** *D*, III, 3 September 1928.

219 **almost canine:** SP, *MB*, where she writes of Stella's 'complete, unquestioning dependence', p. 106.

220 **a battlefield ... mistress and maid:** 'The London Scene', in Bowlby (ed.), *Crowded Dance*, p. 118.

Four. Memoirs of a Lavatory Attendant

This chapter covers the period after Nellie Boxall left in 1934 and until Virginia's suicide in 1941. I have said little about Louie Everest since the book concentrates on live-in servants, but for more, see Glendinning, and Louie's own recollections.

The minute-books for the Rodmell Labour Party, held in the Sussex archive, list attendees and topics but unfortunately give few details of any discussions in the Woolf's sitting room. I would also like to know more about M. Agnes Smith, the unemployed weaver from Huddersfield who wrote to Woolf about *Three Guineas*; her six letters to Virginia are in the archive but we don't have the replies (but perhaps some relative of Agnes has them?). In 1944 Agnes published *A Worker's View of the Wool Textile Industry* through Hillcroft College at which she had studied.

Woolf's stories 'The Duchess and the Jeweller' and 'Gypsy, the Mongrel' can be found in Dick, *SF*, as can the unpublished ['Portraits']; 'Ode Written Partly in Prose on Seeing the Name of Cutbush Above a Butcher's Shop in Pentonville' and 'The Watering Place', a cleaned-up version of 'The Ladies Lavatory', which is in the Berg; 'Anon' and 'The Reader' are printed in Kime Scott. Mrs Gape, Virginia's symbolic charwoman, appears in 'A Letter to a Young Poet' (1932), reprinted by Leonard Woolf in VW's posthumous collection, *The Death of the Moth* (1942); VW also discusses the problem of 'swallowing' Mrs Gape in an actual letter to John Lehmann, *L*, V, 31 July 1932.

The political differences between Quentin Bell and his father are made clear in QB's *Elders and Betters*, while Grace Higgens's low wages are discussed in Spalding, *Vanessa Bell*. The discoveries about Mabel Haskins's later life, the Rileys and George Riley's career are my own, thanks to the Islington Local History Library and the Family Record Office, London.

225 **a fin glimpsed:** *D*, III, 30 September 1926; and 4 September 1927, where she refers again to this vision as an 'important fact' of her life which no biographer could ever guess: 'yet biographers pretend they know people'.

226 **have no screens . . . splinters & mosaics . . . that decoction of illusion . . . It must lack centre . . . The whole world:** ibid., 31 July 1926; II, 15 September 1924; III, 15 June 1929; V, 1 November 1940; SP, *MB*, p. 85.

MRS WOOLF AND 'MRS GAPE'

229 **it is very kind:** May 1934, CHA/1/296, King's.

229 **the Higgenses had to take:** Nicolson, *Among the Bohemians*, p. 197.

229 **a protest against Mrs Beeton:** Huws Jones, *Margery Fry*, p. 127.

229 **artistic colours:** letter from Riley to the Librarian, John Barnes Library, now Islington Local History Library, 26 December 1974; Riley 'searched & searched & eventually found an old shop in Theobalds Road that sold the paints in powdered form' for Fry to use. Fry's painting of Dalmeny Avenue is also stored in Islington.

230 **tall and gaunt:** Garnett, *Deceived*, p. 128.

231 **Marie Bartholomew, Percy's daughter:** interview with author, 30 October 2004.

232 **the complete English Gentleman's home . . . a house should be:** *D*, IV, 9 September 1935.

233 **thus filling up a blank:** ibid., 11 January 1935.

233 **I've been washing up lunch:** VW to VSW, *L*, V, 6 September 1934.

234 **Katherine Mansfield wept:** Nicolson, *Bohemians*, p. 183.

234 **Lytton Strachey's sisters:** Partridge, 'Bloomsbury Houses', p. 131.

235 **a daily cleaning woman:** between the wars she might earn between 3s and 3s 6d for a long morning: Roberts, in Lewis, ed., *Labour*.

240 **Louie read a paper:** VW to Judith Stephen, *L*, VI, 22 August 1939.

241 **badge of servility:** Horn, *Life below Stairs*, p. 157.

242 **very good for my conceit:** VW to ES, *L*, V, 16 November 1935.

242 **telling a French acquaintance:** Jacques-Emile Blanche, *L*, VI, 5 October 1938.

242 **happily, voteless and uneducated:** *D*, IV, 2 October 1935.

244 **writing to Margaret Llewellyn Davies:** *L*, VI, 8 May 1938.

245 **a man lying on the grass:** *D*, V, 11 November 1937.

246 **sinister dwarf city:** 'The London Scene', in Bowlby (ed.) *Crowded Dance*, p. 108.

246 **clammy:** an early example: writing to Vanessa about a budding author who had sent an unsolicited manuscript, 'I'm in daily touch with Doris [Daglish] of Nicosia Rd Wandsworth,' a surburban part of London, 'and find it a clammy proceeding. She perspires – she is without charm,' *L*, III, 17 September 1925.

247 **shoppers off Oxford Street:** *D*, V, 12 July 1939.

247 **householders in a leafy Oxford suburb:** the 'Cutteslowe Walls', erected in 1934 in the Summertown district, pulled down four years later and re-erected in 1939; finally demolished 'by a rampant tank' in 1943: McKibbin, *Classes*, p. 103.

249 **Brown jelly . . . the man in uniform:** *D*, IV, 22 April 1935.

249 **all aesthetic quality:** *D*, III, 5 September 1927.

250 **a kind of fungus:** unpublished sketch, [Portraits], *SF*.

251 **I wanted to live:** 'Mistress and Maid', *Listener*, 23 February 1938.

253 **I must go and see:** VW to Ethel Sands, *L*, III, 1 August 1927.

253 **This foreign body:** e.g., 'the foreign body being of some gross material inimical to thought', *D*, II, 22 August 1922.

254 **the ugly poor woman look:** *D*, IV, 29 June 1932.

254 **fingernails clotted with dirt:** describing Lady Katherine Thynne, 'dressed like a charwoman', *D*, III, 7 December 1925; *D*, V, 23 September 1939, a description of the mind of the journalist and editor Kingsley Martin as 'all pitted & soft as a hot dis[h]cloth – steaming, unwholesome, unreal'.

255 **some said there was a kangaroo:** Clissold Park was so named in 1835 by the Rev. Augustus Clissold who married into the Crawshay family, the owners of the house and estate. It became one of London's first municipal parks in 1889 and was well stocked with animals and birds, including fallow deer, turkeys and wallabies.

255 **its rather like sitting . . . like a doomed mouse:** to Julian Bell, *L*, VI, 2 May 1936; *D*, V, 13 March 1936.

256 **'Immunity' was her word:** See Lee, p.635, where she highlights this, and 'Fascism' for a full discussion of Woolf's politics.

256 **all the surroundings of the mind:** *D*, V, 7 August 1939.

257 **Shall we ever live:** SP, *MB*, 108.

259 **Now margarine is rationed:** *D*, V, 25 July 1940.

259–60 **that fat timid sheep . . . tweed wearing sterling . . . The poor dont understand:** VW to MLD, *L*, VI, 6 April 1940; to ES, 25 September 1940; *D*, V, 1 November 1940.

261 **a gnat on a blade of grass:** *D*, V, 17 August 1938.

264 **Could I write it:** 10 October 1940.

266 **great patriarchal machine:** SP, *MB*, p. 155.

267 **nine-page letter:** 7 November 1938, MHP, Sussex.

268 **Labour Party meeting:** 19 September 1940, LWP II/I/4/i, Sussex.

268 **Servility, and the shame:** I am indebted here to Lee's illuminating discussion of Woolf and Freud, pp.722–5.

269 **Reading Freud . . . the alternately loved and hated:** *D*, V, 8 December 1939; SP, *MB*, p. 123.

269 **She told Octavia Wilberforce:** Wilberforce repeats what she remembers of the conversation in a letter to her companion, Elizabeth Robins, 14 March 1941; Jalland, *Wilberforce*, p. 176.

269 **1914 but without even the illusion:** *D*, V, 14 September 1938; *Downhill All the Way* is the title of that part of LW's autobiography which spans the interwar years.

270 **We do represent:** Forster to VW, 6 June 1935, Sussex.

271 **breach in the bank:** *D*, V, 3 November 1940.

272 **no echo in Rodmell:** ibid., 26 February 1941.

272 **Observe perpetually . . . Haddock & sausage:** ibid., 8 March 1941.

274 **'The Ladies Lavatory':** Berg; the more sanitized version is in *SF*.

275 **she had taken to scrubbing . . . the world of good:** Jalland, *Octavia Wilberforce*, p. 180.

276 **don't go scrubbing floors:** VB to VW, *VBL*, 20 March 1941.

276 **I had never known her want:** Noble, *Recollections*, p. 195.

Five. Afterlives

The opening paragraphs draw on a medley of voices, many anonymous, from Roberts, *A Woman's Place*; Horn, *Life below Stairs*; Taylor, 'Daughters and Mothers', who also gives the memories of Minnie Cowley, Jennie Owen and Mrs Woodburn; and on individual autobiographies, including Foley, *Child in the Forest*; Rennie, *Every Other Sunday*, Powell, *Below Stairs* and Balderson, *Backstairs Life*. For other interviews with servants which have shaped this chapter, see Burnett, *Useful Toil*. The details of Nellie Boxall and Lottie Hope's later lives came from my own interviews with neighbours and family, especially Wendy Court, Nellie's great-niece. The recording of the Ewart Evans's interview with Happy Sturgeon, and of Nellie and Lottie in 'Portrait of Virginia Woolf', are in the NSA. The script for the BBC *Omnibus* programme of 1970 on which Louie appeared is in LWP, Sussex, which also holds Trekkie Ritchie's account of the vicissitudes of Leonard's estate, his will and all other details pertaining to his domestic affairs.

For reflections on the problems to do with interviewing, and 'oral history', Samuel and Thompson, *The Myths We Live By*; Fraser, *In Search of a Past*, where he explores his own complex relation to the servants in the country house of his childhood; and Alexander, *Becoming a Woman*, the last especially valuable for thinking about women's lives in the interwar years.

281 **Haven't we been awful:** Roberts, *A Woman's Place*, p. 52.

281 **I shan't be sorry:** Thompson, *Lark Rise*, p. 155.

281 **When I was thirteen:** Burchardt, 'Stepchildren's Memories', p. 247.

282 **Got your eyes:** ibid., p. 244.

282 **You were just . . . strong-faced:** Taylor, 'Daughters', p. 134.

285 **neither noticed nor cared:** Glendinning, *Leonard Woolf*, gives these details.

285 **When Vanessa learnt:** VB to Jane Bussy, *VBL*, 9 January 1945.

286 **I want you to love me:** Adamson, *Love Letters*, 30 May 1943.

286 **To know you & love you:** ibid., 11 May 1944.

286 **Labour Party branch meeting . . . a couple of years later:** LWP II/I/4/i, Sussex.

287 **When these recollections:** Russell Noble, *Recollections*. Marler

thought they might be 'the most emotionally affecting portion' of the book, *Bloomsbury Pie*, p. 102.

289 **terrific domestic upheavals ... With unlimited quantities:** VB to Jane Bussy, *VBL*, 13 January 1941.

290 **a food inspector:** Christopher Driver, obituary of Hope Chenhalls (Laughton's secretary), *Guardian*, 15 January 1996.

292 **a gifted cook:** *Vanessa Bell's Family Album*, p. 64.

294 **Nellie confiscated Lottie's key:** VW to VB, *L*, IV, 7 February 1929.

294 **At least one friend:** Gerald Brenan in 1967, cited by Sprott, *LLW*, pp. 162–3.

295 **Virginia and Nell were:** Grace Hill, letter to Wendy Court, 27 June 1988. Grace was the daughter of Arthur Boxall, Nellie's brother. She died in 1997.

303 **Jim was still furious:** Jose Buschman interviewed Jim when she was renting Stile Cottage from Jim in the summer of 1992, and published his memories in a Dutch literary magazine, *De Parelduiker* ('The Pearldiver').

303 **Vanessa's 'parsimony':** Spalding, *Vanessa Bell*, p. 329.

304 **Jim Bartholomew had done:** LWP II/I/3/h, Sussex.

304 **the house was called Glazebrooks:** LW to Sir Henry Lintott, *LLW*, 16 January 1963.

304 **Leonard wrote robustly:** LW to Burlington Willes, *LLW*, 2 June 1965.

306 **It was eventually sold:** *The Times*, 11 March 2002.

307 **A French novelist ... a Spanish author:** Daniele Roth, *Bloomsbury, côte cuisine* (Editions Balland, 2001); Alicia Giménez Bartlett, *Una Habitación Ajena* (Editorial Lumen, Barcelona, 1997).

309 **My God, how does one:** VW to VSW, *L*, VI, 3 May 1938. Lee's biography boldly begins with this question and a discussion of Woolf's relation to the form.

309 **the platform of time ... As a child ... Both views true?:** *D*, V, 25 April 1940.

Bibliography

Place of publication is London unless otherwise stated.

WORKS BY VIRGINIA WOOLF

'Asheham Diary', introduction by Anne Olivier Bell, *Charleston Magazine*,
   9, 1994
The Crowded Dance of Modern Life: Selected Essays, vol. II, ed. Rachel
   Bowlby, Penguin, 1993
'Introductory Letter', *Life As We Have Known It*, by Co-operative
   Women, ed. Margaret Llewellyn Davies, Hogarth Press, 1931; Virago,
   1977
The Pargiters: The Novel-Essay Portion of 'The Years', ed. Mitchell A. Leaska,
   Hogarth Press, 1978
Roger Fry, Hogarth Press, 1940; reprinted 1991; introduction by Frances
   Spalding
Virginia Woolf: Women and Writing, ed. Michele Barrett, Women's Press,
   1979
Virginia Woolf's Reading Notebooks, ed. Brenda Silver, Princeton University
   Press, Princeton, 1983
The Waves: The Two Holograph Drafts, ed. J. W. Graham, Hogarth Press, 1976
A Woman's Essays: Selected Essays, ed. Rachel Bowlby, Penguin, 1992
A Writer's Diary, ed. Leonard Woolf, Hogarth Press, 1953

BLOOMSBURY: MEMOIRS, BIOGRAPHIES
AND CRITICISM

Adamson, Judith, ed., *Love Letters: Leonard Woolf & Trekkie Ritchie Parsons
   1941–1968*, Chatto and Windus, 2001

Anscombe, Isabelle, *Omega and After: Bloomsbury and the Decorative Arts*, Thames and Hudson, 1984

Bell, Clive, *Old Friends: Personal Recollections*, Cassell, 1988

Bell, Quentin, *Virginia Woolf: A Biography*, 2 vols., Hogarth Press, 1972

——, *Elders and Betters*, John Murray, 1995

Bell, Quentin, and Angelica Garnett, *Vanessa Bell's Family Album*, Norman and Hobhouse, 1981

Bell, Vanessa, 'The Strange Story of Mary Elizabeth Wilson', *Charleston Magazine*, 3, 1991

——, *Sketches in Pen and Ink: A Bloomsbury Notebook*, Hogarth Press, 1997

Boyd, Elizabeth French, *Bloomsbury Heritage: Their Mothers and Their Aunts*, Hamish Hamilton, 1976

Briggs, Julia, *Virginia Woolf: An Inner Life*, Allen Lane, 2005

Buschman, Jose, 'Virginia Woolfs tuinman en de dood' ('Virginia Woolf's Gardener and Death'), *De Parelduiker*, 4, 2003

Curtis, Vanessa, *The Hidden Houses of Virginia Woolf and Vanessa Bell*, Robert Hale, 2005

Dakers, Caroline, *The Holland Park Circle: Artists and Victorian Society*, Yale, New Haven, 1999

Dell Marion, and Marion Whybrow, *Virginia Woolf & Vanessa Bell: Remembering St Ives*, Tabb House, Padstow, 2004

DeSalvo, Louise, *Virginia Woolf's First Voyage: A Novel in the Making*, Rowman and Littlefield, Totowa, NJ, 1980

——, ed., *Melymbrosia*, Cleis Press, California, 2002

Diamand, Pamela, 'Durbins', in Lee, ed., 1992

Fawell, Ruth, *Joan Mary Fry*, Friends Home Service Committee, 1959

Fry, Roger, 'A Possible Domestic Architecture', *Vogue*, March 1918; reprinted *Vision and Design*, Chatto and Windus, 1920

Garnett, Angelica, *Deceived with Kindness: A Bloomsbury Childhood*, Oxford University Press, Oxford, 1984

——, 'Life in the Kitchen and Elsewhere', in Lee, ed., 1992

Garnett, David, *The Flowers of the Forest*, Chatto and Windus, 1955

Garnett, Henrietta, *Anny: A Life of Anne Thackeray Ritchie*, Chatto and Windus, 2004

Gillespie, Diane F. and Elizabeth Steele, eds., *Julia Duckworth Stephen: Stories for Children, Essays for Adults*, University Press, Syracuse, 1987

Glendinning, Victoria, *Leonard Woolf: A Life*, Simon and Schuster, 2006

Gordon, Lyndall, *Virginia Woolf: A Writer's Life*, Oxford University Press, Oxford, 1984

Henderson, Nicholas, *Old Friends and Modern Instances*, Profile, 2001

Higgens, Diana, *Grace at Charleston: Memories and Recipes*, Lockhart & Co., 1994

Humm, Maggie, *Snapshots of Bloomsbury: The Private Lives of Virginia Woolf and Vanessa Bell*, Tate, 2006

Jalland, Pat, ed., *Octavia Wilberforce: The Autobiography of a Pioneer Woman Doctor*, Cassell, 1989

Jones, Enid Huws, *Margery Fry: The Essential Amateur*, Oxford University Press, Oxford, 1966

Lee, Hermione, *Virginia Woolf*, Vintage, 1997

Lee, Hugh, ed., *A Cezanne in the Hedge and Other Memories of Charleston and Bloomsbury*, Collins and Brown, 1992

Leventhal, F. M., 'Leonard Woolf', in Pedersen and Mandler, eds., 1994

MacGibbon, Jean, *There's the Lighthouse: A Biography of Adrian Stephen*, James & James, 1997

Maitland, F. W., *The Life and Letters of Leslie Stephen*, Duckworth, 1906

Marler, Regina, ed., *Selected Letters of Vanessa Bell*, Bloomsbury, 1993

——, *Bloomsbury Pie*, Virago, 1998

Meisel, Perry, and Walter Kendrick, *Bloomsbury/Freud: The Letters of James and Alix Strachey, 1924–25*, Basic Books, 1985

Naylor, Gillian, ed., *Bloomsbury: Its Artists, Authors and Designers*, Pyramid, 1990

Nicolson, Virginia, *Among the Bohemians: Experiments in Living 1900–1939*, Viking, 2002

Noble, Joan Russell, ed., *Recollections of Virginia Woolf*, Sphere, 1989

Oldfield, Sybil, ed., *Afterwords: Letters on the Death of Virginia Woolf*, Edinburgh University, Press, Edinburgh, 2005

Olsen, Victoria, *From Life: Julia Margaret Cameron & Victorian Photography*, Arum, 2003

Partridge, Frances, 'Bloomsbury Houses', in Lee, ed., 1992

Powers, Alan, 'Roger Fry and the Making of Durbins', *Charleston Magazine*, 13, 1996

Reed, Christopher, ed., *Not at Home: The Suppression of Domesticity in Modern Art and Architecture*, Thames and Hudson, 1996

——, *Roger Fry's Durbins: A House and Its Meanings*, Cecil Woolf, 1999

——, *Bloomsbury Rooms*, Yale University Press, New Haven, 2004

Rudikoff, Sonya, *Ancestral Houses: Virginia Woolf and the Aristocracy*, Palo Alto Press, California, 1999

Scott, Bonnie Kime, ed., *The Gender of Modernism: A Critical Anthology*, Indiana University Press, Bloomington, 1990

Shone, Richard, 'Asheham House: An Outline History', *Charleston Magazine*, 9, 1994

Spalding, Frances, *Roger Fry: Art and Life*, Granada, 1980

——, *Vanessa Bell*, Weidenfeld and Nicolson, 1983

Spater George, and Ian Parsons, *A Marriage of True Minds: An Intimate Portrait of Leonard and Virginia Woolf*, Harcourt Brace Jovanovich, New York, 1977

Spotts, Frederic, ed., *Letters of Leonard Woolf*, Bloomsbury, 1992

Stansky, Peter, *On or About December 1910: Early Bloomsbury and Its Intimate World*, Harvard University Press, Cambridge, MA, 1996

Stape, J. H., ed., *Virginia Woolf: Interviews and Recollections*, Macmillan, 1995

Stephen, Leslie, *The Mausoleum Book*, Clarendon, Oxford, 1977

Sutton, Denys, ed., *Letters of Roger Fry*, Chatto and Windus, 1972

Todd, Pamela, *Bloomsbury at Home*, Pavilion, 1999

Woolf, Leonard, *An Autobiography*, 2 vols., Oxford University Press, Oxford, 1980

BRITISH DOMESTIC SERVICE: MEMOIRS AND CRITICISM

Balderson, Eileen, with Douglas Goodlad, *Backstairs Life in a Country House*, David and Charles, Newton Abbot, 1982

Cullwick, Hannah, *The Diaries of Hannah Cullwick*, ed. Liz Stanley, Virago, 1984

Davidoff, Lee, *Worlds Between: Historical Perspectives on Gender and Class*, Polity, 1995

Davidoff, Lee, and Ruth Hawthorn, *A Day in the Life of a Victorian Domestic Servant*, Allen and Unwin, 1976

Dickens, Monica, *One Pair of Hands*, Michael Joseph, 1952

Firth, Violet, *The Psychology of the Servant Problem*, C. W. Daniel Co., 1925

Foley, Winifred, *A Child in the Forest*, British Broadcasting Corporation, 1974

Fraser, Ronald, *In Search of a Past: The Manor House, Amnersfield, 1933–45*, Verso, 1984

Gardiner, Juliet, *The Edwardian Country House*, Pan Macmillan, 2002

George, Dorothy M., *London Life in the Eighteenth Century*, Kegan Paul, 1925; Penguin, 1976

Gerard, Jessica, *Country House Life: Family and Servants 1815–1914*, Blackwell, Oxford, 1995

Giles, Judy, *The Parlour and the Suburb*, Berg, Oxford, 2004

Girouard, Mark, *The Victorian Country House*, Yale University Press, New Haven, 1979

Harrison, Molly, *The Kitchen in History*, Osprey, Reading, 1972

Harrison, Rosina, *Rose: My Life in Service*, Viking, 1975

Hecht, Jean, *The Domestic Servant in Eighteenth-Century England*, Routledge, 1956

Higgs, E., 'Domestic Service and Household Production', in John, ed., 1986

Hill, Bridget, *Servants: English Domestics in the Eighteenth Century*, Clarendon, Oxford, 1996

Horn, Pamela, *The Rise and Fall of the Victorian Domestic Servant*, Sutton, Gloucester, 1986

——, *Life below Stairs in the 20th Century*, Sutton, Gloucester, 2001

Huggett, Frank, *Life below Stairs*, John Murray, 1977

Kent, D. A., 'Ubiquitous, but Invisible: Female Domestic Servants in Mid-Eighteenth-Century London', *History Workshop Journal*, no. 28, autumn 1989

Lambert, Angela, *Unquiet Souls: The Indian Summer of the British Aristocracy, 1880–1918*, Macmillan, 1984

Marshall, Dorothy, *The English Domestic Servant in History*, History Association Pamphlet, 1949

May, Trevor, *The Victorian Domestic Servant*, Shire Publications, Princes Risborough, Bucks, 1998

McBride, Theresa, *The Domestic Revolution*, Croom Helm, 1976

Meldrun, Tim, *Domestic Service and Gender 1660–1750: Life and Work in the London Household*, Longmans, Harlow, Essex, 2000

Murray, Leonora (Leonora Eyles), 'The Trouble about Domestic Service', *The Nineteenth Century and After*, Jan.–June 1931

Myers, Charles S., 'The Servant Problem', *Occupational Psychology*, April 1939

Powell, Margaret, *Below Stairs*, Pan Books, 1970

Rennie, Jean, *Every Other Sunday: The Autobiography of a Kitchen-Maid*, Barker, 1955

Seleski, Patty, 'Women, Work, and Cultural Change in Early Nineteenth-Century London', in Harris, ed., 1995

Stuart, Dorothy M., *The English Abigail*, Macmillan, 1946

Summers, Anne, 'Public Functions, Private Premises: Female Professional Identity and the Domestic Service Paradigm in Britain, *c.* 1850–1930', in Melman, ed., 1998

Taylor, Pam, 'Daughters and Mothers – Maids and Mistresses: Domestic Service between the Wars', in Clarke, ed., 1979

Turner, E. S., *What the Butler Saw: Two Hundred and Fifty Years of the Servant Problem*, Michael Joseph, 1962

Waterfield, Giles, and Anne French, *Below Stairs: Five Hundred Years of Servants' Portraits*, National Portrait Gallery, 2003

Waterson, Merlin, *The Servants' Hall: A Domestic History of Erddig*, Routledge, 1980

Zmroczek, Christine, 'The Weekly Wash', in Oldfield, ed., 1994

OTHER WORKS CONSULTED

Alexander, Sally, *Becoming a Woman*, Virago, 1994

Berry, Paul, and Mark Bostridge, *Vera Brittain: A Life*, Chatto and Windus, 1995

Boswell, John, *The Kindness of Strangers*, Penguin, 1989

Boulestin, Xavier Marcel, *Myself, My Two Countries*, Cassell, 1936

Briggs, Asa, *Victorian Things*, Batsford, 1988

Burchardt, Natasha, 'Stepchildren's Memories: Myth, Understanding, and Forgiveness', in Samuel and Thompson, eds., 1990

Burnett, John, *Useful Toil: Autobiographies of Working People from the 1820s to the 1920s*, Allen Lane, 1974

——, with David Vincent and David Mayall, *The Autobiography of the Working Class: An Annotated Critical Bibliography*, Harvester, 1984–9

Cantacuzino, Sherban, *Wells Coates*, Gordon Fraser, 1978

Chasseguet-Smirgel, Janine, *The Body as Mirror of the World*, Free Association, 2005

Clarke, J., et al., eds., *Working-Class Culture: Studies in History and Theory*, Hutchinson, 1979

Cruickshank, Dan, and Neil Burton, *Life in the Georgian City*, Viking, 1990

Darley, Gillian, *Octavia Hill*, Constable, 1990

Davidoff, Leonore, and Catherine Hall, *Family Fortunes: Men and Women of the English Middle Class 1780–1850*, Hutchinson, 1987

Davies, Hunter, *Relative Strangers: A History of Adoption*, Time Warner Books, 2003

Davin, Anna, *Growing up Poor: Home, School and Street in London 1870–1914*, Rivers Oram, 1996

Ellmann, Maud, *The Hunger Artists: Starving, Writing & Imprisonment*, Virago, 1993

Ewart Evans, George, *From Mouths of Men*, Faber, 1976

Fishman, William J., *East End 1888*, Duckworth, 1988

Fitzgerald, Penelope, *Charlotte Mew and Her Friends*, Collins, 1984

Forster, Margaret, *Hidden Lives: A Family Memoir*, Penguin, 1996

Giles, Judy, *Women, Identity and Private Life in Britain: 1900–1950*, Macmillan, 1995

Glucksmann, Miriam, *Women Assemble: Women Workers and the New Industries in Inter-war Britain*, Routledge, 1990

Graves Robert, and Alan Hodge, *The Long Weekend: A Social History of Great Britain 1918–1939*, Faber, 1940

Harris, Tim, ed., *Popular Culture in England c.1500–1800*, Macmillan, 1995

Holme, Thea, *The Carlyles at Home*, Oxford University Press, Oxford, 1965

Horn, Pamela, *Labouring Life in the Victorian Countryside*, Alan Sutton, Gloucester, 1987

Hunt, Felicity, ed., *Lessons for Life: The Schooling of Girls and Women 1850–1950*, Blackwell, Oxford, 1987

Janaway, John, *Godalming: A Short History*, Ammonite, Godalming, 1993

John, Angela, ed., *Unequal Opportunities: Women's Employment in England 1800–1918*, Blackwell, Oxford, 1986

Kapp, Yvonne, *Eleanor Marx*, 2 vols., Virago, 1979

Kitteringham, Jennie, 'Country Work Girls in Nineteenth-Century England', in Samuel, ed., 1975

Koven, Seth, *Slumming: Sexual and Social Politics in Victorian London*, Princeton University Press, Princeton, 2004

Lanchester, Elsa, *Charles Laughton and I*, Faber, 1938

Lewis, Jane, *Women in England 1870–1950: Sexual Divisions and Social Change*, Wheatsheaf, Brighton, 1984

——, ed., *Labour and Love: Women's Experience of Home and Family 1850–1940*, Blackwell, Oxford, 1986

Lewis, Roy, and Angus Maude, *The English Middle Classes*, Phoenix House, 1949

Longmate, Norman, *The Workhouse: A Social History*, Pimlico, 2003

MacCarthy, Fiona, *Eric Gill*, Faber, 1989

MacKenzie, Norman and Jeanne, *The First Fabians*, Weidenfeld and Nicolson, 1977

McKibbin, Ross, *Classes and Cultures: England 1918–1950*, Oxford University Press, Oxford, 1998

Melman, Billie, ed., *Borderlines*, Routledge, 1998

Monk, Audrey, and Gabrielle Mabley, *Hambledon*, Gaymonk, Hambledon, 2000

Oldfield, Sybil, ed., *This Working Day World: Social, Cultural and Political History of Women's Lives 1914–45*, Taylor and Francis, 1994

Oliver, Paul, Ian Davis and Ian Bentley, *Dunroamin: the Suburban Semi and its Enemies*, Hutchinson, 1981

Olney, R. J., *Rural Society and County Government in Nineteenth-Century Lincolnshire*, Lincoln, 1979

Parker, Mary, *Memories of Hambledon*, private publication, 2001

Parr, Joy, *Labouring Children*, Croom Helm, 1980

Pedersen, Susan, and Peter Mandler, eds., *After the Victorians: Private Conscience & Public Duty in Modern Britain*, Routledge, 1994

Porter, Roy, *London: A Social History*, Hamish Hamilton, 1994

Prochaska, Frank, *Women and Philanthropy in Nineteenth-Century England*, Clarendon, Oxford, 1980

Rawding, C. K., *The Lincolnshire Wolds in the Nineteenth Century*, The History of Lincolnshire Committee, Lincoln, 2001

Rice, Margery Spring, *Working-Class Wives: Their Health and Conditions*, Penguin, 1939; reprinted Virago, 1981

Robbins, Bruce, *The Servant's Hand: English Fiction from Below*, Columbia University Press, New York, 1993

Roberts, Elizabeth, *A Woman's Place: An Oral History of Working-Class Women 1890–1940*, Blackwell, Oxford, 1984

——, 'Women's Strategies, 1890–1940', in Lewis, ed., 1986

Russell, Rex, *A History of Schools and the Education Provision in Lindsey, Lincolnshire 1800–1902*, Part 3, Lindsey Co. Council, Lincs., 1966

Samuel, Raphael, ed., *Village Life and Labour*, Routledge, 1975

Samuel, Raphael, and Paul Thompson, eds., *The Myths We Live By*, Routledge, 1990

Sichel, Edith, *New and Old*, with an introduction by A. C. Bradley, Constable & Co., 1917

——, *Letters, Verses & Other Writings*, ed. Emily Ritchie, privately printed, 1918

Spalding, Frances, 'Changing Nature: British Landscape Painting', in *Landscape in Britain 1850–1950*, Arts Council, 1983

Thompson, Flora, *Lark Rise to Candleford*, Penguin, 1973

Thompson, Paul, *The Edwardians: The Remaking of British Society*, Weidenfeld and Nicolson, 1985

Vicinus, Martha, *Independent Women: Work and Community for Single Women 1850–1920*, Virago, 1985

White, Jerry, *London in the Twentieth Century*, Viking, 2001

Woolf, Leonard, *Socialism and Co-operation*, National Labour Press, 1921

Wright, L., *Clean and Decent: The Fascinating History of the Bathroom and the Water-Closet*, Penguin, 2000

Acknowledgements

It is a great pleasure to be able to acknowledge all the support I received during the course of writing this book. In Lincolnshire I was privileged to be taken round the villages in search of Sophie Farrell by Rex Russell, whose local history is incomparable; my thanks to him and to Eleanor Bennett for her hospitality. I tracked down neighbours and relatives of Nellie Boxall thanks to David Rose's history column in the *Surrey Advertiser* and Paul Sawtell at BBC Southern Counties Radio. I am also grateful to Surrey local historians Jenny Overton, Elizabeth Rich, and especially to Audrey Monk, who took me on a tour of Hambledon; Clive Downes, historian of Godalming, unravelled many of the mysteries of Boxall family history for me. Without the generosity of Nellie Boxall's great-niece, Wendy Court, Nellie might have remained a purely literary figure. I would like to thank her and Nellie's other relatives and neighbours for their help: Vanessa Hobbs, John Etherton, Joan Hornett, Roger MacDavitt, Margaret Seymour and Robert Atkins. I am also very grateful to Carolyn Phillips, Florence Selwood's grand-daughter, and to other Selwood relatives: Ralph Bessant, Audrey and Alan Stacey, David Stacey, Roger Davis and Veronica Mitchell-Lawrence, and John and Jay Leakey. Marie Bartholomew, daughter of Percy and Lydia Bartholomew, shared her memories and brought Monk's House to life. Erika Lukas made me very welcome at her home, formerly Durbins. Olivier Bell, David Boulton, Pauline Cherry, Basil Comely, Winton Dean, Marion Dell, Henrietta Garnett, Frits van Halewijn, Sir Nicholas Henderson, Hermione Lee, Michael Meredith, Belinda Norman-Butler, Richard Olney, Alan Palmer, Christopher Reed, the Revd Brian Williams, Wendy Hitchmough and Chloe Garner of the Charleston Trust, Stuart Clarke and Stephen Barkway of the Virginia Woolf Society of Great Britain – all answered queries out of the blue and gave their support.

For permission to quote materials in copyright I would like to thank the Society of Authors as the Literary Representative of the Estate of Virginia Woolf, and the Henry W and Albert Berg Collection of English and American Literature at the New York Public Library; Henrietta Garnett, Trustee of the Estate of Vanessa Bell; the Trustees for the Estate of Roger Eliot Fry, and the University of Sussex and the Society of Authors as the Literary Representatives of the Estate of Leonard Woolf. I am also grateful to Lisa Dowdeswell at the Society of Authors; Isaac Gewirtz, Curator of the Berg Collection of English and American Literature; the New York Public Library; Dorothy Sheridan and her team at the University of Sussex Library Manuscript Collections; Martin Tupper and Martin Banham at the Islington Local History Centre, Finsbury Library; Elizabeth Ennion at the Archive Centre at King's College Cambridge; Dominic Persad of Tate Enterprises and the Tate Picture Library; and Pamela Madsen at the Harvard Theatre Collection, Houghton Library, for their help with permissions and with the reproduction of photographs. The librarians and archivists at the London Metropolitan Archives, at the local records offices in Lincoln and Surrey, and the Harry Kreitman Research Centre at the Tate were all unfailingly helpful and courteous. Caitlin Adams undertook initial research on Edith Sichel for me in the British Library; Vicki Tromanhauser hunted up and transcribed material from the Berg Collection; Anna Davin passed on the priceless information about the interview with Happy Sturgeon; Simon Cooke did some last-minute census work in Brixton and Duncan Barrett stepped in at short notice to take a photograph of Sophie Farrell's old home: I warmly thank them all.

Since I first read and studied Woolf's work at Sussex University in 1981, and in my subsequent teaching, I have been heavily indebted to other scholars both here and in the US. It is not possible to acknowledge the myriad books and articles of the last twenty-five years which have constantly reassessed Woolf's achievements as a feminist and as a writer. In particular, though, my reading of Woolf was hugely stimulated by the very different work of Michele Barrett, John Mepham, Jane Marcus, Cora Kaplan, Gillian Beer, Rachel Bowlby, and Julia Briggs. I have also returned on many occasions during the writing of this book to Hermione Lee's magnificent biography of Woolf, a landmark for

Woolf scholarship. Naturally the views put forward, and any errors of judgement are my own.

Mrs Woolf and the Servants has been a long time a-growing. The contract for a book about Virginia Woolf and Nellie Boxall was settled in the spring of 1995, through my then-agent, Rachel Calder, and editor-to-be at Viking, Clare Alexander. I am glad to have the chance to thank them for backing me all that time ago. It made a huge difference. Mary Kay Wilmers and Jean McNicol at the *London Review of Books*, Susanna Rustin at the *Guardian* and Ariane Bankes at *Canvas* published articles which explored some of the ideas in the book, for which I am grateful. At Fig Tree/Penguin my editor, Juliet Annan, has been unfailingly good-humoured and enthusiastic as the work stalled and then morphed over the years. I don't doubt that the book has benefited from her robust criticism and advice. Thanks also to Jenny Lord, Sarah Hulbert and the editorial team at Penguin, to my meticulous and passionate copy-editor, Bela Cunha, and to Caroline Sheard for her index. David Godwin, who took over as my agent, has kept me going with his genial devotion to serious books.

I owe a great deal to the English Department at University College London, where, under the good auspices of John Sutherland and David Trotter, the project got off the ground, and to my colleagues at the Raphael Samuel History Centre at the University of East London where I have been able to finish the work. The writing of this book coincided with many years of mourning and recovery. I wish I could acknowledge each and every student and colleague, family member or friend without whose support I might have given up the ghost altogether, but I must confine myself here to thanking in particular those who, in their different ways, inspired me or spurred me on with literary or historical talk, sharing ideas and sometimes reading parts of the book as it evolved: Sally Alexander, Julia Briggs, Barbara Caine, Peter Claus, Greg Dart, Lee Davidoff,, Paul Davis, Jane Garritty, Dave Glover, Laura Gowing, Catherine Hall, Phil Horne, Maggie Humm, Cora Kaplan, Kathy Mezei, Alex Owen, Lyndal Roper, Ellen Ross, John Shaw, John Styles, Peter Swaab, Barbara Taylor, Pam Thurschwell, Amanda Vickery and Giles Waterfield. Kasia Boddy read most of the draft and offered illuminating criticism; Norma Clarke read all of it, and, as ever, her encouragement was a great boost. Marybeth Hamilton discussed all the final drafts with me; without her wit and imagination this would have been a much less adventurous book, and much, much harder to write. I have learnt more from Sylvia Hutchinson at the Institute of Group Analysis than I can possibly acknowledge; she will know how much this book owes to her. Fran Bennett and I have talked about class feeling and women's lives for more than thirty years and will go on doing so, I hope, for the next thirty: this book is dedicated to her.

Finally, I want to thank my husband, John O'Halloran, who entered the story halfway through, as it were, and became essential to the making of it, listening unstintingly, offering comments on every page, and often doing more than the lion's share of the housework. Among the many invisible presences to whom this book is addressed is the ghost of his mother, Bridget Flannery, who came over from County Mayo as a young woman in the 1930s, found work as a cleaner and brought up her family. It has been such a joy and comfort to know that I never had to explain to her son what this book is really about.

Alison Light, Stoke Newington, London, 2007

Index

Note: page numbers in **bold** refer to illustrations.